# LIBYAN SANDSTORM

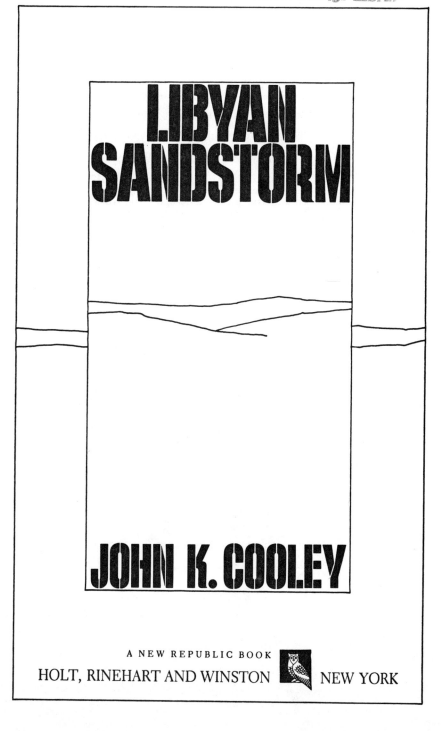

# LIBYAN SANDSTORM

# JOHN K. COOLEY

A NEW REPUBLIC BOOK

HOLT, RINEHART AND WINSTON    NEW YORK

Copyright © 1982 by John K. Cooley

All rights reserved, including the right to reproduce
this book or portions thereof in any form.

Published by Holt, Rinehart and Winston,

383 Madison Avenue, New York, New York 10017.

Published simultaneously in Canada by Holt, Rinehart
and Winston of Canada, Limited.


Library of Congress Cataloging in Publication Data

Cooley, John K., 1927–

Libyan sandstorm.

"A New republic book."

Includes bibliographical references and index.

1. Libya—Politics and government—1969–

2. Qaddafi, Muammar. I. Title.

DT236.C66    961'.204    82–917    AACR2

ISBN-0-03-060414-1


First Edition


Designer: Amy Hill

Printed in the United States of America

1 3 5 7 9 10 8 6 4 2

ISBN 0-03-060414-1

*For my mother*

I did, however, hear a story from some people of Cyrene. . . . These men declared that a group of wild young fellows, sons of chieftains in their country, had on coming to manhood planned amongst themselves all sorts of extravagant adventures . . . one of which was to explore the Libyan desert and try to penetrate further than had ever been done before.

—HERODOTUS, *The Histories*

# CONTENTS

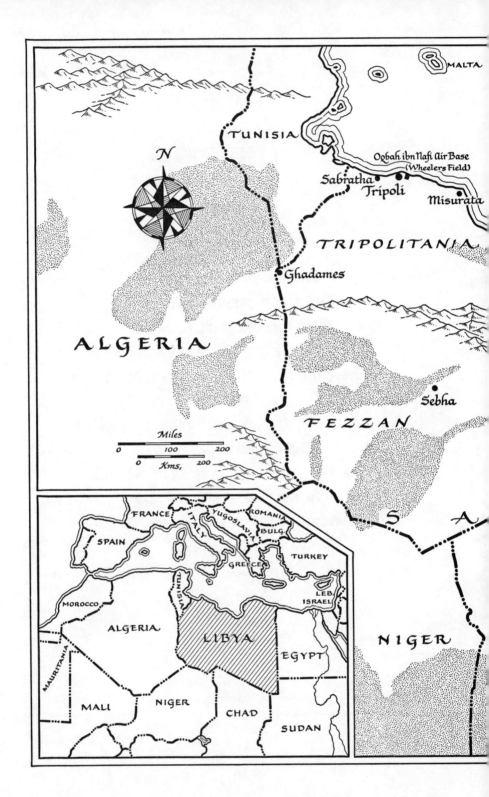

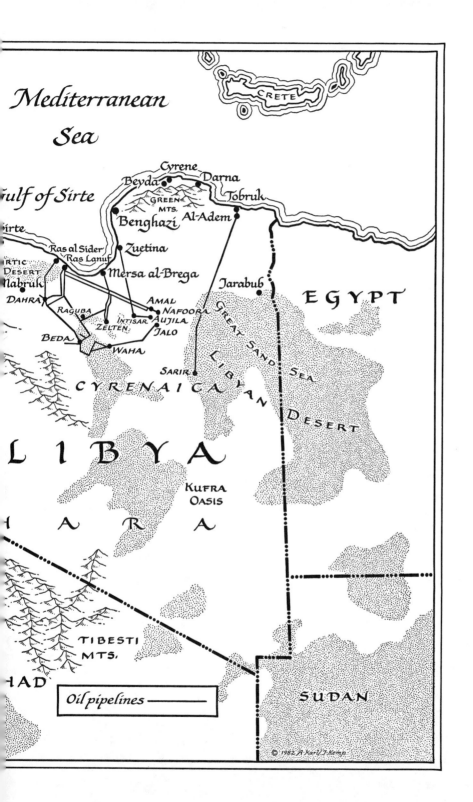

Mediterranean Sea

CRETE

Gulf of Sirte

Cyrene
Beyda
Darna
Tobruk
GREEN MTS.
Benghazi
Al-Adem
Sirte

ARCTIC DESERT
Nabruk
Ras al Sider
Ras Lanuf
Zuetina
Mersa al-Brega
Jarabub
EGYPT

DAHRA
RAGUBA
AMAL
NAFOORA
AUJILA
JALO
INTISAR
ZELTEN
BEDA
WAHA
SARIR
Great Sand Sea

CYRENAICA
LIBYAN
DESERT

LIBYA

KUFRA OASIS

SAHARA

TIBESTI MTS.

CHAD

Oil pipelines ———

SUDAN

© 1982 A. Karl J. Kemp

# ACKNOWLEDGMENTS

Although I lived in North Africa almost continuously from 1955 until 1964 and have visited it many times since then, this book on Libya might never have been written without the help and encouragement of family, friends, and colleagues. The Christian Science Publishing Society, publishers of *The Christian Science Monitor*, made it possible for me, as the *Monitor*'s Middle East correspondent for thirteen years, to travel to Libya and the rest of the Middle East and North Africa. From my reports and commentaries for the *Monitor* and now ABC News, my present employers, there grew the seeds of this book. I owe a debt of gratitude to the *Monitor*'s wonderful and understanding editors, namely Geoffrey Godsell and David Anable, and to ABC executives like Mark Richards and correspondents like Peter Jennings, for helping to make it possible for me to continue following through the years the fortunes of Muammar al-Qaddafi and other leaders of the region.

The Carnegie Endowment for International Peace generously made it possible for me to think, speak, and write about North African affairs in general during the year 1980–81. My special thanks are due to the Endowment's president, Thomas Hughes, and its secretary and foremost Middle East expert, Larry Fabian, as well as to other friends and colleagues at the Endowment too numerous to name here.

It was Marc Granetz of New Republic Books, the editor of this book, who saw the possibilities and the need for an account of contemporary Libya that might inform the general reader without overly displeasing the specialists. His sympathetic editing, patience, and forbearance with my journalistic quirks, as well as the skill and staying power of Sally Smith at Holt, who steered the manuscript through the treacherous, shoaly water of Arabic and African spellings and the confusing mass of differing transliterations, have vastly improved the finished product. Julie Caesay found herself devoting much of her working time to typing the manuscript and, more than that, sometimes making valuable contributions to the research. Mr. G. Henry M. Schuler, former U.S. diplomat in Libya and present expert oil consultant, gave advice on the oil chapters, though I did not always follow it to the letter—with the result that he and others may differ with some of my own conclusions or statements about the tremendous role that oil has played in Libya's development, as well as in the evolution of Colonel Qaddafi's policies.

Arabic transliteration is always any Western editor's or writer's nightmare. As will be seen from the way I spell Colonel Qaddafi's name—not Gaddafi, or Qathafi, or Qaddhafi, or any number of other scholarly or semi-scholarly versions—I have chosen, often arbitrarily, what seemed to be the simplest or most current spelling in English. If this is too "journalistic" for some specialist readers, I hope they will find the book's substance interesting enough not to take me too violently to task for this question of form.

Thanks are due, in both general and specific terms, to many others: Pierre Shamas and Dr. William Mussen of the Arab Press Service, Patrick Seale and Maureen McConville, Omar al-Fathali, David Mack; Daryl Penner, Joseph Montville, Lillian Harris, and many others, including Arab and Western officials and diplomats who are now serving in Libya or other countries who would not wish to be named here. Dr. Majid Khadduri at the Johns Hopkins University, and many friends as well as foes of Colonel Qaddafi in both Western and Mideastern countries kept me, through expert counsel, from straying out of reportage and commentary into the murky domain of polemics.

Vania, my wife, and Alexander, my son, as well as Katherine Anne, my daughter, came to understand what was involved in trying to write current history, some of it as it happened. Their belief that this is possible helped me to see the book through to completion. They share my love and enthusiasm for the Mediterranean world and its people, for they are parts of both.

*Washington, D.C.; Tripoli; Athens; London, 1979–1982.*

# LIBYAN SANDSTORM

# A SEPTEMBER DAWN

**S**eptember 1, 1969. The sun rises early across the Sirtic Desert, ascending into the milk-and-blue sky above the sea like a fiery balloon drifting upward with the wind. At 6:20 A.M., Abu Meniar al-Qaddafi and his wife, Aissha, are already up. Abu Meniar is sipping a glass of thick, black tea at the entrance of their goatskin tent.

This is the day on which Abu Meniar has planned to begin the journey to Misurata, seventy miles to the west. He would travel the coastal road, built by Italian Fascists under Mussolini to move their all-conquering armies along the vast stretches of desert between Tunisia and Egypt. Since he and Aissha had sacrificed their meager savings for the education of their son, it was necessary to sell as many goats as they could at the Misurata market. They needed to buy clothes for the winter, the time when the *gharbi*, the chill wind from the desert's southern reaches, would sting them with its sand and blinding dust. Abu Meniar knows he has a long day ahead of him.

He reaches inside the tent for his transistor radio, the one his son brought him while on a weekend pass from Gar Yunis, the military post outside Benghazi where he was stationed in a signal corps unit. As usual at this hour, the monotonous, nasal yet melodious voice of the muezzin chanting the morning prayers, verses from the Koran, carries on Benghazi Radio. Suddenly, it is interrupted. A burst of military music breaks through static. Aissha comes out of the tent and joins Abu Meniar, listening. Both are electrified by a vaguely familiar voice:

*In the name of God, the Compassionate, the Merciful, O great*
*Libyan people!*
    *To execute your free will, to realize your precious aspira-*
*tions, truly to answer your repeated call demanding change*
*and purification, urging work and initiative, and eager for*
*revolution and assault, your armed forces have destroyed the*
*reactionary, backward, and decadent regime. . . .* [1]

Abu Meniar and Aissha look at one another, instantly dumb. The
speaker announcing the fall of the absent King Idris and the Libyan
monarchy that had ruled for nearly eighteen years is their son, Lieutenant
Muammar al-Qaddafi.[2]

    **. . . W***ith one blow from your heroic army, the idols collapsed*
*and the graven images shattered. . . .*

    Lieutenant Colonel Musa Ahmed switches off the radio in his new
temporary headquarters at the Gurnada Camp. It is time to head back to
Benghazi to begin explaining to the foreign embassies the coup (in which
he has participated) that occurred during the night. Later, he and
Colonel Adam al-Hawaz, the officer who commanded the signal group
at Benghazi, will be reassuring the Americans, the British, and the
French that their citizens and interests—including their oil installations
and workers—are in no danger from the cabal of young military men
that have just seized power.
    As he snatches up the keys to his Land-Rover and downs the dregs of
his coffee, Musa Ahmed hears from the room next door the radio
proclamation continuing:

    *. . . In one terrible moment of fate, the darkness of ages*
*—from the rule of the Turks to the tyranny of the Italians and*
*the era of reaction, bribery, intercession, favoritism, treason*
*and treachery—was dispersed. From now on, Libya is deemed*
*a free, sovereign republic under the name of the Libyan Arab*
*Republic, ascending with God's help to exalted heights. . . .*

The stream of rhetoric from the still-unknown young signal corps
lieutenant seems almost anticlimactic after the night Musa Ahmed has

just spent—a night that was the culmination of months of patient, secret planning and seemingly interminable delays.

Only a few days before, Musa Ahmed was posted to Benghazi army headquarters to head up a forthcoming conscription program to draft young Libyan men for what had become highly unpopular duty in the Royal Libyan Armed Forces. Although the government hadn't meant it to, the transfer helped Musa Ahmed and his fellow conspirators. Their success in putting out of action the British-advised Cyrenaica Defense Force (CYDEF)—the armory and artillery-equipped first line of defense around the king—was central to Qaddafi's whole enterprise. CYDEF's strength lay in Musa Ahmed's new territory. Musa Ahmed and his action group met in the late evening of August 31 at the bar of the Cyrene Motel, which was located among the ruins of the ancient Greek colony Cyrene, whose citizen, Simon, is said to have helped carry Christ's Cross. From Cyrene, one direction led to Beyda, the new capital built by King Idris in Cyrenaica's Green Mountains, and the other to Gurnada, CYDEF headquarters and site of its main arsenal of tanks and heavy weapons.

After some drinks and talk, Musa Ahmed and his friends left the motel and drove in Volkswagens and Land-Rovers to Gurnada, where a recent alert had placed a guard company on standby. The man in charge, Captain Abdallah Shuayb, was, like Musa Ahmed, a member of the Hassa tribe, which had an old quarrel with the Barassa tribe that supported the king. He was, like Musa Ahmed, with the conspirators. He had ordered the alert to be delayed, allowing Musa Ahmed's group, armed only with handguns, to disarm the sentry easily and take the camp. One man was killed, fifteen others wounded, in some confused shooting that turned out to be one of the coup's few violent incidents. Brigadier General Sanussi Fezzani, the CYDEF commander whose loyalty to the absent king was unquestioned, was easily captured at home.[3]

. . . *Extend your hands, open your hearts, forget your rancors. Stand together against the enemy of the Arab nation, the enemy of Islam. . . .*

Miles to the south, in the Fezzan desert city of Sebha, another young lieutenant, Mahmoud Riffi, switches on his radio at about 6:30 A.M. His barracks are near the old fort built by Fezzan's former French occupiers

during and after World War II. Lieutenant Riffi and the other officers in
the Fezzan security force go through their usual morning routine and
breakfast as though this were a normal, dull day of monotonous Saharan
garrison life. But the phrase "enemy of the Arab nation" makes those
who hear it perk up. The Arabic word, *al-adouh*, is an unmistakable code
word. In the rhetoric long used by Radio Cairo's "Voice of the Arabs,"
the program that provided Qaddafi and his fellow conspirators with
much of their intellectual nourishment, the "enemy" meant only
Israel.

> . . . *the enemy of humanity, who burned our holy places and*
> *shattered our honor . . .*

Three weeks earlier, in the Old City of Jerusalem, an Australian
religious zealot, almost under the eyes of the soldiers guarding the holy
shrines since the Israeli conquest of the city, had set fire to the holy
mosque of al-Aqsa, enflaming Muslim opinion around the world
against Israel. The news of the fire had been a major, if late, factor in
the young conspirators' decision to act when they did. Throughout the
summer, fighting had intensified between Nasser's army and the Israelis
who had seized Sinai and the Suez Canal's East Bank in 1967.
Emulating Nasser's own conspiracy, which had overturned the Egyptian monarchy of King Faruk in July 1952, Qaddafi and his fellows
called themselves the Free Officers.

Lieutenant Riffi and a few friends, without firing a shot, find
themselves in full command of the situation in Sebha. Maintaining
close radio contact with Qaddafi and his two main companions in
Benghazi, Captain Muhammad Yusuf al-Mugarieff and Captain Mustafa al-Kharoubi, Riffi assures Qaddafi's Benghazi group of the success
of the revolution in the Fezzan.[4] As he hears the final lines of Qaddafi's
proclamation, Riffi probably muses that this was where it all started—
Sebha, where, in the 1950s, Qaddafi and his fellow conspirators were in
high school together before Qaddafi was expelled for his political
activity.

In Tripoli, Libya's main metropolis and oldest capital, many of the city's
ten thousand or so foreign residents, including Americans manning the
huge U.S. Air Force base at Wheelus Field, awake and eat breakfast
barely aware of what has happened during the night.

The conspirators, led by Lieutenant Abdel Salem Jalloud, Qaddafi's most faithful aide, employed a tactic used by that past master of the *inquilab* (military coup), Abdel Karim Kassem, when he overthrew the pro-Western Iraqi monarchy of the Hashemite family in Baghdad in July 1958. On the day before the planned coup troops of three army armored-car battalions received permission for a night training exercise. Instead of beginning maneuvers, the young officers and noncoms drove their vehicles directly into Tripoli. Well before dawn, they surprised and disarmed the Tripolitanian police and the British-staffed Tripolitanian Defense Force (TRIDEF). They then headed directly for the low-lying radio and television buildings facing the old Italian-built corniche that looked over the harbor. Quickly ascertaining by radio that Qaddafi's men had arrested the CYDEF commander in Cyrenaica and seized his main base at Gurnada, and that other small groups had taken over the post and telegraph building and the radio at Benghazi, they then established permanent radio contact with Cyrenaica. By 6:30 A.M., Tripoli radio was hooked up to relay Qaddafi's triumphant broadcast from Benghazi.

Out at Wheelus Field, which sprawls from the seacoast to the desert just east of Tripoli, Colonel John Groom, the base commander, gets the news from an orderly who tells him at breakfast that the BBC is reporting a "revolution of some kind" in Libya.

Within minutes all U.S. personnel have been restricted to the base and Groom is on the phone to the U.S. embassy. Training flights, by request of the new junta, are suspended. A young attaché, his voice quavering, briefly describes the night's events for Groom on the phone. The base intelligence staff, meanwhile, is working as fast as it can to translate for the colonel the radio proclamation being made by the unknown young man. The proclamation ends with what sounds to the small group of officers like a call to arms:

> *Thus will we build glory, revive our heritage, and revenge an honor wounded and a right usurped. O you who witnessed the holy war of Omar al-Mokhtar for Libya, Arabism and Islam . . .*

The experts soon identify, for those who knew or cared, who Omar al-Mokhtar was: he was the Cyrenaican schoolteacher who had led his faithful followers (including Abu Meniar, Qaddafi's father) in a heroic but finally fruitless guerrilla war that ended when Omar was cornered, captured, and hanged by the Italians in 1931.

Phone calls between the base and embassy office move slowly; the United States had been obliged, like other major powers under the monarchy, to maintain three separate but equal embassy offices in Tripoli, Benghazi, and the king's new mountain capital of Beyda (a token office, only theoretically equal to the other two).

Daryl Penner, a young American consul in Benghazi, is ready to drive to work at his consular office on Green Mountain Square, near Benghazi's heart. Before he arrives, he encounters George Dickerson, the Benghazi embassy's administrative officer, returning from an unsuccessful attempt to drive his child to school. "They've taken over," Dickerson tells Penner excitedly. "Who has taken over?" the younger officer asks. Dickerson explains that there are soldiers manning roadblocks and enforcing an apparent curfew: it has to be some kind of military takeover. Penner sets off for a walk and is soon confronted by a Libyan soldier, guarding a corner near the subdivision of houses where many American families live. No soldier was ever stationed there before.

Penner, who doesn't know Arabic, returns home and turns on his radio. At about 9:30 A.M. he hears a one-line report on the BBC that there has been some kind of military coup in Libya. Later, in mid-morning, he hears scattered shooting from the direction of Benghazi's public buildings, and later some isolated shots, perhaps fired to enforce the curfew. A neighbor heard some small-arms fire from the radio and television buildings much earlier that morning—perhaps warning shots fired when Qaddafi, Kharoubi, and company took over the station to broadcast the proclamation.

In Beyda, Joseph V. Montville, principal and only foreign service officer manning the post, finds himself and several other members of the diplomatic corps barred from entering their offices. Two days later they all celebrate by going on a group picnic in the nearby Green Mountains.

Late in the morning, U.S. embassy political officer David Mack climbs into a Libyan army Land-Rover parked near the embassy's Tripoli office. Sitting in front with the driver is a lean-faced young officer with no uniform insignia. Behind him sit the British and French chargés d'affaires in Tripoli. "Who are you?" asks Mack.

"Call me 'Sergeant Muhammad,' " says the Libyan. "As we told you on the telephone, we're having a briefing at the revolutionary headquarters." Sardined together in the Land-Rover, the driver, Mack, his British and French colleagues, and "Sergeant Muhammad" next drive to the Soviet embassy, only a short distance away. There they find a worried Soviet diplomat observing their approach.

Mack believes he has a good idea of what is going on in the Russian's mind. *What*, the Soviet embassy staffer must have been wondering, *in the name of Marx, Lenin, and all that's holy can the American, British, and French political officers be doing in that Libyan Land-Rover together? This looks like a put-up job. Can the West be muscling in on this Libyan coup?*

Either through "Sergeant Muhammad's" persuasion or because he had prior instructions to do so, the Russian gets over his initial shock and crowds into the packed Land-Rover with the others. Together they drive off to the temporary Revolution Command Council (RCC) headquarters in the radio and television building, on the corniche facing the Bay of Tripoli. There, "Sergeant Muhammad" and several colleagues brief the envoys of the Big Four on the events of the night before and the aims of the revolution. This gives David Mack enough material for his first substantial report of the day on the revolution's initial success and its apparent goals. "Sergeant Muhammad," as the Tripoli diplomatic community is soon to learn, is the revolution's Number 2 leader, Lieutenant Abdel Salem Jalloud.

In Tripoli, Benghazi, Beyda, and Libya's other main towns, top police officers and other officials of the old regime who were on the conspirators' early arrest lists are taken into custody by several hundred young officers and noncoms of the army.[5] By the time the morning sun has risen fully from the direction of Nasser's Egypt, the handful of unknown officers, who had daringly thrown their dice against tremendous odds, have—though few of them know it or dare to think it—won the first round. They wait for reaction—from the Libyan monarch in Turkey, from his appointed successor Crown Prince Hassan al-Reda, and from London, Washington, Cairo, and other foreign capitals.

**K**ing Idris al-Sanussi, the Libyan monarch, is vacationing on the Marmara Coast of Turkey with Queen Fatima. One of his first thoughts upon hearing the news is for the safety of their adopted daughter, Sulayma, who is still in Libya (and who has indeed been detained by the still-anonymous RCC). He is apparently confident, however, that the British and perhaps the Americans will help restore his regime; British writer Ruth First has reported that he told an aide the coup was a "trifling affair" and he (Idris) would soon go home in triumph. Before the end of the day, the Foreign Office in London would receive an urgent request from the king, through the Libyan embassy in Ankara, for

British military intervention "to restore order and peace and to protect lives." (At the time, Tobruk, a last possible royal stronghold in the once loyalist Sanussi heartland of Cyrenaica, still had not fallen; but this was mainly because the garrison there was no particular threat to the revolutionaries, and because Qaddafi and his fellow RCC members simply didn't get around to moving on Tobruk until September 3, when they secured it without bloodshed.)

Idris sends his counselor Omar Shalhi to London the next day for a twenty-minute interview with British Foreign Secretary Michael Stewart. In the meantime, he refuses the RCC's broadcast offer to return to Libya as an "honored citizen." Three days later, on September 5, the Arab world's most prestigious newspaper, *Al-Ahram* of Cairo, whose editor, Muhammad Hasseinine Haykal, flew to Benghazi to identify and sound out the unknown new leaders for Nasser, publishes what it says are the secret clauses of the Anglo-Libyan Treaty of 1953 that provide for British military intervention in the event the Libyan throne has to be defended. Code-named the Radford Plan, these clauses call for British forces to be airlifted—after a four-day alert period—from Britain, West Germany, Malta, and nearby Cyprus. The plan calls for no American participation, and it is supposed to be activated in the case of "Egyptian intervention"—a move by Abdel Nasser's army to take over Libya.

There are several problems about implementing this treaty, Michael Stewart probably explains to Omar Shalhi. First, there has been no Egyptian military intervention. Second, there has been no warning, no time to activate any alert period. Third—and it may be sheer coincidence—there has been some highly unusual Soviet naval activity along the Mediterranean sea-lanes between Libya and both Malta and Cyprus, where the Anglo-French component of the Suez operation against Nasser was mobilized in 1956. On September 4, when RCC control of Libya is assured, an RCC broadcast claims that Britain has refused Omar Shalhi's request to land British intervention forces in Libya because of the universal Arab condemnation of Britain such a move would arouse and because of "the presence of the Soviet fleet in the Mediterranean."

What was in fact happening was a major Soviet fleet exercise in the Mediterranean. It ran from August 19, nearly two weeks before the coup, to September 11, after the RCC had "gone public" and its power was well consolidated. From August 20 to 27, the Soviet *eskadra* in the Mediterranean conducted antisubmarine warfare (ASW) exercises off the coast of Cyrenaica, south of the big NATO bases of Crete. U.S.

aircraft based at Wheelus Field and in Greece and British forces at Akrotiri, the sovereign British base on Cyprus where the Suez expedition had been prepared, were easily able to observe these maneuvers and others connected with landing exercises near Alexandria, on the then hospitable coast of Nasser's Egypt. According to RCC insiders, there was no foreknowledge in Qaddafi's group of the Soviet maneuvers, which moved closer to Libya after September 1. To prepare for coastal landings in Egypt, the Soviets set up an ASW barrier of ships to the northwest of Alexandria between September 1 and 3. This barrier lay directly across the airlift route between the British base of Akrotiri in Cyprus and the one at al-Adem, Libya; and, beginning on September 6, the Soviet ships then moved westward to oppose a simulated U.S. carrier battle group that was supposed to be moving eastward from the area of Sicily. In this way, the Russian fleet units assumed strategic positions to meet either the U.S. Sixth Fleet sailing from the west or a British airlift from the northeast. It is highly unlikely that Qaddafi's group, which included no Libyan naval officers at all, knew of the Soviet fleet moves in advance, or coordinated their action with the Russians.

In Turkey on September 4, John Ellison of the London *Daily Express* succeeds in reaching the royal party at their seaside retreat shortly before they are to depart for a new villegiatura and temporary refuge at Kamena Vourla, Greece, and then for Egypt, where Nasser has guaranteed them asylum and hospitality. The news that the British government has decided not to intervene on behalf of the deposed king has arrived before him. In an interview published by the paper on September 5, the weary king, speaking slowly and carefully through an interpreter, tells Ellison that he is ill, tired, and never really wanted to be king anyway, but accepted kingship only "because of my feeling for Libya and for the Libyan people." More than anything, Idris claims, he wants to "hand on" his royal office. In 1963, he recalls, he had told the presidents of both Libya's legislative assemblies that he "no longer wanted to be king." Then, after going abroad for the summer in 1969, he had told them again, from this same place on August 4: "I cabled the two presidents saying that I wished to abdicate. I said I would give them a formal declaration that I would stand down and leave my crown to Prince Hassan. They replied, 'Wait until your return. Then in November we can discuss the whole matter here.' I agreed to this, but said if they continued to refuse my abdication, then I would go away." At the moment of the September 4 interview, Hassan's stand was still uncertain, and the old king added that whether Hassan took the throne or not "would depend upon him and the Libyan people."

But fifty-three-year-old Crown Prince Hassan al-Reda, who was arrested by the RCC along with scores of other old regime senior figures, announces his support for the new regime on September 5, renouncing all his rights to the throne and calling on the people to accept the new regime without violence.

In Cairo, a dispirited and ailing President Gamal Abdel Nasser is presiding over the first session of an Arab summit conference, discussing a common Arab strategy for rebounding from the humiliating defeat by Israel in 1967 and for confronting the Jewish state yet again in a battle to win back lost territories. General Muhammad Fawzi, the Egyptian war minister, has just reported that with proper inter-Arab coordination, the Arab armies should be ready again for battle with Israel within eighteen months. King Hussein then rises; the news of the coup against King Idris arrives while he is speaking. News of a coup against one Arab king is, of course, bad news for the others: Faisal of Saudi Arabia, Hassan of Morocco, the sultan of Oman, the emirs of Kuwait and the other Gulf principalities. Tactfully, Nasser pays tribute to King Idris. He recalls how when Egypt needed money to buy arms, he had sent his envoy to see Idris. "He promised," Nasser relates, "to give us 20 million pounds straight away on only one condition—that we should return to him a *subha* [rosary] which had been given by one of his ancestors to the al-Azhar mosque [in Cairo]."[6]

But when attention shifts from Idris to the conspirators, there is unexpected fear in the air. Nasser—along with some senior officials in Washington and Moscow—expected a coup in Libya, *but from a different camp*: from Colonel Abdel Azziz al-Shalhi and his followers, who wanted to put Crown Prince Hassan al-Reda on the throne. Their coup was to have been on September 4. Cairo was expecting to hear from Colonel Shalhi's brother, Omar, who may have been part of his brother's coup. Omar at the time was representing King Idris in London.[7]

Feverishly, the summit conferees speculate about the possible political pedigrees of the unknown Libyan conspirators. Are they Nasserites? Arab unionists who might eventually follow Nasser or some other Arab leader? Muhammad Haykal, chief editor of *Al-Ahram*, says his radio monitor picked up from an RCC communiqué from Benghazi the catch phrase "freedom, socialism, and unity." This, claims Haykal, proves that they are not supporters of the Arab Baath socialist party then ruling in Iraq and Syria because the Baathist slogan is "unity, socialism, freedom," "freedom" being last. Haykal tells Nasser that the young Libyans seem "close to us" in their thinking (Haykal liked to think that for Nasser, freedom came first).

Meanwhile, back in Benghazi, the RCC has sent an emissary—none other than Colonel Adam al-Hawaz, who has good contacts with the British and American embassies—to the Egyptian consulate in Benghazi with a message: they want to see an Egyptian envoy as soon as possible. When asked whom, Hawaz can think only of either Nasser himself—who was certainly not going to fly to Benghazi on what might prove at best a wild goose chase, and at worst a trap—or Haykal, whose articles in Al-Ahram were known throughout the Arab world. Nasser phones Haykal and tells him to take off at once.

Haykal sets off for Benghazi with a military officer, a political intelligence specialist, and a photographer in an Egyptian military plane. As they approach al-Adem base, they fly low because of British radar and air defense missiles there. The al-Adem tower asks the pilot to identify himself, his passengers, and his destination. Instead of responding, the pilot asks for instructions. He receives none. He manages to land instead at Bennina, the Benghazi airport. The airport is in total darkness. Then a few landing lights go on to reveal a row of armored cars on both sides of the runway.

First to greet Haykal is Mustafa al-Kharoubi, a member of the RCC group that seized Benghazi with Qaddafi early that morning. Haykal related later that Kharoubi, when told who Haykal was, embraced him and wept, saying, "I can't believe my eyes."

They drive to the Egyptian consulate, where Kharoubi tells Haykal about the revolution. "We are all believers in Nasser," he declares. But who, asks Haykal, is their leader? "You will see him tonight," says Kharoubi. "You can't imagine how pure he is." What, asks Haykal, is the leader's rank? "His rank is lower than mine because he was disciplined," Kharoubi says. "He was a captain like me, but he was reduced to first lieutenant."

At 2 A.M., Muammar al-Qaddafi walks into the consulate. Haykal is shocked at his extreme youth. Qaddafi explains to Haykal that he has named their movement al-Dubbat al-Wahdawiyin al-Ahrar ("The United Free Officers"), in emulation of the Egyptian revolution. They want union with Egypt. After carefully following all the events in the Arab world, they knew that Nasser needed a second front with Israel in the Arab East.

"He is forgetting depth," Qaddafi lectures Haykal. "Libya represents depth. We have hundreds of miles of Mediterranean coastline; we have the airfields; we have the money; we have everything! Tell President Nasser we made this revolution for him. He can take everything of ours and add it to the rest of the Arab world's resources to be used for battle." Qaddafi then tells Haykal to fly back to Cairo and tell President Nasser that "we do not want to rule Libya. All we have done is our duty as Arab nationalists. Now it is for President Nasser to take over himself and guide Libya from the reactionary camp, where it was, to the progressive camp, where it should be."

Haykal returns to Cairo to find a summons from Nasser to see him immediately. Nasser wants to study the photographs of Qaddafi the photographer has taken; Haykal orders them developed for Nasser's eyes only. Qaddafi and his companions, he tells Nasser, are "a catastrophe." Nasser asks whether they are against Egypt. Far from it, Haykal tells him. The problem is that they are "shockingly innocent" and "scandalously pure." They are Nasser's men. They want unity with Egypt, the sooner the better. Haykal, who has been deeply impressed by Qaddafi's enthusiastic yet ascetic personality, reports to Nasser that Qaddafi seems to be offering all of Libya's vast oil resources and strategic space on a platter, to serve in the common struggle against Israel and the Western imperialists. He relays what Qaddafi has said to him about the common background of the young conspirators, and how their organization had begun in secondary school, where they chose to enter military schools and get into the Libyan armed forces, which to them seemed to be the only possible instrument for changing Libyan society.

Nasser makes Haykal relate every detail about Qaddafi; Haykal even goes so far as to disclose the fact that Qaddafi was unshaven. Haykal then goes to get a few hours of sleep.[8] "Judging by all I heard," Haykal wrote in *Al-Ahram* on September 12,

> *I feel that the action prior to [the war with Israel] . . . was only a prelude and that accurate and organized work began after 1967. . . . When they began to learn from the sufferings of the 1967 setbacks by Israel, it was the overpowering conditions prevailing in Libya which fashioned and polished the core of their revolutionary characters. From suppression they derived an urge to spring forward; from observing corruption they gained ideals; and from their isolation they learned the importance of unity.*

That first encounter with Qaddafi in Benghazi deeply stamped Egyptian perceptions of Qaddafi for a long time. Sadat, who began as an uneasy friend of Qaddafi and became a deadly adversary, shared in these initial perceptions. He did not meet Qaddafi himself until a year later in Cairo at an Arab summit conference. He found him an "eye-catching character, with a revolver that never left his belt."[9]

In Washington, President Nixon, Secretary of State William Rogers, and presidential adviser Henry Kissinger are deeply mired in the widening war in Indochina. They realize that the crises caused by the rise of the Palestinian guerrillas in Jordan and the Egyptian-Israeli "war of attrition" on the Suez Canal are distinctly related to the Libyan coup. Libya, one of the Arab world's major oil producers, whose real estate is used for military bases by both the United States and Britain, has suddenly swung sharply and dramatically into the pro-Palestinian camp. Though senior U.S. officials know that the Shalhi coup was brewing, they disclaim any foreknowledge of the Qaddafi takeover. Many do not appear to grasp its significance at once.

The Nixon administration cannot and does not share all of Israel's obvious concern about this threatening new shift of the balance of power. Indeed, the two high policymakers who know most about Libya, Deputy Assistant Secretary of State for African Affairs David Newsom and Ambassador to Libya Joseph Palmer, have what they think are sound reasons for believing that the young Libyan officers would prove to be important assets in the struggle to keep Soviet influence and communism out of the Arab world.

Shortly before the coup, Newsom had exchanged jobs with Palmer. Newsom, as he himself recalls, "was well aware, months before the coup, that things were not going well for the kingdom."[10] The atmosphere of corruption and intrigue, which had spared the respected figure of the eighty-year-old king but tainted many of the courtiers and high government officials, had bred many rumors about plots and conspiracies, some of them true. About a year before the coup, in 1968, Newsom, as ambassador, had warned Idris in a private audience that the U.S. military presence at Wheelus Field and all of the ancillary training facilities in Libya did not mean that the United States—whatever the British attitude might be—would protect his throne. In his first dispatches on the coup, Palmer informs Nixon, Rogers, and Kissinger that the still-anonymous young men of the RCC promise to protect all

Western interests, including the pumping of oil. They have, he adds, proclaimed a kind of Muslim welfare state, drastically raising wages and banning alcohol as a step toward implementing Koranic law in the new republic. Qaddafi (the CIA and the embassy by now know the name of the young lieutenant), now promoted to the rank of *al-aqid*, or colonel, in his obvious Muslim zealotry would certainly be anti-Communist.

The British government, after rejecting intervention to restore the king, began leaning toward recognizing the new junta, although the British wondered how to recognize a new government whose identity was not even known. Three days after the coup, British Ambassador John Freeman calls on Newsom to discuss recognition. Newsom, already respected as one of the most seasoned experts in African and Arab affairs, feels that the new men should be given a chance. Freeman agrees. The United States and Britain, along with most of the other leading powers and the Afro-Asian-Arab nations, soon recognize the new revolutionary government.

But who is being recognized? Who is Qaddafi?

Abu Meniar and Aissha al-Qaddafi, his parents, who had produced two daughters as well, pooled their meager savings to send Muammar to Koranic elementary school and finally to high school at Sebha in the Fezzan. There, at the age of fifteen, he had begun in 1959 to listen to Nasser's speeches on the "Voice of the Arabs" and to discuss them with his classmates. One of them, Ali al-Houdery, was the last chief of the Libyan diplomatic mission when that mission was expelled from Washington by Secretary of State Alexander Haig in May 1981. Other classmates at Sebha who formed the first teenage revolutionary cell with Qaddafi included Abdel Salem Jalloud, who was to become his most trusted deputy; Bashir al-Hawadi; Mustafa al-Kharoubi (Qaddafi's intelligence chief, still surviving in 1981); and Abu Bakr Yunis Jabir (Libyan army chief of staff, and also a survivor in 1981).

Qaddafi insisted that his fellow cell members observe "revolutionary disciplines," avoiding strong drink and dissolute ways. Qaddafi's puritanism, in part a reaction against the creeping corruption spread by the foreign oil companies and contractors that jockeyed for positions and favors under the old regime, went back to his Bedouin origins.[11] He told all of his schoolmates to prepare for a military career, since that was the only way to make a revolution. Qaddafi was expelled from Sebha for political activity, in particular for leading demonstrations against the king for his lack of support for Nasser and the Palestinian cause against Israel. Before transferring to high school in Misurata, Qaddafi set up a series of "first cells" in Sebha. Each member was supposed to create his own study cell, referred to as a "second cell." Members of each cell were supposed to be unknown to each other; membership in the secondary cells required Qaddafi's approval.

At Misurata, one of the large Tripolitanian towns, he broadened the base of the conspiracy by forming "first" and "second" cells there too. Jalloud, who had first planned to attend medical school, was persuaded with others to prepare for the military college. Qaddafi's class graduated from high school in Misurata in 1963 and entered military college in Benghazi almost at once. The proximity of the University of Benghazi, as Qaddafi's former high-ranking government planner Omar al-Fathali points out, made it possible for the conspirators, whose ranks had now been joined by Omar al-Meheishi at Misurata, to have contact with Arab nationalists and other dissidents among the students.

This was the real beginning of the Free Officers' movement as such. Qaddafi and his classmates graduated in 1966. Most were sent abroad for advanced training; newly commissioned Lieutenant Qaddafi went to Beaconsfield, England, for the British signal corps training that served him in such good stead on September 1, 1969.[12]

From his nine-month training course at Beaconsfield, Qaddafi knew well that communications and their control are direct channels to power. After his return from England he was stationed at a series of Libyan army outposts. By means of radio and a simple cryptosystem he himself devised, Qaddafi kept in touch with members of the first and second cells.

The Suez war in 1956 aroused persistent rumors in Libya that the Arab defeat was due partly to British use of its Libyan bases. The trauma of Suez nourished the dreams of the young conspirators in high school at Sebha and Misurata. The subsequent Arab defeat in the June 1967 war rankled them even more. As their secret network of lieutenants and captains exchanged brief coded messages, they spent their evenings listening to Radio Cairo's "Voice of the Arabs" program, with its heady promise of coming revenge. One such broadcast seemed especially for them:

*Dear Arab brothers, raise your heads from the imperialist boots, for the era of Tyranny is past! Raise the heads that are bowed in Iraq, in Jordan, and on the frontiers of Palestine.*

*Raise your head, my brother in North Africa. The sun of
freedom is rising over Egypt and the whole of the Nile Valley
will soon be flooded by its rays. Raise your heads to the skies.*[13]

Based at Gar Yunis near Benghazi, where he could regularly visit his
parents on weekend passes and carefully follow the webs of politico-
military intrigue being woven around the royal court, Qaddafi in early
January 1969 sent a four-line "first alert" to his fellow plotters: Check
control of soldiers, transport, arms, and ammunition. When they
signaled that this was done, Qaddafi set March 21 as the day of
revolution.

As luck would have it, the Egyptian singer Oum Kalthoum, a sort of
motherly Arab version of Marian Anderson and Joan Baez rolled into
one, scheduled a concert that very night in Benghazi. Oum Kalthoum
was and still remains a living legend for the Arabs. Initiating a
revolution on the night of her recital would have been not only in
extremely bad taste, but also even contrary to the Arab cause—Oum
Kalthoum used to improvise long ballads about Palestine, Nasser, and
the martyrdoms of the Arab heroes. And this performance was a benefit
for al-Fatah, the Palestinian guerrilla group. Most of the royal regime's
senior figures, who had to be arrested, would be in the concert until the
early morning hours of March 13. To seize them would immediately
spread the alarm.

Qaddafi called off the coup for that night, and visited his parents in
Sirte instead. Driving back to camp at Gar Yunis at midnight, he and
two companions had a blowout in which their car overturned and was
badly damaged. Buried under the wreckage were plans for the coup.
There were anxious moments among the conspirators when a wrecking
crew arrived and began to raise the junked car. The crew found not the
coup plans, but a bottle of distilled water and mistook it for gin. The
Royal Libyan Military Police did not use breath tests; ironically,
Qaddafi was roundly chewed out for the sinful use of alcohol, a
substance he never touched.

Coup day was then moved to March 24, but again it was postponed:
King Idris visited Benghazi unexpectedly and had extra protection with
him. June 5, the anniversary of the 1967 war, was the next proposed
date. The Shalhi brothers, planning their own coup, sniffed trouble
brewing, and had some of the Free Officers transferred to new posts and
abroad for training. Idris left in July to spend the summer in Turkey and
Greece; on August 4 he announced from Turkey that he planned to step

down. Qaddafi knew the Shalhis and their men were preparing to act no later than September 4. He knew the time for him to act could not be postponed again.

Virtually no Western correspondents were in Libya on September 1. Most of us who were covering the Middle East were preoccupied with the Arab summit in Cairo, the war of attrition along the Suez Canal, or, like myself, were at our base in Beirut between voyages. Libyan embassies mostly ceased to function for several days; as there was no hope of obtaining a visa in Beirut, I flew to Tunis. One young attaché in the Libyan embassy there seemed more knowledgeable and accommodating than his colleagues. "We have no budget and no authority to send visa request cables to Tripoli for you," he said. "We don't know who the new rulers are. The only instructions they have given is that you must send your cables to Tripoli, addressed to the RCC. And make sure they're in Arabic!"

As the Tunisian posts and telegraphs then had no teleprinters for transmitting Arabic characters, I typed out, laboriously, a brief petition in Arabic transliterated phonetically in Roman letters. The young attaché verified that there was no Israeli stamp in my passport; placed an authenticating code word in my message (my somewhat disjointed Arabic text amused him no end); and speeded me on my way to the post office, where I paid for the cable and prepaid the reply (a bill of about one hundred dollars altogether).

During the full week I waited in Tunis, the RCC gradually emerged from their collective shell. On September 8, a week after the coup, with the identities of the RCC members still undisclosed, the RCC formed a cabinet. The two military men with the best contacts with the British, Americans, and Egyptians, Colonels Adam al-Hawaz and Musa Ahmed, got, respectively, the critical interior and defense portfolios. Salah Buassir, became the first foreign minister. None were Free Officers; it soon became apparent that these were front men approved by the revolutionaries.

On September 12, I finally got my visa and flew to Tripoli to call on the new prime minister, Mahmoud Suleiman al-Maghrebi. His last name means, literally, "the North African," though he is not North African but Palestinian. He has proved to this day to be one of the important actors in the entire Libyan drama.[14]

Maghrebi was born in 1935 to a Palestinian mother and a Libyan-Syrian father who moved to Libya in the late 1950s when Qaddafi and his friends were forming their first cells in the Sebha high school. Like most Palestinians, the Maghrebi family realized that education was the key to escape from the hopeless squalor of the refugee camps and they helped Mahmoud to get a first-class secondary-school education and then saw to it that he acquired Libyan citizenship—Palestinians in their diaspora must try to acquire local citizenship in order to qualify to work. Through connections at the American University in Beirut, Mahmoud won a scholarship to George Washington University in Washington, D.C. There he learned the basics of petroleum engineering and geology. He went on to finish law school at Johns Hopkins University, and was then hired by the Esso Corporation to work in Libya. He became a practicing lawyer and a secret Baathist. During the nationalist explosion against the Idris regime that erupted during the 1967 Arab defeat by Israel, he was jailed for nationalist activity, which consisted mainly of organizing oil-company workers in a nationalist union, which he used to try to enforce the oil embargo against the United States. A court sentence of four years in prison deprived him of Libyan nationality; his release in an amnesty came in August 1969, just before the coup. Another trained petroleum engineer, a Libyan named Anis Ahmed Shitawi, became the first minister of oil.

After separate brief conversations with him, I compared notes with my close friend Joe Alex Morris, the Mideast correspondent of the *Los Angeles Times*.[15] "Do you realize," Joe asked me, "that this guy is likely to be the key figure in the new regime as far as working out an oil policy is concerned?" As usual, Joe was right.

Maghrebi repeated to us the assurances already transmitted to the oil companies that their work would continue uninhibited by the revolution, and led us wrongly to anticipate that the new regime would be composed mainly of technocrats like himself.

The doctrinaire young men of the RCC were already imposing their own will on the country. Within a short space of time, several hundred of the remaining Libyan Jews—already victimized in the 1956 Suez and 1967 June war riots—were expelled. Thirty thousand Italian settlers, many of them tradesmen and artisans whose skills the new republic could ill afford to do without, were deported. The proud and ostentatious Italian Cathedral of the Sacred Heart of Jesus in downtown Tripoli was deconsecrated and proclaimed the Mosque of Gamal Abdel Nasser. The Tripoli fire department threw ropes and cables around the stubborn crosses that graced its roof and pulled them down. The RCC purged the government car pools of their Mercedes, which to them symbolized the old regime's arrogance, and drove around instead in Fiats, Land-

Rovers, and Volkswagens. They displayed the riches of the royal palace, which became the People's Palace. The RCC, twelve young men in all, set up shop in the Bab Azziziya military barracks outside the center of town. Qaddafi lived there like a monk in an austere bare room with little more than his Koran and a shortwave transistor radio on his writing table. Later, Bab Azziziya was to become Qaddafi's well-guarded fortress, with a secret tunnel leading directly to his private house.

In the afternoon of September 13, Joe Morris and I wandered down to the Foreign Ministry, a faded, ornate Ottoman-period building with some Italian embellishments. There was little or no security in evidence. Minister Salah Buassir and several dignitaries dressed in white burnooses and red tarbushes chatted with a few officers.

One of the officers stood alone on the balcony just outside the door. He wore uniform khakis without insignia of rank and a cap decorated with gold braid. Joe and I introduced ourselves, trying out our Arabic. The officer looked amused by us, but he was friendly with just a trace of shy aloofness. When I asked him who he was, he answered in English, "Just one of the revolutionary council." His well-chiseled features and flashing eyes looked beyond us, roving restlessly, speculatively over the men in the room. "None of us are giving interviews right now."

We made some more desultory conversation.

"Obviously," Joe said, "your group believes in collective leadership."

"Just like the Algerians," he answered. "You know the Algerians? The Algerian revolution? Like them, we are against the cult of the personality."

Almost a decade earlier, I told him, I had covered most of the eight-year struggle of the Algerians for independence from France, a war that had probably cost a million Algerian dead and would have torn apart France itself if it had not been for General de Gaulle.

He shrugged. "Yes," he said. "General de Gaulle was a great man. But did you know ben Bella and the Algerian leaders?" This was a reminder to us that the local leaders of the Third World are supposed to make revolutions, not accept autonomy, independence, or other favors their colonial masters are prepared to offer them.[16] "We are like the Algerians," said the officer. "We are not after publicity. Maybe you will know our names later, but not now." He moved past us into the room. "Now, if you will excuse me, we have some work to discuss here."

"That one," said Joe as we were gently shooed out of the meeting room by a single security guard who had suddenly appeared, "is obviously someone we are going to hear a lot more about."

Very soon afterward we found out that the officer we had been talking to was Qaddafi himself. The next day, over at Tripoli's broadcasting station, a friend replayed for me the tape of Qaddafi's September 1, 1969, proclamation. Its final words gave a keynote for the time ahead:

> *O you who witnessed the holy war . . . who fought the good fight. . . . O sons of the steppe, sons of the ancient cities, the upright countryside. O sons of the villages . . . the hour of work has come. Forward!*

# TWO

## THE SHORES OF TRIPOLI

On the map Libya looks like an oblong wedge stretching from the Mediterranean shore of Africa down into the Saharan wasteland. It is a country whose landscape, seascape, and artifacts seem to transport you backward into the past, not forward into the future. The trappings of Qaddafi's visionary dreams—the flags, slogans, pictures of him, and other revolutionary paraphernalia that suggest the bleakness of Orwell's *1984* transferred by magic to the coasts of Africa—are everywhere, but once they are out of sight they are out of mind. You need no magic carpet to feel and see around you the timeless Libya, as it was for ages before the Greeks and as it doubtless will be ages and ages hence.

A thin green line of civilization has hugged the Libyan shore between Tripoli and the Tunisian border since ancient times. It was as carefully cultivated by the ancient Romans and their North African subjects as it was by Mussolini's colonists who arrived in the 1920s under the ensign of Fascism. It was neglected by most of the successive waves of foreign conquerors during the two thousand years in between, and it looked then (and still looks now, despite the proliferation of big seaside villas crowding together in some areas nearest Tripoli) rich and full of promise. High, stalky date palms and luxuriant patches of esparto grass, one of Libya's chief exports before the oil boom arrived in 1959, stretch inland as far as you can see.

As the distinguished historian Majid Khadduri has observed, foreign conquerors have often landed but rarely penetrated inland beyond this strip of green in Tripolitania for long.[1] Colonial wars were struggles between the desert and the town. The desert and those who live there always won and returned to the coast to reap the culture and the riches of the departed conquerors. The Berbers of Tripolitania and Cyrenaica inherited the towns and vineyards of Rome and Greece; in 1970 Muammar al-Qaddafi inherited the U.S. Wheelus Field, British military bases, and an oil-empire network stretching from the derricks and drilling sites of the desert north along miles of pipelines to the refineries and tanker ports of the coast.

The key to survival in this arid land, as in the rest of the Saharan countries, is of course not oil but water. Not a single perennial river waters Libya. During the winter rains, flash floods sweep through the wadis, then dry up to a trickle under the merciless sun. Underground water, in some cases great oceans of it, have been discovered by the oil companies in their impatient drilling for the black lifeblood of our industrial world. Water seeps slowly through the underwater rocks, feeding springs and wells that nourish the oases.

Most of Libya's 679,358 square miles is a sea of sand, dust, and rocky hills. Towns and villages are its green islands, with date-palm groves instead of the eucalyptus, citrus, juniper, and lentisk trees of the coast groves. The Jebel Nafusah mountains and the nearby plain of Gefara in the northwest are divided from the Jebel al-Akhdar, or Green Mountains, of Cyrenaica in the northeast by the Sirtic Desert. This desert stretches due south of Sirte, Qaddafi's ancestral home and stronghold. Several plateaus break the monotony of the great sand seas in the southern province of Fezzan, which is bounded on the far south by the forbidding Tibesti mountain range in northern Chad.

The three areas of Libya—Tripolitania, Cyrenaica, and the Fezzan—have always looked at the outside world in widely different ways because of their wide separation and different histories. Until the United Nations created Libya out of the debris of Italian colonization in 1951, inhabitants scarcely thought of the three as comprising one country, even though *Libya* in Latin and *Libye* in Greek were ancient names for the entire known part of northern Africa.

Tripolitania had been under Roman rule; its name comes from the Greek *tripolis*, the "three cities." Tripolitania, Libya's largest subdivision, is Latin for "land of the three cities," which were, in ancient times, Sabratha, Leptis Magna, and Oea. All three were once trading posts run by the Phoenicians from Tyre in today's Lebanon; later Carthage in today's Tunisia. Here the gold and ivory (and later, in Turkish times, the slaves) of inner Africa were brought to market. The

Greek colonizers who followed the Phoenicians therefore named this coast Emporia, or the "land of markets." Leptis Magna became the Roman capital of Emporia in the time of Emperor Septimius Severus, the first North African Berber ever to make it to Rome and wear the imperial purple as Roman *imperator*. Sabratha was probably Greek before it became Roman; it is the oldest part of Tripoli today and stands on the ruins of Oea.

Roman Sabratha now sits in stillness on the Mediterranean shore. The upright columns of its temple of Jupiter frame a blue seascape; the Mediterranean seems to permeate its ruined columns. You can hear the gentle yet insistent undertones of the surf from the open-air gallery of the first-century A.D. theater, which Italian archaeologists carefully restored, and where European troupes played Shakespeare and Pirandello before World War II. There are crude frescoes of the late Roman Empire, already tainted by the heavy influences of barbarian Europe. This is what the area around Pompeii might have looked like had it survived the eruption of Vesuvius and existed another three hundred years.

Cyrenaica, to the east, lies only about 180 miles from Crete, the largest Greek island—which puts Qaddafi's Soviet-made short- and medium-range missiles within range of the largest NATO installations in the eastern Mediterranean. The few Greek traders and sponge fishermen who still live in Benghazi and its surroundings today will tell you that they are the last of an unbroken line of Greeks who first settled in Cyrenaica. According to Greek tradition, the oracle at Delphi instructed the first Greek immigrants in the early seventh century B.C. to leave the overcrowded island of Thera and go to Cyrenaica. Berbers, according to Herodotus, the father of history, guided them to a spot about twelve miles inland where, their hosts told them, a "hole in the heavens" would give them ample rain for farming.

Eight Greek kings ruled the Greek province of Cyrene until it became a republic in 400 B.C. Cyrene became the "mother" of five other cities, called the Pentapolis. The Carthaginians to the west were warded off, but the Persian army of Cambyses, after conquering the Greeks in Egypt, occupied Cyrene briefly. When Alexander the Great entered Cyrene in 331 B.C. the Greek population cheered and presented him with war-horses, but begged him not to drive westward and attack the tough Carthaginians. After the conqueror of the world died in Babylon (present-day Iraq) in 323 B.C., his Macedonian generals got the empire. One of them, Ptolemy, got Egypt and Cyrenaica. Rome acquired the region in 74 B.C. and ruled it, along with Crete, as a Roman province. Meanwhile, Cyrene had become one of the Hellenic world's main cultural centers, producing wine, grain, wool, aphrodisiac herbs, and such learned men as the geographer Eratosthenes and the epigrammatist Callimachus, remembered by those who know their classics for his statement "A big book is a big bore."

Down in Fezzan, which Qaddafi, more than any other ruler in Libya before him, has regarded as the desert bridge to a possible future empire in Black Africa, lived the most intriguing and mysterious of the Berber tribes, the Garamantes. They mechanized desert warfare with their war chariots, and commanded a powerful desert kingdom around 1000 B.C. on the trade route between the western Sudan and the Mediterranean coast. Their inscriptions in *tifinagh*, the geometrical alphabet still used by the Tuaregs of the central and southern Sahara, are practically their only direct traces extant, apart from the writings of Herodotus. From their capital at Germa they controlled the desert caravan routes from Ghadames to the Niger River, eastward to Egypt, and westward to what is now Mauritania.[2] It is the same supply route Qaddafi has used since 1975 to channel arms to the Polisario movement fighting the Moroccan Royal Army in the western Sahara.

The Roman emperors brought with them Rome's mixture of civilized urbanity and savage cruelty. Many Christians and others were tortured and killed by Septimius Severus, the Berber emperor in Rome, and his wife, Julia Domna, heads of the official pagan cult. Later, history's best-known convert to Christianity, Emperor Constantine the Great, whose head appeared on the coin in Sabratha, made it both chic and politic to be a Christian in North Africa. The Church then became an arm of Rome's state power.

The Christian faith's already flaccid hold in Libya was further weakened by Christianity's decisive separation from Judaism. Jews from Palestine had settled in North Africa during the first Roman persecutions of the Jews in Palestine (63 B.C. to A.D. 135). A Cyrenian king-messiah, Lukus Andreas, in A.D. 115–117 led a Jewish revolt that spread eastward into Egypt; then came the revolt of the messianic Jewish rebel, Simon Bar Kochba, against the Roman Emperor Hadrian. Christians in North Africa seem not to have supported the Jewish revolt; gradually, Jews and Christians grew apart. Prominent North African rabbis no longer recognized the Septuagint, a Greek version of the scriptures used by the Christian Church, returning instead to the Hebrew text. In Palestine and Babylon, Jewish schools founded in the second and third centuries produced Talmudic teachings that were brought to North Africa.

The state Christian church soon became riddled with Eastern heresies that questioned official Christian dogma, weakening it for its impending overthrow in North Africa by Islam. In Cyrenaica, the Monophysite heresy and its tedious, bloody quarrels over whether the true nature of Christ was human or divine, finished the job of undermining Christianity. When the Roman Empire was divided into Eastern and Western halves in A.D. 395, the dividing line ran through the Sirtic Desert, leaving Greek Cyrenaica and Latin Tripolitania even more separate than before. After brief periods of rule by Vandals, barbarians from Europe, and the Byzantine Empire, Arab armies conquered North Africa in the name of Islam. By A.D. 700 the coastal cities had been converted to the new faith and social order. Islam appealed to the Berbers, who were weary of the gods of Phoenicia, Greece, and Rome with all their confusing cults and sects. Today Islam appeals to Africans and is making great headway in Black Africa as a missionary faith for much the same reasons: it is simple; it has no real hierarchy or priesthood; and it promises the direct contact with God that North Africans, like so many others in the Afro-Asian world, seem not to find in Christianity or Judaism.[3]

The Arab conquest and the wars between the Arab dynasties, some of which rose out of the Sahara south of Morocco and today's Algeria, delayed the national unity of Libya for a long time—until the intensely nationalistic era of the nineteenth and twentieth centuries. As Adrian Pelt, the High Commissioner of the United Nations who presided over the difficult birth of the Kingdom of Libya in the early 1950s, has observed, some fourteen foreign occupations over the course of three hundred years have had no permanent impact on Libya. Only Ottoman Turkish rule, which began with the Turkish occupation of Cyrenaica in 1517 and the capture of Tripoli from the Knights of St. John of Jerusalem in 1551, and the subsequent Italian conquest in 1911, had really significant effects upon Libya's thoroughly Arabized culture and society.[4]

The Hapsburgs prevailed in Spain and the Turkish naval power in the Mediterranean. Ottoman generals and admirals captured Tripoli and other coastal towns for their sultans, and occasionally mounted expeditions against the Arab Bedouin of the interior. But the Turks kept mostly to themselves. The sultan in Constantinople ruled through a pasha. The pasha's main support was a corps of janissaries (from the

Turkish word *yeniceri*, meaning "new soldier"), Turkish peasants who devoted their lives to a professional military career. If there is still considerable Turkish blood in the veins of coastal Libyans today it is because Turkish military men developed a taste for liaisons and marriages with Arab women; their offspring, called *khoulouglis* ("sons of servants") rose to the top of society. One such *khoulougli*, a cavalry officer named Ahmed Karamanli, became a local leader. From his reign (1711–45) arose a new hereditary monarchy, mainly Arab, that wielded some power in Cyrenaica and Tripolitania. Ahmed Karamanli's successors, faced by falling income from taxes, loans, and tribute collected abroad, were less successful.

Subsequent direct rule from Constantinople in 1773–95, during the time of the American Revolution, was followed by the rule of one of those rare strong leaders in Libyan history who, like Qaddafi, have imposed themselves forcefully on their own country and the world around it. This was Yusuf Karamanli, a Turco-Arab dictator who allied himself with the bey of Tunis and with Napoleon Bonaparte during Napoleon's 1799 invasion of Egypt. During Yusuf's reign, from 1795 to 1832, the first bitter confrontation between the United States and the Arab world occurred. This confrontation helps to explain the stereotypes and ugly caricaturing of Arabs and Muslims that survives to this day in our mass media—television, newspaper cartoons and comics, popular novels like Harold Robbins's *The Pirate.*

This first crisis in Libyan-American and Arab-American relations had its origins in the prosperity of Tripoli and some other North African city-states. North Africa's trade with Europe was flourishing; the stones of Leptis Magna were used to build Versailles and St. Germain des Prés in eighteenth-century France. At the same time, a main source of income for the Barbary states were their pirate ships. The Barbary corsairs conducted piracy as well-disciplined commerce that was an extension of Turkish naval strategy in the Mediterranean.[5] The pirates were usually supported by local rulers like Yusuf Karamanli in Tripoli. The rulers' private and public treasuries (usually indistinguishable from one another) were greatly fattened by the seizure of European and American merchant ships, the enslavement of their crews (some of whom built harbor fortifications at Tripoli), and the holding of American citizens for ransom. In 1799 President John Adams's administration began paying annual tribute to the local potentates in North Africa to ensure immunity for U.S. ships. Yusuf's share of the tribute was eighteen thousand dollars a year.

In September 1800, President Adams sent the frigate *George Washington* to Algiers with an installment of tribute to be paid to the dey of Algiers, the Ottoman sultan's representative in that city. The dey ordered Captain William Bainbridge, the *George Washington*'s commanding officer, to carry an ambassador and a large chest of tribute to the sultan in Constantinople. When Bainbridge refused, the dey told him: "You pay me tribute, by which you become my slaves. I have a right to order you as I may think proper."[6] Surrounded by Algerian guns, Bainbridge was forced to hoist Algerian colors and accept the mission. During the first months of 1801, Yusuf Karamanli in Tripoli upped the ante for annual tribute to $250,000 a year, a very large sum for the sparse federal treasury of the infant United States.

President Thomas Jefferson objected to the Adams administration's policy of appeasing the pashas and pirates. In 1804 he sent a sizable U.S. fleet to punish them. The U.S. Navy, having scarcely recovered from the revolution and already faced with threats from the European powers, was still getting its sea legs in distant places. Blockading Tripoli and the adjoining Libyan coast proved to be a difficult operation. Outside Tripoli harbor, the frigate U.S.S. *Philadelphia* was trapped when it hit a shoal. Its crew surrendered and was captured with the ship. In one of the U.S. Marine Corps's earliest and most successful commando raids (inspiring the words "shores of Tripoli" in their hymn), Lieutenant Stephen Decatur infiltrated the harbor and blew up the *Philadelphia*, ending her use by the Tripolitanians as a gunship commanding the harbor.

The American squadron poured shot after shell into Tripoli. Yusuf, well ensconced behind the thick walls, which were reinforced by the Ottomans and the Knights of St. John, resisted. He pressed the *Philadelphia*'s hapless crew into hard labor to strengthen the fortifications even more; he also had the captain and first officer conduct tactics, navigation, and language courses for the captured junior officers.

President Jefferson, a man of action, decided that enough was enough. He assigned a former U.S. consul in Tunis, Cyrus Eaton, to carry out a plan to overthrow Yusuf and replace him with his older brother, Hamed. Early in 1805, Eaton, Hamed, and a motley group of adventurers, mercenaries, and U.S. Marines marched from Alexandria westward across six hundred miles of desert. With fire support from the reinforced U.S. naval squadron in the Mediterranean they captured the Cyrenaican port of Darna. Jefferson's special envoy, Tobias Lear, negotiated a peace accord with Yusuf: Yusuf dropped his demand for regular tribute payments, and accepted $60,000—half his original demand, but still a tidy sum for those days—as ransom for the *Philadelphia's* crew. The United States, in turn, dropped Hamed's claim to the throne. The settlement received mixed reactions in the United States as it was something less than complete victory, but dovish sentiment prevailed and the agreement was accepted. Operations at sea against the corsairs, however, continued until 1815. Not until 1970, when Colonel Qaddafi sent the U.S. Air Force base packing from Wheelus Field, was there any but the normal and casual contact between Libyans and Americans.

It was under the often careless Turkish rule of the nineteenth century that Cyrenaica experienced the religious revival that has determined Libya's fate down to the Qaddafi period. The family that brought it about came not from Libya but from Algeria, which from 1830 on was under the guns of its French conquerors. This family was the Sanussi, founders of the Sanussiya religious order. The founder was Sheikh Muhammad ibn Ali al-Sanussi, born in the Berber village of Mazouma in western Algeria. After religious studies in Fez and Morocco, and a pilgrimage to Mecca, Sheikh (pronounced "shehk," not "sheek," and used here in the sense of a religious teacher) Muhammad settled in the oasis of Beyda, Cyrenaica. To purify the faith and strengthen resistance to the encroachment of the infidel (the Christian European), he founded a series of *zawiyas*, or religious lodges, each one a hostelry, school, and sometime trading post rolled into one. The first was in Mecca, and the first one in Libya at Beyda.

Europeans, especially casual travelers and explorers in Libya, were sometimes kidnapped or shaken down by tribesmen using the Sanussi name, often mistakenly called Sanussi fanatics. Actually, the Sanussi were quite different from fanatics. Instead of practicing begging or extreme asceticism, Sanussi followers were expected to work for a living. The mystical and extreme practices of the Muslim Sufi orders and brotherhoods—processions, self-flagellation, and dervish-type whirling and dancing—were forbidden. The Sanussi's aim was to study the Koran, live pious lives, help their brethren, and purify the faith. This stern, truly ascetic approach had far more appeal to the rational-minded desert Bedouin than did the esoteric practices of the Sufis. It won great respect for Sheikh Muhammad, whose followers called him "The Grand Sanussi." They believed he possessed the quality of *baraka*, a kind of personal blessing or white magic, said to be a quality of any successful, charismatic leader.

In the far south of the Sahara, Sheikh Muhammad's successor, the second master of the order, Muhammad al-Mahdi, led a similar revival movement and a missionary drive southward into Black Africa. Soon the movement took on a political cast: it aimed at resisting European, at the time mainly French, encroachment. By 1867, fifty Sanussi lodges covered the Barca plateau in Cyrenaica. By 1897, the Sanussi had established one at Bir Allali, in the north of what is today Chad; Mahdi was killed when the French army captured Bir Allali. French army captain Gentil Lamotte, one of the early French Arab-language specialists attached to the colonial troops, wrote prophetically in 1902 that

> Islam had brought immense progress to all of the [Central African] populations, but it is a serious danger for us: never will a Muslim accept, without serious reservation, Christian domination, and this truth appears more certain because, in the center of Africa, the influence of the Sheikh al-Mahdi ibn Sanussi is considerable. As distinguished from other Muslim brotherhoods, this one has pan-Islamic dreams. It wishes and pursues above all else the expulsion of the infidel from the Dar al-Islam [the Land of Faith], and for a long time it has been preparing for this goal.[7]

While the Sanussi fought French influence in their own way, the Turks along the Mediterranean coast had another approach: the military reconquest of Libya. In 1835, as the French threat from Algeria grew, the Turks deposed the last of the Karamanlis and reestablished direct rule by the sultan in Constantinople. To complicate matters, Arab resistance to the Turks was growing everywhere. In the interior it was led by the prestigious chief of the Awlad Slaiman tribe, Abdel Jalil Seif al-Nasr, who had gradually taken over the Fezzan during Yusuf Karamanli's war with the U.S. Navy and the last years of Karamanli rule that followed. Abdel Jalil went on to unite the tribes of Tripolitania and the Sirte region against the Turks as well.

One of these tribes was the al-Qaddafa, which was eventually to produce the parents of Muammar al-Qaddafi. The Qaddafa was one of a group of clans that were forced out of Cyrenaica by stronger tribes and that fell under the spellbinding influence of the Sanussi orators. Despite the zeal and cunning of their chiefs, the Arabs of the regions that resisted were eventually subdued by a Turkish general, Ahmet Pasha, who adopted ruthless, earth-scorching tactics.

Before he died, the Grand Sanussi founded the order's central lodge at the oasis of Jarabub, near the Egyptian border. There the North

African pilgrims' overland route to Mecca intersects with the Saharan trade route over which the gold, the ivory, and the slaves of Black Africa came to the Mediterranean coast. Just before his death in battle with the French, Mahdi moved the order's headquarters to the oasis of Kufra, about four hundred miles to the south. Kufra, as we shall see later on, became so sacred to the next master of the order (he became King Idris I) that Occidental Petroleum's shrewd overlord from California, Armand Hammer, was able to make its development in the 1950s and 1960s a principal focus of his successful effort to fashion a worldwide oil and commercial empire.

Turkish rule was to give way to Italian. Italy, with its swaggering soldiers and mercantile-minded adventurers, was the next foreign power to carve out a piece of North Africa at the expense of the Libyans. Italian traders, explorers, and missionaries had been visiting Libya for many centuries. With France and Britain racing for colonial dominion throughout much of the rest of Africa, the Italian kingdom decided by 1911 that its turn had come: if it did not take Libya, someone else would. The British were already in Egypt; and the French were well established in Algeria, Tunisia, and the vast lands south of Libya, then called simply the Sudan (not to be confused with the Anglo-Egyptian Sudan, south of Egypt). The diplomatic stage was set by several understandings with other colonial powers: an Anglo-French convention in 1899 conceded that Italy had a sphere of influence in Tripolitania; in 1909, Czar Nicholas of Russia agreed not to oppose Italian plans. Italian emigration to Tripolitania was expected to relieve southern Italy's population pressure. Liberals and socialists, however, wondered whether Libya really offered Italy any strategic or commercial advantages.

Italians began writing popular songs about *Tripoli, bel suolo di amore* ("Tripoli, fair land of love"). Paintings depicted the African shore in romantic terms. The chauvinist Right won out. In an almost festive atmosphere in October 1911, the Italians delivered to the Turkish authorities in Libya an ultimatum that no honorable soldier could accept, and with a forty-hour deadline.

After a short but thunderous bombardment of Tripoli harbor, Italian troops landed near the city on October 7. At the moment, Turkish armies were heavily committed in the Balkan wars in southeastern Europe. The Italian navy easily captured the Greek islands of the Dodecanese group and Rhodes, then under Turkish occupation. Libya, however, proved not to be an easy conquest.

Said Pasha, the grand vizir who ran the empire for the sultan in Constantinople, faced a serious logistical problem. His dilemma may contain some lessons for any power contemplating war in Libya. Italy controlled the sea-lanes, and the Dardanelles were blocked. The Turkish navy was almost out of action, with several armored cruisers wallowing helplessly in the mud of Constantinople's Golden Horn. The only communication lines to Libya lay across the land routes through Syria and Egypt. There was no way to send troop reinforcements; only individual officers could risk the overland route. Two senior Turkish generals, Enver Pasha and Ali Fethi Bey, were assigned to Libya. So was a still relatively unknown young nationalistic captain named Mustafa Kemal (his name meant "maturity and perfection"), already a member of the secret revolutionary organization called the "Committee of Union and Progress." Like Qaddafi sixty years later, Mustafa Kemal was dreaming and plotting of power; after World War I, he emerged as Mustafa Kemal Ataturk, the savior and father of modern Turkey.

With two friends, Mustafa Kemal crossed Asia Minor, Syria, and Palestine only to learn that the British occupiers of Egypt, by rights a Turkish province, had declared Egypt to be neutral in the Libyan war and had closed the frontier, even to individual Turkish military personnel. Mustafa Kemal dressed in Bedouin clothes and took the train westward from Alexandria. The Egyptian officer at the Libyan border post, detesting the Italian Christian imperialists as much as the British ones, let him pass. Kemal's comrades-in-arms received him jubilantly, promoted him to major, and gave him command of the sector of Derna. *Jihad,* or holy war, against the Christian invaders was proclaimed from the depths of the Sahara to the shores of Tripoli, and the Arab tribes of the interior rallied to the aid of their Turkish overlords, now seen as brethren of the same faith. Despite his personal rivalry with Enver Pasha, the future Ataturk managed to distinguish himself as a fierce field commander in a land he already knew from a tour of duty in Libya in 1909.

To bolster their own ranks and give their side a Muslim flavor too, the Italian generals threw in Muslim troops from Eritrea, Italy's first colony on the Horn of Africa. The Libyans and Turks considered them mercenaries and traitors to Islam. This redoubled the ferocity of the Libyan-Turkish resistance.

The highly professional Turkish soldiers at first stood their ground near Tripoli, and the Italians made little progress inland. Next the Italians tried a fresh seaborne landing at Misurata, but still made little progress. And they were severely beaten at Rumeila. Yet at the end of 1911 the Italians announced the annexation, on paper, of Tripolitania and Cyrenaica, despite their failure to advance southward from the coast. "If any nation of Europe has the right of possession or protectorate in this land," trumpeted the royal government in Rome, "that nation is Italy."

Unfortunately for the Turks and Libyans, Turkey was defeated in the Balkan war and signed a peace with its European opponents, including Italy, in October 1912 at Lausanne. One of the conditions of the peace treaty was that the Turkish sultan give up his rights in Libya, though he did not have to recognize Italian sovereignty there. (A guarantee of "administrative autonomy" for the Libyan Arabs, also written into the treaty, was never realized.) Although the main Turkish forces sailed home, the Turks continued to send the Sanussi guns, ammunition, and other supplies. Most of the Tripolitanian Arab resistance fighters surrendered and were disarmed before the outbreak of World War I in 1914; in Cyrenaica, however, the story was different. The Sanussi master, Ahmed al-Sharif, took command and brought faithful Sanussi cells in Tripolitania and Fezzan under his Cyrenaican command. In Misurata, a local chieftain, Ramadan al-Suheili, joined the war, after seeming to desert to the Italians. As the guns of August thundered in Europe, a general Libyan offensive forced the Italians back to their coastal strongholds at Tripoli, Homs, Zuara, and the ports of Cyrenaica.

The Sanussi allied themselves with the Central Powers, Germany and Austria-Hungary, against Italy in World War I. The Germans used Misurata as a submarine base; arms and ammunition for the resistance movement arrived there aboard German submarines. The Italians in Libya and the British in Egypt became allies in 1915, when Italy formally entered the war on the Allied side. The Germans, allied with the Turks, stepped up supplies to the Libyan fighters. Prestigious Muslim leaders, including Nuri Pasha from Turkey and Abdel Rahman Azzam from Egypt (later the secretary-general of the Arab League, formed during World War II), arrived in Cyrenaica to join Ahmed al-Sharif at his Sanussi headquarters. The Turco-German objective was to pin down the Italian forces in Libya and then attack the British in Egypt. The Italians hoped the British would help them to conquer Libya, but the British kept their operations centered in the desert confines of Egypt and Cyrenaica. Spurred on by Nuri Pasha, the Sanussi tried to take on the British army but were badly beaten in the Western Desert of Egypt.

As a result of this defeat, Ahmed al-Sharif handed over the reins of power in the Sanussi movement to Sayyid Muhammad al-Idris. In 1918 he became new Grand Master of the Sanussi order; in 1952 he became King Idris I. Ahmed al-Sharif fled to Constantinople aboard a German submarine.[8]

The defeat of the Sanussi in Egypt ended serious resistance to the Italians. Idris and other Cyrenaican leaders in 1917, with advice and help from the British government, signed a kind of armistice with the Italians near Tobruk. Fighting ended, and both Italian and Sanussi zones of influence were recognized in Cyrenaica, with each side responsible for security in its own zone. Sayyid Idris became the paramount leader of the Cyrenaican Libyans. Italy, one of the weakest and weariest of the 1918 Allied victors, was unable to mount overseas military expeditions, and therefore granted limited self-government to Tripolitania and Cyrenaica. Provincial Libyan councils were supposed to advise and assist the Italian administration. A little more peacetime was bought with two new agreements, in 1920 and 1921, that gave Idris the hereditary title of *amir* ("prince") in Cyrenaica. Conflict between Sanussi Libyans and the Italians was increasing, however.

Between 1918 and 1923, the Tripolitanian Arabs tried to establish and operate their own republic, based at Gharian, with Abdel Rahman Azzam, the Egyptian statesman, as adviser. In 1922, faced with renewed warfare with the Italians, the republic offered to make Idris the amir of Tripolitania; after some hesitation, Idris, already hampered by his failing health, accepted. In his acceptance letter, Idris first mentions "the unification of the fatherland" as an aim of his national policy.[9] But he returned to Egypt and remained an absentee leader, not to return to Libya until the Allied victory in 1943.

In Italy, the political ferment that followed World War I produced the new and heady brew of Italian Fascism. Benito Mussolini came to power in 1922 with a program of frank and aggressive imperialism. The new Italian governor-general in Libya under the first Fascist government, Count Volpi, and the Italian army commander, Marshal Badoglio, embarked on a vigorous drive to occupy and govern all of Tripolitania. In Cyrenaica the going was much rougher for the Italians. A rural schoolteacher named Omar al-Mokhtar, who was to become the legendary hero and leader revered by Qaddafi and his generation, took over the leadership of the growing guerrilla resistance to the Italians. As the Italians advanced farther and farther south from their strongholds at Benghazi and Tobruk, Omar al-Mokhtar's partisans harassed their supply lines and punished them with surprise attacks.

The Italians realized that in order to conquer the coastal towns and the Cyrenaican hills and plains to their south, they would first have to deprive the Sanussi partisans of their desert bases in the southern oases. Using air power and new desert fighting vehicles that resembled old Ford trucks with great sheets of boilerplating riveted onto their frames, they occupied Jarabub oasis in 1925, and from there moved southward to take Zella, Aujila, and Jalo in 1927.

The town-dwellers of Cyrenaica played a largely passive role in the resistance. Omar al-Mokhtar, who had begun fighting the Italians back in 1911 under Ahmed al-Sharif, and had then spent the years until 1923 with Idris in Egyptian exile, commanded a force of between two and six thousand guerrillas, mainly nomads. Political leadership in Libya was supplied by Idris's brother, Reda, until Reda's capture by the Italians and banishment to Sicily in 1928. After that, Omar al-Mokhtar was the effective governor of the unpacified territory by night, moving men and supplies and collecting both taxes and recruits for the resistance movement. In 1925, an Italian-Egyptian agreement gave Italy undisputed sovereignty over the Sanussi strongholds of Jarabub and Kufra oases, making it easier for Italy to seal off the Egyptian frontier and thereby cut off the guerrillas from their privileged sanctuaries and sources of supply in Egypt.

Omar al-Mokhtar's devoted guerrilla bands continued to resist, attacking Italian troop convoys, communication lines, and supply trains. By 1929, Marshal Badoglio had become governor-general and Marshal Rodolfo Graziani, another war veteran, had become supreme field commander. Graziani's forces occupied the Fezzan oasis of Mizda, pressing the Libyans farther and farther into the Sahara. He used the same search-and-destroy tactics that the French and Spanish armies were employing against another notable North African nationalist leader, Amir Abdel Krim, in the Rif mountains of northern Morocco, though on a much larger scale. Folk literature of the North African desert recounts how some of the captured Libyans were dropped alive from airplanes. Water wells were plugged with concrete and stones. The Italians slaughtered herds of camels, sheep, and goats. Whole tribes, their livelihood thus ended, were herded into concentration camps in the desert. This savage behavior by the Italian military, and the subsequent seizure, settlement, and colonization of Libya's arable pasturelands, and oases have never been forgotten or forgiven by Libyans of Mokhtar's generation, or Qaddafi's. Such cruelty goes far to explain the punitive measures that both the royal regime and Qaddafi eventually took against the remaining Italian settlers.

In 1930, Graziani began operations in Cyrenaica by building a two-hundred-mile-long barbed-wire fence along the Egyptian border, from Bardia oasis on the seacoast to just north of Jarabub oasis, to halt all resupply and reinforcement operations from Egypt's Western Desert. Anyone who harbored or protected the guerrillas faced ruthless vengeance from the Italians; the nationalist leaders were gradually killed or captured. On September 11, 1931, Omar al-Mokhtar, pinned beneath his horse during a clash in the Green Mountains, was cornered, wounded, and captured. After a confrontation with Graziani, he was hanged before a crowd of twenty thousand Libyans.

With Italian conquest virtually complete, Mussolini proceeded to establish the North African portion of what Mussolini saw as the new Roman Empire. His goal was to make Libya into what he called the "fourth shore" of *mare nostrum*, "our sea." Tripolitania and Cyrenaica were divided into the new provinces of Tripoli, Misurata, Benghazi, and Derna. The antique name, Libya, was revived and given to the entire territory. Fezzan was designated as South Tripolitania. The Italians called it a "military region" and gave it a separate military administration, in much the same way that France and Spain had set apart the southern regions of their Moroccan and Western African (Spanish Saharan) protectorates and colonies.

Rome ruled the colony directly, with Italians holding all administrative posts. Mussolini poured billions of lire into building a modern system of roads, public works, port facilities, and rural irrigation, all for the benefit of Italians, not Libyans. By 1940, 110,000 Italian settlers, many of them landless peasants, had been brought to Libya. Much more ambitious colonization projects would have raised the Italian population to over half a million by the 1960s, had World War II not intervened.

During Fascist rule, Italy concluded with neighbors two territorial agreements that are still remembered by those neighbors today. An agreement with Britain and Egypt transferred a corner of the Anglo-Egyptian Sudan known as the Sarra triangle to Libya in 1934. In 1935 an accord called the Mussolini-Laval Agreement moved the Libyan border with Chad (then a French colony) about sixty-five miles south to include the so-called Aouzou Strip (Qaddafi reoccupied this strip in 1973–75). This territorial concession to Italy was never ratified by the French parliament, which was keenly aware of Mussolini's greed for a slice or two of the French colonial pie. In 1939 Mussolini formally incorporated Libya as a province of metropolitan Libya in the same juridical relationship that Algeria had to France.

After Hitler invaded Poland, forcing World War II upon the reluctant

West, Libyan Arab leaders gathered in Alexandria in October 1939. They saw Italy's likely involvement in the war (which came about only in June 1940) as a golden opportunity for liberation. Idris was chosen as leader of the nationalists; and the Cyrenaican leaders, already in touch with the British in Egypt, announced support for the Allies. By August 1940, British-Libyan military cooperation had begun, despite the reluctance of the Tripolitanians to enter into an alliance with a power that seemed far away and unlikely to win the war, or to admit the supremacy of the Sanussi, whose strength lay not in Tripolitania but in Cyrenaica. The British commander in Egypt, Sir Henry Maitland Wilson, organized formation of the Libyan forces, who fought under the Sanussi flag and a British commander. Britain refused Libyan requests for a guarantee of Libyan independence after the war, but Foreign Secretary Anthony Eden assured the House of Commons that "at the end of the war the Sanussi in Cyrenaica will in no circumstances again fall under Italian domination."[10] Recruiting Cyrenaicans who had fought against the Italians in the colonial wars, Wilson raised five Libyan battalions.

The tide of desert war rolled back and forth three times across the Cyrenaican desert. The forces of the Italians, bolstered and finally led by German General Erwin Rommel's Afrika Korps from February 1941 on, as well as the British Empire forces of Generals Wavell, Montgomery, and Auchinleck, fought modern history's first great tank battles in the desert. With air and naval support, they left a trail of devastation along the Mediterranean littoral, from al-Alamein in Egypt to Qaddafi's Sirtic homeland in Libya. To this day Qaddafi's government insists that the World War II combatants, especially Germany, Italy, and Britain, must pay Libya reparations for the minefields and unexploded bombs and shells that have taken a toll of hundreds of Libyan dead and injured since 1943, occasionally still doing so in remote areas. Once the Americans and Free French had joined the North African battle by landing in Morocco, Algeria, and Tunisia in November 1942, Montgomery's British Eighth Army captured Benghazi in November 1942 and Tripoli in January 1943. In the south, de Gaulle's General Jacques Leclerc de Hauteclocque led the French forces from the south into the Fezzan. All of Libya was then free of Axis troops. Separate British military governments in Tripolitania and Cyrenaica and a French military regime in the Fezzan took over the administration until the independent Kingdom of Libya came into being in early 1952, under United Nations auspices.

Before the Allies signed the Italian peace treaty in February 1947, Italy giving up "all claims to its African possessions," there were many rounds of Big Power bickering over what was recognized as a prime piece of strategic real estate.

Soviet dictator Joseph Stalin, realizing Libya's tremendous strategic importance during either a war or the armed peace with Western Europe that followed World War II, bid early for a Soviet foothold in Libya. Though Mussolini had fallen in 1943, and Britain had promised Idris in 1942 that Cyrenaica would never again fall into Italian hands, the Big Powers did not really face up to the question of the future of Libya and Italy's other colonies until 1945. At the Potsdam Conference in 1945, the Soviets put in a strong bid for a trusteeship over Tripolitania. Already the future outlines of the Soviet-NATO confrontation over Libya were evident: the Italian government asked for return of all Libya to its control. It was willing, it indicated, to concede strategic base areas to Britain and the United States, provided it could have sovereignty.[11] At Potsdam, the foreign ministers seemed to favor a U.S. trusteeship for a ten-year period, after which Libya would become fully independent.

The Soviets had a different idea. Foreign Minister Vyacheslav Molotov asserted that Moscow had "wide experience in establishing friendly relations between different nationalities" (at that moment, the Soviets were tightening their grip on the "friendly nationalities" liberated from Nazi control at the war's end in Poland, Hungary, Rumania, and Czechoslovakia, as well as East Germany and Austria). If the Soviets were given the administration of Tripolitania during the ten-year period, Molotov added, he could assure the Council of Foreign Ministers that "the Soviet system would not be introduced into this territory, apart from the democratic order that is desired by the people." In a moment of rare candor, Molotov added that the USSR would like to have a sea outlet on the Mediterranean, and such bases in Tripolitania under Soviet control would serve that purpose. The Western powers were swift to reject this.[12]

By the time of the next Council of Foreign Ministers meeting in Paris in April 1946, Britain had proposed immediate independence for Libya. Molotov watered down Stalin's original trusteeship bid; this time, he suggested a joint trusteeship. The Italian colonies would be divided into four units, with Italy exercising joint authority in each with one of the Big Four—the United States, the Soviet Union, Britain, and France— until later independence. Molotov proposed that the Soviets and Italians jointly administer Tripolitania. This rejected, Molotov, doubtless with an eye on the rising bid for power of the Communist party in Italy, suggested that Italy alone should have trusteeship in Cyrenaica. There was no agreement on this. The final decision, at the Paris Peace Conference, was that the Big Four governments should try to determine the fate of the Italian colonies together, and if they were unable to, they would finally accept the recommendations of the United Nations General Assembly.[13] A four-power commission that visited Libya was unable to agree on final recommendations. The issue of Libya's future was also complicated by Egyptian territorial claims for "security" reasons along the border. Egypt claimed that this strip of territory, reaching from the Mediterranean frontier to the frontier of Sudan in the Sahara and including the plateau of Sollum, the oasis of Jarabub, the port of Bardia, and the oases of Arkinu, Uwaynat, and Sara, was part of Egyptian territory Britain had ceded to Italy when both Egypt and Libya were under foreign rule. The Egyptian claims were never accepted, but they have remained a dormant issue that any Egyptian president could easily invoke in a determined offensive against Qaddafi; this was foreshadowed by Egyptian attacks on some of these places, which the late President Sadat had called "nests of terrorists," in the brief Egyptian attack of July 1977.[14]

After months, indeed years, of wheeling, dealing, and maneuvering, it became clear that the Soviets and the West were sharply divided on the Libyan issue, as on so many others. The Truman administration and the British evidently agreed in the summer of 1949 that they had to convince Italy that total independence for Libya was the wisest step. Ambassador Henry Villard, later the first U.S. ambassador to the independent Kingdom of Libya, explained that a UN trusteeship would have precluded Libya's future role in Western defense. However, an independent Libya, under Western influence, could "freely enter into treaties or arrangements with the Western powers looking towards the defense of the Mediterranean and North Africa."[15]

The Korean War, erupting in 1950, was soon to reconfirm for the Truman and Eisenhower administrations what Villard already knew, and what Ronald Reagan's administration had to rediscover in 1981: the North African coast and hinterland are of tremendous strategic importance. An enemy established there could soon end Western control of the Mediterranean sea-lanes and communication lines to the Persian Gulf. In the months after the outbreak of fighting in Korea in 1950, the United States rushed a multimillion-dollar construction program to expand the base facilities it was already using with British consent in Libya (Wheelus Field and related installations), and to build a chain of new bases in Spain and Morocco for use by the U.S. Strategic Air Command (SAC) as part of its nuclear deterrent against the Soviet Union.[16]

In any case, a UN General Assembly resolution decided in late 1949 that Libya, including Cyrenaica, Tripolitania, and Fezzan, should become an independent and soverign state no later than January 1, 1952. A UN commissioner, Adrian Pelt, was appointed to assist the Libyans in preparing a constitution and the other attributes of statehood. A council including representatives of Egypt, France, Italy, Pakistan, Britain, and the United States was appointed to assist him. Though the Soviets protested that Libya ought to get immediate independence, and France had reservations about the short transition period, the General Assembly adopted the resolution by a vote of forty-eight to one, with nine abstentions.[17]

Independent Libya's new constitutional monarchy thus began operation with the blessings of the United Nations and the good wishes of the superpowers, despite the Soviet disappointment over Libya's retention within the Western zone of influence. The system of palace government in some ways resembled an American-type federal system, but it did not alter the traditional tribal nature of Libyan society. The elected house of representatives, or the appointed senate, or the king himself could initiate laws. The king could also veto laws, dissolve the parliament, appoint the provincial governors, and take other measures, such as declaring a state of emergency, when needed. Islam and the religious legitimacy lent to Idris by the long tradition of the Sanussi in history were key elements in this palace rule.

After one hotly contested election in February 1952, when a traditional nationalist politician named Bashir Bey Sadawi and his National Congress Party conducted a tumultuous and occasionally violent campaign in Tripolitania, the king suppressed and banned political parties, and deported Sadawi. This and the suppression of the Omar al-Mokhtar Club, an elitist political group in pre-independence Cyrenaica, sounded the death knell of party politics in Libya, even of the limited quasi-Western type practiced after independence in Egypt, Morocco, and several other Arab countries. From now on, politics were conducted in a conspiratorial, semi-clandestine way. This helped to create the conditions for Qaddafi's coup in 1969. Qaddafi's continuation of the royal practice of banning all political parties and Western-style politicians, which he and the RCC consider hopelessly corrupt and decadent, seems to ensure that if any new political movement success-fully unseats them from power it too will have had clandestine roots.

A second feature of the eighteen-year-old Kingdom of Libya that was decisive in bringing about its fall to Qaddafi was its welcoming of Western military bases. For a time, a succession of Libyan prime ministers, the most notably successful of whom was undoubtedly Mustafa ben Halim (in office from 1954 to 1957), managed to strike a delicate balance. That balance, at least in words and diplomacy, saw an anti-Zionist and anti-imperialist Arab state accept de facto membership in the Western defense system because of the presence of British and American bases.[18]

Wheelus Field had been operated by the U.S. Air Force from 1944 to 1947, when flights were suspended until reactivation during the Korean crisis in 1950. At first, the field functioned primarily as part of MATS (Military Air Transport Service). After ben Halim successfully negotiated the base treaty with the U.S., Wheelus, named for a U.S. pilot killed in the Pacific War, became a main training base for NATO. The Strategic Air Command, with an eye on the easy flight plan across NATO partner Turkey to the southern USSR, found it was a natural base for B-47s and other aircraft that could deliver a nuclear payload in case of World War III. In 1956, the year when the Suez War first stirred major Libyan nationalist riots against both the United States and Britain, the U.S. Seventeenth Air Force transferred its headquarters from Rabat, Morocco, to Wheelus. Gunnery and bomb-practice ranges and a Mediterranean communications center flourished.

Libya's twenty-year defense treaty with Britain, signed in 1953, had helped provide the impetus for the Eisenhower administration to regularize Wheelus's existence with a similar accord signed with ben Halim. The American treaty was due for review in 1970, the very year when Qaddafi forced evacuation of both the British and American bases. Libya was supposed to receive about $40 million in U.S. economic aid for twenty years. Annual U.S. subsidies were later increased in a military aid agreement signed in 1957, two years before the first major oil strikes. The Kingdom concluded other treaty arrangements, including defense and military-supply relationships, with France, Italy, Greece, and Turkey.

To counter the effects of Radio Cairo's "Voice of the Arabs," which so fascinated Qaddafi and his fellow conspirators, the United States helped to finance a Libyan station in Benghazi. The United States hoped—in vain—that its influence would replace Cairo's. As a result, a European observer reported in 1970 after Qaddafi's takeover, what was then known as "the radical Arab bloc" had "two powerful stations—in Cairo and in Benghazi—the former originally financed by the British and the latter by the Americans."[19]

There was plenty of other American influence in Libya for Qaddafi to root out. In the period between 1957 and 1959, on the threshold of the oil age, the U.S. aid mission in Libya had grown to be one of the largest in the world, perhaps the second largest after the one in South Korea. American advisers and technicians, mostly non-Arabic speakers who depended on Palestinian translators, operated in Libyan federal and provincial government departments from agriculture to education. With British advisers, they trained Libyan police. Libya joined the International Monetary Fund (IMF) and the World Bank (IBRD) in September 1958.

Soon, however, the American aid advisers and most of their Western colleagues would be leaving. An oil boom was on the way that would provide the Libyans with all the funds they needed to buy what they wanted. The technology, military hardware, and expert advice they could buy with their newfound oil money were destined to turn their vast, rustic, and dirt-poor kingdom into a wealthy nation, into a power to be reckoned with in the Third World.

# THE GREAT OIL BOOM

The story of modern Libya is the story of oil. Under the seas of sand and stony wasteland lie vast quantities of oil and gas, and nearby is an oil-thirsty Europe. Oil and energy sources have been the keys to Qaddafi's power; they have also brought fabulous fortune and wealth to a few of the Western world's oilmen and financiers who had secured a position in Libya during the monarchy. High-quality light oil with little sulfur—ideal for Caribbean and North American refineries that make the high-octane gasoline on which the American motorist depends—is the main reason why neither President Ronald Reagan nor any of his predecessors could lightly contemplate overthrowing Qaddafi even for his support of terrorism. Libya's oil is both a weapon and a shield. No one dealing seriously with the country in commerce, politics, or war can fail to consider the oil or the far-reaching effects it has had on Libya's economy, people, and politics.

The account of Libya's oil boom, from the first oozings found by Mussolini's scholarly seeker Professor Ardito Desio up to the 1980s, begins as a tale of long ignorance and hesitant, timid starts. In our own day, it unfolds as a story of growing prosperity for a people who had known only grinding poverty, and of political and financial power that neither the Libyans nor anyone else could have dreamed possible a generation ago.

At the end of World War I, when oil strikes in Arabia and Persia had already lured the British and the Americans into many of their fateful rivalries and adventures in the Middle East, nothing was known of any oil in North Africa. Nowhere in the French, Spanish, Italian, and British Protectorates, which stretched along the African shore from Gibraltar to Sinai, were there surface signs of petroleum—no flickering gas fires as in Iran, no sluggishly flowing asphalt ponds as in Iraq.

It was Professor Desio of Milan University who made the first detailed geological map of Libya and then, in 1935, began watching water wells, drilled by Italian crews to irrigate the land for Italian farmers, for traces of oil or natural gas. [1] The Italian state company divided the country into zones of exploration and began serious drilling, especially in the Sirtic Desert, in 1940. But, like the Soviet equipment used forty years later in the Middle East, the Italian rigs were simply not up to the task of penetrating the desert's tough hide. The outbreak of war in Libya and Egypt brought the search to an end; neither the Axis nor the Allies had time to drill holes. Then, a year after independence, the royal Libyan government granted the first eleven reconnaissance permits. French oilmen, after considerable exploration of their own in the Algerian Sahara, struck oil at Edjeleh, on the border of an area assigned to France in a 1955 treaty signed by Mustafa ben Halim, Libya's third prime minister, and French Premier Pierre Mendès-France. Each side gained from the agreement, and that had a number of consequences. France— and the future Algerian state—got an added area of about 10,000 square miles in return for financial help to Libya. There was an assurance for Libya that French troops still occupying the Fezzan would leave. In return for the promise of evacuation of French troops from Fezzan, Libya promised to employ French civilian technicians at the airfields there, including Sebha, Ghat, and Ghadames. France was guaranteed the right to continue using an airfield at Edjele that abutted on territory assigned to Libya. What this amounted to was a continued French military and surveillance presence near areas the French knew were being used for smuggling arms to the Algerian nationalist FLN, which was in full revolt against France. [2]

These arms transports were being discreetly arranged by the same Prime Minister ben Halim who—while under fire from critics at home for handing over the rich oil-bearing territory to France—was helping the Algerian nationalists in any way he could. By the 1980s, the treaty threatened to destroy the good relations between North Africa's two most "revolutionary" states, Algeria and Libya. In a new Libyan atlas published in 1976, the old pre-1956 boundaries were shown. They included portions of Niger and Chad as well as Algeria. By 1981, Qaddafi was threatening to cause major problems with the Algerians by having his national oil company order an American firm holding a concession on Libyan soil to drill in a pocket of nearby territory claimed by Algeria.

As things stood in August 1956, when the Libyan-French treaty was ratified, ben Halim had already finished what was his greatest achievement for Libya and, at the same time, the most solid basis for Qaddafi's later power over oil. This was a well-thought-out, detailed Petroleum Law. It ensured that no single foreign company or group could gain a monopoly in Libya, as an American company had done in Saudi Arabia, or a British one in Iraq.

Oil companies interested in taking their chances in Libya were able to get the first prospecting permits under a 1953 law. Those companies that responded and carried out surveys were then consulted by the ben Halim government on how best to draw up the new Petroleum Law. When their comments were in, ben Halim appointed Anis al-Qasim, a Palestinian attorney and Libyan government official, to head the drafting committee. Oil company representatives took part in the work, and the law was written, passed by parliament, and put into force on July 18, 1955.[3]

To appreciate the shrewdness and foresight of ben Halim and his advisers, and how this was to pay off for Libya down through the next generation, it is well to remember how the United States and the world stood with regard to energy back in those pre-OPEC days (OPEC was not created until 1960; Libya joined in 1962). Oil was still cheap, selling at around two dollars per barrel or less. Cheapest of all was oil from the Middle East. This made it easy for the "majors" or "Seven Sisters"—the giant companies of Exxon (then Esso), Mobil, California Standard, Texaco, Gulf, British Petroleum (BP), Royal Dutch-Shell—and the smaller Compagnie Française des Pétroles (CFP)—to keep their control of world oil supplies, since only they were established in the Arabian Peninsula, the Persian Gulf, Iran, and from wherever else the cheap oil came. It was difficult for the smaller companies ("independents") who wanted to challenge the giants of Big Oil to muster the financing or the organizational strength to break into the Mideast market. Besides, there was always the strong possibility that the Seven Sisters would use their Mideast oil as a weapon to gain new territory and business at the expense of the independents. The independents, however, profited from the opportunity offered by the Iranian crisis of 1952–54, when nationalist-minded Premier Muhammad Mossadeq (eventually destroyed by the Shah and the Western companies and regimes) tried to nationalize the oil fields, and the British-owned consortium shut them down. When a new Iranian oil consortium was set up, the United States insisted that Exxon, Mobil, and also several American independents be given shares in it. This gave several independents the opportunity to acquire crucial organizational and political experience.

In Iran and Saudi Arabia, the local governments had dealt with the big companies *en bloc*. To avoid this, ben Halim and his experts divided Libyan territory up into many small concessions and parceled them out to as many different companies as possible. This was to give future Libyan governments the option of dealing separately with each company on concessions and for whatever oil was actually found. After 1969 this enabled Qaddafi to acquire both carrots (new concession arrangements and non-nationalization of equity) and sticks (the companies' large dependency on Libya as a principal source of crude). The Petroleum Law encouraged exploration and commercial pumping of oil. Since the law also obliged the oil companies to turn concessions back to the Libyan government where they were not active, it was in the companies' own self-interest to pump out as much of the profitable Libyan crude oil to the nearby European market as possible.[4]

Libya's map was divided into grids, and irregularly shaped concession blocs were superimposed on them. The more independents who wanted in, the more the Libyan treasury would take in customs duties, surface rents, and other payments. Libya itself (if not ben Halim, who was already a successful engineer and contractor) and other members of the ruling oligarchy were poor. The money was urgently needed for development, and to free themselves of dependence on the military-tied subsidies of the United States, Britain, and, in the earlier years, France. Also, the greater the number of companies taking part, the more local patronage and payoff money there would be to help hold Libya's fragile federal structure together.

The majors wanted territory close to the Mediterranean, to avoid the cost of building long pipelines to oil tanker posts. These and other transport expenses increase as one moves farther into the desert places of Libya's interior. Ben Halim's team had anticipated that. They saw to it that Libyan law limited the size of concession plots nearest the sea to 30,000 square kilometers apiece. The less attractive sites, down in the Sahara, were much larger. In this way, the royal government was able to grant plots close to the water to a great number of oil companies. This meant more competition, more payments, and more patronage.

As it turned out, the biggest oil finds came not from the coastal concessions in the fifty-mile-wide strip from the Tunisian to the Egyptian border but inland from there, in the Sirtic Desert. To spread around the new income, the Libyan royal government obliged companies to include large expanses of Saharan territory, in Fezzan and southern Cyrenaica, where there had been little drilling activity even by the start of the 1980s. A few fortunate companies received coastal concessions shaped like long, narrow tongues extending from the shore down to the Sirtic Basin. In this way Exxon gained the rights to its fabulously rich Zelten field; Amoseas acquired Nafoora ("fountain"); Mobil and its partner Gelsenburg of West Germany got Amal ("hopes"); and Oasis obtained a rich field with the Italian name of Gialo. The parent companies of the Oasis group, known originally as Conorada, bid independently of one another, acquired choice acreage, and later pooled their acquisitions.

This oil policy has remained unique in the Middle East and North Africa until today. Its uniqueness has become Qaddafi's main strength. In every other important oil-producing state of North Africa and the Islamic states of the Middle East, oil production has been either totally nationalized or retained by one large concessionaire that has kept most other companies out. This has ended the kind of changing relationship with the host government, like that of ARAMCO with Saudi Arabia in former years. The Saudi kingdom has more recently become ARAMCO's owner by gentle stages with profit to all. The major concessionaire formula prevailed in Saudi Arabia, Iran, Iraq, Qatar, Abu Dhabi, Bahrain, and Oman, to be replaced later by partnerships and joint ventures. Independents and smaller companies have staked out roles in some Persian Gulf states, Egypt, the neutral zone between Kuwait and Saudi Arabia, and elsewhere. Nowhere, however, did independents' production become dominant. In Libya, by contrast, many of the oil concessions given to both majors and independents became productive in almost equal degree, right from the start.[5]

A brief, prosaic news release from the Esso Corporation in Libya on April 12, 1959, brought what to experts was startling news:

> Esso Libya announces its Zelten No. 1 well flowed approximately 100 barrels in one hour of sour 37 degree gravity oil stem test at a depth of approximately 54,000 feet. This well is located in Cyrenaica on Esso's Concession No. 6 and is

*approximately one hundred miles from the Mediterranean and two hundred miles south of Benghazi. The well is currently being drilled to a greater depth.*[6]

This signaled the spectacular phase of the Great Libyan Oil Boom, like nothing seen since the California Gold Rush in 1849. All of the companies that had obtained concessions under ben Halim's laws raced to move their equipment in and begin drilling as quickly as possible. The Libyan method of dealing with the companies separately encouraged all manner of competition. Once confidence in Libyan oil was strong, one ingredient of this competition became a rivalry as to who could get to which Libyan officials and bribe or buy them first. Concession brokers and influence peddlers operated in the near fringes of the royal court. The sudden infusions of huge amounts of cash were dramatic in a poor country that, by some estimates, had only a forty-dollar per capita income as it completed its first years of independence. Within a few years, hundreds of Libyan families began to live like millionaires and to consort with Libyan's Western residents. For poor tent-village-dwelling families like that of Abu Meniar and Aissha al-Qaddafi this was rubbing salt into the wounds of poverty.

Breaking the ground in Libya for later American concession brokers was Wendell Phillips, an adventurer, scholar, promoter, and specialist in exotic countries and regimes. Born in 1921 in Oakland, California, Phillips studied his way through a dozen or so universities and colleges in the United States and Belgium and Korea, and picked up numerous honorary degrees at many other institutions of higher learning. Archaeology, journalism, anthropology, marine biology—practically no scientific discipline or humanistic study seemed beyond the range of his serious study or his constant dilettantism. Phillips was also, at heart, a born businessman and something of a gambler. He recognized at an early age that Big Oil held the promise of great riches for those enterprising enough to seek them.

He prospected first in Indonesia and other parts of the southwest Pacific, then organized and led archaeological expeditions in southern Arabia in the 1950s. He photographed and reconstructed the travels and adventures of the biblical Queen of Sheba in Saaba and Kataba in the Yemen, and explored the ancient spice route of the Hadramaut region, where the riches of southeast Asia were carried westward in medieval times.

Phillips ingratiated himself with one of the Arab world's leading misanthropes, the miserly old Sultan Said ibn Taymour of Muscat and Oman, who kept his ancient kingdom isolated from the outside world and kept out the oil companies. Phillips eventually obtained oil concessions from Sultan Taymour before the British and the sultan's son, Qabus, overthrew the sultan and opened the country to the outside world in 1970. Ironically, however, it was Shell, and not Wendell Phillips, who found and developed Oman's major oil sites.

During the early 1950s, Phillips became friendly with the Secretary of the U.S. Air Force, Harold Talbott, who knew Mustafa ben Halim and other prominent Libyans well through the negotiations ben Halim had conducted with the Eisenhower administration for the use of Wheelus Field. Wendell Phillips eventually got to see King Idris and secured entry to Libya for Texas Gulf, an independent American oil firm that came into Libya under the name of Libyan-American Oil Company. Texas Gulf land was later to yield Raguba field, which by the time of the 1973 Arab-Israeli war and the resulting oil embargo had yielded over 350 million barrels of oil. Before Phillips's death on May 5, 1975, in Honolulu, where Wendell Phillips Oil Company was based, he became an extremely wealthy man. Before his death his company formed a group with Sinclair. Together, this group composed the Libyan-American Oil Company, which took on Exxon as equal partner to develop one of Libya's first-discovered oil wells, Mabruk.[7]

Conorada, which later became the Oasis Oil Company, won the most diversified concession acreage in Libya. Oasis and other independent company executives argued that since they lacked the large crude-oil resources of the majors they would be more energetic in seeking Libyan crude. Developments bore this out, but their performance records, during the early years, were not sufficient to win them the richest concessions; they had to resort to prominent Libyan agents of influence. These were usually government ministers like Prime Minister ben Halim or members of the Shalhi family, the most powerful men in King Idris's entourage. Right down to the start of the 1980s, when some of them were either members of the émigré opposition to Qaddafi or benevolent toward this opposition, they drew many others into the Libyan political whirlpool.

Ben Halim, educated in Egypt, was trained as an engineer and then as a Libyan government bureaucrat before he became prime minister in 1954. As we saw earlier, he probably accomplished more in that office for his country than anyone who preceded or followed him until Qaddafi's time. In May 1957 he resigned, tired out by the delicate business of steering Libya gingerly through the 1956 Suez crisis, when both Britain and Egypt might have involved Libyan territory in actual warfare but for the skill of ben Halim and some others. Ben Halim at first served as ambassador in Paris, then returned to private life in Libya, founding his own engineering firm, Libeco. His engineering work enabled him to come in contact with the big Texas construction group Brown & Root. Later ben Halim survived a melodramatic postrevolutionary kidnap attempt by a Palestinian gang in Beirut, and experienced the (for him) happy outcome of sanctuary in Saudi Arabia, the benefits of Saudi citizenship, and finally, success in becoming a confidant of the Saudi princes.

During the late 1950s, major American contractors were angling in Libya for a share of the huge contracts that they already knew or sensed would result from the coming oil boom of the 1960s. The Bechtel Corporation of California had already built two major Mideastern oil pipelines and Algeria's first one (it ran from the Edjeleh area signed over to France in the 1956 agreement to La Skhirra in Tunisia). In 1967–69, the West, as a result of the June 1967 Arab-Israeli war, had a foretaste of the Arab oil embargo of 1973–74. The Suez Canal was closed, increasing the desirability and the price of North African oil west of Suez. Much earlier, in 1961, Bechtel completed the pipeline from the Exxon concession in Zelton to Mersa al-Brega on the Mediterranean coast, and later built projects for the development of the oil field.

When the Oasis oil group sought a contractor to build two sea berths at the Mediterranean port of Sirte and an eighty-six-mile pipeline from Dahra to Sirte, Bechtel's bid ran into tough opposition from ben Halim, now operating as a private individual. Bechtel accordingly decided to join forces with ben Halim and formed a joint venture, giving ben Halim a large share of the resulting work. This included construction of a residential community at the Oasis terminal, and a large share of the work on the oil-gathering system at Oasis Oil's Dahra field, southwest of Sirte. Bechtel's relationship with ben Halim, who had left Libya before the 1969 revolution, was to continue through the first two years of the Qaddafi regime, until 1971. After the relationship was terminated, Bechtel retained his brother, Abdul Hamid ben Halim, as counsel. Between 1960 and 1969, Bechtel, which had the friendship or participation of leading U.S. Republicans and Brown & Root of Texas, which latter had in turn the blessings of Lyndon B. Johnson, built together with ben Halim much of Libya's oil infrastructure—Mobil's Sirtica pipeline, further branch pipelines, a road from the Raguba field to Zelten, and pipelines and other projects for Oasis.

By the mid-1960s, the international oil companies, big and small, were swarming like bees to the Libyan honeycomb. Libya was a new source of oil, close to the Western markets. After 1967 it had the advantage of being free of dependence upon the Suez Canal, which the late President Sadat reopened only in 1975. The West began to learn its lesson about the need to diversify its Mideast energy sources in the Iranian crisis of 1951–54; the first closure of the Suez Canal in 1956–57 was a red-light warning of the vulnerability of Mideast oil to the stormy forces of war and politics. When the Libyan oil boom began, Libya still appeared to oil companies and their respective governments to be a pro-Western power. There were still British and U.S. military bases there to protect the oil fields. Its logistics looked secure too. The short journey to European ports, and the longer Atlantic voyage to the Caribbean refineries that provide Americans with some of their gasoline and other refined needs, including low-pollutant fuel oil, were both along sea-lanes protected by Western navies and deemed relatively safe from Soviet interference. Libya had less political turbulence than its North African neighbors. As the four-year-old Algerian revolution for independence from France and the resulting return to power of General de Gaulle in Paris threatened new instability in Western North Africa in 1958, twelve Western companies received roughly sixty separate concessions in Libya. Included were the Seven Sisters and the French Compagnie Française des Pétroles, which was anxious to expand its new operations in the Algerian Sahara further westward.

Besides the American majors, there were new American independents coming into the international game for the first time. The Oasis group, now well established alongside the majors, consisted of three of these independents: Continental Oil (Conoco), Marathon, and Amerada Hess. Nelson Bunker Hunt of Texas operated separately, of which more later. Occidental Petroleum too was to appear on the Libyan scene later on.

Conoco was a tiny oil company before the big strikes it made as part of Oasis in Libya in 1958. Conoco's Leonard F. McCollum, hired away from Standard of New Jersey (later Esso and now Exxon) in 1947, began marketing oil in Western Europe. The Libyan bonanza helped Conoco to buy, by 1964, one thousand gasoline stations in Britain, West Germany, Austria, Luxembourg, and Belgium (where it soon found itself in tough competition with the Soviet Union's highly capitalistic Belgian marketing enterprise and the filling-station chain run by the Soviet company Nafta-B). Eventually, in 1966, Conoco was able to buy Consolidated Coal, making Conoco the coal company with the largest reserves in the United States. The chairman since 1979, Ralph E. Bailey, is a professional coal man.[8] Conoco, it was reported in industry circles, found some oil around 1978 in remote portions of Chad—soon to become inaccessible because of the civil war there and because of the occupation of the country in the winter of 1980–81 by Colonel Qaddafi's troops. In 1981, after a heated takeover battle, Conoco was bought by DuPont.

The Hunts of Texas, especially the late H. L. Hunt's son, Nelson Bunker, were among the next American oilmen to help shape Libya's future. It was Nelson Bunker Hunt who discovered in Libya the largest lake of underground oil in all Africa, the Sarir field. For the Hunts, this looked like the gateway to Aladdin's cave; Sarir far exceeded the size of the East Texas field, the largest oil field in the United States. Sarir lay under the Sand Sea of Calanscio in the midst of Libya's desert, nearly three hundred miles from the Mediterranean coast in eastern Cyrenaica. It was this Libyan oil field, rather than their future silver dealings, that brought the Hunts to the attention of Qaddafi and other leaders in Libya, and to the rest of the world as well.

Haroldson Lafayette Hunt, born in Ramsey, Illinois, on February 17, 1889, died in Dallas, Texas, on November 20, 1974, one of the wealthiest men in the world. He began his career with a $5,000 inheritance and ended it with assets worth $2 billion. His first major successful oil ventures were lucrative leases of oil properties in Arkansas and Louisiana. His skillful negotiations for leases in Rusk County, Texas, helped make him into a multimillionare before his son went to Libya.

Nelson Bunker Hunt was established in Big Oil in his own right by the time the Hunt Oil Company had vainly sought oil in Pakistan, and then moved into Libya where its bright future lay. He was born, appropriately it would seem, in El Dorado, Arkansas, on February 22, 1926, the second of H. L. Hunt's fourteen children (H. L. had three wives). Unlike his father, Nelson Bunker does not drive an old car or carry his lunch in a paper bag, though he does like to fly economy class and save money in other ways.

In an early concession awarded in Libya, Hunt Oil got the easternmost. It was Concession No. 65, the Sarir field, in which British Petroleum (BP) gained a 50 percent interest by purchase in 1960. (BP had been scouting the territory west of Suez for oil, but had discovered none in the eight Libyan concessions it already held.) As an operator with Hunt, BP in 1961 brought in the first producing well in Sarir, and soon the extent and richness of the field was evident. BP, however, was dragging its feet about getting Sarir into production because of a surplus of crude oil in its Persian Gulf fields.[9] Sarir went onstream in 1967, though, after Hunt leaked to the Texas-based *Oil and Gas Journal* the intelligence that Sarir had recoverable reserves of 7 to 9 billion barrels and could easily exceed production of 400,000 barrels per day (bpd), whereas BP had said it could produce only 200,000 bpd. (Indeed, Sarir was to reach a sustained peak production of 470,000 bpd by the time Qaddafi began his pressure tactics against the companies in 1979.) The Hunt-BP combine built its own pipeline from Sarir to the Mersa Hariga terminal at Tobruk, the easternmost of Libya's Mediterranean oil tanker terminals, only about sixty miles away from Egypt.

In 1965 the government of King Idris was ready to shuffle its deck of old petroleum concessions and deal new concession cards to anyone able to afford a seat at Libya's petroleum poker table. Most of the new concessions were territories relinquished under the 1961 amendments to the old 1955 Petroleum Law (one-quarter of holdings five years after award, and further relinquishments after eight and ten years). Esso was king of the Libyan producers. It had been the first to go onstream, and by 1965 was producing around 400,000 bpd. Some 540,000 bpd, including other companies' oil, was moving through. Mersa al-Brega, on the Gulf of Sirte about two hundred miles south of Benghazi, was the site of Esso's oil export terminal; it was connected by a thirty-inch pipeline to its prolific Zelten field. Esso had also built a major natural-gas liquefaction plant at Mersa. Libya had become a major oil exporter in the few years since an Esso tanker, the *Canterbury*, loaded the first crude-oil cargo for Britain on September 12, 1961.

What was happening by the time the new 1965–66 concession awards came around is well described by Wilbur Eveland, a former CIA officer and oil-company consultant, in his book *Ropes of Sand: America's Failure in the Middle East.* Eveland, who himself negotiated a contract in Libya for the Vinnell Corporation of California (not an oil company), discovered that he had to make large payments to Libyan agents of influence. Eveland describes "oil company greed, internecine rivalries, subordination of corruption" as beginning in Libya in earnest.[10] It became next to impossible for any American or European firm to do anything in royalist Libya without sponsors, patrons, and payoffs. By relying on agents of influence, the oil companies were able to obtain their concessions and contracts, but only at the cost of being associated in Libyan public eyes with the most corrupt elements of the local society. Such associations added grist to the conspiratorial mills of Qaddafi and his fellows already forming their first and second cells for the coming revolution. The concessions awarded in February 1966 brought in new, unknown companies to work in Libya alongside Esso and the other giants. Two of the choicest concessions, relinquished by Oasis and Mobil, and bid for by nineteen companies, went to a California-based firm that many in Libya had never heard of: Armand Hammer's Occidental Petroleum Company. The company's bid was wrapped in the Libyan national colors and was sweetened with a series of offers that no Libyan government of that day could refuse—including a proposal to invest 5 percent of its profits in an ambitious project to water the desert around Kufra oasis, the birthplace of King Idris and once a stronghold of Omar al-Mokhtar in the southern desert.

To win the oil fields that were to make its fortune, Occidental paid close attention to fourteen "preferential factors" that Libya's new Petroleum Council had listed for the bidding companies. Occidental accepted several crucial ones: an offer to notify the oil minister of all contracts worth over half a million dollars; promises to keep local funds in local banks, and a commitment to build refineries, petrochemical plants, and other "downstream" activities in Libya that would enable the country to win its freedom from Western controls over these operations.[11]

But just what was Occidental and who was this Armand Hammer? "None of us knew anything about him at the time," recalled Mahmoud Suleiman al-Maghrebi, who was by that time already laying the foundation for the Libyan oil-industry strike of 1967 that was later to help Qaddafi use oil as a political weapon.[12] Hammer, in fact, has proven from a commercial point of view to be one of the greatest friends Qaddafi—or the Soviets—had in the United States.

Armand Hammer was born May 21, 1898, in New York City to Dr. Julius and Rose (Robinson) Hammer. Julius's father was a Russian émigré who had won and then lost a fortune in Russian shipbuilding before moving to the United States in the mid-1870s. Julius, a gynecologist and general practitioner, sold pharmaceuticals and household goods wholesale, and later went into the drugstore business in New York. Armand and his two brothers expanded their father's business; Armand found it difficult to keep up his medical studies at Columbia University because of the tending the family business required. He did graduate, though, and with top honors, in 1921. He may have been the first medical student ever to earn a million dollars while still in school.

During the suffering and epidemics brought by the tides of revolution and attempted counterrevolution in the Soviet Union, Hammer bought a surplus U.S. Army field hospital and moved it to Moscow. His first business deal, forged amid his humanitarian activities, was to offer a shipload of surplus American wheat in exchange for Russian caviar and furs. Lenin received Hammer and urged him to apply capitalism, not medicine, to Russia's revolutionary wounds. He offered Hammer the concession of an asbestos mine, which eventually became productive. Hammer went on to obtain from Lenin sales concessions for many top U.S. firms: Ford, U.S. Rubber, Allis-Chalmers, Underwood Typewriter. As Communism settled in, departing Western businessmen sold Hammer promissory notes. Hammer's luxurious Moscow mansion, Brown House, was soon filled with priceless art treasures acquired with the help of Hammer's younger brother Victor. Brown House became a gathering point for celebrities from the Western world visiting the young Communist state. When Hammer left the USSR in 1930, he took the art treasures and the Soviet promissory notes—which the Red commissars, true to their word, later paid in full.

Hammer's next ventures included whiskey distilling, cattle, control of the Mutual Broadcasting System (which he bought in 1957 and later sold for a profit, after getting it out of the red). In 1956 he moved to California, intending to retire. A friend suggested he finance two wildcat oil wells being drilled in Bakersfield, California. The company drilling them was Occidental Petroleum Corporation, with total assets of about $120,000. Hammer bought up the stock, financed the wells, and took a stock option at $1.50 a share. Two of the wells, south of Los Angeles, brought up oil. Hammer came out of retirement and charged into the oil business, becoming president and chairman of Occidental, or "Oxy," as many call the firm.[13]

Hammer had prepared carefully for the 1966 Libyan bid awards, and insiders watching the Libyan oil scene were not surprised when Occidental won the former Oasis and Mobil concessions. Hammer had flown to Libya shortly after the concession law was updated in 1961 to see the new oil strikes for himself. He employed geologists who knew Libya. In December 1963 a Libyan government official had tipped off one of these geologists that Occidental could win friends and probably influence the king in his favor if Occidental could make Libya an offer to use the natural gas associated with crude oil, which the big oil companies were flaring and wasting, to produce ammonia that could be used for a fertilizer plant to help turn Libyan desert places into farmland. Hammer listened attentively and immediately set up an international fertilizer marketing corporation—Interore. He tempted the royal government with the hint that if Oxy were to get a choice concession in the next awards, it would *try* to build a fertilizer plant in Libya to put to work Libyan natural gas that the other companies were simply burning up.[14]

In the 1960s, however, there was more than just the possible fertilizer plant to sweeten the package for the Libyans. Hammer also offered an Occidental-patented nitrogen-preservation system to truck and store fresh farm produce in Libya. A third offer was an investment in Libya of 5 percent of profits from any oil produced in developing Kufra oasis, the ancestral Sanussi home. Above and beyond these temptations, Occidental relied on the well-known Libyan agents of influence—in this case chiefly Taher Ogbi, minister of labor in 1966 when the contract awards were made, and Omar Shalhi, the all-powerful and growingly influential minister at court. Both received commission fees, including an "overriding royalty" of 3 percent of the sales price of every barrel of crude oil Occidental exported from Libya (monies were to be deposited in a Swiss bank). A certain self-styled "General" Pegulu de Rovin, of French or Spanish origin, sued Occidental in a Libyan court, claiming that he was entitled to a fee for introducing Ogbi to Occidental. De Rovin claimed that Hammer had agreed to pay an initial $100,000 (which de Rovin admitted receiving) and $300,000 more from the proceeds of subsequent Occidental oil exports from Libya. De Rovin could not document his claim, and the case was dismissed.[15] An Occidental representative meanwhile was cultivating Fuad Kabazi, the Libyan oil minister, who pressed Occidental's case before the king and cabinet, and who upon occasion communicated with one of Hammer's men in a secret code.[16]

Hammer's company grew quickly and mightily. One discovery well on acreage relinquished by Mobil yielded 70,000 bpd on test, helping to transform Occidental overnight into a major international energy company. By 1967, when anti-Western riots troubled some Libyan cities during the June Arab-Israeli war and the Libyans halted oil exports to the United States for twenty-seven days, the midget California firm of 1957 had reached a net worth of $300 million on gross income of almost $662 million and net earnings estimated at $22.7 million. Three years later, during the first year of Qaddafi's regime, thanks to Libyan and to a lesser extent Californian oil and diversification into chemicals, coal, and fertilizers, Occidental's earnings were reported to be $175 million on sales of over $2 billion.[17]

The formula of acquiring relinquished oil acreage proved so success-

ful in Libya that Hammer tried it out elsewhere. When Peru expropriat-
ed Exxon's oil fields, Occidental offered to operate them on a service
contract, as the Soviet Union was doing for nationalized oil fields in
Mideast countries like Iraq. Oxy also made important discoveries in the
North Sea, Nigeria, Venezuela (offshore in Lake Maracaibo), and
Ghana.

Along with the Bechtel Corporation, Hammer negotiated the sale of
oil field and fertilizer technology to the USSR, with the Nixon
administration's blessing. Hammer donated over $100,000 to Nixon's
1972 presidential campaign, paying $46,000 in cash himself and
channeling another $54,000 through the former governor of Montana,
Tim Babcock, then an Occidental executive in Washington.[18] Occidental obtained the help of Bechtel and ben Halim in developing its Libyan
fields. During the period 1967–71, out of the royal regime and into the
Qaddafi era, Bechtel got the main contract for engineering, procurement, and construction of oil fields and pieplines at Mersa al-Brega.[19]
The pipeline contract was especially lucrative for both Occidental and
Bechtel; its original price of $43 million escalated through cost overruns
and other factors to $147 million. Occidental began exporting oil in
early 1968 and by the end of that year these exports reached nearly
600,000 bpd.[20] Esso, the biggest exporter of oil from Libya between
1961 and 1965, exchanged first place for second with Oasis twice before
the Qaddafi revolution in 1969. Occidental's growth was so meteoric
that it was challenging Esso for second place in 1970, after only two
years of production.

In achieving this spectacular new international status, however,
Occidental helped lay the foundations for its own and other companies'
later weakness with Qaddafi, and, much more important, for the
upswing in world prices and for the gradual creation of Libyan oil power
on the world scene. Occidental neglected some of the promises it had
made to the Libyans in its campaign to win its valuable concessions.
Among the biggest commitments to Libya had been a quasi-promise to
construct an ammonia plant, if both parties desired it. Each side, Oxy
and Libya, was to bear equally the expected cost of about $30 million.
Libya was to supply the natural gas that the project used as feedstock;
Occidental agreed to pay Libya the prevailing rate for the gas. At first,
during the early months of Occidental crude-oil exports from Libya, the
royal government did not press Hammer to move ahead with the plant.
Then, in June 1968, it raised the issue in a way Hammer had perhaps
not foreseen: Occidental's gas production was supposed to play an

important part in planning for the Exxon terminal at Mersa al-Brega. But there were early symptoms of an ammonia glut on the world market. Fertilizer prices dropped sharply. The ammonia plant idea looked less and less attractive to the Oxy board in California. In addition, Oxy was undergoing a temporary slump in its fortunes, with its stock prices down to $10 a share toward the end of 1968. Occidental decided the plant would lose money, and told the Libyans it would not be feasible. The Libyans were bitterly disappointed; they had hoped to build a major southern Mediterranean center for manufacture of ammonia fertilizer and sell it to other Mediterranean countries. Neither offering the Libyans an old ammonia plant owned by an Oxy subsidiary in Plainview, Texas (to be shipped in pieces and reassembled in Libya), nor building an aluminum smelter, a mineral- or gas-processing plant placated the Libyan government. When it finally became apparent to Occidental that it could gain more relinquished oil acreage only by agreeing to construct the ammonia plant, it began to do so in January 1969. But Libya was obligated to provide the natural gas to fuel the plant, and since no gas was readily available, the plant was never built.[21]

One of the promised projects Hammer did not neglect was the Kufra oasis. He announced that he had discovered a "new Nile" under the desert: a reserve of one quadrillion barrels of water. Occidental's experts had been carefully studying the thousands of existing wells of hundreds of farms in the Kufra area. As early as World War II, experts had detected underground water there. As the company prepared to spend $13 million on the project in 1969, some Libyan officials objected that this was only a showpiece, that the money would be better spent on projects along the more populated Mediterranean coast, where more people would benefit. However, Hammer did go ahead with the Kufra project, and it is one of the few major oil company development projects in Libya to survive the revolution. (The new Qaddafi regime eventually took it over.) With the help of two U.S. government hydrogeological consultants named Tipton and Kalmback—among the first U.S. civilian officials to help the Qaddafi government—the earlier Occidental idea of irrigated grain cultivation, aimed at making Libya more self-sufficient in food, was put aside in favor of a scheme to raise 250,000 Barbary sheep, fed by alfalfa irrigated by the center-pivot sprinklers used in California, Israel, and elsewhere. It cost tremendous sums, and later Libya found it cheaper to import sheep from Bulgaria. Southern Libya's livestock population grew, and so did the area of irrigation around Kufra. Between 1973 and 1975 similar methods were applied in the area of the Sarir oil field. By 1977, Kufra was again under cultivation for grain production. Kufra and Sarir attracted foreign and unskilled labor from the Arab world, south Asia, and both Western Europe and the East bloc states.[22]

The Hunt BP group already had a plant to separate liquid petroleum gas from the oil-associated natural gas that Occidental was flaring (and thus wasting), because there was no economical way for using it at the time. Occidental decided to follow their example and build another. Bechtel did the feasibility studies for the plant and eventually built it.

What was important was that by 1969, Armand Hammer and Occidental Petroleum had carved out for themselves a major stake in Libya. A few other oil companies could say the same. What no one could say or even surmise was what the still-unknown revolutionaries led by Qaddafi would do with Libya's newfound resource—oil.

# FOUR

## OIL: WEAPON OF REVOLUTION

**B**y the time Lieutenant Muammar al-Qaddafi's revolutionaries had secured Libya's oil ports, pipelines, and loading terminals on September 1, 1969, and reassured their Western owners and operators that they could go on with "business as usual," Libya was, after barely one decade of production, the world's fourth largest oil exporter.

Crude oil was loaded and shipped out by tanker from five different Mediterranean sea terminals that were connected to the various fields by pipelines. Esso's first major terminal had operated at Mersa al-Brega on the Gulf of Sirte since 1961, and the Esso group also operated a refinery and gas liquefaction plant near the same terminal, processing gas for shipment in liquid form to Italy and Spain. The Oasis group, operating the Hofra field in western Cyrenaica, piped their oil to Ras al-Sider, west of Mersa al-Brega. Mobil Oil and the West German firm of Gelsenburg built another pipeline to Ras Lanuf, in Qaddafi's Sirte homeland a few miles east of Ras al-Sider. Ras Lanuf is now often mentioned as a possible site for a new Libyan capital city, as well as the center of a new complex of petrochemical plants whose construction has advanced in the early 1980s. The Sarir oil field, still operated in 1969 by Hunt and BP but eventually to be nationalized, sent its oil to a fourth terminal at Mersa Heriga, near Tobruk, through another pipeline. Lastly, a new terminal was opened in 1968 at Zuetina, south of Benghazi, to export the take of Occidental's Aujila and Intisar fields. The majors were doing well in Libya: profits were soaring, and so was the value of their stocks. Most American oil and gasoline consumers little knew or cared that higher stock dividends for stockholders would be followed abruptly by higher prices at the pump.

The cheapness of Libyan oil, one of its greater virtues for the West, was its greatest vice in the eyes of other producing countries and the major oil companies. Before the Iranian crises and the advent of fifty-fifty profit sharing between ARAMCO and Saudi Arabia in the 1950s, the Seven Sisters had always acted together to establish a single world price for oil. This was based on the Gulf of Mexico oil price set by the U.S. oil companies. Since Mideast oil was much cheaper to produce than Gulf of Mexico oil, the majors made windfall profits in the Mideast.

By the time of the Libyan oil discoveries of 1959–60, however, Arabian Light oil had replaced Gulf of Mexico oil as the pricing yardstick for the rest of the world. When war closed the Suez Canal in 1956, the price of Saudi Arabian Light soared to the new high of $2.12 per barrel. Mideast oil-producing countries briefly tasted the sweetness of wealth, and they liked it. When, in 1959–60, just as Libya's oil was about to begin flowing, the companies cut prices drastically again— without consulting the producer governments—it came as a rude shock.[1]

U.S. independent companies with no permanent markets for crude oil outside the United States and Canada had to find markets for their large Libyan production. But in 1959 the Eisenhower administration decided to limit oil imports by 12 percent of demand in any one year. This cut off the markets in the United States for Libyan oil, and obliged the independents to sell at low prices—sometimes as low as $1.30 a barrel—in Europe. This price-cutting deprived the Libyan government of revenue and helped undermine world prices generally.

There was no immediate reaction in Libya, but on the larger world oil stage, the reaction to price-cutting by the companies led to the creation of OPEC, the Organization of Petroleum Exporting Countries. OPEC was conceived at the first Arab Petroleum Congress of April 1959; it was fathered chiefly by two oil ministers, Abdallah Tariki of Saudi Arabia and Perez Alfonso of Venezuela, and was born at a crisis meeting of Iran, Iraq, Saudi Arabia, and Kuwait in Baghdad in 1960. Libya joined in 1962, and other members by the 1970s included Qatar, Indonesia, Abu Dhabi, Ecuador, and Gabon. In Libya as in the Mideast the government decided to base its revenues on taxes on income based on the "posted" price of the companies (subject to slight discounts allowed by OPEC elsewhere in the Mideast) rather than the actual realized market price (at that time, the market price was often lower than the posted price). Seven of the companies working in Libya opposed the change because it meant less money for them. Government action, still relatively gentle and gradual, obliged them to accept, and Libya's oil revenues went up from about 67 cents on a barrel in 1964 to 96 cents in 1966.[2]

Next came the 1967 oil embargo, during which Libya lost nearly $40 million during a twenty-seven-day shutdown of Libyan oil exports. The companies in Libya realized they were not immune to the backwash of the Arab-Israeli war. As Libyan officials became shrewder about oil, external factors were helping to make Libyan crude oil extremely desirable. Closure of the Suez Canal from 1967 to 1975 enhanced the value of Libyan oil and also increased the government's take per barrel. Another factor that favored Libya from 1969 on was the periodic shutdown or interruption of the flow of oil through ARAMCO's Tapline (Transarabian Pipeline) from Saudi Arabia to Sidon on the Mediterranean coast (that raised freight rates considerably, and freight rates were then a large part of the oil cost). From 1966–67 on, the Biafra war virtually halted Nigeria's oil exports for a time. Finally, environmentalists in Europe were gaining more influence over regulatory processes. Libya's low-sulphur crude became more and more desirable.

For a few weeks after Qaddafi came to power, the only restrictive action felt by Western oil companies in Libya was the banning of liquor. But they were soon to feel more significant pressures. In December 1969 Qaddafi's Libyan National Oil Company negotiated a technical accord with Algeria, which was having trouble with Western oil firms. President Houari Boumedienne's government was unhappy with the small rate of investment of the companies and the resulting slowness of new-reserve discovery. Then Texas oilman John Paul Getty entered the Algerian scene in October 1969. Getty, a crusty Minnesotan born in 1892, had made between $2 million and $4 million in oil in part by persuading his widowed mother to relinquish control of George F. Getty, Inc., his late father's company. He had recently scored big in both the United States and the Middle East, chiefly by securing half-interest in the Neutral Zone oil acreage that Saudi Arabia shared with Kuwait. The Algerians and Libyans were both glad to see Getty's company in Algeria; though in private life Getty was reputed to be so miserly that he once installed a pay telephone booth in his London mansion for the use of guests, in Algeria he was willing to offer better terms than either the majors or the smaller French companies. Qaddafi took note of such largesse. After the first OPEC meeting attended by the Libyan revolutionaries in December 1969, other OPEC members offered strong support to both Algeria and Libya.[3]

Even so, the Libyan revolutionaries handled the oil companies gingerly. There would be no nationalizations and no confiscations, they told an Egyptian newsman who asked how far oil could be regarded as a "weapon in the battle" against Israel. In response oil minister Shitawi said: "Use of oil for concession of pumping [in the 1956 and 1967 embargoes] . . . was the only remaining weapon, though it affected state revenues. However, if a crisis similar or analogous to the June 1967 crisis happens, we shall act, as we did then, according to what we deem appropriate in such circumstances." Shitawi warned the companies that they had "no excuse" to exert pressure "now that the Revolution has declared that it shall be bound by all agreements concluded."[4]

Qaddafi made his first move against the companies in January 1970. It was a simple request in line with the royal government's earlier efforts to raise the tax reference price of Libyan crude by about 10 to 20 percent, something Qaddafi's Algerian and Venezuelan friends had advised was perfectly just and feasible for Libya's choice crude oil. The companies at first dragged their feet and did not reply. The Libyans in the meantime sought new oil advisers in every part of the world, such as Canadians in Alberta Province, who had developed techniques to conserve the oil found in their carbonate reefs. Then Qaddafi toughened. Though the new tax demands had been presented to all the companies, Qaddafi's oil advisers decided to concentrate on only two companies: Occidental and Exxon. In May Occidental was ordered to cut back its oil production by 300,000 bpd. This was the first time that had ever happened in the Mideast or North Africa. The Libyans insisted that the cutbacks were ordered for technical reasons, that Occidental had been pumping out its fields faster than sound engineering practice would have dictated.

Occidental and Exxon overcame their reluctance to talk about prices, and offered Libya initially small and then gradually larger annual increases. To protect Oxy, Armand Hammer flew to New York to see Exxon's new chairman, J. Kenneth Jamieson, a Canadian from Medicine Hat, Alberta, the heart of Canada's own oil country.

The conversation, it appears, went something like this:

*Hammer:* We won't give in to Qaddafi if you won't. But we don't have any outside crude to spare if Qaddafi cuts us off. Can you help?

*Jamieson:* How?

*Hammer:* By letting Oxy have Exxon crude from non-Libyan sources—at a good discount, of course.

Jamieson at this point consulted Exxon advisers. They reminded him that Hammer had been only too ready to operate Exxon's former field in Peru when it had been nationalized. Besides, they pointed out, Exxon's position in Libya was much less vulnerable than Oxy's. Exxon had plenty of crude from all over the world.

*Jamieson:* Sorry to keep you waiting. Why don't you talk to our crude-oil sales staff? They'll be happy to give you the standard outsiders' discount. By the way, you may remember this consent decree. [He shows it to Hammer.] We signed this a few years ago with the U.S. Department of Justice. We promised to refrain from future actions to fix prices or restrain trade, though we didn't admit to any such actions in the first place.[5]

On those terms, Hammer wasn't buying from Exxon. This left him without extra oil for maneuverability, and so he moved in another way: first he slowed down construction of a $60 million liquefied petroleum gas (LPG) plant and lines in Libya, and finally he closed it down.

A kind of cold war developed. The Libyans cut back on visas and travel permits for Oxy and Bechtel personnel (Bechtel was doing most of Oxy's engineering work). Libyan police began to stop and search Occidental personnel on their way to work. The Oil Ministry then imposed another production cut of 60,000 bpd. By the first anniversary of the Libyan revolution, on September 1, 1970, Oxy was producing only 440,000 bpd, just over half of what its peak output had been.[6]

A series of three Libyan negotiating teams went into action. The third and most effective of these was headed by Abdel Salem Jalloud, Qaddafi's faithful aide who had helped take over Tripoli on Revolution Day and was now prime minister. Jalloud reminded the Oxy and Exxon people that the posted price of choice Libyan crude from Zelten or Zuetina had not changed from 1961 until 1970, remaining at $2.23 per barrel. This was equivalent to that of lower-quality Iraqi crude, delivered at Mediterranean terminals in Syria and Lebanon.[7] Jalloud called this neither fair nor just. Therefore, the companies had to grant an immediate price rise of 30 cents a barrel; a further hike of 10 cents over a five-year period, and an increase in the tax rate (the government's chief source of revenue) from 50 to 58 percent (this was largely to absorb payments into the Kufra oasis fund, which the government was then taking over).

Facing possible expropriation and without other substantial sources of oil, Hammer instructed his representatives in Libya to give in, provided Jalloud would permit Oxy to go back to 800,000 bpd production. Jalloud approved 700,000 bpd.[8]

On September 4, 1970, Qaddafi celebrated the revolution's first anniversary three days late by announcing what Western oil experts gloomily predicted would bring the first major rise in crude-oil prices in thirteen years, and the biggest one ever: terms similar to Oxy's for everyone. On September 18, the three independent Oasis partners agreed to similar terms, but without their major partner, Shell. When Shell refused to sign, Qaddafi took away its one-sixth share of Oasis production. Hunt and Mobil resisted, but Exxon, Texaco, and Standard of California (Socal) caved in, one by one. Although the British government was willing to stand behind BP, the U.S. State Department was not inclined to take a strong stand in support of the American companies, feeling that existing good relations with Qaddafi, who was proving to be as fervent an anti-Communist as he was an Arab nationalist, ought to be preserved. Two of the partners in another combine called American Overseas Oil Company (Amoseas), Standard of California and Texaco, were not getting any other choice low-sulfur oil from Nigeria, the other principal source of such oil west of the still-closed Suez Canal. Arabian Light crude from the Persian Gulf was not getting through the Tapline because the Syrians had cut that ARAMCO-owned pipeline. Qaddafi held the whip hand, and he knew it.

**B**ack in the United States, the first reaction to the Tripoli agreements, as oilmen came to call the new price hikes, arose from an unexpected quarter. At 7:00 A.M. on November 11, 1970, American consumers awoke to the unwelcome news that the Gulf Oil Company was raising its price asked and charged for *domestic* crude oil by 25 cents per barrel, approximately a 10 percent increase. Gulf gave no reason or justification. It could not blame the Tripoli agreements because Gulf produced no oil in Libya. The fact remained, however, that by Christmas 1970 every producer and refiner in the United States, whether it had Libyan production or not, had followed Gulf's lead by raising prices 25 cents a barrel. Shortly after New Year's Day 1971, gasoline retailers began the upward price spiral of the coming decade with an initial .7 cents increase. President Nixon, who by now was getting used to living both with Qaddafi and with American Big Oil, expressed concern about the price hikes, but did nothing effective to counter them. Paul Mc-Cracken, chairman of the Council of Economic Advisers, claimed that the state of Texas had acted as Qaddafi's ally: the Texas Railroad Commission, which regulated Texas oil production, had cut down allowable production once in November and a bit more in December— despite the Libyan price hikes and the shutdown of Tapline, which had now lasted 270 days.[9]

What had impelled Gulf to take this free ride on the crest of Qaddafi's price wave? Gulf had been among the first concessionaries in Libya before the revolution, and had even discovered some small fields in western Tripolitania, but it never wanted to develop them and finally gave them up. It was not North African but Kuwaiti oil that had made Gulf into an international giant earning two-thirds of its profits overseas. Ever since the 1920s and 1930s, when Gulf was one of the majors pioneering development of Persian Gulf oil, the company had been fueling its operations with a rich mixture of domestic and Mideast politics. Gulf developed a subsidiary in the Caribbean that channeled money to many politicians. Claud Wild, Gulf's Washington representative, testified that for ten years he gave $10,000 a year to Senator Hugh Scott, Republican leader in the Senate. In 1971, a few months after the Tripoli agreements and Gulf's ensuing price hike, Wild was reportedly solicited by Maurice Stans, a chief fund-raiser for Nixon; Wild contributed $100,000 to the Nixon committee for the reelection of the president. Details of "slush fund" payments abroad in Kuwait, South Korea, and elsewhere disclosed in a long Securities and Exchange Commission report led to the resignation of Gulf president Robert R. Dorsey and three other Gulf executives in December 1975 at the request of the board of directors. The subsequent chairman, Jerry McAfee, apologized to stockholders and has brought Gulf more and more into the uranium business.[10] The only conclusion many observers can reach about the 1970 Gulf price hike, which had such a domino effect in the United States, was that Gulf had needed a reason or a pretext to raise prices. The Tripoli agreements were as good a pretext as any other.

Qaddafi and Jalloud had good cause to be satisfied with their first year of directing Libyan oil policy. At home, despite the production cutbacks imposed on Hammer and other major operators, Libyan crude-oil production in 1970 had reached a record level, 3,318,000 bpd. Revenues had jumped from $1.132 billion in 1969, the last year of royal rule, to $1.295 billion (and were to continue rising except in 1972 and

1975). In a law promulgated by Qaddafi on March 15, 1970, Libya's old Libyan General Petroleum Corporation (LGPC), created in April 1968 by the royal regime as a 100 percent state-owned oil company, was renamed the Libyan National Oil Company (LNOC), and designated the future instrument to guide and direct petroleum operations. Alone, or with foreign partners, LNOC was given the power to "develop and manage oil resources and invest in all stages of the oil industry" as well as manage downstream activities like petrochemicals and other oil-based industrial activities. During the takeovers and nationalizations that began in 1971, LNOC was gradually to increase its share of Libya's production from only 0.33 percent of the total in 1970 to 61.53 percent in 1974, the year when the Arab oil embargo cut most deeply into the West's industrial growth.[11]

Abroad, the Tripoli price hikes of late 1970 spurred OPEC's other members to forge ahead with their own demands. In June 1970, Algeria took over the operations of several oil companies, including Shell and Phillips, and in July imposed a raise of 72 cents a barrel on the French companies. By the end of the year, the Shah of Iran was pressuring the Western consortium working in Iran to pay him more and invest more in the Iranian oil industry. Most of the other OPEC members began demanding a 55 percent tax base (instead of the old fifty-fifty arrangements existing before Hammer bowed to Qaddafi) and a 30 percent increase in posted prices. OPEC met in December in Venezuela and summoned the companies to meetings in January to meet its demands, which ran along Libyan lines. By now, it was clear to the majors that the producing countries in the Persian Gulf—Saudi Arabia, Iran, Kuwait, the Arab emirates—would want to surpass the Libyans if they could in price demands. Libya would then move to new increases to keep its lead, and "leapfrogging," as the oil trade calls it, would result, with disastrous results for the Western oil consumer. Some of the "radical" producer governments like Iraq, Syria, and now Libya, were included to accuse "conservative" producer governments like Saudi Arabia of being soft on the oil companies. In order to prove they were not, the Persian Gulf members of OPEC had to ask for at least as much as they had won.

What the oil companies realized at this point was that they would probably have to give at least this much to the rest of OPEC in the end. However, as Hunt oil ex-representative in Libya Henry Schuler has pointed out,[12] if the companies had been able to hold the line there, they would oblige all the OPEC members—including Libya—to settle for these terms and expect no new rises in the near future. But it was not to be.

Shell took the initiative of calling the companies to meetings in London. To protect themselves from U.S. federal prosecution under the antitrust laws, the U.S. firms first got a formal clearance from the Justice Department. Some twenty-five American, British/Dutch, French, Belgian, German, Spanish, and Japanese companies participated. The independents in Libya, including Armand Hammer, asked for and received assurances that the majors would back them if they had to stand up to Qaddafi. On January 15, 1971, the U.S. Justice Department gave qualified approval to a Libyan Producers' Agreement. It guaranteed that the big companies would "take care of" the independents if Qaddafi gave them the choice of cutting production or being expropriated. The next day, the companies delivered a message to all the OPEC states and OPEC headquarters in Vienna calling for "stability in the financial arrangements with producing governments in the long-term interest of both the producing countries and consuming countries alike, as well as that of the oil companies." It requested "all-embracing negotiation" between the companies and OPEC.[13]

What happened, however, was that the major companies stopped short of providing the "safety net" the independents wanted. They were willing to provide money, but not crude oil, to any company Qaddafi threatened. (Gulf was soon to demonstrate this by refusing to sell replacement oil to Armand Hammer's Occidental, because Gulf said Hammer had knuckled under to Libya and was being paid with its increased allowance from 500,000 to 700,000 bpd production.) At the same time, the Nixon administration in effect undercut the companies' solidarity effort against Libya. U.S. Under Secretary of State John N. Irwin traveled to Tehran to see the Shah and U.S. Ambassador Douglas MacArthur III. The Shah assured Irwin that the Gulf states would sign and stick to a five-year price agreement, separate from the North African countries. The State Department relayed to the companies the suggestion that separate and parallel talks be conducted with the more "moderate" Gulf states and the more "extremist" North Africans. The London group wanted more comprehensive talks, but gave in to the State Department's wishes. Later Irwin, who contributed $50,000 to Nixon's 1972 reelection campaign and who later became U.S. ambassador to France, admitted that he lacked experience in oil matters and on his way to Iran had not seriously tried to stop over in Libya to see Qaddafi to get the Libyan view.[14] When Exxon's George Piercy arrived in Tripoli, Oil Minister Ezzedine Mabrouk (who was later to leave the Qaddafi regime and set up shop as an oil consultant in the United States) refused to see Piercy except as a representative of Exxon alone—not as a representative of all the companies.

According to Schuler's 1974 testimony, the London group's Tehran and Tripoli teams worked separately and did not coordinate Gulf and Mediterranean strategies, as they had agreed in the beginning to do. The Libyans consistently refused to negotiate publicly in the same conference room with the "reactionaries" and "feudalists" of the Persian Gulf. Iranian minister Jamshid Amouzegar's team gave the companies a virtual ultimatum to impose a new price solution on the companies by February 15, and they would follow the imposition by an embargo in "crude oil and petroleum products" if the companies did not return to the negotiating table by then. The threat was probably an empty one, but the companies yielded and on February 14, 1971, signed the Tehran agreement with the Gulf producers. They got increases that amounted to about an initial 30 cents a barrel, with further smaller increases over the five-year period to follow. In exchange, the companies believed, or talked themselves into believing, that they were getting security of supply and stability.[15]

A week after the Gulf agreement, Qaddafi summoned the companies to Tripoli and presented them with a new set of price demands. Dennis Bonney, an elegant Englishman with a Midlands accent who represented Standard of California (Socal), described for Senator Frank Church's investigating subcommittee in 1974 how Jalloud repeatedly summoned the company men to late-night meetings, handed them written demands or proposals, then sent them home, only to phone them later in their hotel rooms and, on one occasion, even threaten them with nationalization that same night if they did not give in.[16] At one meeting Jalloud walked in with a submachine gun over his shoulder, demanding that the Western governments sell Libya arms.

The Libyan position was strong and growing stronger. World oil supplies were getting tighter. Tankers to haul the oil to refineries and consumers were becoming more scarce. Western Europe was increasingly thirsty for Libya's high-quality nearby oil. The American companies in Libya had obligations to those European customers, as well as to the American oil consumer. The companies gave in, granting Libya hefty premiums for its low-sulfur crude, with the posted price rising another 80 cents per barrel and the Libyan government's share of the additional take another 54 to 63 cents. This led Lord Strathalmond, the chairman of BP, to declare that the Western oil industry was becoming a "tax collecting agency" for the producer governments.[17]

Few of the leading U.S. oil executives in Libya at the time would have been willing to admit that the companies were either tax collectors or fat, docile cows waiting to be milked by Qaddafi. Before the Tehran agreements, the majors and the principal independents had announced formation of a common front for the negotiations they faced. What was not then known or announced, however, was that seventeen companies working in Libya also concluded a secret "Libyan Producers' Agreement." If it had worked, the history of Big Oil inside and outside Libya, and the consequences for the Western consumer, might have been quite different.

The companies agreed among themselves that it must be "all for one and one for all." Each company promised to sign no agreement with the Qaddafi regime without the consent of all the others. If Qaddafi required one company to cut back its production, as he had started out doing with Occidental in 1970, each company would contribute a quota of oil in certain specified proportions for which the company under pressure would pay. Such "safety net" provisions did not work out as the independents had hoped, however; the majors inserted language in the agreement's text that required them to provide firms being punished by Qaddafi with only 25 cents for every barrel of Libyan oil they lost. The independents did not care for this at all, but they had to swallow it.[18] And a major test of the agreement, and of the enlightened self-interest of the companies, a test that proved to be bad news to the Western oil consumer, was coming much sooner than probably even Colonel Qaddafi himself than suspected. This test was the second phase of Libya's use of oil as a revolutionary political weapon.

It all began before dawn on November 21, 1971, about one thousand miles to the east of Libya, in the Persian Gulf (or *Arab* Gulf, as Qaddafi, the Kuwaitis, Saudis, and other Gulf Arabs like to call it in defiance of the late Shah of Iran). For years, the Shah had been demanding that the British remove their protective gunboats. In 1968, when a British Labor government resolved to withdraw its troops and end British defense commitments east of Suez, the Shah in Tehran saw the Gulf, especially three tiny but highly strategic islands in the Strait of Hormuz that controlled the Gulf's entrance, falling into his lap like ripe apples. All the Shah had to do, in fact, was shake the tree ever so gently.

A few days earlier, Britain had officially removed her defense umbrella from the three islands—Abu Musa, and Big and Little Tunb. Abu Musa was under the suzerainty of the emir of Sharjah. The state of Sharjah was a postage-stamp-size member of what was soon to become the United Arab Emirates on the Arabian mainland. Abu Musa is twelve miles or so of pleasant, sandy beaches, palm trees, and assorted greenery arising unexpectedly from the glum, flat expanse of the Gulf. Fishing and working at a mine that produces red iron oxide for paint pigments are the main activities of its few hundred Arab inhabitants, a peaceable lot of people who mind their own business. Big Tunb and Little Tunb, on the other hand, are little more than barren rocks (Big Tunb has a lighthouse, important for navigators of the treacherous waters of the Strait of Hormuz). The Tunbs were under the rule of another Arab leader on the mainland, the sheikh of Ras al-Khaimah. It is doubtful whether even Sinbad the Sailor would have found any material there to contribute to Scheherazade's tales of the *Arabian Nights*.

On that dark morning in November 1971, sea and airborne forces of Iranian marines suddenly swooped in on all three islands from helicopters and landing ships. At Abu Musa, the landing was almost unopposed because the emir of Sharjah had already been "sweetened" by the Shah with a promise of co-sovereignty over the island, and probably some financial consideration as well. He was allowed to fly his flag over the Arab fishing village at one end of the island. Iran's imperial red-lion-and-sun ensign fluttered defiantly over the helicopter pad and airstrip that Iranian combat engineers had hastily erected near the other end.

At Big Tunb, however, the irascible old Sheikh Kassimi of Ras al-Khaimah had ordered his garrison of thirty or so turbaned gendarmes to resist the Iranians. Several Iranian marines and a number of the Ras al-Khaiman garrison were killed in the landing. Well before noon it was all over: the islands and therefore the inner entrance of the Persian Gulf, beyond the rugged coast controlled on one side by the sultan of Oman and on the other side Iran, were securely in the hands of the Shah. There were cheers in Tehran, quiet chuckles of satisfaction in Washington and London, and howls of outrage from Arab capitals, where there was much talk of new "aggression" by their ancient Persian enemy.

Qaddafi and the Libyan broadcasting and newspaper media thundered at Britain, which they said had "sold out" the Arab cause in the Gulf for a handful of Iranian rials and, probably, Israeli shekels as well (Israel was commonly perceived by then as one of the Shah's principal allies, and a conniver in all of his imperial majesty's dastardly acts). Of course the United States, which by then had, with Britain, been expelled from its Libyan bases, came in for its share of Qaddafi's scorn, as the government that Libya said had appointed the Shah to be the "gendarme and agent" of the Nixon regime in the Middle East. But Britain, which Qaddafi, Jalloud, and their companions believed to be plotting against them to restore the old regime in Libya, was the blackest villain of all. It was upon British interests that Qaddafi's wrath would fall.

At the time that Britain and Iran thus changed the guard in the Persian Gulf, the new trend in OPEC politics was "participation." This meant to acquire by persuasion, purchase, or *force majeure*, where necessary, at least a 51 percent share in the assets of the companies operating in the OPEC member countries. Qaddafi and his oil advisers now sniffed both a chance for revenge on the British for the actions of perfidious Albion in the Gulf, and an opportunity to strike another revolutionary blow in oil policy against the West. The weakening of the U.S. dollar on world markets in August 1971 had already caused Libya and other OPEC members to demand extra revenue to compensate for the dollar's losses. In October, just before the Shah's seizure of the Gulf islands, the members of the secret Libyan Producer's Agreement and other companies gathered to stonewall the Libyan demands. Qaddafi retaliated by removing the amount in dispute, a trifling one million dollars, from Esso's bank account in Tripoli. On December 7, the Organization of Arab Petroleum Exporting Countries (OAPEC), the more exclusive club including only the Arab members of OPEC, announced in Abu Dhabi that they would require increasing host government participation in both the capital and management of oil companies, with 20 percent of total equity their first goal.

Simultaneously, the Tripoli government announced that in retaliation for the British "treachery" in the Arab Gulf, it was nationalizing the interests of BP in Libya's Concession No. 65 (this had been a fifty-fifty joint venture between BP and Nelson Bunker Hunt of Texas). Neither Hunt's interest nor six other nonproducing BP blocks were taken over. Qaddafi announced creation of the Libyan Arab Gulf Exploration Company and transferred the nationalized BP interests to his new national firm, created as a subsidiary of LNOC. Qaddafi promised compensation and eventually set the amount at $100 million. BP and the British Foreign Office resolved to fight the action tooth and nail, and soon brought test cases to block marketing of the "hot" or "stolen" oil.

The U.S. government and the major oil companies tried to cooperate.

Qaddafi, apparently delighted with this opportunity to diversify his oil sales, then began what proved to be a long and growingly interesting commercial relationship with the Soviet Union. He offered and sold oil from the nationalized BP Sarir concession to the Soviets, Bulgaria, Rumania, the Brazilian state oil company Petrobras, and the Italian state oil company ENI, all of which were only too delighted to do business with him. (Italy in particular was susceptible. True to form, Qaddafi was pressuring the most vulnerable companies, one of which happened to be the Italian state firm of AGIP, then preparing to start pumping from its Bu Attifel concession through a branch pipeline to Occidental's main pipeline to the Zuetina sea terminal. The Libyans would permit AGIP to begin only after it agreed to equal participation.) This marked the beginning of the end of the old-style European oil concessions in Libya.

Once again, Western resistance to Qaddafi collapsed almost before it could be organized. When the U.S. State Department asked the American oil companies not to buy the "hot" BP oil, they replied, "We would be delighted not to take the oil, if you can show us where we can get some oil."[19] After complicated legal action by BP against the Libyans and any buyer of the nationalized oil, BP-Libyan negotiations finally led to conclusion of agreements in September 1972 and November 1974, after the embargoes of the stormy year of 1973–74 had passed. The "net book value" of BP's assets was set at $150 million, but all the company finally got was $42 million, after deductions of $108 million in taxes, royalties, and other money due the Libyan government. BP, in return, stopped its legal proceedings against Libya.

Thus, Qaddafi proved to Libya and the rest of the world that oil was indeed a political weapon, and that he could successfully use it, especially when it was to his commercial advantage to do so. None of the BP story, however, meant much to the average American oil consumer. Even if he was vaguely aware that BP was marketing gasoline and other products in the United States under its own name and that of Sohio (Standard of Ohio) and Boron, the average American also neither knew or cared that Qaddafi's actions against BP, which was 46 percent owned by the British government, were heightening BP's interest in access to the American gasoline market, and above all to Alaskan crude oil.

In 1968 Sohio, a relatively small company, signed an agreement with BP to develop the Arctic oil fields of Alaska's North Slope. So eager was the company, then headed by chairman and chief executive officer Charles Spahr, to get into the Alaskan action that it sold 53 percent of its company to BP. The British firm owned a majority of the North Slope acreage, but wanted much more access than it had to the American gasoline market. BP setbacks in the Middle East, especially in Libya, had made the British company doubly determined to ride the Alaskan boom out for all it was worth.[20] By that time, Sohio's assets had soared to more than $9 billion. It owned a third interest in the Trans-Alaska Pipeline, wells in the southern and southwestern United States, and a coal company.[21] For both BP and Sohio, putting eggs in the Alaskan basket instead of the North Africa–Mideast one paid off very well.

For Qaddafi's oil experts, meanwhile, the period prior to the October 1973 Arab-Israeli war and the resulting embargo and price revolution was a busy one. In general it was a time of declining production but increasing income; Qaddafi's initiatives helped world prices to soar. From a peak of well over 3 million bpd in 1970, production dropped continuously until 1975.[22] Yet during the same period, Libyan oil revenues increased from $1.3 billion in 1970 to $2.3 billion in 1973; and leaped to $6 billion in 1974 as a result of the post–October war price increases.[23] American companies had built up a tremendous stake in the boom, and with it, of course, in the survival of the increasingly stable Qaddafi regime. U.S. oil companies were reported to have invested well over $1.5 billion in Libya at the time of the revolution, and this investment continued. So did the profits: the LNOC chairman estimated that while in 1972 oil companies in Libya were reporting current earnings of 15 percent on invested capital, a more realistic figure would be 20 percent. Company sources estimated profits in 1972, the year following the nationalization of BP, at between 30 to 40 cents per barrel of oil pumped.[24] For the companies, this was among the most profitable oil operations in the world. It was, therefore, small wonder that they were willing to put up with occasional harassment and political lectures by Jalloud and others on the need for the United States to change its policy concerning the Palestine question, Israel, and similar matters.

By the beginning of 1973, the war year, Qaddafi's oil planners knew they could get more control. As an official U.S. government report noted: "it was clear that the worldwide impact of the Libyan moves had affected the majors' crude supply to the point that the [London] Producers' Agreement was a dead letter. Libya saw its leverage and knew how to use it. In the fall of 1972 several of the Persian Gulf states obtained 25 percent participation in the equity of the private oil companies operating in their territory."[25] Qaddafi, once again, felt that revolutionary ethics would hardly permit him to be softer on the companies than the "reactionaries" of the Gulf. With the new fifty-fifty Italian government agreement behind him, he returned to the old tactic, started with Armand Hammer in 1970, of applying pressure to the more vulnerable companies. One of these was clearly Oxy itself, as well as the American companies of the Oasis group (Conoco 33.3 percent, Marathon 33.3 percent and Amerada Hess 16.7 percent).[26]

Qaddafi began his campaign for a total takeover of these groups in May 1973 (when, unknown to him, Presidents Sadat of Egypt and Assad of Syria with King Faisal of Saudi Arabia were already preparing for the October war with Israel). Libya stopped Hunt's tanker loadings and notified the company that it would no longer be able to produce or export oil on June 1. Then Qaddafi seized one of his favorite perennial occasions—the June 11 anniversary of the American evacuation of the Wheelus Field air base in 1970—to announce nationalization of Hunt's assets as a "strong slap on the cool arrogant face" of the United States for its backing of Israel. Other companies, he warned, should take note of the action as an example of what could happen to them if they did not accept Libyan terms. It was also, he said, a warning to the United States "to end its hostility to the Arab nation." (At the same time, King Faisal and the Saudi oil minister, Ahmed Zaki Yamani, had begun their long series of much more courteous but nonetheless explicit warnings that if a new war broke out with Israel, oil exports to the West would be curtailed or cut off.)[27]

On August 11, there was some bad news for Armand Hammer, as well as for the smaller American independents. The Libyan government announced nationalization of 51 percent of Occidental's assets in Libya and the interests of three out of the four companies of the Oasis group. The 16.1 percent of Oasis that belonged to Shell was not affected, and the Libyans proposed a participation agreement with Shell. After hesitating a day, Hammer agreed on August 12 to the nationalization and announced with LNOC the formation of a joint venture to continue work on two of Occidental's concessions. The Libyans paid $135 million to Occidental, calculated on what was supposed to be the value of the nationalized interests. Occidental was given the right to purchase the Libyan government's 51 percent share of the oil produced for the duration of its concession. The price was to be set by common agreement at the time of the sales negotiations. On August 16, it was the turn of the three Oasis group companies to consent to the nationalization and sign an agreement with Libya similar to Occidental's. Marathon received $39.5 million, Conoco $36.6 million, and Amerada Hess $18.4 million in compensation. Shell, however, held out and refused to sign the partcipation agreement the Libyans proposed.[28]

Under the 1971 Libyan Producers' Agreement, Hunt was not entitled to help in the form of extra oil from the majors. Mobil and Shell were short themselves, and could not oblige. Gulf, which was being rationed on its take of oil in Kuwait, its principal source, could not help either. Texaco, Socal, Exxon, and BP were able to provide Hunt with some oil until September.[29] Then came the hardest blow of all for the majors. Only one month before the outbreak of the October Arab-Israeli war and the embargo measures that followed, Qaddafi took over majority control of those major companies operating in Libya that had turned down his 51 percent participation proposal. On September 1, 1973, a Libyan law nationalized 51 percent of the assets of Esso Standard of Libya, Inc., and Libyan American Petroleum Co. (owned by Esso Sirte with 50 percent, Atlantic Richfield with 25.5 percent and Grace Petroleum with 24.5 percent). Shell received the same treatment for its interests in the Oasis group, as did Mobil and West Germany's Gelsenburg, and Amoseas (jointly owned by Texaco and California Asiatic Oil Company, each with 50 percent). The companies were given a one-month deadline to accept or reject. If they accepted, they would get participation agreements similar to those of Oasis and Occidental. If they rejected the offer, Libya reserved the right to nationalize 100 percent of their interests. Gelsenburg and Grace Petroleum gave their consent in late September, just before the war's outbreak. Mobil and Esso waited until the end of the oil embargo crisis in April 1974 to agree.

Through the eventful winter of 1973–74, Qaddafi proposed further measures against the companies. He fully nationalized the remaining assets in Libya of Texaco and Socal in Amoseas and Atlantic Richfield; he created a subsidiary of LNOC called Umm Gawaby, to take over the interests of Amoseas. Texaco, Socal, and Atlantic Richfield all submitted their cases to the International Court at The Hague for arbitration. The court was finally, in April 1977, to award Atlantic Richfield an $80 million arbitration award. In September 1977, Texaco and Socal settled out of court with Libya. Together, they received a compensation of $152 million to be paid in the form of crude oil deliveries over fifteen months.

Shell, however, refused to come to terms with Qaddafi. The giant international conglomerate, Royal Dutch/Shell, has traditionally been one of the companies said to be "crude short," which means it produces less oil than its refining and marketing organizations can use. In Libya, Shell had spent hundreds of millions of dollars on exploration without finding any really big fields. It finally had bought into one half of Amerada's one-third interest in Oasis for a reported $64 million after entering into a long-term crude contract with Amerada. But Shell had ample crude-oil resources outside Libya, unlike a company like Occidental. In 1965 American Shell Oil's president Monroe E. Spaght, who became the first American to serve as managing director of the larger Royal Dutch/Shell group, was quoted as saying, "What'll we do now? What's our next step? How do we make more money?" On March 30, 1974, while Libya was still maintaining the embargo relaxed by the other Arab states, Qaddafi fully nationalized the company's remaining assets in Libya. Then, on June 13, 1974, Shell announced that it had reached an agreement with the Libyan government on the compensation to which it was entitled. This was not published, but apparently took the form of discounts on the price of future purchases of Libyan crude from the LNOC.[30]

One of Qaddafi's last post–1973 war victims in Libya was Amoco Libya Oil Company, a subsidiary of Standard Oil (Indiana), which oilmen sometimes like to call the "oil company of Middle America"; its headquarters are not in Indiana, where John D. Rockefeller founded it, but in Chicago. Though it has always stressed developing U.S. oil reserves, Indiana Standard, as Amoco, had successfully worked in Iran and Latin America and in the pre-1970 Egypt of Nasser, who, while thundering about "American imperialism" and "America the ally of Israel," was quietly allowing this U.S. company to develop Egypt's Red Sea oil fields. In any case, Libya fully nationalized Amoco Libya on March 31, 1976, and transferred its assets to LNOC. The sum total of these nationalizations brought LNOC's share in total crude-oil production from a microscopic 0.33 percent, or 11,000 bpd, in 1971 to 65 percent, or 1,255,800 bpd, in 1976.[31] Truly, the frequent calls by Qaddafi and Jalloud for the use of oil as a political weapon in the "revolutionary" battle against Israel and its Western allies had paid off.

In the turbulent time between the Tripoli agreements of 1970 and the world oil-price revolution of 1973–74, the big multinational oil companies rapidly lost their control over prices as well as production throughout much of the Third World, especially in the Middle East and

North Africa. Again and again Libya showed the other producers that toughness, boldness, and timing were of the essence in securing recognition of "rights" that OPEC had often been unable to secure, and Libya repeatedly took the lead in such actions. Even so, Qaddafi remained careful not to nationalize fully the foreign oil companies, because they continued to supply needed expertise. Estimates in 1981 of how much equity Libya had actually taken over ranged from 60 to 70 percent. As the flurry of nationalizations of the Yom Kippur/Ramadan war period died down, the Libyans granted new exploration concessions —the first since the 1969 revolution. Generally, these took the form of a sharing of production that favored Libya by a ratio of a little over 80 to a little under 20 (81 to 19 in the case of Occidental). Armand Hammer's powerful group was the only important operator that made totally new discoveries in the 1970s.

In 1976 European companies making offshore soundings about sixty miles due north of Zuara in the Mediterranean discovered a very large oil field near the offshore median line. The demarcation line was disputed with Tunisia, Libya's oil-poor neighbor. Tunisia badly needed the production, by then about 45,000 bpd, of this offshore field (which had the picturesque name of the old Phoenician goddess Astarte) to supplement oil from its El Borma field near the Algerian border, which is where the first Tunisian oil was found in 1964 and which by the early 1980s was well past its peak.

In their dispute over the continental shelf in the Gulf of Gabes—not unlike the one between Libya and Malta in 1980 that cost Qaddafi his good relations with that strategically important island republic—Tunisia and Libya took their dispute to the International Court of Justice at The Hague. In February 1977 the first serious Libyan-Tunisian tension flared: the Tunisian navy sent its frigate, the *Bourguiba* (named after that nation's president), to the disputed area to halt Libya's drilling there. Italian personnel, working aboard an offshore rig called the *Scarab Four* for a joint venture between LNOC and the Italian state oil firm ENI, were the target. The Tunisian warship fired warning shots. The Libyans sent one of their own gunboats. The Italians finally towed the rig away, because they could not get security guarantees for the seventy-man crew. The dispute dragged on into the 1980s, and together with the Libyan-based guerrilla attack on Gafsa, Tunisia's phosphate-mining center, on January 26, 1980, has convinced President Bourguiba's government that Qaddafi, who in 1974 unsuccessfully tried to unite with Tunisia, is determined to destroy the little country's pro-Western, liberally oriented regime.[32]

While the Sadat-Assad-Faisal bloc was secretly preparing for the October 1973 war with Israel, Qaddafi continued his pressure on oil prices. By the eve of the war on October 1, 1973, the posted price of the best-grade Libyan crude oil had reached $4.60 a barrel. This was partly because world oil supplies had tightened and partly because tanker space to haul oil over long distances was at a premium, and Libya's oil was valued highly for its nearness to the ports of Western Europe. On October 16, 1973, ten days after the Egyptians had surged across the Suez Canal and Syrian tanks had thrust across the Golan Heights, Libya joined the other nine Arab oil exporters in the embargo on the United States and the Netherlands (judged to be the Western countries most strongly supporting Israel) in what was announced would be progressive monthly cutbacks of 5 percent in production for all customers of the Arabs. Libya's own output was cut from about 2.4 million bpd in mid-October to about 1.7 million bpd in mid-November. Qaddafi threatened, but never executed his threats, to deprive Europe of Libyan oil completely (he wanted the Europeans to exert pressure on the Nixon administration in Washington).

This was also the time of the great OPEC price gouge, led not so much by the Arabs as by Venezuela and the Shah of Iran. But Qaddafi got his share: Libyan crude doubled in price on October 16, from $4.605 to $8.925. Some Libyan oil went on the spot market for $20 a barrel. Just at the time in January 1974 when some production cuts had been partly restored (Kissinger's shuttle diplomacy had begun to work in disengaging the Egyptian and Israeli armies in Sinai and along the Suez Canal), OPEC again jumped the price of Saudi Arabian light "marker" crude, the oil supposed to serve as the yardstick for world prices, from $5.119 to $11.651, retroactive to January 1, 1974. Jalloud claimed that Libyan oil's "real" price should be between $20 and $25, but he actually raised it "only" to $15.768 as of January 1.[33]

From this point on, Libya's role as a spearhead of price militancy in OPEC began slowly to decline. Overpriced oil and the world recession, bringing some Western industrial economies down to close to zero growth in 1974–75, also brought down the demand for oil. Tankers were suddenly more available again. With its geographic advantage less important, Libyan crude in 1974 could no longer compete with the Gulf varieties that were cheaper to produce. Accordingly, Libyan production began to drop, and was less than 1.5 million bpd for all of Libya in that recession year of 1974. Qaddafi was finally forced, at the start of 1975, to lift the embargo on sales to the United States and the

Caribbean refineries that supplied the United States (the other Arabs had lifted the embargo ten months earlier). Continued drops in production and resultant price-cutting finally brought about an upswing in production and sales again, but the effect of the slump brought to Libya its first serious financial crisis. This led in turn to Libya's worst political crisis since the revolution—the attempted overthrow of Qaddafi by one of the key members of the RCC and until then a Qaddafi intimate—Omar al-Meheishi. (We will have a close look at the Meheishi affair later on.)

From 1975 on, new factors made life more complicated for Libya's oil planners: the coming of North Sea oil; competition from Nigerian fields; the need to conserve Libya's reserves, which might not last more than another thirty years at the 1974 production rates. Throughout the late 1970s, however, Qaddafi and his mortal enemy the Shah of Iran remained leading price hawks in OPEC. At home, Qaddafi cajoled and pressured the foreign oil companies to continue providing the expertise and training that he hoped one day would give him control over the "downstream" activities like petrochemicals, transport, and refining.

What was left of Libya's oil revolution by 1981, in the final analysis, was impressive enough: an annual income, for a population of fewer than three million people, of about $20 billion—enough for spectacular, if wasteful, development at home, with many billions left over to finance the causes of liberation, terrorism, and the Muslim faith throughout much of the world.

To carry out those grand designs, Qaddafi needed something he would never acknowledge but that was essential to his very survival. A truly nonaligned leader, as he proclaimed himself to be, could not afford to seek the open protection of any superpower. But in those early years he could, and did, enjoy discreet protection from the intelligence and security services of the one superpower he most antagonized later on: the United States of America.

# QADDAFI'S WESTERN PROTECTORS

In the first three years after Qaddafi's revolution, the United States had regarded the Libyan colonel, a certified Libyan patriot and definitely an anti-Communist, with fairly benign approval. For reasons that will soon be apparent, he enjoyed the protection of an American shield.

That shield, however, had failed to protect either America's allies and friends or America's own diplomats from Libyan plots. This was why, at a moment late in 1977, President Jimmy Carter sat in the Oval Office of the White House, writing a note by hand on a piece of White House stationery. It was destined for the eyes of only one man, Colonel Muammar al-Qaddafi. A diplomatic courier sped the note to Tripoli.

There was no time to lose. Carter and the National Security Council had learned that the life of the U.S. ambassador in Cairo was in mortal danger. Herman Frederick Eilts, the capable, taciturn Arabic-speaking envoy appointed by President Nixon to work with Secretary of State Henry Kissinger in easing President Sadat's history-making shift to friendship with the United States, was the target. The plot was a Libyan one.

Eilts's distinguished career, during the time when the U.S. government had been shielding Qaddafi, had included a tour of duty to Saudi Arabia. There he had done much to win the friendship and confidence of King Faisal, despite Saudi-American differences over the Israeli question. Qaddafi appears to have considered Eilts a dangerous man. He was upset that Eilts had also won Sadat's confidence and was helping to steer Egypt into what Qaddafi regards as the "imperialist-Zionist camp."

Three Libyans, trained in one of Qaddafi's schools of terrorism, were to infiltrate Egypt as agricultural exchange technicians. They were to track Eilts's moves and kill him. Sadat's security advisers and police, who had grown used to elaborate Libyan conspiracies to assassinate Sadat and instigate violence in Egypt's cities, had never seen a plot as intricate or well thought out.

An American "mole" inside Qaddafi's terrorist training establishment had learned the details of the plan bit by bit, and swiftly relayed them to Washington. Almost certainly, the mole was training or pretending to train terrorists himself. The American was a double agent, working for Qaddafi and reporting to Washington.

There was agony in the White House and among the very few top members of the U.S. intelligence staff who knew of the plan to kill Eilts. At what point should the U.S. agent be recalled? If it were done too soon, or if visible security precautions were taken in Cairo to protect Eilts, Qaddafi would sniff the existence of the mole. The agent's life, and possibly the lives of others among the more than two thousand U.S. oil contractor and business people working in Libya, would be endangered. Besides, the White House had to know the final details of the plot in order to act in liaison with Egyptian security to save Eilts.

President Carter himself resolved to act. He waited until the deadline for the Eilts operation set in Tripoli was only days away and then handwrote a note to Qaddafi. In it he warned the Libyan leader curtly that the United States was aware of the details of the plot. To authenticate his warning, Carter listed a few details, naming the prospective assassins and describing their cover.

There was silence for a time. Then an answer came back from Qaddafi. the whole thing was a fantastic fable; the President had been misinformed; the three Libyans involved were innocent and had been set up by someone.

The three-man squad never did enter Egypt. The American mole successfully escaped from Libya. "Operation Eilts" had been thwarted. The few Carter White House staff members who knew sighed their relief.

The Eilts assignment and its thwarting remained a well-kept secret. But it was a turning point for the Carter administration and for U.S. policy toward terrorism, whether of the Libyan or other varieties. Qaddafi's respect, if not his esteem, for Carter and his administration seemed to take a quantum leap. And the incident also fixed firmly in the President's mind the conviction, later understated in typical Carter-esque fashion in his report to Congress in the affair of his brother Billy's involvement with Libyan influence-peddlers, of Qaddafi's evil ways. It added immeasurably to the pain caused Carter by his brother's antics. Carter wrote:

> *There are few governments in the world with which we have more sharp and frequent policy differences than Libya. Libya has steadfastly opposed our efforts to reach and carry out the Camp David Accords [between Israel, Egypt, and the United States, signed in 1978 and 1979]. We have strongly differing attitudes toward the PLO and the support of terrorism. . . ."*[1]

President Ronald Reagan's administration has taken great pains to stress that the Soviet Union seems to stand behind the world "terror network," described minutely and graphically by Claire Sterling in her book of the same name.[2] During the first few months of the Reagan administration, Secretary of State Alexander M. Haig frequently indicated that the Soviets were somehow behind most of the evil that terrorists were doing throughout much of the Western world and elsewhere, including Latin America and the Middle East. As one administration spokesman put it in June 1981, "Governments such as the Soviet Union, Cuba, and Libya—which directly or indirectly sponsor, train, finance, and arm the terrorists—must be clearly told that their behavior is unacceptable in a world seeking peace and prosperity. . . ."[3]

Early in the Reagan administration, Secretary Haig, appalled at the 1980 scorecard of world terrorism—760 international terrorist acts, killing 642 people and wounding 1,078—announced that the United States would never again negotiate with terrorists, as it had done to secure liberation of fifty-four U.S. diplomatic hostages of Iran's revolutionary government in the winter of 1980–81. Haig set up an interdepartmental group on terrorism and ordered an "intensive" review of U.S. counterterrorist methods.

One other thing he did, much more crucial, was nevertheless not reported in the public media at the time. Haig ordered an immediate investigation of any possible CIA links to Qaddafi's regime and the terrorism Qaddafi had supported around the world. It was time, if enough U.S. officials had the knowledge, courage, and will to do so, to probe Qaddafi's ace in the hole—his American connection.

During the Carter and Reagan administrations, relations with Qaddafi grew strained and antagonistic. But we must remember that that is not the way U.S.-Qaddafi relations began. Qaddafi's eventful rule of Libya has been little known and understood by Americans. But both the colonel's supporters and those who consider him one of the greatest threats to humankind since Genghis Khan tend to agree on this fundamental truth: Qaddafi is at least in part an American responsibility.

U.S. oil companies and others with powerful allies in earlier U.S. administrations became associates of Qaddafi's revolution, after having contributed to the corruption of the royal regime he overthrew. But U.S. involvement goes beyond this commercial collaboration with Qaddafi. During the first years of the revolutionary government, at least until the first major arms deal Qaddafi and Major Jalloud concluded with the Soviets in 1974, the United States and Western European intelligence services protected Qaddafi from his enemies, and most assuredly helped him to remain in power.

Long before two former American CIA operatives, Frank Terpil and Edwin Wilson, made their 1976 commercial deal with Qaddafi to sell Libya their U.S. intelligence expertise, contacts, and gimmickry, it appeared to Arabs in the Middle East that Qaddafi had indeed "made a pact with the Devil" and was enjoying American CIA protection. Qaddafi, a Lebanese editor friendly with many of the Western correspondents based in Beirut used to comment, "is an American agent. He must be on the American payroll. How else can you explain some of his actions?" Many Arabs shared this view.

The editor was wrong, of course. Qaddafi was no one's agent but his own. What gave him the reputation, especially among Arab leftist and Communist circles during the early years of his regime, as "America's Man" were two things. First was the series of anti-Soviet and anti-Communist actions he took: frequent criticism of the Soviet Union and Communism in his early speeches and in the Libyan media; denunciation of the Soviet role in the 1971 Indo-Pakistan war as "conforming to Soviet imperialist designs in the area" and also of the shipment of F-5 planes to Pakistan; criticism of the 1972 Soviet-Iraqi treaty (though Qaddafi had himself signed an economic and technical agreement, but not yet an arms treaty, with the Soviets a bit earlier). According to his former advisers, he had also approved Egyptian President Sadat's expulsion of the Soviet military from Egypt in July 1972. Second, and what was equally or even more evident from the start, was what amounted to CIA protection of Qaddafi's regime and person.

First to learn, to their grief, of this protection were two Libyan colonels, Adam al-Hawaz and Musa Ahmed, the defense and interior ministers in Qaddafi's first government formed in September 1969. Neither man was part of the inner circle, the first and second cells of revolutionaries who originally planned the coup; both had been brought into the RCC fold at the last minute. Both were Cyrenaicans with good army contacts. Above all, both were friendly with the British and Americans. Their explanations of Qaddafi's revolution to Westerners and to Nasser's envoy, Muhammad Haykal, were reassuring, and had helped to sell the coup to London and Washington and win assurances of nonintervention and recognition from those two key Western capitals.

Before the end of September 1969, Qaddafi, Jalloud, and the other ten RCC members had moved out of their first headquarters in the broadcasting station to the Azziziya Barracks, near the gates of Tripoli, for greater protection. Soon it became apparent that all was not well in the RCC. There was quarreling over priorities, jobs, and other matters; precisely what happened with Ahmed and Hawaz may never be known. It is clear that Qaddafi, inclined to be overcautious to the point of paranoia about people he didn't completely trust, knew or thought he knew that some kind of conspiracy was brewing among the "outsiders" —men like Ahmed and Hawaz who had operated on the fringes of the RCC, and who now controlled the security forces in the defense and interior ministries. At some point in early December 1969, either the CIA station chief himself or another U.S. agent operating under military or corporate cover, warned Qaddafi that there was indeed a conspiracy brewing against him and that his least trustworthy associates were Ahmed and Hawaz, the two pro-Western senior officers.[4]

On December 11, Qaddafi's personal security men seized Hawax and Ahmed. They were tried and, with six others, sentenced to prison terms that were later increased at a new trial held "by popular demand" in October 1970. At almost the same time as the Hawaz-Ahmed affair, someone, perhaps the CIA, carried out a rather successful "black propaganda"[5] operation against the Soviets. The Kremlin was already in a bad posture in Libya; it had taken somewhat longer than the Americans and the British to recognize the new regime. An Arabic translation of a Soviet book that was highly critical of Islam began circulating in Tripoli. Usually in such cases, the offended party—either the United States, which has also suffered from such "black" operations, or the Soviet Union—claims forgery. In this case, the Soviets could not deny the book's authenticity. They did insist, however, that it had been intended only for internal use in the USSR.

All this helped send the message around the Middle East that Qaddafi was the Americans' man. That key leaders such as Nasser knew better had little effect on the ordinary Arab newspaper reader or transistor-radio listener. After all, hadn't the CIA penetrated Nasser's own RCC in Egypt, and known of his July 1952 revolution well in advance?[6]

Although Qaddafi had in 1970 quickly closed the British and American bases, the Nixon administration found reasons to consider Qaddafi a good man not to cross, if not even to befriend. In the Indo-Pakistan war of 1971, for example, Qaddafi did more than simply denounce the Soviet role: he sent Pakistan several of Libya's squadrons of Northrop F-5 "Freedom Fighter" fighter-bombers, delivered before the revolution to the royal regime. In August 1971 he cooperated with President Sadat of Egypt in crushing the coup by Sudanese Communists against President Jaafar al-Nimeiry; he intercepted and forced to land in Libya a British airliner carrying two of the coup's key leaders, and handed them over to Nimeiry in Khartoum to be hanged.

In the following year, Qaddafi intervened in Yemeni politics in a way that was entirely pleasing to the United States. Yemen was recovering from its long civil war in which Saudi Arabia (and European mercenaries) had supported Yemen's royal family against a "republican"regime supported by Nasser and the Soviet Union. The war had ended its acute international phase when the last Egyptian troops pulled out in 1967. That left the Yemen divided into the north, run by tribal-supported rulers backed by Saudi Arabia, and the south, turning increasingly, to Qaddafi's chagrin, to Marxist-type internal revolution and goverment.

Two rival Yemeni delegations came to Tripoli to seek Qaddafi's support. To win it, Qaddafi told them, they must achieve what he had alrcady begun to prescribe for all of the Arab states: unification. Since the superpowers sought to divide the Arabs, he argued, Arabs must resist and unite instead. In Tripoli, Qaddafi literally locked the two delegations in a room and informed them they could not emerge until they had achieved a unity agreement supported by a basic law for a political organization set up along Islamic but not Marxist lines, and modeled after the newly created Libyan Arab Socialist Union—Qaddafi's early copy of Nasser's single ruling political party.[7]

The Yemeni delegates, if only to obtain relief from being locked in together, signed some kind of document. However, in Yemeni politics, nothing is ever decided for keeps. Qaddafi continued to ship arms to both sides (favoring one when he felt it was threatened by the other), and at the same time arming, for a brief period, another British and American ally, Sultan Qabus of Oman, against the Dhofar guerrilla movement that the southern Yemeni Marxists supported.

Besides following such foreign policy lines, Qaddafi managed also to soothe Washington with sweet strains of anti-Communism not unlike those heard from Nasser's Egypt, where Communists were still being interned (along with Muslim Brothers and other assorted enemies of the regime) in concentration camps. Qaddafi's abolition of all political parties in Libya meant the rigid prohibition of Baathists, whether of the pro-Iraqi or pro-Syrian persuasion, socialists of various sorts, and of course Communists. Thus, Washington felt, even if Qaddafi were somewhat wild in his attitude toward Israel and on the Palestine question, he was a staunch foe of Communism and would never allow the Soviets to obtain any kind of bridgehead—military, political, or ideological—in North Africa.

**N**one of these considerations carried any weight with Qaddafi's Libyan enemies, nor with the foes he was making by his subversive activities in the name of Arab unity in Morocco, Tunisia, later Egypt and the Sudan, and Chad, and other neighboring Black African states. They wanted to kill Qaddafi. Patrick Seale and Maureen McConville in their book *The Hilton Assignment*[8] relate one such story in full, changing only the proper names of some of the cast of characters. Their narrative, though offering no conclusive proof of Western opposition, leads almost to certainty that the CIA, working with British and Italian services, thwarted an elaborate, well-planned plot to assassinate Qaddafi. European mercenaries were to have landed on the coast near Tripoli and attack the main prison, code-named the "Hilton" (there is no Hilton hotel in Libya). They were to have freed and armed several hundred Libyan political prisoners, mostly of the old regime, for an attack on Qaddafi and his companions in the Azziziya Barracks, only a couple of miles away.

The story, as told by Seale and McConville, opens in London in late July 1970. "Steve Reynolds," a South African soldier of fortune, contacts retired colonel David Stirling, the hero of many a highly irregular guerrilla operation in North Africa and elsewhere during World War II. Libyan exiles in Rome were led by former royal councilor Omar Shalhi (the same Shalhi whose brother, Abdel Azziz, had planned a coup of his own, and the same Omar Shalhi who had flown to London to ask for British intervention against Qaddafi in September 1969). The exiles wanted to hire a band of expert European mercenaries for a quick strike against Qaddafi. "James Kent," an associate of Stirling's with experience in Yemen and other places where mercenaries had seen action, felt that since there was no Communist involvement, and many people besides Shalhi and his Libyans would like to see an end to Qaddafi, the operation should be perfectly feasible.

Since 1967 Stirling had run Watchguard, a private security organization. Watchguard sold military and antiterrorist training to African and Mideastern rulers who wanted more personal security than their own bodyguards could provide. Though Watchguard itself was not enlisted in the Hilton enterprise, some of its veterans of Britain's tough, secretive Special Air Services (SAS), an elite commando force, were available. Stirling had tried to convince the CIA to create an American variant of Watchguard. The CIA, already burned by the Bay of Pigs with Cuban exiles and assorted other mercenaries in Cuba, Vietnam, and elsewhere, had not done so.

Stirling and Kent felt that neither Americans nor Britons would object to Qaddafi's removal, especially if it were done according to the Hilton plan, with the mercenaries only triggering what was basically a Libyan action by Libyans. This was reinforced on May 18, 1970, when a retired senior British official discussed the Qaddafi situation with Kent and Stirling. In subsequent conversations, they drew up a short list of six men capable of leading the anti-Qaddafi strike force. One of them, by coincidence, was none other than Omar Shalhi, whom Reynolds had already met in Rome.

Omar Shalhi lived in a lavish, fortresslike villa outside Geneva. The fortune he had made in acting as an agent of influence for the oil companies and other foreign firms during the Libyan oil boom of the 1960s was safely locked in a number of banks in Switzerland and elsewhere. Since the refusal of Britain and the United States to use their then still existing bases in Libya for overt intervention, Shalhi had resolved to get the job done covertly if possible.

In late July 1970, Steve Reynolds flew to Rome to meet Shalhi for the second time and to inform him that manpower and technology for the Hilton assignment were available in England. Then, on August 9, 1970, Reynolds met Stirling at Keir, the Scottish country home of the Stirling family, where Stirling was convalescing from an automobile accident. Kent arrived and the three agreed to set the assault on the

"Hilton" for mid-September 1970. Kent recruited for the operation's London base two former Watchguard men.

After considering and discarding such options as overland incursion from Tunisia by car, and regular or special aircraft flights from Europe, it was decided the strike force must be landed from the sea.

The Kent-Stirling team set about recruiting men who had the necessary military skills and would join the raid for the five thousand dollars a head being offered by Shalhi. Two team leaders passing themselves off as businessmen flew to Tripoli to reconnoiter the prison and its surroundings. Their job was to draw maps and requirements for a fast attack and, once the 150 to 200 senior military and police officers and politicians of the old regime had been liberated, armed, and unleashed, to move against Qaddafi for an equally swift getaway. After casing the prison, the two men reported to Reynolds, who arranged to order arms and explosives, including antitank weapons, from Omnipol, the Czech arms firm that handles much of the Soviet bloc's "commercial" arms exports. As a cover and a way to secure Libyan cooperation, Reynolds discovered and reported to Qaddafi's authorities that a small airline was using Libyan airspace for flights from Luxembourg to South Africa, violating the African boycott of the apartheid regime in Pretoria. This pleased the Libyans and won their confidence.

Kent flew to Valetta in Malta on August 15 to inspect that country and assess its possibilities as a place where a ship might be hired, and casualties, if any, evacuated to after the operation. But he found that Reynolds had preceded him, and that Reynolds's secretary, whom Seale and McConville in their account call Tracey, was talking too much about the team's needs and had perhaps already breached pre-operational security. In the meantime, senior British officials—despite Reynolds's earlier assurance to Kent that both the CIA and Britain's Secret Intelligence Service (SIS) had agreed to the plot and that U.S. Ambassador to the Court of St. James Walter Annenberg had attended one of the planning sessions—had begun to warn against using any British personnel. Qaddafi was not popular in Whitehall, seat of the British Foreign Office and Ministry of Defense, but Her Majesty's Government had no intention of being blamed by Qaddafi, his then ally Egypt, and the rest of the Arab world if things went wrong.

Believing that the job could still be done with non-Britons, Kent paid off the British team, postponed the operation, and flew to Paris to recruit French mercenaries instead. With difficulty, Kent located "Marcel," a

French "fixer" who was a screenwriter down on his luck. Marcel said he knew the right people for the Hilton assignment.

Through Ahmed Shawkat, a Lebanese financier reputed to have good CIA contacts, and Yassin Ubaid, a wealthy Libyan émigré who peddled both oil and hot intelligence information in Rome, Kent learned to his horror that Qaddafi's counterintelligence services wanted to kidnap Shalhi and bring him home alive to stand public trial as the regime's most dangerous enemy. Shawkat and Ubaid wanted to do exactly what Kent was doing—hire a gang of European mercenaries. Their purpose: to seize Shalhi and send him home to Tripoli in irons. Would Kent do this for a two-million-dollar fee?

Kent cautiously agreed to return to Rome to discuss the matter further. Resolving to play for time, he used Marcel to meet "Léon," a French veteran of Indochina and of the French generals' *putsch* of April 1961 (in which mutinous officers in Algeria unsuccessfully tried to overthrow General de Gaulle in France and thus thwart de Gaulle's plan to grant Algeria the independence that was finally to come in July 1962). Léon set about recruiting a French team.

Kent flew back to Rome in September to meet the Libyan counterplotters and string them along. He discovered that Qaddafi's new GID (General Investigation Directorate), reporting to RCC member Major Abdel Moneim al-Hony (later himself to become a defector and one of Qaddafi's most dangerous opponents in the 1980s), had thoroughly penetrated the mysteries of Shalhi's Geneva defense. Kent promised to submit a detailed proposal for Shalhi's kidnapping to Hony by October 15, 1970.

Having won this respite, Kent deposited five thousand dollars for each member of the French team recruited by Léon in a safe-deposit box in Geneva. Shalhi brought in another Libyan merchant, code-named William, to work out the financial arrangements. D-Day was now reset for November 6. Eleven days earlier, on October 26, Shalhi gave Kent a letter to be delivered to King Idris (Egypt's guest in exile) that declared that if the Hilton assignment succeeded, Idris would have his kingdom back. A second letter, to Omar's brother Abdel Azziz, one of the prisoners in the "Hilton," instructed him to pay Kent "four million dollars for his contribution to our cause."

Kent again stalled the Libyan GID men, after a message from Hony forced the postponement of their date in Tripoli. This time he demanded a four-month sixty-thousand-dollar "feasibility study" in which Shalhi would be under surveillance. Meanwhile, Reynolds had begun assembling the men and arms in Europe. He chartered a ship, which was to load the arms at Ploče, Yugoslavia. The rendezvous was set for Bari, Italy, on November 5; members of the team traveled by different trains from France. The ship was supposed to anchor outside Bari harbor, where the hit team would board at midnight and sail from Tripoli.

But as the team members waited anxiously, very bad news arrived. The boat had been delayed in Yugoslavia by engine trouble. Then Kent's London office phoned to tell him that President Tito's police had impounded the huge arms cargo at Dubrovnik and also arrested the local Yugoslav agent. The entire operation had fallen apart. Kent had to pay off the French team, as he had paid off the British one. On November 8, 1970, he flew to Geneva for a laborious postmortem with Shalhi.

After some recrimination over two hundred thousand dollars spent for no results, Shalhi agreed to a new plan. Kent dropped the talkative Reynolds. Through Léon, he bought a boat in Toulon, the *Conquistador XIII*, which was powered by two Mercedes engines that could do eighteen knots. Kent bought Panamanian registry for the boat, and then hired the services of a four-man crew.

The first arms cargo was lost to the Yugoslav authorities. With great difficulty, Kent assembled a new group of arms buyers who purchased, again from Omnipol, a new load of weapons for forty-five thousand dollars of Shalhi's money; the money was to be delivered at Dubrovnik. Kent had to fly to Prague to handle the arrangements, which included many payoffs to Czechs and others. The team was to be collected at Catania, Sicily, after the *Conquistador XIII* had picked up the arsenal at the small Yugoslav port at Ploče, which, unlike Dubrovnik, was licensed to export arms.

This time, the French mercenaries were told to report to Catania. There, once on board and at sea, they were to test their weapons, Zodiac landing boats, Tokai transceivers, and other battle equipment. Under the cover of an alleged alcohol-smuggling operation, three French mercenaries would hire a car in Tunis, drive to Tripoli masquerading as travel agents, and drive the trucks needed for the operation. Seale and McConville describe in minute detail the carefully thought-out diversionary attacks and antitank defensives against Qaddafi's armored vehicles, which would roll out from the Azziziya Barracks. Shalhi was to go along in person to rouse the prisoners once the gates and walls had been breached, and to lead the attack himself. The mercenaries were to withdraw to their ship and escape.

After many new meetings with Shalhi and the other principals in Germany and Austria, Kent flew to Vienna on January 7, 1971, to draw up final plans and set the final date, which they decided would be one month later. Kent personally completed the arms arrangements in Prague. In Abbeville, France, a final meeting was held with the *Conquistador XIII* personnel.

The ship sailed from France, reaching Brindisi on January 25. On January 27, Kent and a Yugoslav agent, Gregor, checked out the crates of arms stored in Ploče, and paid off the Yugoslav customs agents. All seemed well until the next day; in Rome one of the mercenaries, "Jeff Thompson," reported that from the time the *Conquistador* XIII had arrived on Bari on January 26, the Italian police had begun heavy surveillance of him and of the ship's movements.

On Friday morning, January 28, Jeff was awakened in his hotel room by a black-suited Englishman who carried a rolled umbrella and implied that he represented the SIS. He recited full details of Jeff's military record and family history and said it could get very unpleasant for Jeff if Jeff continued with the Hilton assignment. When Jeff drove to Trieste the next day to await the *Conquistador XIII*, he got an unfriendly phone call from the same SIS man, announcing that he would visit Jeff again at eight the next morning. Jeff left for the Austrian border before the SIS man could arrive, and discovered that two Italian police cars were tailing him. They then saw to it that he left Italian territory. Jeff flew to meet Kent in Frankfurt. There he quit the Hilton assignment.

Kent faced a dangerous situation. Shalhi and his friend William, whom Kent suspected might be a double agent for Qaddafi, were more nervous than ever after Jeff's defection. In Paris, the SDECE, the French equivalent of the CIA and SIS, had warned Léon that he should take care since "the Americans seemed to be taking a growing interest."

Up to then, Kent had believed the big powers were either benevolent or indifferent but probably not hostile to the operation. Nothing had leaked to the media. The CIA, SIS, or others could have intervened earlier, in ways that might have gone beyond warning British personnel or specific individuals, but they had not done so. On the other hand, the SIS and Italian police appeared to be hot on their trail.

After flying to London on February 8, 1971, Kent discovered that the British authorities too had been checking up on other members of the team—even Stirling, who had given up any active role in the Hilton assignment a year earlier (the foreign secretary, Sir Alec Douglas-Home himself, had questioned Stirling, an old friend). Kent decided to test the waters by provoking a meeting with an SIS contact. This man wanted to know everything Kent knew; Kent refused to tell him. The SIS man then informed him that Omar Shalhi was not exactly Britain's favorite Libyan. Kent was left with the feeling that the earlier official British enthusiasm for the plot had cooled rapidly.

Italian hostility, and the seeming cooperation of the British and Italian authorities, was a different matter. Italy was quickly acquiring a new economic and investment stake in its former colony, even under the new Qaddafi regime. The Servizio Informazioni Difesa (SID), the Italian counterintelligence service, certainly employed individuals not unfriendly to Qaddafi, as did the Servizio Informazioni Operazioni Segrete (SIOS), the Italian secret military intelligence services. Leaks about the first arms shipment of the Hilton planners could have reached Qaddafi's services from either one or both.

However, as Seale and McConville point out, and as newsmen who have covered Rome know well, it is neither the Italian secret services nor the extreme right (least of all its pro-Arab or pro-Israeli components) that set the policies and attitudes of Italy's bewildering series of shaky cabinets. It is the factional bosses inside the Christian Democratic Party, the financial-industrial complex largely controlled by the CDP, and the managers of ENI, Italy's well-heeled national oil company. At the very time the final attempt by the Hilton plotters was under way, ENI was making final a concession agreement with Libya that was to give the company an estimated twelve million tons of oil a year. Only this explains why the Italians in those early years kept the pressure up on anti-Qaddafi Libyan émigrés. It could also go some way toward explaining why they tolerated the presence of Palestinian guerrillas like Wael Zuaiter (who was later murdered in Rome on October 16, 1972, probably by Israeli agents, because of his suspected activity on behalf of Black September, the secret terrorist component of the PLO).

Despite the overwhelming opposition, and despite between a half and one million dollars down the drain, Kent and Shalhi decided on one last try. They believed it was not Libyan opposition but outside interference and some bad luck that had thwarted them so far. Now that Qaddafi seemed to be moving closer to Sadat in Egypt—on November 8, 1970, he and Sadat had announced their intentions to merge Egypt, Libya, and the Sudan no later than September 1, 1973—the Egyptian security services were taking an even more active interest and role in Qaddafi's protection, making the Egyptians the objective allies of the Americans, the British, and the Italians, if not the French.

At a clandestine meeting in Hamburg on February 19, 1971, the discussion turned to how best to cope with the possible opposition of the CIA, which could thwart any seaborne landing at the moment the three components of the operation—mercenaries, ship, and arms—were brought together in a critical mass. At that time, discovery by a hostile security service might mean a disastrous ending. Kent and Shalhi decided on a rendezvous at sea, in international waters north of Tunisia. Shalhi elected to use *Conquistador XIII* again, but this time used a second ship to collect the hit-team members from a Moroccan port. Léon's French team would be picked up at Tangier, while the Arab components of the team would board from Algeciras, across the Strait of Gibraltar in Spain. The explosives were still at Ploče in their crates, and could presumably be collected there.

But Léon had trouble with his team, losing some members and therefore having to recruit new ones. His SDECE contacts warned that the Americans were now openly hostile even though no U.S. personnel were involved. The sea rendezvous between the chartered boat from Morocco and the *Conquistador* XIII was set for March 28, after the *Conquistador* XIII picked up the arms in Yugoslavia, and the final assault on the Hilton was set for March 31.

An Italian government decision made in Rome, however, wrote finis to the whole venture, once and for all. When the *Conquistador XIII* prepared to cast off from her berth at Trieste on Sunday, March 21, 1971, squads of well-armed Italian police and carabinieri poured aboard, arresting the captain and crew and questioning everybody. At their headquarters in the Frankfurt airport hotel, Shalhi, William, and Kent admitted defeat, and drowned their sorrows in champagne.

There was an important epilogue, which Seale and McConville relate in part. It deals with Morocco and King Hassan—perhaps Qaddafi's most implacable enemy in all of North Africa—and also with the late General Muhammad Oufkir, the sinister Moroccan security chief who later betrayed Hassan and was probably killed by Hassan in retribution. The bizarre Moroccan epilogue to the Hilton assignment also involved Qaddafi's American mercenaries. It was perhaps the first of any such appearance, coming well before Frank Terpil and Edwin Wilson & Co.

After their farewell party, Kent, Shahi, and William separated. William returned to Frankfurt airport hotel on April 3 only to learn that two Americans had visited the hotel seeking information about him; they had tried unsuccessfully to get a key to his room before being thrown out by German police summoned by the manager. Shalhi,

Kent, and William all agreed that very probably the two Americans worked for Qaddafi's intelligence, and were hit men sent by Yassin Ubaid's office in Rome. Had the CIA leaked information to Qaddafi again? Or was the CIA or some other Western service using Americans directly involved as Qaddafi allies?

Without discovering the answer, the three conspirators knew enough to convince them that the United States, Britain, and Italy were all hostile to the Hilton assignment, and might go to any lengths to keep Qaddafi out of harm's way. Shalhi was still determined, however, not to give up. To pursue the operation further obviously required a partnership with some real enemy of Qaddafi, not with Qaddafi's Western sympathizers. Shalhi surveyed the Persian Gulf oil emirates, the oil companies themselves, and other Arab political exiles. None offered real support.

The events at Skhirat, a beach resort in Morocco where King Hassan has a summer palace, on July 10, 1971, provided the break Shalhi believed he needed. Hassan was celebrating his forty-second birthday in leisurely style. His guests included many senior army officers and government officials, as well as virtually the entire senior level of the Rabat diplomatic corps. Suddenly a force of military cadets from the Ahermoumou military academy in Morocco's Middle Atlas mountains, arriving by truck, surrounded the palace and opened fire with small arms and heavy weapons. Simultaneously other cadets stormed the state radio studios in Rabat and took over, broadcasting that the "tyrant Hassan" had been overthrown, and calling on Moroccans to rise up in the name of Islam and establish a people's republic.

By official count, 92 people were killed and 133 wounded. Hassan escaped by locking himself in one of the toilets. The rebels lost their nerve. With the quickness of mind that had distinguished most of his acts of state, Hassan turned the tables on the rebels, pardoning some of them on the spot (many professed they had been drugged and led to believe they were attacking a group that had threatened the king), and turning full authority to deal with the insurrection over to General Oufkir, the ruthless chief of security who had made a name for himself with the French army in World War II and Indochina.

The Rabat radio station was recaptured within a few hours, but not before Qaddafi's broadcasts in Tripoli had cheered on the revolt with promises that Libyan "shock troops, paratroopers, bombers, and huge troop carriers would soon fly to help the Moroccan people." As Oufkir had dozens of army officers summarily shot and others tried by drumhead courts and imprisoned, Hassan accused Qaddafi of complicity and brought relations to a total break.[9]

Shalhi quickly got himself invited to Rabat, where he met with Oufkir. Oufkir and Shalhi decided that James Kent should fly in to brief Oufkir and turn over the Hilton assignment plans to the Moroccan kingdom.

Kent and a female assistant met Oufkir at Oufkir's Rabat home. Oufkir learned from Kent of the previous plans and of a new standby team of Belgian mercenaries Kent had secretly assembled in case Léon and the French withdrew. Oufkir approved of the operation, though he said it would be better simply to murder Qaddafi rather than to attack the prison.

Oufkir offered reinforcements of Moroccan commandos to help complete the job. He flew Kent to al-Hoceima, a small Mediterranean port east of Tangier. Kent thought of storing the arms and explosives in the chalets of the nearby Club Méditerranée, but the first step was to get them transferred. In early October 1971 he chartered a ship from Ploče and moved the arms to al-Hoceima where they were stored in a Moroccan military camp.

During the winter, as Hassan himself later related, Oufkir reported to him prophetically about an official visit Qaddafi was due to make to Mauritania, Morocco's Saharan neighbor to the south. Qaddafi's plane had to fly over the Sahara, later a battlefield between Hassan's Royal Armed Forces and the Saharan guerrillas supported by Qaddafi and the Algerians. Oufkir told the king, "If we could find out Qaddafi's flight plan ahead of time, why not send an F-5 to smash him into the desert?" Hassan says he asked Oufkir if he were mad. Even if the whole operation went like clockwork, an inquiry would find traces of the cannon shells and rockets, which only Moroccan F-5s would be firing. "Can you imagine the international uproar if Morocco were accused of piracy against a head of state?"[10]

Oufkir's enthusiastic cooperation with Omar Shalhi, through James Kent, was never tested against Qaddafi's British and American protection. Oufkir moved against his king instead, and his betrayal of Hassan was punished by death (the manner of the betrayal was the reason for Hassan's revelation about Oufkir's plan against Qaddafi). On August 16, 1972, several Moroccan F-5s ambushed King Hassan's personal Boeing jetliner as it was returning him to Rabat from conferences in Paris. Hassan, his brother Prince Abdallah, and three of his children were aboard. When the first cannon shells tore into the plane, Hassan took charge and ordered the pilot to land at once. Disguising his voice, he broadcast an announcement that the king had been hit and other passengers seriously wounded. (When the plotters later discovered the ruse, the F-5s made repeated strafing runs against the royal palace in Rabat, hitting no one.)

Summoned to the palace by the king, who knew of Oufkir's complicity, Oufkir "committed suicide," in the words of the palace announcement. Those who saw Oufkir's riddled corpse believed differently. Meanwhile, the Libyan media had again reacted enthusiastically to the coup attempt and showed disappointment when it failed. As so often, the United States did not escape blame: a Lebanese newsman interviewed one French garage mechanic working near the Kenitra base where the U.S. Navy still helped the Moroccans train pilots.[11] The Frenchman attested that the "Americans" had armed the F-5s with their cannon shells and rockets. Quick on the trigger, the Beirut news hawk cabled his paper, *Al-Nahar*, that there was "serious evidence" of U.S. involvement in the plot against Hassan.[12]

In the backwash of the Hilton assignment and the waves of conspiracy and counterconspiracy that followed between Hassan and Qaddafi, Morocco's role as a safe base for Qaddafi's future opponents looked secure. How secure, and how important it really was and is, are subjects we will return to later.

There was a further episode evidencing American protection of Qaddafi. This was a second early anti-Qaddafi plot, thwarted while Kent and his band were still trying to prepare the Hilton assignment. This time, the United States dissuaded Israel from backing what was, patently, a crackbrained scheme. It was one of the rare occasions when Israel's proud Mossad and the American CIA did not see eye to eye, and where the United States may have saved Mossad from a grave embarrassment to the Jewish state. As for Qaddafi, he never chose to make public any Israeli role, if indeed he was aware of it.

Following the June 1967 war, General Zwi Zamir was appointed head of Mossad; his previous post had been as defense attaché and head of the Israeli Defense Ministry's military mission. At a London cocktail party shortly before leaving to take up his new post in 1968, he told a questioner he was going into the "textile business." This was not too far off the mark, since Israel's nuclear research station at Dimona, where the Jewish state acquired its nuclear weapons capability, was presented at the time as a "textile factory." "Textiles" is also a word favored by the Israelis to mean clandestine intelligence activities.

Zamir was promoted to major general and given the title of *Memuneh*, used for the anonymous chief of Mossad whose identity is usually kept secret by Israel while he is actually serving in office. In the winter of 1968–69, the year before Qaddafi's coup in Libya, Israel's greatest security problem was the ban that President de Gaulle had imposed on export to Israel of French Mirage fighter-bombers—the kind that de Gaulle's successor, President Georges Pompidou, was soon to sell to Qaddafi. That ban had been imposed because Israeli commandos, in retaliation for an attack at Athens airport on an El Al Israeli airliner in December 1968, had raided Beirut airport and burned up a number of Lebanese airliners partially owned by Air France. De Gaulle termed Israeli actions "insolent" and moved increasingly toward new aid and support to the Arab world and the Palestinian cause. The embargo on French aircraft and arms, especially the Mirages, threatened Israel's air superiority over its Arab neighbors, according to the estimates of the Mossad and the separate Israeli military intelligence service. It was important to be able to build a prototype of the Mirage in Israel itself. To this end, a Swiss engineer named Alfred Frauenknecht was successfully recruited to steal the plans of similar Mirages delivered to Switzerland, and an Iraqi pilot, Munir Rofa, was induced by both Mossad and CIA agents to defect to Israel in his Mirage.

None of this, however, helped Mossad penetrate the plans or operations of either Qaddafi or his enemies. This became an urgent task for Zwi Zamir, because, like any Israeli planner, he was eager to exploit the divisions between the Arab states rather than encourage their unity. The CIA, through its own close Libyan connection, was probably able to help: this was the period of intense CIA-Mossad collaboration, often run by the CIA's efficient counterintelligence chief James Angleton. According to Richard Deacon, an admiring chronicler of Mossad activity, Zwi Zamir set Mossad agents in Communist Eastern Europe to discover anything the new Qaddafi regime might be planning against Israel or Libya's Arab and African neighbors.

In Sofia, Bulgaria, Israeli intelligence is said to have learned that Dr. Salah Saraya (an Egyptian close to Qaddafi who attempted a coup against Sadat in 1974) and some other Egyptian intelligence officers were on Qaddafi's payroll. Eventually, Saraya and his coconspirators were arrested after Mossad, according to Israeli sources, tipped off Sadat through CIA or other channels. Sometime before Libya's first big arms purchases from the Soviets in May 1974, Mossad had learned through their careful surveillance of Jalloud's frequent European travels that Qaddafi was already in the market for arms from the Soviet Union—the arms he was unable to buy in Western Europe after Israeli protests of the January 1970 sale to Libya of over one hundred French Mirage fighter-bombers. (The bombers were manufactured by Avions Marcel Dassault, which until the de Gaulle embargo was a loyal friend of and supplier to the Israeli air force.)

According to Deacon, Mossad agents learned of the Hilton assignment early on. A man Deacon describes as an active free-lance Israeli agent appears to have either penetrated James Kent's organization or carefully observed its operations; apparently he helped organize at least one load of arms supplies from Omnipol in Prague. The arms were shipped to Yugoslavia, from where they were to be transferred to Douala, in Cameroon, and ultimately to Chad.

According to Deacon, the Mossad agent intercepted a letter dated May 10, 1971, from one of the Yugoslav intermediaries to a Vienna transit agent confirming receipt of a small arms shipment from Omnipol. It was probably the second one, sent to Ploče on behalf of Kent and his men. But the shipment was so small that the Mossad man concluded it would be useless to count on that particular operation to overthrow Qaddafi.[13] One former high CIA official, however, recalls that at roughly this time, Mossad developed a strong interest in another operation in which Omar Shalhi was involved. Also central was Prince Abdallah al-Abid al-Sanussi, a relative of King Idris. Prince Abdallah al-Abid had figured prominently in a scandal of the royal era concerning bribery, nepotism, and overpayments for a new highway being built to the Fezzan. Because of his name, al-Abid ("black man"), and his dark skin, Western oilmen, diplomats, and sometimes other Libyans called Abdallah the "Black Prince."

The Black Prince's attempt, which Israeli intelligence closely followed and may have actually supported or contemplated actively supporting, depended upon the use of Libya's big southern neighbor, Chad, as a territorial base. The story of this attempt to repeat the World War II feat of the Free French forces of entering Libya by its southern Saharan borders is certainly one of the reasons for Qaddafi's obsession with Chad and his 1980–81 military occupation of the country. With reason, he has always regarded any hostile presence there as a major threat to his security.

In February 1970 the Black Prince began meeting with Shalhi and other émigrés in Rome. Among the conspirators were the Seif al-Nasr family, who had dominated Fezzan's politics in the royal era; retired officers of the old Libyan security forces; and some Libyan businessmen and contractors who had prospered under the old regime.

Though Chad had been politically independent from France since 1960, French military presence and economic influence was still strong there. Chad's population is divided between the Muslim Toubou and other desert dwellers in the north, and the black Sara people, some of whom were Muslims, others of whom were Christian and animist, in the south. A Muslim liberation front, calling itself by the French acronym Frolinat, and headed by Dr. Abba Seddik, was supported by both Algeria and Libya. There was also a frontier dispute, arising from early Sanussi expansion southward, and from the frontier "adjustment" between France and King Idris's government of 1955–56. Qaddafi therefore quickly sheltered and "adopted" both Frolinat and the refugees from the Muslim rebellion in Chad. During this period, Qaddafi appears to have promised the Pompidou government in France not to aid Frolinat too actively if the Mirage aircraft sale to Libya went through.

Besides the French military presence in Chad, another sharp thorn in Qaddafi's side was Chad's diplomatic relations with Israel. The Libyans complained of the presence, from time to time, of Israeli economic and military missions in Fort Lamy (now N'Djamena), the capital and stronghold of the southern Sara rulers. In September 1971 Chad President François Tombalbaye, whom Qaddafi later attempted to convert to Islam, was to charge that Qaddafi had sent arms and trained agents to evict him from power.

The Black Prince and his coplotters felt that here was a springboard back to power in Libya—an opportunity to restore the monarchy by moving up from Chad. Arms were smuggled, perhaps with Israeli help, from Chad into southern Fezzan.

The strike was scheduled for sometime in the summer of 1970. The plan was to recruit a force of foreign mercenaries, more than those of the Hilton assignment but probably no more than two hundred (though Qaddafi's counterintelligence people talked in terms of "thousands" after the plot ended in debacle). Chartered aircraft were to lift the troops and weapons to an airstrip near Sebha. From there, with local complicity assured by the Seif al-Nasr clan, the rebel force was to make their pronunciamento on Sebha radio. Then they would distribute arms to the local tribes and march northward, hoping to touch off anti-Qaddafi revolts in Tripoli and Benghazi.

The CIA special operations directorate, in its infinite wisdom, seems to have examined the plan and found it somewhat less than practical.

This opinion was passed on to Mossad (which must have had its own qualms about the plot) with a clear indication of American disapproval. And, once again, someone—perhaps this time only his own counterintelligence, led by the still loyal Major Abdel Moneim al-Hony—tipped off Qaddafi.

When an advance planeload of the Black Prince's mercenaries landed, Qaddafi's forces were waiting to capture them all. Twenty Libyans went on trial, including Shalhi and three others living abroad who were tried in absentia. All were sentenced to long prison terms, but none was executed. There was some colorful testimony at the trial, including "confessions" by the defendants that the strike force consisted of five thousand airborne European mercenaries "armed by the CIA" and equipped with armored vehicles, artillery, and poisoned daggers.

Of Israel, Zwi Zemir, or the Mossad, there was no mention in Libyan offical pronoucements.

Years later one of Israel's former chiefs of military intelligence (different from Mossad) answered the question "Is Qaddafi a *real* threat to Israel?" by saying:

> *Look, in the long run, of course we have to take Qaddafi seriously. He is a man with a single purpose: the destruction of Israel. In the long run, he has the money, the arms, and the means to cause us all serious harm, including you in the West.*
>
> *In the medium and short runs, it's a different story. You might even say that for Israel, Qaddafi can be a kind of asset. Who else, in all his frantic attempts to unite the Arabs, is keeping them divided to the extent Qaddafi is? He is a strategic threat, but perhaps a tactical asset; an agent of division in the Arab World.*[14]

The comment carries an enormous irony. For ever since Qaddafi and his fellow high-school students in Sebha had dreamed and planned for the liberation of Palestine, their watchword had been the same cause of their idol, Gamal Abdel Nasser. For Qaddafi and his comrades, Palestine's liberation would be achieved only through one grand event: the unification of the Arabs into a single power bloc. From his earliest moments of power after September 1969, Qaddafi turned a major portion of his energies toward that goal.

# THE QUEST FOR ARAB UNITY

One idea above all others obsesses Qaddafi: the unification of all Arabic-speaking peoples. Only in total Arab union, he says, can there be Arab strength; and the Islamic faith is necessary to create that union. Nearly everything Qaddafi has said, written, or done since his classroom days in Sebha can be explained in terms of this dream. In order to achieve it the state of Israel, which Qaddafi regards as the last and most odious of the Western colonial implantations in the Arab body politic, must be eliminated; and the four million Palestinian Arabs must return to their original homes, or those of their families, in historic Palestine. Anything that contributes to those causes is right and just. Anything that works against them must be circumvented or eradicated. President Sadat's murder in Cairo on October 6, 1981, when the United States and Israel still depended heavily on Sadat to implement the Camp David peace process, was therefore seen by Qaddafi as a great victory for himself, even though he lacked direct responsibility for the Egyptian murderers.

During the very first weeks of his consolidation of power at home, Qaddafi had already begun to plan for what he believed would lead to a unified Arab future. That plan, he felt, had to be shaped in brotherhood with his idol and mentor, Nasser. President Jafaar al-Nimeiry of the Sudan, another young officer who had seized power in his giant country only three months before Qaddafi seized Libya, might be included as a junior partner. All three Arab leaders claimed to believe in the same principles of "Islamic socialism" as stepping-stones toward Arab unity.

On December 27, 1969, in a Tripoli that had barely awakened to the reality of its own revolution, it was easy for the three to sign the Tripoli unity pact. To the fascinated news media of the Arab world and to the skeptical onlookers in Israel and the West, they proclaimed the purpose of the pact as "a tight revolutionary alliance whose goal is to thwart imperialist and Zionist intrigues."

During the twilight months of Nasser's presidency in 1970, as the Palestinian guerrilla movement waxed strong and challenged King Hussein for supremacy in Jordan, all seemed to be going well between Egypt, Sudan, and Libya. Even when Nasser, tired and ill with the diabetes that was sapping his once seemingly limitless strength, agreed on August 4 to the cease-fire with Israel on the Suez Canal sponsored by Secretary of State William Rogers, Qaddafi remained fiercely loyal to his senior "brother." He denounced Arabs, especially among the Palestinians, who accused Nasser of treachery or of signing the "American" cease-fire. At the same time, Qaddafi made it clear that he himself would *never* make peace nor come to any kind of an understanding with Israel.

All through this period Nasser's friends and aides, including Sadat and Muhammad Haykal, were getting to know Qaddafi. Haykal described Qaddafi, whom he had first met in Benghazi a year earlier, as having a "personality of fascinating complexity." Invited once by Nasser to dine, Qaddafi found that the main dish was *gampari*, the giant Egyptian shrimps caught in the Mediterranean at Abukheir, near Alexandria. Qaddafi asked, were they locusts, or what? Haykal explained that they were creatures from the sea, like fish. Qaddafi answered indignantly, "I can't eat fish. It hasn't been killed according to Muslim ritual, with someone saying *Allah akhbar* [God is great] at the instant of slaughter. These have just been allowed to die. I couldn't eat them."

Later, at a meeting with Nasser and Haykal, Qaddafi explained that he had decided to send help to the IRA in order to fight British colonialism. What should be done, Qaddafi wanted to know, about East Bengal, the Muslim country seeking liberation from the West Pakistani army? Haykal tried to explain that the IRA was not a liberation movement in the true sense of the word. Bangladesh, on the other hand, was the political expression of the ethnic Bengali people, a nation in its own right. Qaddafi would have none of this. He considered it a rebellious separatist movement aimed against the unity and integrity of Pakistan, the world's largest Muslim state. Bangladesh was, in fact, for

Qaddafi, a kind of Israel.[1] This was why, in the subsequent Indo-Pakistan war of December 1971, Qaddafi was to please the Nixon administration by tilting toward Pakistan, even sending it some of the F-5 jets the United States had supplied to the deposed King Idris.

During another discussion of the superpowers, the conversation got onto U.S. national security affairs adviser Henry Kissinger and Soviet premier Alexei Kosygin. Qaddafi announced that he could not differentiate between one "K" and the other: both were enemies. Nasser answered, "But Muammar, we can't put the Soviet Union and the United States on the same footing. The Soviet Union may, as you say, be an atheist state, but it is with us. And although the United States is a Christian state, it is against us." When Haykal tried to convince Qaddafi that Marxism was a vital part of contemporary political thought, Qaddafi refused to accept this. Only Islam, he said, had any validity as a complete social theology, a system for all seasons.[2]

Nasser's death on September 28, 1970, was probably a greater blow to Qaddafi than to any other Arab leader. It followed immediately the Cairo Hilton peace conference to settle the Palestinian-Jordan war, a conference during which, President Sadat recalls, the revolver-toting Qaddafi "attacked King Hussein constantly, describing him as a madman who should be confined to a lunatic asylum."[3] "Madman" was a word Sadat very soon would be using to describe Qaddafi.

Nasser, beloved leader and brother, was gone, but Qaddafi resolved to persevere in the work toward unity. On November 8, 1970, Qaddafi met with Sadat, now president of Egypt, and Nimeiry in Cairo to "coordinate the policies of the three countries." Qaddafi was impatient to find a formula for total Arab union. The Sudan was not ready, because it was still working out its own constitutional arrangements. (Egypt, though Sadat skipped over this fact, was also not ready.) A new partner was admitted: President Hafez al-Assad, who had just come to power in Syria. In his capacity as air force commander he had shown skill in averting both U.S.-Israeli intervention and a possible U.S.-Soviet confrontation by denying air support to the Syrian tank division that Baathist generals had clumsily ordered into a losing battle against the Jordan army. Assad, interested in unity with Egypt, Libya, and Sudan, joined their conference.

The Cairo meeting led to a "close community" known as the Confederation of Arab Republics that intended to become the "core of Arab unity." Later in November Egyptians, Syrians, and Libyans continued the unity talks in Benghazi; according to Sadat, they succeeded in drafting a formula for future unity because Qaddafi, at the last minute, proved cooperative. On April 17, 1971, Egypt, Libya, and Syria agreed to form a Union of Arab Republics; Nimeiry had bowed out because of internal problems in Sudan. Sadat, Assad, and Qaddafi agreed that September 1, 1971, should be the date of referendum in all three countries.

Events in Egypt and the Sudan threatened the unification plans. In Egypt, Sadat arrested three of his chief aides—Vice-President Ali Sabry, security chief Sharawi Gomaa, and intelligence chief and presidential office director Sami Sharaf—charging them with being Soviet agents and with opposing the Union of Arab Republics.[4] Sadat, using the tactics of surprise that he was to perfect with such stunning success in the years that followed, then signed a long-expected Soviet-Egyptian friendship treaty on May 27, 1971; with Ali Sabry and his friends in jail, Sadat, who needed Soviet help to rebuild his forces for the next confrontation with Israel, was showing the Soviets that he was signing the treaty uncoerced. In the Sudan a Communist coup on July 19, 1971, had to be combatted; Egyptian and Libyan military and intelligence agencies helped restore the ousted Nimeiry to power and to crush ruthlessly the resistance of the powerful pro-Soviet Sudanese Communist party.

But the Egyptian and Sudanese internal situations calmed to a reasonable degree, and the presidents of Egypt, Syria, and Libya were able to sit down together in Damascus and approve a constitution to govern the future federal Arab state they were combining to form. A referendum, showing the usual percentages of 90 percent or better, approved the document, as planned, in all three countries on September 1, 1971.

On October 4, the federation's three leaders met in Cairo. Sadat, as expected and wished, was chosen president, and Cairo was designated capital. The new state was officially to come into being January 1, 1972. On paper its institutions looked impressive: a presidential council, a federal government and assembly, and even a federal constitutional court to handle top-level judiciary matters. However, there was a "kicker": each member state had not only the right but the duty to intervene to "reestablish order" in case of turmoil in any of the other states.[5]

With his Arab relations looking better and better all the time, and with high hopes of winning the friendship and eventually the support of the United States, Sadat proceeded to expel the Soviet military from

Egypt on July 18, 1972. The massive Soviet military presence, which also troubled Qaddafi, had been growing more and more unpopular with the Egyptians. Qaddafi was delighted by Sadat's action. He had been pondering for months the possibility of a real, not just a paper, union between Egypt and Libya—the same union he had proposed to Haykal and Nasser the day after his September 1 revolution—and he had presented his unionist ideas to Sadat in detail months before, in February 1972, when Sadat stopped in Libya on the way home from one of his frustrating arms-shopping expeditions in Moscow.[6] Sadat's expulsion of the Soviets prompted Qaddafi to propose again, in concrete details, a "total union" between Egypt and Libya. Qaddafi made some remarks to this effect on July 23, and then sent a formal proposal to Sadat four days later. Sadat, feeling there was some serious material for discussion, flew to Benghazi to meet with Qaddafi. On August 2, Qaddafi and Sadat agreed to "create a unified state and to establish a unified political command to bring about in stages the merger of the two countries by September 1, 1973."

Sadat was surprised and pleased to discover that even the Libyans had desired to appoint him as president of the new merged state. Qaddafi was supposed to be vice-president and armed forces commander. But Sadat explained to Qaddafi that he didn't approve of appointing Qaddafi the military commander-in-chief. Egypt had had bitter experience with politicians who also ran armed forces in the 1956 Suez war, the disastrous Egyptian campaign in the Yemen, and finally the 1967 war with Israel. The armed forces, said Sadat, should be professional and shouldn't dabble in politics at all. Qaddafi agreed. Sadat also said that uniting Egypt's poverty-stricken population of over 35 million with Libya's oil-opulent 2.5 million would be grossly unfair to Libya if done right away. Sadat's gradualist approach was adopted.[7] Joint committees were to draft a new constitution, coordinate the economies and the legal and educational systems, and create a common legislature. Against the considered opinion of some Egyptians, who remembered the ill-fated 1958–61 Egyptian union with Syria that had been called the United Arab Republic (UAR), the same name was chosen for the Libya-Egypt marriage.

The marriage was doomed, for many reasons.

First of all, the committees were bureaucratic by nature and there were many formalities. Second, the abilities of many of the committee members were limited. Third, the societies of the two countries were fundamentally different, and xenophobia was rife. To Egyptians,

Libyans were rather crude and rustic fellows with a lot of money who came to Cairo to gawk at the tall buildings, carouse in nightclubs and cabarets (which were forbidden in Libya), buy up Egyptian real estate, and chase Egyptian women who were independent and sophisticated, and occasionally available, at least on a commercial basis. To Libyans, Egyptians—and there were about three hundred thousand Egyptians working in Libya as teachers, postal workers, and technicians in all walks of life—were rude and overbearing.[8] When Qaddafi, as a guest in Egypt, held discussions with Egyptian women's groups, he was dismayed to find that they would not buy his stated opinion that women were simply inferior to men, and ill-equipped for military combat or other traditionally masculine functions. Fourth, and perhaps most important, was the incompatibility of temperament between Sadat and Qaddafi. Sadat claimed shortly before leaving for the Arab summit conference in Rabat in 1974 that Qaddafi was probably mentally unbalanced, and certainly immature.[9] Qaddafi, over time, became convinced that Sadat was neither a true revolutionary in the Nasser tradition nor really interested in the liberation of Palestine. As Muhammad Haykal has observed, Qaddafi and Sadat doubted each other's sincerity in seeking the union. Qaddafi accused Sadat, later on, "of not in his heart wanting unity." Qaddafi said he would resign once the union was carried out; Sadat simply did not believe this.[10]

The union idea, going nowhere fast, was soon to be buried by events.

On February 21, 1973, a Libyan Airlines plane en route to Cairo lost its bearings. The pilot overflew the Nile Delta and continued on his errant way over Sinai. Israeli radar of course spotted the plane and apparently concluded that it was up to no good—perhaps on a photo-reconnaissance mission, or even some kind of kamikaze-type raid in which it would try to crash into an Israeli city or the top-secret Israeli nuclear reactor at Dimona in the Negev desert. In any case, Israeli fighters intercepted the aircraft and shot it down. One hundred eight people, all the passengers and the French crew, were killed. Salah Buassir, the former Libyan foreign minister, was one of the victims.

Qaddafi, beside himself with rage and facing a shocked Libyan population as well as considerable Western sympathy, phoned Sadat to consult him about reprisals. Sadat counseled moderation. Egypt, he told Qaddafi, had already begun to prepare for a war with Israel that would help to wipe out all of the past humiliations of the Arabs. If Libyan planes attacked Haifa, as Qaddafi suggested, the Israelis would surely respond by hitting the Libyan airfields, which were essential to Arab strategy. As for rumors that Egyptian fighters could have flown to the rescue of the Libyan plane, Sadat explained that they didn't because of bad weather. Qaddafi then asked why the weather was good enough for the Israelis to fly. But he yielded to Sadat's advice, and did nothing.

Turmoil erupted in Tripoli and Benghazi when the victims of the airliner were flown home. Salah Buassir's son had leaflets printed that accused the Egyptians of treacherous cowardice. Qaddafi arrested and jailed him, but that didn't prevent anti-Egyptian demonstrations that led, on February 23, 1973, to an attack on the Egyptian consulate in Benghazi. Relations between Qaddafi and Sadat grew strained.

Another incident helped make them worse. Wealthy Jews and other supporters of Israel from the United States and Europe, anxious to celebrate the anniversary of Israel's independence on May 15, had booked passage on a special sailing of the *Queen Elizabeth II*. The *Queen* set sail from Southampton for the Israeli port of Ashdod on April 15. Two days later, Qaddafi summoned the young commander of an Egyptian submarine, one of the Soviet-supplied Egyptian naval units still stationed in Libya under the old joint defense arrangements Qaddafi had made with Nasser.

Qaddafi confronted the commander with a map of the Mediterranean and a plan, and reminded him that the submarine and its crew were part of Libya's armed forces and that he, Qaddafi, was the commander of all of Libya's armed forces. He wanted the Egyptian officer, whom we will call Captain Shukry, to intercept the *Queen* and sink her with two torpedoes. Shukry asked to have the order put in writing. Qaddafi complied.

Shukry returned to his ship and ordered an immediate departure for a secret operational mission. Outside Tripoli harbor, in conformance with Qaddafi's instructions, the submarine submerged. After nightfall, though, Shukry had his ship surface and he radioed a coded report to the main Egyptian naval base at Alexandria, describing Qaddafi's order. Quickly the message was passed up the Egyptian chain of command to Sadat, who ordered the submarine back to Alexandria at once. "It seems," Sadat told Haykal on the telephone, "that Qaddafi wants to put us on the spot. He is trying to sink the *Queen Elizabeth II*." Sadat said nothing to Qaddafi until the *Queen* reached Ashdod safely; then he notified Qaddafi that the submarine had been unable to spot the *Queen*, let alone sink her.

Qaddafi was not fooled by Sadat. Cheated of his revenge for the airliner, he fell into one of his fits of depression and told his colleagues on the RCC that he was resigning. One Libyan insider recalls that "Qaddafi at this point became like a different person. He withdrew into the desert, raging at anyone who tried to speak to him. If ever he showed signs of being a manic depressive, it was after the submarine incident."[11]

When the RCC refused to accept Qaddafi's resignation, he had it printed up and took the copies out into the streets of Tripoli, where he distributed them himself to passersby. After days of inconclusive discussions with Jalloud and other RCC members, Qaddafi agreed to withdraw to Egypt and try to end the misunderstandings with Sadat by appealing directly to the Egyptian people. With all his books and clothes, and accompanied by his small child and his wife, Tahia, a nurse who had once attended him and for whom he had divorced his first Bedouin wife, Qaddafi flew to Cairo on June 22.

Sadat realized that he had to handle his unwelcome guest as diplomatically as possible. After all, the unity project was still, on paper at least, running its course. It was important that Qaddafi should come to know and understand what Egyptians and Egypt, an eminently hospitable country, were really like. Sadat first installed Qaddafi in the Tahra Palace (later the site of many Egyptian-Israeli meetings during the lead-up to the Camp David peace accords), and then encouraged Qaddafi to tour Egypt, and meet groups of women, students, and the various professionals. During these meetings, Qaddafi met with skepticism about his strict Islamic principles concerning the inequality of women and many other matters. These experiences depressed him; he returned to Tripoli on July 9, and notified the RCC that since there was no hope of true unity with Egypt he was sticking to his resignation. Demonstrations, spontaneous or otherwise, by crowds of Libyans who pleaded with him to remain—as crowds in Cairo had pleaded with Nasser to withdraw his resignation after the lost 1967 war with Israel—changed Qaddafi's mind.

The day after Qaddafi returned to Tripoli, Sadat preserved the thinning pretense of accord by agreeing in principle to two referenda concerning the Egypt-Libya merger. The first, setting the principles and bases, was scheduled for September 1, 1973, the anniversary of Qaddafi's revolution. The second, a year later, would approve the constitution of the new united state and the selection of its president.

Ink had scarcely dried on the accord when Qaddafi—or, as Haykal suspects, someone in his entourage—decided to promote a "people's march" on Cairo to force unity down the throats of the Egyptians. On July 18, 1973, thousands of Libyans in festive moods assembled at Ras Jedir in Tripolitania near the Tunisian border. The worried Tunisian border guards soon saw, to their immense relief, that the demonstration was pointed the other way, toward the east.

Gathering new marchers as they progressed, the crowd swelled to twenty thousand and then twice that number as the column moved eastward along the Litoreana road toward Cyrenaica and the Egyptian border. When reports of the march reached Sadat, he sent a message asking Qaddafi to "adopt a firm and wise attitude"—in other words, to halt the march. A Sadat emissary, Hafez Ghanem, flew to Tripoli July 19 to try to reason with Qaddafi; Egyptians feared that the Libyans would be armed, and it was rumored that once they arrived in Cairo, they would launch an orgy of puritanical violence against the bars, cabarets, and restaurants on the road to the Pyramids. Qaddafi told Ghanem that since he had resigned (once again) as of July 11, he could do nothing to stop the "march of the people." The Egyptian authorities blocked the coastal road with a railway car, and mined a portion of the road farther on. At Fuka the marching Libyans, after some dickering with the local Egyptian authorities, were finally halted on July 21.

Egypt, meanwhile, was busy celebrating the anniversary of its own 1952 revolution. The occasion was not lost on Qaddafi: he announced on July 23 that "the merger with Egypt is inevitable, even at the price of civil war." He added that there should be a "people's revolution" to end "corruption, bureaucracy and favoritism which reign in Egypt today."

From that moment on, Sadat realized that he was dealing with an irrational and potentially dangerous adversary. But Sadat, now deeply involved in the secret preparations for the October 1973 war that was to catch the Israelis by surprise on Yom Kippur and to plunge the Western world into crisis, temporized with Qaddafi. On August 29, after much talking, the Egyptian-Libyan Unified Political Command announced a series of paper unification measures scheduled to take effect September 1, 1973. On September 10, the Higher Council of Planning was established with "resident ministers" replacing the ambassadors of the two countries in Tripoli and Cairo.

Appearances had been saved, barely.[12]

**M**uch of the secret Egyptian military planning for the October war, and especially the role of various Arab leaders—Qaddafi's nonrole led to further Libyan-Egyptian bitterness—has been told in the little-noticed but invaluable political and war diary of former Lieutenant General Saad al-Shazly.[13] Shazly is the brilliant U.S.-trained Egyptian staff officer who planned and led the successful Egyptian assault across the Suez against the Israelis on October 7. Sadat gave him Egypt's highest military decoration for the effort, and sent him off to be ambassador first in London, then in Lisbon. After a time, Shazly broke with Sadat and took up residence in Algiers, where in 1981 he quietly led an anti-Sadat Egyptian political organization. Upon Sadat's murder, Shazly surfaced and all but claimed responsibility for the killing.

From Qaddafi's initial efforts toward political and military union with Egypt on, Shazly supported Qaddafi. At an April 1971 meeting of Egypt's Supreme Armed Forces Council, a kind of Egyptian equivalent of the U.S. National Security Council, War Minister Muhammad Fawzi, along with nine other officers, opposed the Libya-Egypt-Syria union. Shazly, outranked by all of the others, spoke for the agreement, and emphasized one clause—the one that gave any two of the signatories the right to intervene to topple a regime in the third country that opposed the union. Surely, argued Shazly, it was Libya, not Egypt, that ought to fear this. Egypt had nothing to fear from Qaddafi, he pointed out, whereas "Libya could never withstand an Egyptian assault."[14]

Sadat, who in his crackdown on the Ali Sabry faction in May 1971 dismissed his chief of staff, summoned Shazly to replace the man. Shazly's first task, as he recalls, was "to push the Soviets into supplying us on a larger scale than ever before." A Soviet delegation that included an air force general, an admiral, and General Vasily Okunev, the chief Soviet adviser in Egypt, arrived on May 19. The delegation had come to ask for more Soviet navy facilities than the Soviets already enjoyed at Alexandria and Port Said. To house two hundred Soviet military families, they demanded the San Stefano Hotel, on Alexandria's beach. Marsa Matruh port, near Libya, was to be deepened, and housing for two thousand single Soviet personnel was to be provided there. Marsa Matruh airport was to be expanded to take a Soviet fighter brigade and an air defense brigade. New radar stations were to be built. Essentially the Egyptians agreed, but they insisted that the Soviet facilities be placed under Egyptian command.[15]

Shazly looked at the balance of forces between the Arabs and Israel in the same way Qaddafi did. "The Arab world," he wrote, "with a population of 110 million, generated a GNP [Gross National Product] of $26 billion. Israel, with a population of three million, had a GNP of $3.6 billion. Averaged across the Arab world, per capita annual income was $236; in Israel it was $1,300. Facing that discrepancy, the Arabs could surely afford no waste. They had little choice . . . but to coordinate their efforts."[16]

As early as 1971, the Egyptian general staff had begun planning for a giant equipment pool for the next war with Israel; Libya's first squadron of French Mirages was included. In February 1972 Shazly talked Sadat into letting him visit North Africa to begin preparing Egypt's left flank for the next war with Israel. First he healed a rift with President Boumedienne of Algeria that had existed since the 1967 war; Algeria had made a considerable contribution of men and machinery, and much of its heavy equipment was still sitting in Egypt. Boumedienne told Shazly that Sadat was welcome to keep it "as long as you give me a receipt so that we can close our books." Shazly wrote out the receipt. By December 1972, as the Egyptian buildup was beginning, Algeria was ready to send the Egyptians twenty-four new pieces of medium artillery.

Shazly's biggest surprise was the enthusiastic reception he got from King Hassan of Morocco, who was anxious to join the Arab effort despite his distance from the Israeli front. General Oufkir (by then involved in both the Hilton assignment to destroy Qaddafi and a betrayal of his own king) escorted Shazly to Hassan. The king said: "The Moroccan armed forces are at your disposal. Every person in the country will rejoice to see our forces fight for the Arab cause." Hassan was obsessed with the supposed enmity of Qaddafi. "His radio spends more than an hour a day reviling and attacking us. Why? What does he want of us? What have we done to him? Is it more sensible to expend our energies attacking each other or to direct them against our common foe?" Hassan agreed to commit an armored brigade and a squadron of his American-made F-5s to the coming battle with Israel.[17]

Shazly next flew to meet with Qaddafi in Tripoli. The meeting took place in a bare, austere office, apparently in the Azziziya Barracks. With Qaddafi were Jalloud, deputy chief of staff Major Mustafa Kharoubi, and Abdel Moneim al-Hony, who, though still interior minister and outwardly loyal to Qaddafi, was most probably reporting on the meeting to Sadat or the CIA, or both. Everyone at the meeting wore combat fatigues. It was, says Shazly, "like a meeting in some distant desert outpost," which is the kind of atmosphere Qaddafi loves. Qaddafi explained that his own armed forces were so small that he could offer little but the Mirage III fighter-bombers already assured Egypt and some of which had probably already been secretly transferred. Apart from some artillery and armored personnel carriers (APCs), there was little Libya could offer; earlier Qaddafi had offered Libyan passports and a Libyan base of operations to a squadron of Egyptians trained in France. When told of Hassan's promise of substantial Moroccan support, Qaddafi was skeptical; he doubted whether Hassan would keep his promise. Shazly said he knew human nature well enough to know that Hassan would deliver. Although Qaddafi said he suspected Hassan mostly wanted to get Moroccan officers and men out of the country because they were a threat to Hassan, Qaddafi admitted, "Brothers, it seems that the Arabization of the battle we were calling for is going to happen after all."

Shazly reported on his mission to Sadat, who was skeptical about the support pledged by the North Africans. He refused a condition requested by Boumedienne—that Algeria should be notified fully three months before the attack—as an unacceptable security risk.[18] Later Sadat flew to Morocco and Algeria himself to firm up the arrangements; he skipped Libya and Tunisia because they had been little help in past Arab-Israeli wars.

At a meeting of Egypt's Supreme Defense Council on October 25, 1972, Sadat's newest war minister, General Abdel Ghani al-Gamassi, reported that Libya was readying "everything they have" for the coming war. "They have put at our disposal a squadron of Mirages; twenty-four self-propelled 155 mm. guns; twelve 120 mm. mortars mounted on tracked vehicles and 100 armored personnel carriers."[19] When, on October 7, 1973, the war did come, all of the promised Libyan equipment and more was already inside Egypt. There were not one but *two* Libyan Mirage squadrons, one with Egyptian pilots and another with Libyans. A Libyan armored brigade was also on hand to fight with other units from Algeria, Morocco, Iraq, Tunisia, Syria, Kuwait, and Saudi Arabia.

**D**espite Libyan support—bolstered later by a reported half a billion dollars in cash—Qaddafi was very unhappy with the way Sadat conducted the war. He resented from the outset not having been let in on the secret planning for it, which King Faisal of Saudi Arabia and Assad and all of his top advisers had been in on as early as June 1973. Then, near the eve of the war, a contretemps arose between Qaddafi and Sadat. Libyan students at Alexandria University had asked that Qaddafi address them on September 28, the third anniversary of

Nasser's death. Qaddafi, who asked Sadat's permission, was told that since Sadat had to make a speech in Cairo on the same day, it might look odd. Sadat proposed appearing on the same platform together in Cairo September 28, after which Qaddafi could have the last word with the students in Alexandria the next day. Qaddafi agreed. In Cairo he first visited Nasser's mosque tomb and called on Nasser's widow, where he took the ritual *iftar* supper to break the traditional Ramadan fast, and then returned to Tahra Palace to wait for Sadat to pick him up. He found instead a message from Sadat asking him to join him at the meeting where they had to speak. Qaddafi, insulted, drove to the Saidna al-Hussein mosque in the center of Old Cairo and disappeared into the crowd, never showing up for the joint speech with Sadat. The next morning he flew home, also snubbing the university students.

But when Egypt and Syria launched their attack on October 7, Qaddafi put as good a face on things as he could. Affirming that "Libya will put its oil revenues at the disposal of the battle," he joined the Arab states' oil embargo. Qaddafi's aides ransacked Libya for food, medicine, and supplies of all descriptions, and dispatched them by truck convoys along the al-Alamein road, the only artery open into Egypt. At the same time, Qaddafi proclaimed his "disagreement with the war's strategic objectives": for him, the retaking of a strip of Sinai or expulsion of the Israelis from Syria's Golan Heights were far too modest and limited objectives.

During the first few days of the war, Qaddafi, unable to endure being kept in the dark by Sadat, decided to send two emissaries to observe the war. His choice could hardly have been worse for him: Abdel Moneim al-Hony and Omar Meheishi, both of whom were to defect to Egypt in 1975, probably used the occasion of this trip to strengthen their contacts with Sadat. Furious when Sadat agreed to a cease-fire after Israeli forces had crossed to the west bank of the Suez Canal and established a bridgehead there, Qaddafi gave Sadat his criticisms of Egyptian tactics by telephone. He then flew to Cairo, and protested when Sadat excluded him from the operations room while several Saudi princes were inside.[20]

In November 1973 Qaddafi's fury with Sadat over not pushing the Egyptian offensive in Sinai and in agreeing to disengagement talks with Kissinger and the Israelis reached a peak. Qaddafi refused to attend the Arab summit conference held in Algiers at which the next steps the Arabs should take in their oil embargo and their attitude toward Israel and the West were considered. On December 1, Qaddafi temporarily recalled his chief of diplomatic mission in Cairo. Egypt followed suit. Both Presidents Assad of Syria and Bourguiba of Tunisia tried to mediate between Sadat and Qaddafi, but with little result. Bourguiba's efforts were soon disrupted by his abortive union agreement with Qaddafi, which he signed in haste January 11, 1974, on the island of Djerba apparently under the influence of Muhammad Masmoudi. On February 18, 1974, Egypt suspended its own military aid to Libya (chiefly naval and security forces there, since the flow of money and equipment had all gone from Libya to Egypt during the war).

During one of his conciliatory moods, Qaddafi—who, according to his aides, was now behaving with increasing moodiness—flew to Cairo on February 19 and tried to patch things up with Sadat. "Those who imagine," he said, "that Egypt is moving away from Libya and that Libya is moving away from Egypt because of minor differences between them are wrong and are deluding themselves."[21] Though they reported Qaddafi's remarks, the Cairo news media stepped up their criticisms and attacks on him.

A crisis in Sadat and Qaddafi's relationship broke into the open on April 18, 1974, when an extremist religious group, which Egyptian and CIA reports showed had connections with Libya, attacked the Cairo Military Academy, hoping to trigger a coup against Sadat. Sadat held Qaddafi personally responsible. Qaddafi indignantly denied the charge, and sent Khaweildi Hamidi, an RCC member and interior minister, to Cairo to try to pacify Sadat. But Cairo editors, carefully tuned to Sadat's thinking, did not abate their attacks on Qaddafi. A message sent by Sadat to Qaddafi, published May 24, next accused the Libyan leader of making Libyan economic aid to Egypt dependent on "unacceptable conditions," which almost certainly involved breaking off the disengagement talks with Israel and the United States and renewing hostilities against Israel. Jalloud flew to Cairo in another attempt at reconciliation May 12, but in vain.

On June 4, 1974, Sadat announced that all Egyptian civil servants were forbidden to travel to Libya for jobs or any other purpose. Although this hurt the Egyptians—the workers who had gone eased Egyptian unemployment, earned salaries much larger than they could have at home, and brought back with them all sorts of consumer goods unavailable in Egypt—it was a setback for Qaddafi, whose own civil service and educational systems were short on the skills brought to Libya by the Egyptians. The decision triggered Libyan reprisals. Libya banned all Egyptian books and television films concerning the war, and closed down the Egyptian cultural center in Benghazi. A bomb explosion in an Alexandria nightclub on July 26 was blamed on Libyan agents. The next day, Libya protested the behavior of Mahmoud Abu Wafi, an Egyptian parliamentary deputy and brother-in-law of Sadat, for allegedly stirring up Libyan border tribes against the Tripoli government. On August 6 Sadat made it clear that the last shreds of cooperation were gone: he disclosed for the first time that Libyan Mirages had been sent to Egypt during the 1973 war—contravening clauses in the French supply agreement with Libya—and that some were still in Egypt; he also accused Qaddafi of sending agents to try to blow up his summer villa in Marsa Matruh and assassinate other Egyptian political leaders.

Other Arab leaders, fearful that a Sadat-Qaddafi split would polarize and divide the Arabs once again, tried to mediate. Following one initiative by wily old Sheikh Zayed bin Sultan, president of the United Arab Emirates, Qaddafi flew to Alexandria, met with Sadat briefly, and agreed that "exchanges of information between Cairo and Tripoli will henceforth be objective and avoid futile quarrels." Sudanese President Nimeiry, venturing back into the arena for the first time since the halcyon days of 1971, met first with Qaddafi and then Sadat on December 10, 1974. The formation of another committee was announced—this time an Egyptian-Sudanese-Libyan Committee supposed to find solutions for their tripartite differences.[22]

For a time there was calm. Egyptian workers flowed back into Libya. Cooperation resumed in agriculture, housing, and a new start was made toward meeting Libya's continued need for skilled Egyptian manpower with Egypt's unlimited supply of people for export.

But there were just too many political problems. Sadat's Egypt had begun its long march toward peace with Israel, shepherded along at almost every step of the way by Henry Kissinger and Herman Eilts, the capable U.S. ambassador in Cairo whom Qaddafi was fast growing to detest (and probably, by then, to plot against). On April 12, 1975, Sadat broke their temporary truce by telling an Arab editor from the prestigious Kuwaiti newspaper *Al-Siyasah* that Qaddafi was "one hundred percent mad." The Libyan colonel, Sadat charged, was trying to push Egypt to break its ties of friendship with the Arab oil states. The RCC in Tripoli responded collectively with a memorandum on April 16 that threatened to break relations with Cairo if Sadat did not cease his attacks.

Cairo next accused Tripoli of working to annex the disputed oases in the Western Desert. Egypt organized meetings of the heads of tribes in the oases near the frontier to counter the "Libyan annexation projects." Once again the Egyptian workers in Libya came under fire, with expulsion of 265 of them and the death of one as a result of alleged bad treatment by Libyan police; the death was a subject of long angry debates in the Arab Socialist Union and the Egyptian parliament. Some deputies called for withdrawal of all 200,000 to 300,000 Egyptians from Libya, and breaking of relations with Tripoli. Qaddafi was personally blamed. Then, on April 30, one Libyan and eight Egyptians were accused of being paid by Qaddafi to murder several Egyptian journalists who opposed him, including the renowned Egyptian novelist, editor, and man of letters Ihsan Abdel Qaddus, and the Amin brothers, Ali and Mustafa, who had played important parts in the politics of the Nasser period. Tripoli denied the charges and accused Egypt, in connivance with the Americans, of plotting against Libya. On May 10, 1975, a mob sacked the Libyan diplomatic mission in Cairo. In a protest to the Arab League, Libya blamed the Egyptian authorities and forbade entry into Libya of any Egyptian not obtaining a Libyan work permit in advance. Relations worsened when President Sadat met with President Gerald Ford three weeks later at Salzburg.

By now a violent civil war was raging in Lebanon, with various Arab states and factions intervening on one side or the other. Sadat accused Qaddafi of inflaming the Lebanese situation and of being a "mindless terrorist." The Libyans responded with anti-Egyptian demonstrations in principal cities, denouncing the "capitulationist" attitude of Sadat toward Israel and the United States. For the first time the Cairo media began to denounce the growing military ties—involving tanks, planes, and other heavy equipment—between Libya and the Soviet Union. Egyptian intelligence released evidence to the Cairo newspapers that Qaddafi had set aside a sum of eighty million dollars to finance subversion in the Arab countries as a whole. Sadat's interior ministry expelled a Libyan diplomat accused of distributing anti-Sadat propaganda in Egypt.

Then, something odd happened. Qaddafi was most quiet when he was expected to be loudest.

Toward the end of the summer, as Kissinger pushed his peace shuttle toward a second and lasting Sinai disengagement treaty that the State Department was to call "Sinai II" (after Sinai I, the immediate post-cease-fire arrangements of early 1974), the Libyan-Egyptian controversy seemed to be cooling. Although Syria and the Palestinians loudly denounced Sadat's "treachery" in signing Sinai II on September 1, 1975, Qaddafi did not utter a word of protest. This was even stranger than usual because for once no other Arab leader was mediating between Sadat and Qaddafi when the agreement was concluded.

Arab editors in Beirut and other capitals thought they understood why: Sadat, they said, perhaps with the help of the Israeli intelligence, Mossad, had tipped off Qaddafi to the coup planned by Omar al-Meheishi. (Meheishi soon after went to Egypt and claimed Sadat's protection and hospitality.) Therefore, the Arab grapevine insisted, Qaddafi owed Sadat one and eased up on him. Maamun Abu Zeyd, the skillful foreign-affairs adviser of Sudanese President Nimeiry, even succeeded in temporarily halting the hostile propaganda that had been crackling along the air waves between Cairo and Tripoli. The Egyptian and Libyan prime ministers exchanged visits; Jalloud, always glad to sample the delights of Cairo nightlife after the glum austerity of Qaddafi's capital, was a happy guest in Cairo.

But the calm was only temporary.

Qaddafi and his security advisers, working with their friends Terpil and Wilson, were busy at their conspiratorial looms during the first weeks of 1976. In the webs they were spinning they hoped eventually to trap Sadat, Ambassador Herman Eilts, Nimeiry, Bourguiba, and others whom Qaddafi considered key adversaries.

On March 8, 1976, the Egyptian security authorities announced the apprehension of a seven-man Libyan commando group, charged with bringing Omar al-Meheishi, dead or alive, back to Tripoli. Around the same time, Italian police were able to capture, at Rome's Fiumicino airport, three other Libyans planning to hijack an airliner on the Cairo-Rome run. They had intended to seize Abdel Moneim al-Hony, by then extremely active in opposition to Qaddafi abroad from his Cairo base. On March 20, 1976, the Egyptian media reported another Libyan plot. This time a twenty-member commando group was arrested in Egypt as it prepared to murder various Libyan opponents of Qaddafi, including Meheishi and Hony. Egyptian counterintelligence hunted down and arrested numerous Libyan infiltrators on sabotage or murder missions. On July 1, 1976—one day before a carefully prepared coup attempt in Khartoum against Sudanese President Nimeiry—Milhoud Seddik Ramadan, Libya's senior diplomat in Cairo, was accused of organizing propaganda and secret cells to subvert Sadat, and was expelled.

The focus of Qaddafi's offensive to achieve Arab unity by installing "people's governments" friendly to him shifted temporarily from Cairo to Khartoum. Early on July 2, 1976, rebel troops in the Sudan occupied public buildings and military installations, trying to seize power for the Sudanese National Front, a political party of conservative, if not fundamentalist, Muslims. The coup failed. Both Nimeiry and Sadat blamed Qaddafi and the Soviets. Khartoum filed complaints against Libya with the Arab League and the UN Security Council, and on July 6 broke its diplomatic relations, air links, and all its bilateral agreements with Libya. In August Nimeiry received Meheishi in Khartoum, and called on the Libyans in repeated radio broadcasts to revolt against Qaddafi. In speeches or statements on December 26, 1976, and on April 28 and May 1, 1977, he rejected Arab offers and accused Libya and Ethiopia of working with the Soviets to overthrow both himself and Sadat. Nimeiry also boycotted a major summit of Islamic heads of state from May 16 to 22 chiefly because it was held in Tripoli. A "four-day" desert war, as it came to be called in North Africa, erupted between Sadat and Qaddafi in July 1977. The Sudan was the only Arab country to side openly with Egypt.

The July 1977 conflict was fought out along the desert frontier where in the 1920s Marshal Graziani's Italian legions had battled the Sanussi leaders and the Libyan tribesmen of Omar al-Mokhtar. Described by one Egyptian who was close to it as a "major bloodletting," the "four-day" war proved to Qaddafi that Sadat was in deadly earnest about trying to halt Libyan subversion. But it also demonstrated to Sadat and the Egyptian military staff that Qaddafi's Soviet armament, many of the 1974 purchases by then delivered, had become a formidable arsenal, one that had very possibly already altered the power balance in North Africa and the central Mediterranean.

When in January 1977 Cairo and most other major Egyptian cities erupted in rioting caused by the loss of subsidies that sent the prices of basic foods rocketing, Cairo newspapers included Libya among the culprits. A bombing on February 21 in Alexandria was blamed by the Egyptian authorities on Libya. Cairo discovered a network of eight pro-Libyan Egyptians who were supposed to sabotage the Afro-Asian conference scheduled for Cairo in early March; seven were executed. On April 10, demonstrators in both countries attacked each other's diplomatic missions in Alexandria and Benghazi; diplomats from both countries were interned and forbidden to leave for home for some days.

The head of the Egyptian mission in Benghazi, Nabih Dayruti, accused Libyan authorities of organizing the plunder of the mission in Benghazi in order "to divert the anger of the Libyan people provoked by the execution of forty-five officers at the beginning of April."[23] At the same time, the Egyptian government formally blamed Libya for the first time for the Vienna kidnapping of the OPEC ministers in December 1975, and charged that Qaddafi was preparing "acts of sabotage" against foreign ambassadors in the Arab countries. Egyptian War Minister Gamassi warned that Egypt would respond to any attack by taking reprisals against Libya. Qaddafi answered this by calling for an emergency meeting of the Arab League Council to discuss the "danger arising" from the Egyptian labor force in Libya, which he accused of being a fifth column. On May 7 Qaddafi told Saudi, Kuwaiti, and United Arab Emirates representatives that any aid given to Egypt would be considered an act of hostility toward Libya. Jalloud followed that with a warning on May 19 that Egypt was preparing an attack on Libya, using the supposed plight of the Egyptian workers as a pretext.

Sadat made gestures of public hospitality toward a number of Qaddafi's opponents who had sought asylum in Egypt. Abdel Hamid Bakkouche, who had been Libyan prime minister before the September 1969 coup, was welcomed in Cairo on May 17 and immediately given asylum. A Libyan air-force cadet, Ruhum Asfar, flew his training aircraft to Egypt, joining Meheishi, Hony, King Idris, and many others in their new sanctuary. In middle and late May, three more Egyptians convicted of belonging to a pro-Libyan sabotage ring were sentenced to death, and in early June Libya announced the dismantling of two Egyptian rings accused of planning to blow up the conference room prepared for the May 16 Islamic summit. About this time, according to some published reports, Israel's Mossad warned Sadat of a new Libyan assassination plot. War clouds were clearly darkening the Eastern Desert.

The threat of war between Egypt and Libya alarmed the leaders of Black Africa. On July 7 General Eyadema, the president of Togo, one of the French-speaking states of the former French colonial empire, tried to mediate. He met both the Libyan foreign minister Ali Abdel Salem Tariki, and Tariki's Egyptian counterpart Mahmoud Riad. The next day, Eyadema announced that an agreement had been worked out that would be submitted to the two governments for ratification. On July 9 Riad returned to Cairo and declared that there had been no agreement at all. So much for Togolese mediation.[24]

Meanwhile, the perennial conflict in Chad erupted to muddy North African events even further. Libya and Chad were old enemies, and since winning independence in 1960 the government of the former French colony continued to be on mostly bad terms with Libya. The Muslim Toubou tribes in the north, who had traditional and historical religious and commercial ties with Libya, had been in revolt against the central government in N'Djamena where the southern, partly non-Muslim Sara black people predominate.

At the start of Qaddafi's tangled relationship with Chad in December 1972, the religion of Chad President François Tombalbaye, a Christian, became an affair of state. While Tombalbaye was a guest in Tripoli, Qaddafi offered him two million dollars plus liberal Libyan financing for badly needed development projects to convert to Islam. Tombalbaye refused politely, but did reportedly accept about one hundred million dollars of Libyan funds in return for Libya's annexation of a sixty-mile strip of northern Chad, believed rich in minerals, called the Aouzou Strip. Following the affair of the "Black Prince," when Tombalbaye and Qaddafi traded accusations about Israeli and French involvement in the area, Tombalbaye apparently believed that by ceding Aouzou to Qaddafi, he could relieve some of the pressure generated against Chad by Frolinat, the northern Muslim nationalist movement supported by Qaddafi and, to a lesser extent, Boumedienne.

The Chad situation complicated the Egypt-Libya conflict. On July 11, 1977, Egyptian Vice-President Husni Mubarak, who later succeeded Sadat as president, arrived unexpectedly in N'Djamena, amid charges by the Chad government that four thousand Libyan troops had invaded northern Chad and were fighting with the Frolinat forces to establish a Toubou state in northern Chad. Libya denied these accusations, but Egypt and the Sudan proclaimed their support for the Chad government. Qaddafi's information media described the N'Djamena-Cairo-Khartoum statements as a "declaration of War."

For both Egypt and Libya, their July 1977 conflict had clear-cut military and political aspects. Along with Angola, Ethiopia, and Cuba, Libya was declared by the Egyptians to be an instrument of Soviet policy. The possible implications for the superpowers were reflected in pronouncements from several capitals. In a memorandum to a number of Arab countries, published on April 28 by the Cairo newspapers, the Soviet Union warned against an Egyptian attack on Libya, without specifying what the Soviets might do in response. Ismail Fahmi, the Egyptian foreign minister, asserted on May 14 that what he had charged was that the presence of three thousand Cubans in Libya and Ethiopia (most of the Cubans, said U.S. intelligence, were actually in Ethiopia) justified the presence of Egyptian troops on Libya's frontier. Touching the crucial base of domestic politics as well, Egypt accused Libya of subversive operations against Sudan and Chad, and blamed Libya for aid it had allegedly supplied to the fanatical Muslim fundamentalist sect Al-Takfir wal-Hajra, which the Egyptian government had ordered dissolved following discovery of a plot in Cairo.

After July 21, Egyptian and Libyan military communiqués announced hostilities in progress, but gave radically different versions of each day's events. The first Egyptian statement described an incident on July 16 in the desert about sixty miles south of the Egyptian border town of Sollum, sparked by a Libyan patrol that had killed nine Egyptian soldiers. Egyptian units reportedly crossed the frontier in hot pursuit of the Libyans, and went as far as the small oasis of Musaid. The Egyptians claimed forty Libyan tanks and two aircraft destroyed, twelve Libyan soldiers and thirty "saboteurs"—presumably cross-border guerrilla or commando troops—taken prisoner. Libya's version had it that fighting began July 14 when Egyptians attacked Libyan border posts, and took twelve prisoners. After addressing protest notes and demanding liberation of the prisoners, Libyan forces captured a twelve-man Egyptian patrol on July 16. The next day, the Libyans said, the Libyan commander of the border zone proposed an exchange of prisoners and warned the Egyptians to evacuate the areas their forces had occupied "for several months." When the ultimatum expired, the Libyans said, they captured the areas. During the fighting, twenty-two Egyptian soldiers were killed and thirty-three others taken prisoner, and an Egyptian plane was brought down over Sidi Amr. The Libyans claimed to have shot down two Egyptian planes in an attack on the village of Barada. On July 22 the fighting heated up as Egyptian planes heavily bombed al-Adem air base. Libya reported shooting down five attacking planes, and claimed an attempted Egyptian paratroop attack on the town of Kasr Jidda. Cairo denied it. On July 23 Libya reported new Egyptian air raids against Tobruk and Kufra, and the villages of Mussaid, Jarabub, Barada, and Kasr Jidda. It claimed eight more Egyptian planes downed. Cairo admitted only an artillery duel near Sollum. On the final full day of heavy fighting, July 24, the Libyans announced that during a new Egyptian air raid, Egyptian pilot Major Abdel Hamid Effat was captured alive.

The air raid on the al-Adem base, in which Cairo admitted Egypt lost two planes, was intended to destroy a radar station operated by Soviet experts. This was being used, the Cairo newspaper *Al-Goumhouriya* reported, not only to observe movements of the Egyptian army, but also the U.S. Sixth Fleet and NATO forces in the Mediterranean. President Sadat later claimed that a Soviet helicopter carrier in the Mediterranean had used its jamming and electronic countermeasures gear to monitor and disrupt Egyptian war communications as well as to observe nearby American naval movements.

President Sadat ordered a cease-fire July 25; Colonel Qaddafi never did. Major Jalloud said on August 1 that Libyan losses had been twenty-seven dead, nine missing, nine tanks damaged, and two aircraft lost. Cairo never published any casualty figures, but estimates of diplomats stationed in North Africa were that Egyptian losses had been high.

It was most probably Egypt's losses, rather than Arab mediation, that caused Sadat to halt what might have otherwise become a wider North African war. But Arab mediation played a role. PLO chairman Yasir Arafat made the first, unsuccessful mediation effort on July 20. Sadat demanded, through Arafat, that Tripoli dismantle guerrilla and saboteur training camps near the frontier, halt infiltration of terrorist and sabotage squads into Egypt, and move major military bases further inland. Syria, Kuwait, and Iraq tried their hands at mediation. Then Boumedienne gave some veiled hints that Algeria might have to intervene on the side of Libya if the Libyans invoked a 1975 defense treaty between the two countries. Morocco, many observers believed, might then take the opportunity to move against Algeria, which by then was actively supporting the Polisario guerrillas fighting the Moroccan army in the Western Sahara. After firing stopped, Arafat managed to obtain an exchange of prisoners and an agreement between Libyan minister of state Taha al-Sharif ben Amer and Egyptian foreign under secretary Muhammad Riad to halt hostile propaganda and study frontier problems. By August 23, Cairo was able to announce officially that after "secret and direct contacts," Egypt and Libya had agreed to establish border control posts.[25]

The political background of this Qaddafi-Sadat conflict, little noticed in the West, is worth careful attention today for what it discloses about the growing Soviet role in Libya.

As the fighting was announced July 22, Sadat accused Qaddafi of acting as "the agent of a foreign power known to all" (meaning the Soviet Union) and also of agreeing to "sell off Eritrea to Ethiopia." This referred to a switch Qaddafi had recently made from supporting, with other Arab states, the mainly Muslim guerrilla movement in Eritrea to supporting the new Marxist revolutionary regime of Mengistu Haile Miriam, supported by the Soviets, in Ethiopia. Anti-Soviet struggle and opposition to Soviet influence in Africa were constant themes in pronouncements of Sadat and other Egyptian leaders. Sadat tried to give a pan-African flavor to his military action: in a reference to evidence that Qaddafi had begun to train African and Arab dissidents in guerrilla camps to overthrow their governments and install in power "people's" governments favorable to Qaddafi, Sadat said he was acting "in the name of the fallen martyrs of Tunisia, Sudan, Chad, Niger, Egypt, and Morocco" (all countries where Qaddafi had meddled). Egyptian Prime Minister Mamduh Salem and War Minister Gamassi both accused Libya on August 2 of having become a Soviet base. Though he denied having territorial ambitions against Libya, Sadat remarked on July 26 that one oasis, near the town of Sina, had been ceded to the Italians by Egypt only in 1930.

For Qaddafi, President Sadat was leading his people in a military adventure to divert their attention from Egypt's internal economic woes, and wanted "to prove to the Americans that he was capable of doing something." Official Tripoli commentaries denied the presence of Soviet or Cuban experts and said Sadat was acting as the "instrument of an American plan." On August 1, Jalloud repeated the accusation of U.S. support and claimed the Libyans had shot down four U.S. pilotless aircraft, or drones, over Bardia, a claim never confirmed by any U.S. or Egyptian spokesman. Qaddafi asked for Arab volunteers to support Libya in case fighting was resumed, and he mobilized reservists. The hostilities also galvanized the People's Congresses, supposed to be running the country instead of the former government, into developing an enlarged militia force. Over one hundred Palestinian guerrillas belonging to the more leftist guerrilla groups responded to Qaddafi's call for volunteers and left Beirut for Tripoli, traveling through Cyprus.[26]

The superpowers gave restrained support to their favorites. The United States on July 27 announced its intention to supply arms to Egypt, Sudan, and even Chad. The USSR sent the Soviet chief of staff on a visit to Libya and Algeria and warned on August 23 against any renewal of fighting. During the September 1, 1977, Revolution Day ceremonies in Tripoli—even as Sadat had begun secret sound- ings for his history-making peace visit to Jerusalem—Qaddafi's regular armed forces paraded with new Soviet T-62 tanks, equipped with laser range finders, and Soviet medium-range missiles with a 160-mile range.[27]

Sadat believed that he had demonstrated to the world that Qaddafi was a threat, and that he, Sadat, was willing to do something about it. Qaddafi believed that he had given the Egyptian armed forces a warning, if not a beating, and that they would know what to expect if they ever ventured to tackle their "brothers" to the west in another military engagement. His new Soviet equipment, especially air defense systems, had served him well. The United States and the Soviet Union, as well as other regional actors, had learned that North Africa was not a dormant area of secondary importance where no dramatic crises were to be feared or expected. Lessons had been learned by some. But there were still others who had to learn.

President Bourguiba's Tunisia, like Morocco and Algeria a former colony of France, believed in minding its own international business. Bourguiba, it was true, had some original ideas about ending the Arab-Israeli conflict that got him into trouble with Nasser in the early 1960s.[28] But internationally Tunisia had the reputation of moderation, prudence, and fairly effective use of the large quantities of French, American, and other Western economic aid it had been receiving since 1956. With its parliamentary-type façade that barely masked the one-party government of its charismatic, patriarchal hero-leader President Habib Bourguiba, Tunisia was something of an annoyance to Qaddafi. During the years of his fascination with Nasser's dream of a united Eastern Arab world, Qaddafi had no time for the dream Morocco's King Muhammad V, Tunisia's Bourguiba, and Algeria's leaders all shared: a united Maghreb, or Arab West. Less than three months after signing the December 1969 Tripoli Pact with Nasser and Nimeiry, Qaddafi pulled Libya out of the Permanent Consultative Committee for the Maghreb, which King Idris had joined.

Like Egyptians and other Arabs, Tunisians were drawn to Libya's prospering oil economy by the promise of well-paid jobs and abundant goods that could, like the cash, be sent or taken home with them. Since 1970 a yearly average of thirty thousand or so Tunisians worked in Libya. Qaddafi's ecstatic calls for Arab revolution and unity were anathema to Bourguiba. With his rather Mussolini-like jaw and stubborn ways, Bourguiba wanted to preserve both his charisma and his Western, secular convictions. Qaddafi never appreciated the fact that Bourguiba became the first Arab head of state to abolish polygamy, establish equal rights for women, and even challenge the value, in terms of human energy and productivity, of the Muslim fast month of Ramadan. Like the relationship between Sadat and Qaddafi, the relationship between Bourguiba and Qaddafi promised early on to be a volatile one.

And so it was. In February 1971, when Qaddafi paid his first official visit to Tunis, he found that Bourguiba either couldn't or wouldn't return in time from one of his European convalescences to meet him. Qaddafi tried again in December 1972. Almost certainly, he had been informed by Bourguiba's foreign minister, the Machiavellian Muhammad Masmoudi (who either admired Qaddafi or was on his payroll) that Bourguiba and some of the younger Turks of his ruling Socialist Destour Party might be susceptible to siren songs about Arab unity. On December 16 Qaddafi addressed a capacity crowd in a Tunis cinema, the Palmarium, proposing the unification of the two countries. Bourguiba, who had been watching the speech at home on television, jumped into his Mercedes to be driven immediately to the Palmarium. There, to Qaddafi's delight and that of the crowd, he mounted the stage and engaged the young Libyan in a lively political debate: Of course, he said in effect, we are all for the unity of the Arabs. But unification is something we simply cannot be rushed into!

Just the same, when Qaddafi departed, the joint communiqué issued December 17 emphasized the "determination of the two governments to develop their cooperation and extend its scope to cover all domains: political, economic, cultural, social, and others." One by one, conventions were signed during 1973 that concerned trade, customs duties, transfer and guarantee of investments, a joint shipping company, professional schooling, social security, and the activities of Tunisian firms and workers in Libya. On September 1, 1973, while Libyan misunderstandings with Egypt multiplied, Bourguiba was the only Arab head of state to celebrate the Libyan revolution's anniversary.

Masmoudi and Qaddafi felt Bourguiba's mood was mellowing. On January 11, 1974, Qaddafi arrived on Tunisia's beautiful Mediterranean island of Djerba, which has, ironically for Qaddafi, the oldest continuous Jewish community in North Africa. Bourguiba joined him the next day with a large delegation. After one forty-five-minute meeting, Bourguiba signed a document agreeing to creation of an "Arab Islamic Republic." It was to have a "single constitution, a single president, and a single army, and the same legislative, executive, and judicial powers," following a referendum to be held in both countries on January 8, 1974.

Those who turned on Radio Tunis the next day to hear morning prayers were probably astonished to hear the radio identify itself as the "Radio of the Arab Islamic Republic."

On January 12 Bourguiba, after consulting with his canny prime minister, former Tunisian Central Bank governor Hedi Nouira, seemed to have realized the enormity of his mistake. He began backtracking; he had the state broadcasting station announce that the referendum would be postponed to March 20 and that the union project would be implemented in steps. The next day Bourguiba dismissed Masmoudi, who dropped into an almost permanent state of disgrace.

"We have been knifed," said one very prominent politician, who by 1981 had become one of the bidders to succeed Bourguiba when his life presidency ends, "by the combination of a silly old man, an enthusiastic fanatical young man, and a conniving schemer of a foreign minister." By January 15, the Socialist Destour Party was declaring that not only would the referendum be delayed longer than March 20, but to hold one the constitution would have to be amended, and this would require at least four months. Besides, added the Destour's political apparatchiks, the Djerba document "should be viewed as a political declaration, not as a treaty."[29]

Bourguiba decided that he needed another rest and flew to Switzerland. Undaunted, and determined to rescue the union if he could, Qaddafi followed him there, to no avail. Furious with the failure, Qaddafi blamed it on pressure from Algeria, and was probably not far from wrong since President Boumedienne and his ruling army officers had never felt they could tolerate a single, strong state on their eastern borders. On February 10, Qaddafi delivered a speech attacking Maghreb leaders "who stand in the way of inevitable unity." After the more than decent interval of nine months, a Libyan delegation visited Tunis on November 30 to try to breathe life back into the merger project, again in vain. Despite ratification of all the 1973 paper agreements, relations quickly went from bad to worse. In early March 1976, Libya expelled 6,837 workers who, the Tripoli authorities said, lacked proper work and residence permits. On March 12, Qaddafi found one of his more Castro-like phrases—Qaddafi and Castro were yet to have their first meeting but they already had something of a mutual-admiration society going—for Tunisia: "the *comprador* of American capitalism."

Then the classic pattern of subversion and terror began. This time, instead of Egypt, Sudan, Chad, or Niger, Tunisia was the target. On March 21, 1976, Bourguiba announced the arrest of three members of the Libyan *mukhabarat* (intelligence service) who he said had come to Tunis to murder him and his prime minister, Hedi Nouira. Tripoli, as usual, issued a denial and expelled eight Tunisian diplomats. Tunis retaliated in kind, and both ambassadors went home, though there was not a total break in diplomatic relations.[30]

An offshore-oil dispute then vastly complicated the political controversy.[31] Tripoli finally accepted, in August 1976, the contention of Tunis that the drilling dispute should be submitted to the World Court in The Hague, but neither side kept a pledge given then to undertake joint drilling operations at the offshore site. The dispute heated in January 1977 when an Italian firm operating for Libya, SAIPEM, moved a drilling platform to the disputed site. (In May of the same year, it withdrew it after a vigorous international diplomatic campaign by the Tunisians.) New complications arose, in the form of an American firm, Reading and Bates, that ventured to install a new platform for Libya in the disputed zone. Two Libyan gunboats and a submarine escorted it. After a complicated series of maneuvers by both sides, and mediation by the Arab League, the Tunisian and Libyan foreign ministers on June 10, 1977, signed a compromise, again agreeing to submit the problem to The Hague, and to accept the World Court's decision. Again economic cooperation projects were revived; Libya loaned Tunisia about $70 million; Tunisian workers began to emigrate anew to the promised land of oil. At the beginning of November 1977, Tunisian foreign minister Habib Shatti even visited Libya to discuss politics, especially the coordination of policy on the Palestine problem and the new crisis brewing in inter-Arab relations over Sadat's impending journey to Jerusalem.

When that journey came about, the two countries parted ways in their reactions to it. Libya cried treachery and Qaddafi convened a Tripoli summit conference in December 1977 that resulted in an Arab "Front of Steadfastness" that included Syria, Algeria, Iraq, South Yemen, and the PLO. All of these were to reject what was to become, during the following three years, the Camp David peace process sponsored by the United States. Tunisia's own attitude, even though Tunis was soon to become a focus of Arab militancy when the Arab League headquarters was transferred there from Cairo in 1978 and 1979, was more restrained, even cautiously favorable toward Sadat.

On January 26, 1978, Tunis suffered the worst rioting it had ever known. For hours the normally peaceful city was under a state of siege that began as a general strike ordered by the Destour Party's associated labor syndicate, the Union Général des Travailleurs Tunisiens (UGTT). Bourguiba and his cabinet did not directly accuse Qaddafi of responsibility, but the one-day insurrection was described as a "conspiracy" and accusations were made against Masmoudi and the rather pro-Libyan secretary-general of the UGTT, Habib Ashour, of deliberate instigation. On February 7 Qaddafi employed his favorite tactic—surprise—by flying unannounced to Tunis. Bourguiba, pleading that he was "fatigued," did not see his unwanted visitor. Instead he hurriedly dispatched Nouira, who managed to intercept Qaddafi before he left the airport. Nouira appears to have given Qaddafi some vague assurances for the life of Ashour, who was later put under house arrest. The immediate crisis subsided.[32]

From then until the Gafsa affair, which raised the specter of direct Libyan aggression, Tunisians lived in the grip of a vague but growing fear that if ever their big neighbor to the west began swallowing other countries in the name of Arab unity, Tunisia might prove to be a victim. Like Qaddafi's other Afro-Arab neighbors, the Tunisian leaders resolved to make themselves as indigestible as possible for the seemingly hungry colonel.

Qaddafi's "cultural revolution" in Libya, which he felt should be exported to a waiting world, added a new dimension of the threat to Tunisia and Qaddafi's other Arab neighbors.

## QADDAFI'S NEW SOCIETY:
## *THE GREEN BOOK*

"Thank God," said my young official guide during a visit I made to Libya in 1974, as Qaddafi's "Green Revolution" was getting under way. "Nobody is poor. Everyone has a house or an apartment. I've got a car, because I've got a job and a salary. Ten or even five years ago, no one could have guaranteed me any of these things. Now they're guaranteed to everyone."

Anyone who remembers Libya as it was before 1969 sees little resemblance today to daily life then. Before 1969 Libya was one of the poorest countries in the Third World. The Mercedeses and Cadillacs of the elite few who were made wealthy by oil raced through Tripoli and Benghazi streets ignoring the donkey carts, burden-laden camels, and shacks of the overwhelming number of people who lived at bare subsistence level. Beggars, voluntary car-watchers seeking baksheesh, panhandlers, pimps, and pickpockets roamed the towns in search of largesse from foreigners or the occasional handout from a rich Libyan. Central parts of a Libyan town in those days resembled in some respects today's slums in Cairo, Casablanca, or Algiers. Only a fool or a willfully blind person, however he feels about Qaddafi's politics, could deny that the colonel from the desert has wrought these changes for his country.

Today a foreign visitor coming to Tripoli from the airport passes row upon row of ocher- or lighter sand-colored blocks of new apartment houses and small detached four-family housing units in what was once empty desert. The only tents or shanties visible now are those being used by construction workers, who labor for generous wages to build new houses, schools, mosques, bridges, highways, hospitals (all providing free cradle-to-grave medical care). Beggars and the other miserable or parasitical folk of the streets have disappeared. You carry your own bags at an airport, taxi stand, or hotel because Qaddafi's revolution has called for the end of menial services. When I visited Tripoli in August 1981 the government had just published a decree forbidding domestic servants. On my last morning in the city, the guide and driver assigned me by the Foreign Liaison Bureau, a helpful young man named Omran Ramadan, moved heaven and earth to get me to the airport on time, saw me through the outgoing airport police controls, then left me to handle the careful outgoing customs check and baggage inspection myself. Still living with old habits and reflexes acquired while living for many years in other Mideastern countries, I asked Omran whether my passage through the queue at customs might be speeded if I slipped one of the watchful inspectors a dinar or two. Not quite scornfully, Omran waved his hand in a wide expansive gesture. "We don't have that kind of thing here," he said. "We stopped that long ago." We said good-bye, and I picked up my bags and waited on line with everyone else.

Many foreign observers have borne witness to the dramatic material changes that oil wealth and Qaddafi's cultural revolution have brought to Libya. Dr. John Mason, an American anthropologist educated at Boston University who did field work and had a lectureship in Libya in 1968–70, lived just before the revolution in the sleepy, Arabized Berber oasis of Aujila in Cyrenaica. In those days, he found life there harsh, with only rudimentary transport, shelter, and machinery to ease the hard tasks of living and of raising the oasis crops of tomatoes, onions, and dates. After seven years' absence, Mason returned to Aujila in June 1977. He found that the once pastoral oasis "had become a bustling town overnight." Five new schools, including a high school, a Koranic school, and a girls' school, had been established. Four full-time resident physicians—an Egyptian, a Palestinian, a Sudanese, and an Indian— cared for the inhabitants, "in contrast to the once-a-week visiting doctor of eight years ago." New public housing, some of it for the foreign workers who have poured into Libya since the start of the oil boom, and new or rebuilt mosques have created a new California-like skyline against the groves of date palms. During fifteen minutes in the main village's public square Mason saw "more cars parked than he had seen formerly in the oasis in a year's time." Small shops offered the villagers, who had plenty of money, most of the goods they could have found in a big city (in 1980 and 1981 "People's Supermarkets," with their heavily government-subsidized and abundant foods, were to appear in great numbers only in the cities and towns). Television sets and refrigerators, unknown in 1970, were in many homes. The affluence in Aujila, Mason found, came not directly from jobs with oil concessions in the area but from new openings in both public and private sectors. Since marketing facilities for farm produce were better, vegetable production had improved. Farmers were buying seeds, fertilizer, and equipment at reduced prices in an agricultural cooperative. Within a "few years," Mason reported, a vast new water supply system would make up for the diminishing underground water that had supplied the oasis in the past.

Perhaps most spectacular was the improvement in the way people lived at home. Mason found that old houses of mud bricks, like one he had lived in, were being replaced rapidly by concrete-block houses. Whereas the few affluent farmers had previously built new homes on their farms, they were now building second homes in the villages where they came from. Many people commuted to markets and farm plots by car.

Mason saw women and girls still more or less confined to the home. But several Aujila girls had entered public life. "A few" had graduated from high school. One was working as a receptionist in the local government office. Another was a telephone operator, and a third was a nurse in one of the public clinics.[1]

Multiply the Aujila example by several thousand villages and towns —and many foreign observers in Libya give assurance that Aujila's growth is in some ways typical—and Qaddafi's satisfaction with the material progress he has brought about in Libya appears well justified.

Before examining in some detail the tenets of Qaddafi's Green Revolution we need to glance backward at internal developments in Libya before 1973, the year it really began.

Omar al-Fathali, who worked as one of Qaddafi's social and political planners before leaving Libya in 1979 to teach at the University of Florida, found Qaddafi's young RCC colleagues in 1969 with power in their hands but scarcely a clue as to how to go about using it. They had no mass following. They had imprisoned or disenfranchised many of the old order's most important people—the people who could make commerce, industry, agriculture, or government machinery work. The RCC, reported Fathali and his colleague, Monte Palmer, had opposed all of the established political, social, and economic groups in Libya.

Their main goals became four: to dismantle the old Libyan social elite; to turn the army into a strong political weapon; to make the revolution acceptable to as many Libyans as possible by spreading around, rapidly, the available revenues from oil; and to "legitimize" the regime by turning Qaddafi into a charismatic figure, as Fathali and Palmer show in their political studies of Libya.

Qaddafi's first domestic political target was the old regime. He began his dismantling of it with arrests of most of the senior armed forces officers, except for five or six top officers (two of whom, Colonels Ahmed and Hawaz, were picked up later, in December 1969, as anti-Qaddafi plotters). Some, considered to be neutral or friendly to the revolution, were soon given diplomatic posts abroad or even jobs in the bureaucracy at home. Italian settlers were deprived of Libyan citizenship; most were sent to Italy, and their properties were sequestered and made available for distribution to the lower- and middle-class supporters of the revolution. In a series of hearings, a "People's Court" carefully examined the files of members of the old regime to determine how they had obtained their wealth. Some were sent to prison and had their estates confiscated if it appeared that they had accumulated wealth through bribes and corruption; others were given a clean bill of health. [2]

Toughest to deal with, as Fathali and Palmer point out, were the traditional tribal chiefs, who had prospered under the reign of King Idris. Since they were potential sources of counterrevolution, and *ancien régime* figures like Omar Shalhi and the Black Prince, Abdallah al-Abid al-Sanussi, were likely to try to use them in countercoup attempts, the RCC moved against many of the tribal leaders, especially in Cyrenaica and Fezzan. Tribes as political institutions were abolished, and tribal boundaries were no longer recognized on maps as administrative boundaries. Tribally based local governors and other officials were dismissed and replaced by educated members of tribes with less social standing—in other words, the have-nots of the old regime replaced the haves.

Religious leaders, including that mainstay of the monarchy, the Sanussi order, had to be rooted out too. Some leaders had supported the Black Prince in his 1970 countercoup attempt, and the prestige of the Sanussi, established in the colonial and World War II periods, remained strong among the conservative people of the eastern and southern deserts and mountains. The RCC established its own firm religious credentials. It did this by enforcing the puritanical Muslim antialcohol prohibition that had been lax under the monarchy, and by fasting during Ramadan and encouraging prayer and other strict observance. Later, under the constitution that established Islam as the state religion and the Koran as the ultimate source of law, strict Islamic punishments, such as stoning and the amputation of hands or feet, were put in the law books, though these seem never to have been enforced.

Political parties, labor unions, and student organizations were all at first banned; then, later, the RCC carefully supervised the reconstitution of loyalist labor federations and student organizations. To this day, one of the problems Qaddafi experiences in improving relations with Baathist-ruled Iraq and implementing his recently declared union with Syria is the bad name the Baath party had among Qaddafi and his colleagues. Mahmoud al-Maghrebi, first revolutionary prime minister and finance minister, was a known Baathist (as well as being half-Palestinian); Fathali says that Qaddafi appointed him as part of "early desperate attempts to press all known leaders of the opposition into his service."[3]

In dealing with the army, the RCC's second major target, the RCC carefully surveyed the junior officers and NCOs, and promoted those who followed the revolution and weeded out those who did not. High-ranking high school students were encouraged to enter the military academy and offered foreign study or training, such as attending an American university or learning specialized military subjects in Italy, France, Britain, Sweden, and, after the 1974 arms deals, the Soviet Union.

Despite the beginnings of the oil-price increases and the measures Qaddafi and the RCC took to gain more control over Libyan oil and its revenues,[4] during the first two years after the revolution there was not a great deal of money available to spread around to as many Libyans as they wanted. Until the early weeks of 1972, the RCC largely improvised its economic and social planning, using trial and error. Then, in 1972, it began implementation of a three-year six-billion-dollar development plan. Realizing that imported food, as well as exported oil, might be used as a weapon against Libya by her adversaries and that the great weakness of Nasser's Egypt (as it was to be of Sadat's) was its ever-growing dependence on imported food, the RCC planners gave very high priority in their first development plan to becoming as self-sufficient as possible in food.

The final of the RCC's four major goals, lending the regime legitimacy by converting Qaddafi from an unknown, puritanical leader into a charismatic, even messianic figure, is one that the regime has perhaps pursued most successfully. The RCC ideologues and Qaddafi himself have consciously emulated other successful Third World models, some of whom they knew or had observed: Gamal Abdel Nasser in Egypt, Kwame N'Krumah of Ghana, Indonesia's Sukarno, and Guinea's Sekou Touré, to name a few.[5]

The RCC has been fortunate. Qaddafi, first of all, is a handsome man. He speaks with the soft, magnetic voice of Arabic-speaking people; he commands attention with eloquence and his facility with Koranic verses and folk proverbs. His foreign admirers, many of them women such as journalist Oriana Fallaci (who later lost her admiration) and Ann-Marie Cazalis (who has written an almost adulatory book entitled, in English, *Qaddafi, the Knight Templar of God*), have contributed heavily to the buildup of Qaddafi's charisma. In an often-quoted passage, Cazalis describes why, in her view, Qaddafi could never convert Libya into a Communist state no matter how near he might draw politically and militarily to the Soviet Union:

> *Koranic law heeds the slightest details of everyday life. Marxist does not. Capitalism doesn't give a damn. Muammar Qaddafi reveals to the Arab world and to others that God has given into our hands all that needs to be known in order to construct a just society.*[6]

Qaddafi has always remained the dominant figure in both the formal and informal structures of Libyan government. Throughout the earlier years of his regime, and possibly even in the numerically diminished RCC of more recent times, the RCC has been a collegial body like its Egyptian and Algerian prototypes. All important matters are supposed to be discussed until a consensus is reached. Anyone still opposing that consensus once it is reached ultimately becomes a dissident, an outcast, and an enemy of the state.

The RCC appointed the members of Libya's regular cabinets, or Councils of Ministers, and the cabinets were collectively responsible to the RCC. The RCC could dismiss the prime minister or other ministers individually; the prime minister's resignation would automatically mean resignation of the entire cabinet. If RCC decisions, which have the force of law, required new laws to carry them out, the cabinet had the job of drawing them up. Since there was no parliament or national assembly, the RCC would promulgate new laws by decree.

Cabinets are composed of military and civilian elements. In January

1970, after the commotion of the first plot against him, Qaddafi became prime minister. By 1972, however, he was leaving the administrative work largely to Major Jalloud, always his faithful deputy. In July 1972 Jalloud became prime minister. Contrary to ill-informed speculations in some of the Arab and Western media, Qaddafi did not lose his position of primordial power: he remained chairman of the RCC, commander-in-chief of the armed forces, and president of the first mass political organization he experimented with, the Arab Socialist Union (ASU).

Like so much else in Qaddafi's early political and social thinking, the ASU was modeled upon the organization of the same name set up in Egypt by Nasser. Imitating the wording of the Egyptian model, the Libyan ASU charter, as set up in 1972, honored peasants, workers, soldiers, intellectuals, and "national capitalists" (which in Egypt meant businessmen who had somehow managed to perform the personal, financial, and political acrobatics necessary to coexist with a vaguely "socialist" regime by submitting to progressive taxation and becoming pro-Nasser businessmen). The ASU was supposed to abolish both class distinctions and the Marxists' concept of class struggle. Some 50 percent of the ASU's members, who could be any Libyan man or woman over eighteen not disqualified by the RCC, had to be peasants and workers, as in Egypt. The structure was pyramidal with the RCC at the top.

At the ASU's founding conference, one speaker, as quoted by Ruth First, challenged Qaddafi's concept of socialism as meaning mainly social justice. "How," the man asked, "can we build a pyramid at the top when the foundation is unsound?" On Qaddafi's rejoinder that this was not the heart of the matter, the speaker claimed that the revolution's main duty was to "build freedom and democracy." Qaddafi told him he was mistaken. Consulting the workers, Qaddafi explained, would result only in getting worker-oriented decisions that would be "unfair for the other sections of the people's working forces." Democracy was "nonexistent in Islam," and God had told the Prophet Muhammad to consult people, but then "when determined" about a matter, to go ahead and do it and "rely on God."[7]

The ASU never really got off the ground. A Qaddafi insider has disclosed how after Qaddafi had rebuked many of his followers for their lack of revolutionary enthusiasm and their interest in money, power, and advancement, he would fall into fits of depression. In a sullen mood, he would withdraw from his RCC colleagues to his family home in Sirte or to some anonymous retreat elsewhere in the desert, there to brood and sometimes to meditate and write. Some of these withdrawals and retreats helped lead to the reports, current among his foreign opponents such as the late President Sadat, that he is "insane." One important figure in the PLO has insisted that Qaddafi was secretly treated for a pathological condition, perhaps either schizophrenia or paranoia, by an Italian psychiatrist who visited Libya several times.[8] According to another persistent story, Qaddafi, possibly when he followed Tunisian President Habib Bourguiba to Switzerland in the winter of 1974 to try to persuade him to implement their ill-fated union agreement of that January, was treated secretly and anonymously in a Swiss sanatorium. Although this story was checked out carefully with Swiss and other sources who should know, there seems to be no trace of proof of it. Yet the reports persist.

Qaddafi's most important tiffs with his fellow RCC members, and his depressive behavior on those occasions, began to occur in 1971. On January 24, a few days before a scheduled referendum (which was never held) to approve establishment of a kind of pre-ASU national charter like those of Egypt, Syria, and Sudan, Qaddafi announced that he would not run as a candidate for the presidency of the proposed Libyan Arab Republic. According to what seemed to be an authoritative account in the Beirut newspaper *L'Orient*,[9] this was related to some opposition by Jalloud and other RCC members to the emphasis Qaddafi was putting on instant unions with other Arab countries. Then, on January 26, Qaddafi said he was ceding to "popular pressure" and would be a candidate for president after all. In the event, there was no election and no president. On October 7, 1971, after rumors that he had been injured in a car accident September 18 and his subsequent twenty-day absence, Qaddafi announced that he had submitted his resignation to the RCC sometime in September "to protest the shortcomings of the administrative apparatus in carrying out social, economic, and industrial projects," as Tripoli Radio and newspapers said. He had withdrawn his resignation "in accordance with the wishes of the people," but would "not remain at the head of the Revolution for one more month if the present domestic situation persisted."

New disagreements seemed to arise in July 1972 between Qaddafi and other RCC members, most probably Hony and Meheishi (who were to defect in 1975) over formation of a new cabinet and the planned union with Sadat's Egypt. Even Jalloud, who had been asked to form a government and who had support from most other RCC members, advised Qaddafi that his wish for immediate total union was inopportune and impractical. While Jalloud wanted an all-military government, Qaddafi apparently wanted to include some civilians. Qaddafi again withdrew to the desert, this time for ten days. Qaddafi got his way. The new seventeen-member cabinet formed on July 16 included only two military men; and, on August 2, Sadat and Qaddafi signed their ill-starred agreement for total union.[10]

At another crucial time, when he was proclaiming the details of his cultural revolution, Qaddafi used the threat of resignation skillfully to get his way. On April 15, 1973, in a speech at Zuara, Qaddafi presented his program and then threatened to resign if the "people" chose not to follow his directives.

April 15 was, appropriately enough, *Mouloud*, the Muslim religious holiday commemorating the birthday of the Prophet Muhammad. Qaddafi used the occasion to warn that the revolution was in danger. Libyan guerrillas sent to fight "in Palestine" had been unable to do so. Young Libyans who had to fight if Arab states bordering Israel would not, were not enlisting in the Libyan all-volunteer army. What was more, Qaddafi said, Libyans were refusing to work in the salutory agricultural and other developments being established in remote areas of the country. University students, never a breed held in high esteem by Qaddafi, included in their ranks "perverts" who were engaging in subversive activities.[11] Qaddafi enunciated a five-point program of recommendations for the new Libyan cultural revolution:

1. Suspending all laws in force in Libya. Every legal case would henceforth be examined on its individual merits, in the light of *Sharia*—Muslim religious law derived from the Koran.

2. "Struggling against the political illnesses" of the country, such as Communism, the clandestine Muslim Brotherhood, Baathists, and others suffering from similar "infirmities."

3. Arming the population to assure "the defense of the revolution." (This was one of the early hints of Qaddafi's ultimate intention, announced several times since, to dissolve the regular armed forces and rely on the popular militia forces. It was a sign that he feared the regular army's officer corps.)

4. Proclaiming an "administrative revolution" since the bureaucracy had been growing fat and idle and "become cut off from the people."

5. Launching the cultural revolution on the university campuses "to fight the demagogic spirit and foreign cultural influences."[12]

Qaddafi assured newsmen in May 1973 that these principles differed basically from the Chinese cultural revolution because they did not introduce new thoughts like those of Chairman Mao or seek to suppress opposition but simply returned to the Arabic and Islamic heritage tainted by Libya's colonial era.

There is absolutely no question of whether Qaddafi really believes his own rhetoric; he does. He believes that through the application of money, ideology, and techniques for the "mobilization of the masses," the material situation of his people has vastly improved, and that that improvement should be a guidepost to other peoples around the world. Qaddafi is a believer in Qaddifism.

**A**nyone who wants to understand Qaddafi's political and social thinking has to wrestle with the tenets of *The Green Book*, the three-volume work in which he sets out his Third Universal Theory, the framework in which his precepts for running government and organizing human affairs are laid out.[13] Inspired, as he always is, by the presence of an attractive and skillful female interviewer, Qaddafi told Italian journalist and Third World supporter Oriana Fallaci: "The day of revolution has inevitably arrived, thanks to *The Green Book*. In the whole world, the masses will take power and their guide will be *The Green Book*. *The Green Book* is the product of the struggle of humankind. It's the new gospel, the gospel of the new era, the era of the masses. . . ."[14]

*The Green Book, Vol. 1: The Solution of the Problem of Democracy* is what many Americans, including Billy Carter, were given copies of at the "Libyan-American Peoples Dialogue" held in Tripoli in October 1978. The book modestly claims to present "the final solution to the problem of the instrument of governing." Since all world political systems are products of "the struggle for power between instruments of governing," one of these instruments—group, party, or class—always wins. This, says Qaddafi, means "the defeat of the people, i.e., the defeat of genuine democracy."[15]

If a candidate in a "false democracy"—one with a parliament or Congress and people who vote—wins 51 percent of the vote, this is dictatorship disguised as democracy, since "49 percent of the electorate is ruled by an instrument of governing they did not vote for." Thus parliaments, electoral systems, votes, referenda and plebiscites, and the political party system are all bad. Representation, says one of the marginal slogans printed in green type, is a "denial of participation" and a "falsification of democracy." Majority rule means misrule of the unrepresented minority. Proportional representation is less bad, but here too small minorites are still left unrepresented. "Since the system of elected parliaments is based on propaganda to win votes," Qaddafi asserts, "it is a demogogic system in the real sense of the word, and votes can be bought and falsified. Poor people fail to compete in the election campaign and it is always the rich—and only the rich—who come out victorious. . . . [The] most tyrannical dictatorships the world has known have existed under the shadow of parliaments."[16]

Political parties are bad too, Qaddafi decided during his desert musings. "The party is the contemporary dictatorship." (None had been legal nor had operated in Libya since the early days of the monarchy, when Qaddafi was still a child.) Parties basically represent only specific interest groups or classes, and so operate as factions: "The existence of many parties escalates the struggle for power and this results in the destruction of any achievements of the people and of any socially beneficial plans."[17]

Qaddafi obviously prefers what he calls "direct democracy." He would, perhaps, approve some of the devices of direct democracy as expressed in our old-fashioned New England town meetings, or perhaps in some aspects of the present government of Switzerland, but these systems are not mentioned or evaluated in *The Green Book*. Qaddafi's governing principle is *"no representation in lieu of the people"* (italics are mine). This is one of *The Green Book*'s slogans often seen on posters, on Libyan television, and posted in government offices or public places like airport terminals or bus stations. There is at least a faint flavor of George Orwell and the slogans of his futuristic novel *1984* ("Truth is falsehood," "Freedom is slavery") in all of this.

What Qaddafi calls "the class political system" is just as bad as the party, tribal, or sectarian systems in that "a class dominates the society in the same way that a party, tribe or sect does" (hence his concern with wiping out all these different aspects of Libyan society). The class, like the other aspects, is only a part of the "people" and not the whole. "Plebiscites," even though they purport to consult all the people, "are a fraud against democracy" because "those who say 'yes' and those who say 'no' do not, in fact, express their will" and "have been allowed to utter only one word: either 'yes' or 'no.' " Parties, representing as they do only specific interests or classes, are simply the pieces of a society, the sum of which is a multiparty system, which is factional by nature. In the same way, for Qaddafi, a single-party state simply institutionalizes the dominance of a single class, faction, or interest. Qaddafi's "final solution" is the creation of popular congresses, "the only means to achieve popular democracy." Any other solution is "undemocratic."

With one of *The Green Book*'s main slogans, *"no democracy without popular congresses and committees everywhere,"* Qaddafi explains that people should first be divided into "basic popular congresses." Each of these chooses its secretariat, which in turn chooses other congresses, which together "choose administrative people's committees to replace government administration."

In practical terms, he explains, public utilities, like the electric company, would be run by a people's committee responsible to the basic popular congresses, which are supposed to "dictate the policy followed by the people's committees and supervise its execution." Thus is true democracy born: *"Democracy is the supervision of the people by the people."*

Citizens who are members of the popular congresses "belong, professionally and functionally, to categories" and "should establish unions and syndicates." Major policy subjects—which, in practice, have turned out to be subjects like whether and how to switch to nuclear energy for generation of electricity, or new departures in agricultural planning—are supposed to take "final shape" in the General People's Congress that has been held annually since 1976. Decisions of this central body are in turn to be passed back down the line to the popular congresses, people's committees, syndicates and unions. The people's committees are then supposed to start "executive action." While most executive action accounts for most of the constructive work in housing, new water supplies, and countless other development matters, such action also includes the 1978 seizure of the homes and villas of foreigners for a while.

*The Green Book, Vol. 1*'s final section deals with what Qaddafi describes as "The Law of Society." He calls the "natural law of any society" its "tradition (custom) or religion." Constitutions are not the law of society because they are man-made, and "based on nothing more than the views of the instruments of the dictatorial rule prevailing in the world, ranging from the individual to the party." Traditional law is better because "it imposes moral, not material penalties, that are appropriate for man. . . . Religion does not acknowledge temporal penalties, except in extreme cases, where these are necessary to protect society." Although, says Qaddafi in another often-repeated slogan, *"Society is its own supervisor,"* and "the era of the masses" that will liberate everyone from "the shackles of the instruments of governing" is approaching, he warns that we may also be entering "an age of anarchy and demagogy if the new democracy, which is the authority of the people" should fail and "the authority of the individual, class, tribe, sect or party again comes to predominate."

At the very end of *The Green Book, Vol. 1*, Qaddafi inserts what most of his critics consider the real kicker, the justification of continued rule by the single, charismatic leader. "Theoretically," he says, everything that he has been describing is the "genuine democracy." But realistically, the strong always rule; "the stronger part in the society is the one that rules."

Much of this appears to be derived from Qaddafi's perhaps wide but certainly random reading of Arabic translations of a mixed bag of philosophy, sociology, history, and pseudo-history—Locke, Montesquieu, a dash of Houston Stewart Chamberlain, a whiff of Fascist theory as applied in the "corporate states" of Mussolini in Italy and de Oliveira Salazar in Portugal. To most Arabs in most Arab societies outside Libya, none of Qaddafi's philosophy makes much sense. Edouard Saab, a highly respected Lebanese editor and correspondent of *Le Monde*, said, "What Qaddafi serves up is a mishmash of half-baked ideology and romantic idealism. Surely he himself must be too shrewd to take it seriously."[18]

This, however, is the heart of the problem: Qaddafi *does* take his Third Universal Theory seriously. He takes it so seriously that he is ready to crusade for its realization everywhere that he can reach. Before the publication of the second volume of *The Green Book, The Solution of the Economic Problem*, and the third volume, *The Social Basis of the Third Universal Theory*, Qaddafi and the RCC set about constructing the political institutions required by *Green Book, Vol. 1*. Throughout 1973 and 1974, zealous activists set about creating the local people's committees in neighborhoods, villages, places of work, the university, and the administration, in order, as Qaddafi put it, that "the people might take power into their own hands." This was a period of trial-and-error experimentation. The best known of the early committees was the crucial one dealing with radio, television, and the Libyan News Agency (later called the Jamahariya News Agency, or JANA, after Libya's new official name, Jamahariya, best translated as "the state of the masses").

In a speech on June 11, 1973, Qaddafi took a look at the work done so far. Apparently, he saw that it was good. The cultural revolution, he said, was experiencing "a new upsurge which is expressed through the people's takeover of the management of instruction, agriculture, the administration and culture."[19] There was less spontaneity in the early months of the great experiment than Qaddafi would have hoped. Government officials down to the lowest levels were obliged to join the committees. The RCC continued to be the directing authority and brain of the vast, unwieldy "people's power" machine being built according to the wishes of "The Leader," al-Qaid. At first used sparingly, this term has become standard nomenclature for Qaddafi. Formerly he was most often called al-akh al-Aqid, or "Brother Colonel," on Libyan state radio and television.

By 1976 some of the initial difficulties had been ironed out. John Mason briefly describes how the system of people's government evolved over the years in the oasis he had come to know so well. Though unable to speak for the rest of Libya, he reports, "the new political structure . . . has been highly effective in Aujila."[20] At the lowest level, people's committees (al-Mu'tammar ash-Shaabi al-Asasi) meet regularly to discuss the needs of villages and families. These are passed upward to a regional committee, congress, or council (al-Mu'tammar ash-Shaabi al-Baladiya) composed of ten members of each of the local committees from the three main subdivisions of the oasis, Aujila, Jalo, and Ijkherra. These divide up funds and resources among the three. For larger questions, each local committee sends to Tripoli three members of the General People's Congress, or collective council, as Mason calls it (al-Mu'tammar ash-Shaabi al-'Am). This is the political part of the new spectrum, as it works in Aujila and hundreds of villages like it.

Besides the political part, there is also an administrative portion. The basic administrative unit is the People's Committee, or al-Lejna Shaabia. Local committees for each major residential unit are supposed to run the basic services: education, agriculture, popular housing, water, electricity, and so forth. On the larger scale, the pyramid of power extends upward through regional and national committees.

Mason reports that the whole system has had beneficial effects in Aujila; it has broken down the traditional hierarchy of authority under the boss (mudir) and the tribes (qubail). Schoolchildren study the system for two hours every week. "Almost all" the people Mason talked to in Aujila were "very enthusiastic about the new system and the many positive changes it has brought about."

Partly because of the difficulty the RCC found in stimulating the Libyan "masses" into enthusiastic acceptance of a system at such complete variance with centuries of history and tradition, the first annual General People's Congress was created after some delay and finally held in January 1976. In the meantime, the Arab Socialist Union was reorganized and then finally scrapped. On April 6, 1974, Qaddafi seemed to relapse into one of his periodic moods of depression and intense thought. On that day, the Foreign Ministry (not yet replaced by the newer Foreign Liaison Bureau) announced that Qaddafi, at his own request, had been relieved of his ceremonial, political, and administrative functions, and that Major Jalloud would handle them in the future. But only a few naïve Western newsmen were beguiled into thinking that Qaddafi might actually have relaxed his grip on the reins of power.

In 1977 a new constitution was promulgated; it began to take effect in March. Libya was divided into 46 municipalities, each run by "Municipal People's Congresses," and about 187 "Basic People's Congresses" (the exact number varies from year to year). The General People's Congress includes three delegates from each of the 187 or so Basic People's Congresses. The General People's Committee replaced the old-style ministerial cabinet; it is assisted by the five-member General People's Secretariat, a new name for the old Revolutionary Command Council (RCC).

The "Jamahariya" was officially proclaimed in March 1977; Libya's official name was changed to the Socialist People's Libyan Arab Jamahariya (*Al-Jamahariya al-Arabiya al-Libya al-Shaabiya al-Ishtirakiya*). By 1981 authority at the local level rested in the 187 Basic and 46 Municipal People's Congresses. The Municipal People's Congresses in turn appointed Popular Committees to implement policy. Officials of these congresses and committees, when they go to Tripoli for the annual General People's Congress, form the membership of that body, which is supposed to be supreme in policymaking. Qaddafi usually, though not always, announces to the Congress that he is going to submit vital questions, such as whether to use the "oil weapon" against the United States or whether to embark on some new agricultural or industrial expansion program.

The General People's Congress, true to the tenets of *Green Book, Vol. 1*, appoints its own General People's Secretariat and the General People's Committee. Members of the latter head the twenty or more government departments that are supposed to do the actual work of keeping the country running. The secretary-general of the General People's Committee functions like a prime minister. Since a reorganization in March 1979, Qaddafi has kept his designation as leader of the revolution, but neither he nor his former RCC colleagues hold any official posts in the new administration.

When the General People's Congress meets, its sessions are broadcast and televised live and are also taped and played and replayed during the coming year, whenever debate on a particular subject needs, in Qaddafi's judgment, to be brought before the nation. During most of the year, when the General People's Congress is not in plenary session, its various agencies (the most powerful being the General Secretariat) run the affairs of state.[21]

Voting is by a show of hands. The government departments in the General People's Committee supervise the bureaucracy and the municipal-level committees. The General People's Congress can hire and fire the secretaries when it wishes (practically speaking) or when Qaddafi and his fellow former RCC members on the General People's Committee so decree. Omar al-Fathali and Monte Palmer, comparing these Libyan institutions to Soviet ones, find that the General People's Committee corresponds to the Soviet cabinet; the General Secretariat would be roughly the equivalent of the Soviet Politburo. Qaddafi's "Third Road," neither capitalism nor Communism, does, however, also contain features of the Western parliamentary systems that he condemns.[22]

As this unique system of "people's government" was implemented in 1976 and 1977, Qaddafi was working on *Green Book, Vol. 2*, which he calls with his usual modesty *The Solution of the Economic Problem*. This is the best definition that exists in all of his speaking and writing of just what he means by his brand of Islamic "socialism." To understand the ideological baggage that Qaddafi's economic planners are forced to carry around with them to board meetings and planning sessions, one must be aware of his economic theory.

*Green Book, Vol. 2* begins by discussing relationships between workers, who produce, and employers, whom he calls "owners," an early signal of his basically anticapitalist attitude. Qaddafi admits that the workers' lot has definitely improved since the Industrial Revolution in the West. "Fixed working-hours, wages for additional work, different types of leave, minimum wages, profit sharing," worker "participation in administration," the outlawing of arbitrary dismissal, and the right of social security are all gains, he says, along with the right to strike and "whatever provisions are found in almost all modern labor laws. Of no less significance are the changes in the field of ownership and transferring it to the state."

Despite this progress, Qaddafi says, "the economic problem still exists" because "the wage-worker is like a slave to the master who hires him," even if the state owns the enterprise and the income from it goes to the community (as under Marxist or Communist systems). Instead of the Marxist slogan, "to each according to his need, from each according to his ability," Qaddafi's dictum is *"He who produces is the one who consumes"*—in other words, only the man or woman producing wealth should have the right to enjoy that wealth.

Instead of contributing to the employer's (or owner's) profit, the worker producing the goods or services should be a partner in the production process. This gives rise to the *Green Book* slogan, seen more often than any other in Libya: *"Partners, not wage earners."* Qaddafi insists that fulfilling this goal would be the "ultimate" and desirable way of "abolishing the wage system." This would "emancipate man from its bondage and return to the natural law which defined relationships before the emergence of classes, forms of government and man-made laws." Like the Marxists, Qaddafi says that "the exploitation of man by man and the possession by some individuals of more of the general wealth than they need" departs from "natural law." It is also the "beginning of distortion and corruption" (which Qaddafi saw so much of under the old regime, but which his critics and opponents contend now flourishes in Libya under the new system too).

No one, Qaddafi maintains, can be free "if somebody else controls what he needs to lead a comfortable life." Everyone is entitled to a house, a vehicle, and an income. But he should not work for wages, since he would then be under the control of his employer; nor should he have an extra house to rent. In renting property out to someone else, he would be exercising control over that person's primary need. Echoes of the Marxist theory of surplus value appear at this point: a worker works "solely to satisfy his needs," not to create a surplus to make a profit.

Along with the withering away of the conventional government apparatus implied and required by *Green Book, Vol. 1*, Qaddafi in *Green Book, Vol. 2* foresees the disappearance of conventional labor unions because mechanization and computerization have changed workers from "a multitude of ignorant toilers into a limited number of technicians, engineers, and scientists." (Qaddafi apparently ignores the continued existence of millions of "toilers" in his own country and the rest of the world.) In Qaddafi's coming Utopia, "trade unions will disappear to be replaced by professional and technical syndicates because scientific development is an irreversible gain to humanity. Through such scientific development, illiteracy will be eradicated and the ordinary worker as a temporal phenomenon will gradually disappear. However, man, in his new form, will always remain an essential factor in the process of production."

Qaddafi envisions the eventual disappearance of both profit and money (the former is also a Communist tenet; the latter is not), as his great society of the future meets all of man's basic needs. He doesn't spell out just what would replace money. Qaddafi does not exactly say that the rich should be despoiled and their riches given to the poor, but rather that society should give to each individual whatever share of the wealth that individual has helped to produce.

*Green Book, Vol. 2* goes a step beyond Qaddafi's original proclamation of the new republic's economic principles in 1969. In that, he recognized public ownership as "the basis of the development of society" and private ownership too, provided it is nonexploitive. *Green Book, Vol. 2* was published in early 1977, and in May of that year its theories about property and ownership began to be translated into law: every Libyan has a right to own one home, or a piece of land on which to build a home. (The state, in subsequent measures to ease the terms of loans, has since then made it easier to do this.) However, no Libyan may own more than one home, or collect rent.

On September 1, 1978, the revolution's ninth anniversary, Qaddafi exhorted Libyan workers to "liberate the wage owners from their slavery" and become full partners in production by seizing "the public and private means of production." Hundreds of firms—except in the oil sector, which until today has remained privileged and outside Qaddafi's entire "Third System," which he says is different from either capitalism or Communism—were taken over, and eventually put in the hands of people's committees, in most cases composed of the company workers.

The result of this bizarre combination of socialism and corporatism—the people's committees in each enterprise are supposed to be represented in the General People's Congress, along with those from municipalities, regions, and professional associations—was considerable economic confusion, and a sharp drop in productivity. Perhaps the hardest-pressed in this system, along with small industrialists and factory owners, are the retail merchants. Ever since the end of 1978, Qaddafi has been urging them to give up their shops and enter "productive" work in agriculture or the construction industry.[23] By early 1982, however, orders to close *all* private shops had been delayed or suspended.

One of the final prescriptions of *Green Book, Vol. 2*, which Qaddafi dramatically describes as the "struggle to liberate domestic servants from their slave status and transform them into partners outside the houses, in places where there is material production," was being implemented just before the twelfth anniversary of the revolution. A special decree abolished the institution of domestic servitude. The government announced that it would enforce *Green Book, Vol. 2*'s prescription that "necessary house service" should "not be through servants, with or without wages, but through employees who can be promoted while performing their house jobs and can enjoy social and material safeguard like any employee in the public service."

**W**hat may become the apotheosis of Qaddafi's thinking about history, society, women, religion, and the family are set forth in *Green Book, Vol. 3, The Social Basis of the Third Universal Theory*. Its opening, by implication, makes Qaddafi's idea of his own role in history perfectly clear. "Heroes in history," he says in the second paragraph, "are persons who have made sacrifices for causes," but only those causes (or persons) "which have a meaningful relationship with them." Qaddafi, of course, is thinking and talking here about his own relationship with the Palestinian cause, and what he conceives to be his own, central heroic role in the fight for Palestinian victory.

Doubtless trying to compare the Palestinian struggle with Libya's own battle against colonial domination, he asserts that "group movements" of the good kind "are always movements for independence in order that subjugated or oppressed groups may attain self-realization." With a possible note of prophecy about what might occur in Libya, he continues that struggles for power occur "within the group itself down to the family level."

Either Qaddafi or his ghost writer (if, as some suspect, he had one for *Green Book, Vol. 3*) betrays himself as at least an amateur student of Hegel, the German philosopher of history, and Marx. "Contemporary national liberation movements," he declares, "are themselves social movements. They will not come to an end before every other group is liberated from the domination of another group. . . . [Now] the world is passing through one of the regular cycles of the movement of history, mainly, the national struggle in support of nationalism." Nationalism consists of a lot more than mere patriotism. It is the sum total of family, tribal, and ethnic feeling; and "nations whose nationalism is destroyed are subject to ruin."

For Qaddafi, nationalism is a fundamental "social factor" that colors all of human history. Its only rival in strength is "the religious factor, which may divide the national group or unite groups with different nationalisms." Qaddafi appears at times to be looking at history through the wrong end of a set of very personal binoculars. He speaks of a golden age, buried in the distant past, when "originally, each nation had one religion" and "this was harmony." The troubled history of the world, he says, is largely a result of "differences [in religion] which became a genuine cause of conflict and instability in the life of the peoples throughout the ages."

Every nation, says Qaddafi, should have its own religion just as every human being should. "When the social factor is compatible with the religious factor, harmony is achieved and the life of groups becomes stable and strong and develops soundly." Everything Qaddafi has tried to accomplish in his life indicates that he believes Islam the proper religion for all Arabs and other right-minded people. When he meets a person he really cares about influencing, Qaddafi often tries at once to convert him to Islam. Once he received Eric Rouleau, the well-informed correspondent of *Le Monde* in Paris; Rouleau, an Egyptian Jew by birth, was educated in Europe and held in high esteem throughout the Arab world. Brandishing a Koran in a good-natured way, Qaddafi told Rouleau: "Here is the truth. Here is where you will find your best stories!"

Qaddafi, it should be noted, never mentions Islam by name in *The Green Book*, only religion itself as an abstract but all-important governing force in human lives. On the family he is far more specific: "To the individual man, the family is of more importance than the state. . . . The state is an artificial economic and political system, with which mankind has no relationship and has nothing to do." So vital is the family that "societies in which the existence and unity of the family are threatened, in any circumstances, are similar to fields whose plants are in danger of being swept away or threatened by drought or fire, or of withering away."

Though he has done everything he can to stamp out tribalism and tribes as political or administrative units in Libya, Qaddafi is convinced of the vital importance of the tribe (some Western sociologists might prefer to call it the clan) as a moving force in history and the destinies of nations. His definition of a tribe is simple: "A tribe is a family which has grown as a result of procreation. The nation, then, is a big tribe. So the world is a nation which has been ramified into various nations." However, as human relationships move from the lower level of man-to-man, woman-to-woman, or man-to-woman to the higher ones of family, tribe, or nation, "the degree of warmth diminishes. . . . The social bond, cohesiveness, unity, intimacy, and love are stronger at the family level than at the tribal level . . . stronger at the tribal level than at that of the nation, and stronger at the level of the nation than at that of the world." Therefore (this paragraph, like others Qaddafi or his editor consider to be essential, is set in green type, to stand out from the rest of the book, which is set in black type) human society must keep the family, tribe, nation, and world welded together "by solidarity, cohesiveness, unity, intimacy, and love."

Lest Qaddafi be accused of being a fuzzy-minded "one-worlder," he next speaks out clearly in favor of his favorite conceptual entity, the nation. Its society, he says, "is better than world society as regards fellowship, affection, solidarity, and benefit." If there is any lingering admiration for European fascism in Qaddafi—even though as a child he learned to hate Libya's Italian Fascist occupiers—it shows up in his statements about the importance of the concept of "blood," used by him in the sense of ethnic origin. He calls blood "the prime factor in the formation of the tribe" but adds "it is not the only factor because [political or secular] affiliation is also a factor in the formation of the tribe. With the passage of time the difference between the factors of blood and affiliation disappears, leaving the tribe as one social and physical unit. But it is a unit of blood and origin more than any other."

Qaddafi equates the nation with a large family. Tribalism, he says, is bad, because it "weakens national loyalty." In one of the most candid remarks he has ever made, and one that might be interpreted by some as self-criticism, he adds: "National fanaticism is essential to the nation but at the same time it is a threat to humanity." Although national fanaticism, which Qaddafi defines as "the use of national force against weak nations," or the type of progress that results from "plundering" other nations "are evil and harmful to humanity" the "powerful individual who respects himself and is aware of his own responsibilities is important and useful to the family. . . . Equally useful to the whole world is the progressive, productive, and civilized nation." Only a nation in which the members of each basic unit take care of that unit, whether family or tribe, will be strong and survive because "the social factor . . . is the genuine and driving force of history." In other words, trying to set up a political system not based on social reality—as Qaddafi sees that reality—is useless and won't work.

Ever since his disastrous discussions with Egyptian women's groups in Egypt over the place of women in society, Qaddafi's thought on this subject, which is one of his favorites, has been evolving slowly but surely away from a position of what looked like classic male chauvinism toward one of favoring women's liberation—especially liberation of Muslim and Arab women in their own societies. At the September 1, 1981, anniversary of the revolution, Qaddafi made a speech that, in fact, raised to the front rank "woman's lib" advocates.

In the *Green Book*, *Vol. 3*, however, he has not yet reached such a point. Men and women, he says, are different because they have different natural functions. The functions of menstruation, breast-feeding, pregnancy, and the feebleness that attends childbirth seriously reduce women's physical abilities; "all these innate characteristics form differences because of which man and woman cannot be equal" and therefore must fulfill different roles or functions in life. But the woman's life-giving role is essential and good: "There is a deliberate intervention against conception [birth control] which is the alternative to human life. In addition to that there is a partial deliberate intervention against conception, as well as against breast-feeding." Qaddafi likens nurseries where children are placed to relieve their mothers of the burden to "poultry farms in which chicks are crammed after they are hatched." Natural parenthood is best: "in a family where true principles of motherhood, fatherhood, and brotherhood prevail," the maturing child will be as superior to one reared in nurseries or orphanages as meat from wild or naturally bred animals is superior to that of animals raised on mechanized farms.

Another *Green Book* slogan chosen for frequent public display, *"In need, freedom is latent,"* sounds sibylline and enigmatic and was probably meant to. Qaddafi loves an air of mystery. The context in which this phrase occurs is this: women's natural role is raising children in a natural way, and "a woman who needs work that renders her unable to perform her natural function is not free and is compelled to do that by need, for in need freedom is latent." In Qaddafi's opinion, the condition of need requires freedom to release one from that condition. He also means that a person's freedom is hemmed in by economic constraint.

Women, Qaddafi says, should not be obliged to perform harsh physical labor, especially when pregnant or breast-feeding. There should be agreement in a divorce case, and "neither the woman nor the man can remarry without a previous agreement on divorce." Qaddafi adds, "The woman is the owner of the house" because it shelters her and her children.

Critics of Qaddafi might deride this as simply restating, for his own society, the age-old Western cliché that "Woman's place is in the home." Not so; for Qaddafi next gives the first signals of his coming involvement with women's liberation in the Muslim world. In *Green Book, Vol. 3*, it still consists only of demanding a "revolution" that will keep women from being driven to do men's work, but printed in green type is this: "All societies nowadays look upon woman as no more than an article of merchandise. The East regards her as a commodity for buying and selling, while the West does not recognize her femininity." The question of whether women work or don't work "is a ridiculous materialistic presentation. Work should be provided by the society to all able members—men and women—who need work, but on condition that each individual should work in the field that suits him and not be forced to carry out unsuitable work." Equally bad is child labor or the compelling of women to work under the same conditions as those of men; both constitute "injustice and dictatorship." Qaddafi sums this up: "There is no difference in human rights between man and woman, the child and the adult. But there is no absolute equality between them as regards their duties."

More surprises followed *Green Book, Vol. 3* on the issue of women. On September 1, 1981, Qaddafi made an emotional appeal, totally unnoticed in the West and scarcely heeded in the Arab world, for liberation of women in the Muslim world from their "shackles." For several months, Qaddafi had been seen, though not photographed, with a partly feminine troop of bodyguards, apparently young women specially trained by the East German contingent in armed and unarmed combat and the use of light weapons. Also on Revolution Day 1981 Qaddafi presented to his nation and the world the graduates of a girls' military academy in Tripoli that had opened in 1978. The graduation ceremony was held in the presence of armed forces commander Brigadier General Abu Bakr Yunis Jabir, the academy's commandant, and other armed forces officers. Qaddafi announced that Libya's own gradual "mobilization," begun shortly before the air battle with U.S. planes over the Gulf of Sirte on August 19, 1981, was the "precursor of the patriotic mobilization of all the Arab nations' combat forces." His discussion of the role of women in Libya's defense led into an extraordinary appeal:

*Junior high school graduates ought to enroll in military high schools of all branches of the service. . . . This will soon become a reality because proof is here before us today. . . . In the past it was impossible to have a girls' military academy. Detractors said it is impossible for any woman to come forth and join such an academy. But this proved wrong. Revolutionary transformations have surpassed such mentalities and created a new individual.*

*We are proud that the first military academy for girls in the world is today graduating officers here in the Jamahariya. This is something novel. . . . Whereas in the American Army, 150,000 women are enrolled, this giant force is not a combat force and is also not respected in the American Army. . . . This group is used for recreational purposes and assigned to menial jobs as a sign of condescension toward women. We, the Arabs, the Muslims, Orientals, we the new force and we the builders of the new civilization cannot accept women being bought and sold.*

*Ever since its inception, the revolution has attacked all phenomena where women, especially European women, are bought and sold as a cheap commodity in reactionary, backward societies, including the bygone monarchical regime which had opened nightspots of pleasure where women were traded. European women who wrongly believe they have been liberated are in fact still being bought and sold, and are items of recreation in European armies.*[24]

In the same speech, Qaddafi then had some ridicule for former French President Valéry Giscard d'Estaing. In order to buoy his popularity in the opinion polls, Giscard, claimed Qaddafi, had for the first time allowed women to enroll in the elite parachute brigade of the French Foreign Legion. However, Qaddafi added, Giscard explained to the traditionalist males in the Foreign Legion that enrollment of women was only "recreational" and meant "to raise general morale." French women had felt slighted, and this didn't help Giscard in the coming elections. Qaddafi continued:

*We in the Jamahariya and the great revolution affirm respect for women and are raising their flag. We have resolved to totally liberate women in Libya, thus . . . removing them from the world of oppression and subjugation, so that they may be masters of their own fate in a democratic milieu where they have equal opportunities with all other members of society.*[25]

The girls' military academy would be the "cornerstone" for liberation of women in Libya, the Arab world, and beyond. Other air, naval, air defense, and secondary military schools would be opened for boys and girls. The female half of the 150 million people in Arab nations are both "oppressed and paralyzed." Only a revolution can free this oppressed half of the Arab population, which "falls within the circle of world colonialism":

*The men and women of the Arab nations are being subjected to an attempt at subjugation. But inside the Arab nation, women have been in fact dominated by forces of oppression, feudalism, and profit. We call for the outbreak of a revolution for the liberation of women in the Arab nation. . . . This is a bomb that will rock the entire Arab region and will drive the female prisoners of palaces and market-places to revolt against their jailers, exploiters and oppressors. This call will no doubt have deep echoes and repercussions throughout the Arab nation and the world. Today . . . is not an ordinary day . . . but will be the beginning of the end of the era of harem and slaves and the beginning of women's liberation in the Arab nation.*[26]

After recalling that *Green Book, Vol. 3* called for women to be respected, Qaddafi added:

*Women now are not respected. What goes on at present does not agree with the true constitution of any Islamic society. Islam means freedom, equality, and a humane society. Current practices are no more than insults. Marriages and divorces and other social activities currently being practiced are all contrary to the Koran, Islam, freedom, and humanitarianism. Unfortunately, Oriental societies espousing Islam have harmed our religion and are the most reactionary and infidel of societies. . . . We are determined to see this revolution destroy the citadels of reactionaries and their castles, and raid these high palaces where Arab women are being enslaved, destroying the palaces and liberating women, from the [Atlantic] Ocean to the [Arab] Gulf. . . . We would like to announce that Libyan military colleges, and Libyan military schools are wide open not only for Libyan Arab girls but for all the girls of the Arab nation and Africa. And the fight continues.*[27]

Qaddafi's attitude toward minorities, especially blacks, is of compelling interest because of his extensive dealings with black African rulers and states (who generally hold his motives to be suspicious) and because of his repeated expressions of interest in American blacks and Indians. In *Green Book, Vol. 3* he defines two types of minorities. One—and here he has American blacks in mind—"belongs to a nation which provides it with a social framework." The other—and the Palestinians are clearly meant—"has no nation and forms its own social framework." The second kind of minority, says Qaddafi, will "eventually constitute a nation by virtue of a sense of belonging and a common destiny." Encroachment by the majority on the rights of a minority "is an act of injustice. . . . Its political and economic problems can only be solved by the masses in whose hands power, wealth, and arms should be placed."

In dealing with the subject of blacks and the liberation of Black Africa, Qaddafi, like most Arab leaders, is totally silent about the past generations of Arab slaveowners and slave traders. Neither phenomenon had been seen in Libya since Turkish times, though it has continued up to the present in Mauritania and some other parts of Africa in which Qaddafi has a strong interest. His green-type heading in *Green Book, Vol. 3* is unequivocal: "The Blacks Will Prevail in the World." Forgetting, perhaps, that sub-Saharan Africans, American blacks, and others consider Arabs to be whites, "the latest age of slavery," he says, "is the white race's enslavement of the black race. The black man will not forget this until he has achieved rehabilitation." Qaddafi briefly skims over this subject in two short pages, pausing only to note that blacks now face the problem of "rehabilitating a whole race" and have a "motivation to vengeance and domination." Reverting to his simplistic way of looking at history, Qaddafi says the yellow race once dominated the world "when it marched from Asia against the rest of the continents" (here he is probably thinking of the migration of the American aborigines from Asia via Siberia). "Then came the role of the white race, when it carried out a wide-ranging colonialist movement covering all the continents of the world. Now comes the black race's turn to prevail."

His final comment about the status of black people sounds a bit like that of a paternalistic American white, espousing the pious generalities of post–Civil War American society:

> *The black race is now in a very backward social situation. But such backwardness helps to bring about numerical superiority of the blacks because their low standard of living has protected them from getting to know the means and ways of birth control and family planning. Also their backward social traditions are a reason why there is no limit to marriage, leading to their unlimited growth, while the population of other races has decreased because of birth control, restrictions on marriage and continuous occupation in work, unlike the blacks who are sluggish in a climate which is always hot.*[28]

Qaddafi's final subjects of concern in *Green Book, Vol. 3* are education, music and art, and sports. His own bitter memories of his high school days in Sebha, where he probably spent more time dreaming of the revolution than he did in study, make him impatient, as he has repeatedly told audiences at the universities in Tripoli and Benghazi, with traditional classroom work. "Education or learning," he says, "is not necessarily that methodized curriculum and those classified subjects in textbooks which youth are forced to learn during specified hours while sitting on [sic] rows of desks." That is a type of education which goes "against human freedom." Compulsory education "suppresses freedom because it deprives man of free choice, creativity, and brilliance." Compulsory, "methodized" education is "coercion."

If Johnny or Ahmed is not to learn according to a set curriculum, what should he learn? In response, Qaddafi trails off into what must, for his admirers, be infuriating vagueness: "All methods of education prevailing in the world should be done away with through a worldwide cultural revolution to emancipate man's mind from curricula of fanaticism and from the process of deliberate adaptation of man's taste, his ability to form concepts and his mentality."

This doesn't mean closing schools, but rather providing "all types of education, giving people the chance to choose freely any subjects they wish to learn." This calls for a tremendous increase in the number and variety of schools, something that Qaddafi is indeed pursuing. He takes a hard slap at traditional Arab societies like those of Saudi Arabia or the

Gulf states, and Arab and non-Arab Marxist countries as well: "Societies which prohibit the teaching of religion as it actually is, are reactionary societies, biased toward ignorance and hostile to freedom. Societies which monopolize religious education are reactionary societies, biased toward ignorance and hostile to freedom." In a slap at the West and what Palestinian-born Columbia University Professor Edward Said has called the tradition of "Orientalism" in Western scholarship and journalism, Qaddafi condemns as "reactionary and biased" the "societies which distort the religions, civilizations, and behavior of others in the process of teaching those subjects."

Everyone, says Qaddafi, is entitled to knowledge unless "a person himself does something which deprives him of that right." In the future Utopian society, ignorance will end "when everything is presented as it actually is and when knowledge about everything is available to each person in the manner that suits him."

Like all Arabs, Qaddafi is fascinated by language and its use. The central importance of the Arabic language, which in traditional Arab societies is so special that literates and illiterates alike treat any scrap of paper with Arabic writing upon it as an object of reverence, is a central part of Qaddafi's philosophy as expressed in Green Book, Vol. 3. "Man is still backward," he says, "because he is unable to speak a common language." World education has not produced or even aimed at producing a world language, and so human behavior remains "based on the reaction produced by the feeling the language creates in the speaker's mind."

People who do not understand one another's language are compared by Qaddafi to groups of people who wear different colors to express grief when mourning (black as opposed to white). One group hates the black color, the other group hates the white, and "such a sentiment leaves its physical effect on the cells as well as the genes in the body" and will be transmitted by inheritance. This, Qaddafi assures us, is the reason why people are comfortable only with their own arts and cultural heritage, even if they share a common language with others who have a different artistic and cultural heritage. Learning the languages of others or understanding their culture is no problem. The real problem is the impossibility of a real intuitional adaptation to the language of others.

Qaddafi might, in a moment of candor, admit that his own knowledge of English, which he speaks with bare military competence and frequent mispronunciation, reflects this principle—it's superficial knowledge. Nonetheless, he seems to have an "intuitional" understanding of English as evidenced in his addresses and speeches in English. What Qaddafi and other Arab leaders would prefer is that more people from Western cultures come to know, appreciate, and use the Arabic language (although the Arabic language isn't mentioned in *Green Book, Vol. 3*). "Mankind is really still backward because man does not speak with his brother one common language which is inherited and not learned. However, it is only a matter of time for mankind to achieve that goal unless civilization should relapse."

Qaddafi's final chapter in *Green Book, Vol. 3* deals with a pet peeve. Sport, he says, is either private or public, but if of the second type, "must be practiced by all people and should not be left to anybody to practice on their own behalf." This is a passage that has puzzled many of Qaddafi's closest friends and collaborators, because in Libya ordinary people are as fond of watching football (soccer), displays of horsemanship, and other competitive sports as they are anywhere else. It is just as "stupid," says Qaddafi, for crowds to watch other people eating in a restaurant or praying in a church as it is to "watch a player or a team without participating." It is also "equally illogical . . . to allow an individual or a team to monopolize sports while the people as a whole pay the costs of such a monopoly for the benefit of one person or a team."

Since Qaddafi is, if nothing else, a political animal, he finds an application in politics and so returns to the antiparliamentary theme of *Green Book, Vol. 1*: people should not allow anyone else (person, party, or parliament) to replace them in deciding their own fate. He equates sporting clubs with parliaments or other political organizations. People who "queue to vote for a candidate" to represent them will end up finding themselves "robbed of their will and dignity . . . reduced to mere spectators" like those at a sporting event. Qaddafi's idea of an ideal sports arena is similar to that of the people's council in the political sphere, a gigantic assemblage where everybody participates. The grandstand of a public playing field is to Qaddafi like the figurative political "grandstand" from which most people in most societies watch their politicians and legislators perform. This has got to change: "When the masses march and play sport in the center of the playing fields and the open spaces, stadiums will be vacated and destroyed. . . . The grandstand will disappear when no one is there to occupy it."

At this point, Qaddafi's ideal hero-figure seems to be waiting in the wings. But before this suspiciously Qaddafi-like figure makes his appearance, the *Green Book*'s author tells us what a hero is *not*:

*Those who are unable to perform the roles of heroism in life, who are ignorant of the events of history, who fall short of envisaging the future and who are not serious enough in their lives are the trivial persons who fill the seats of the theaters and cinemas to watch the events of life and to learn their course. They are like pupils who occupy school desks because they are not only uneducated but also illiterate.*[29]

Not so the leaders and heroes, who for Qaddafi are men who ride onto history's stage on horseback:

*Those who direct the course of life for themselves do not need to watch it working through actors on the stage or in the cinemas. Likewise, horsemen who hold the reins of their horses have no seat in the grandstands at the race course. If every person has a horse, no one will be there to watch and applaud. The sitting spectators are only those who are too helpless to perform this kind of activity because they are not horsemen.*[30]

Qaddafi's favorite people, his own Bedouin, behave differently from the more bourgeois and sedentary city folks: "The Bedouin peoples show no interest in theaters and shows because they are very serious and hard-working." Serious people "ridicule acting" and, instead of watching spectator sports, "take part in joyful ceremonies because they naturally recognize the need for these activities and practice them automatically."[31]

*The Green Book*, Qaddafi seems to feel, has provided the main script for his own role as the lonely superstar of modern history. He sees himself as the central figure on the stage, providing guidance and direction to the "masses" who crowd onstage and into the world political arena, enthusiastically cheering his name and proclaiming the era of "people's power" now at hand.

To establish that "people's power," any means, including violent wars of liberation, is justified, provided the particular cause in question is regarded as just by Qaddafi. In order to discourage or eliminate his enemies, help his friends, and promote the power of the "people" everywhere, Qaddafi has been willing to hire and use all manner of foreign experts—even those who come from the very center of world "imperialism": the United States of America.

# TERROR, INC.

**Y**e *shall know the truth*, says the motto etched large on the white marble walls of the main lobby of the CIA's headquarters in Langley, Virginia, *and the truth shall make you free.* In the case of postrevolutionary Libya, the twists and turns of U.S. policy seem to indicate to many thoughtful insiders that the motto has been distorted: *Ye shall ignore the truth, and your ignorance shall make it easier to put the blame on someone else.*

Qaddafi's contractual arrangements with several former CIA officers and members of the U.S. Army's Special Forces ("Green Berets") ranged from electronic surveillance to outright murder of Qaddafi adversaries and critics. Americans helped Qaddafi set up his foreign terror network. The same, and other, Americans sold him—often at tremendous profit to themselves—the gimmickry and tools of terror and subversion. Americans lobbied in their own capital for remission of the embargoes that the Ford and Carter administrations had imposed (often reluctantly) on U.S. military-related exports to Libya, things like Lockheed C-130 transport planes and heavy trucks. In the Arab world and Africa, these actions helped spread the myth that the U.S. government, long after the Hilton assignment and other early anti-Qaddafi plots, remained the more or less acknowledged ally and good friend of the Libyan colonel.

Although Qaddafi obviously valued his American connections highly, he was concerned about the possibility that uncontrolled leaks could reach Washington. By 1973, the year when Qaddafi's final falling-out with Sadat and, indirectly, with the United States began, the Libyan authorities were beginning to insist that some Americans who had been serving in Libya long enough to learn good Arabic and make highly placed friends should go home. Such people had become security risks for Qaddafi: they might learn too much. Despite this, according to former CIA officer Miles Copeland, Libyans who wanted to work for the CIA, like nationals of other countries with the same wish, managed to get through to the Agency and establish the connection without too much trouble.[1]

By the time the Arab-Israeli war of October 1973 broke out, relations between Qaddafi and Sadat were deteriorating. By agreement with President Hafez al-Assad of Syria and King Faisal of Saudi Arabia, Sadat and Assad had not let Qaddafi in on the secret war preparations.

The Nixon administration was in something of a quandary over Qaddafi; he was proving to be a first-class nuisance. French President Georges Pompidou, continuing the new French tilt toward the Arab world begun by President Charles de Gaulle after Algeria won independence, concluded a deal with Libya for one hundred Mirage fighter-bombers in January 1976. More than any other early action by Qaddafi (or Pompidou), this deal troubled the Nixon administration because there were very few Libyans trained at that time to fly such advanced combat jets. The deal indicated, as Henry Kissinger noted in his memoirs, that Qaddafi intended these planes for other Arab states, especially Nasser's Egypt. There were outraged protests from Israel's supporters in the U.S. Congress. When President and Mrs. Pompidou visited the United States in February, Israel's friends organized demonstrations everywhere they went, with blows falling upon both Mr. and Mrs. Pompidou in a Chicago crowd. Only President Nixon's announcement that he would attend a New York dinner for Pompidou prevented the French president's abrupt cancellation of the rest of his trip.[2] The Pompidous cut short their Chicago visit and returned to New York. Kissinger, who calls the violent incident "inexcusable," concludes that it weighed heavily upon Pompidou's future attitude toward the United States.

Was it possible, wondered some Nixon administration officials, that Qaddafi was not going to turn out to be such a white knight of anti-Communism after all? Aside from the annoyance over the Mirage deal (for which Pompidou's government was blamed in Washington far more than was Qaddafi), the Libyan government had begun its pressure tactics against the U.S. oil companies to get them to meet Libyan price and production demands.

On the morning of October 7, 1973, the Egyptian forces, supported by both Libyan and Egyptian pilots flying some of the same French Mirages, began pummeling the Israeli forces in Sinai. President Nixon and Henry Kissinger had to consider Libya in a new light when they met with the U.S. Action Group (USAG) that was hastily formed to deal with the Mideast war. Wasn't there danger, someone asked, that Qaddafi would now order attacks against U.S. property, assets, and citizens? After all, his information media were as usual blaming the United States for its supposed support of Israel (which at that time had not begun, at least in the form of the U.S. airlift of military supplies).

But what happened along the Libyan-Egyptian border, Egypt's only practical land entry and exit after the closing of Egyptian ports and airports, assuaged their doubts. Qaddafi's authorities carefully helped Americans leaving Egypt to cross Libya in protected safety, and fly out of Benghazi or Tripoli to havens in Western Europe or the United States. This caused a modest flutter of gratitude in Washington, and the Nixon administration sent Qaddafi a message of thanks.[3] The Libyans showed similar care and solicitude toward American oil and other workers who left Libya when asked to do so by the Reagan administration in December 1981.

With such a residual friendly constituency in the United States, it is not difficult to imagine how and why the likes of Frank Terpil, Edwin Wilson, and Qaddafi's score or more of American "mercenaries" were able to prosper in their lucrative business deals with Qaddafi. In the mid-1970s—ironically enough, at the very time that Qaddafi began to turn away from the West and, apparently losing hope that Western Europe would follow up the Mirage deal with new arms, began to deal with the Soviets—Libya became one of the overseas areas where former CIA men and Green Berets, usually with Vietnam service records, could carry on such business.

It was the new Reagan administration in 1981 that began to take public notice of this business. Even as Secretary of State Alexander M. Haig and other administration spokesmen were sermonizing about *Soviet* support for international terrorism, the *United States,* in the words of a confidential report published in 1981, had in effect "become a major supplier of [military] hardware and technology in support of worldwide terrorism. Former Central Intelligence Agency personnel, military Special Forces personnel [the Green Berets], and U.S. corporations combine to supply products and expertise to whomever can pay the price."[4]

Miles Copeland, who while with the CIA Cairo station in 1952 helped to forecast the successful coup of the Egyptian Free Officers around Nasser, has jokingly referred to himself as "the only ex-CIA officer who uses the CIA as a cover for his business activities."[5] There are few more apt descriptions than that of the role of that astonishing American pair who enlisted in Qaddafi's service, Frank Terpil and Edwin Wilson. For years, both have been fugitives. On June 15, 1982, Wilson was apprehended in an elaborate Justice Department plan. His trial promised to be a tangle of intelligence intrigues. Terpil, still at large, was seen in Beirut. He may still be promoting terrorism, or he may be in hiding, if Qaddafi suspects him of being an American "mole."[6]

It is from the extremely intricate and complicated relationship between the two men and the Washington power structure that Qaddafi seems to have derived many of his conclusions about how to use the United States and channel American power to his own ends.

Francis (Frank) E. Terpil was born in Brooklyn in 1940. Those who have met him have found that he hasn't lost the rough-and-ready manner and insolent self-assurance of New York street life. He completed his U.S. Army service in 1965 with an honorable discharge and then joined the CIA. Like Qaddafi, Terpil put his army training in communications and cryptography to good use in the Agency. He became a repairer of code machines and other communications equipment. Terpil is remembered well by one of his former U.S. associates, Michael L. Infante, president of Oceanic International Corporation, the "import-export" firm that handled some of Terpil's transfers of American military and security equipment abroad. Infante characterizes him as a "stocky man with a mustache, who was always tinkering with radios" and who was constantly disappearing abroad for weeks or months at a time and then suddenly reappearing with wild tales of adventures in Africa or elsewhere.[7]

In 1971 Terpil was forced to resign from the Agency after indiscretions that apparently went beyond mere boasting in Virginia bars. One episode supposedly involved trying to smuggle contraband liquor into India, a country that strictly regulates alcohol.[8] Terpil then resolved to go into business for himself. He decided that to operate successfully in the international arms and security market, he needed a partner—if possible, a partner who had better and higher contacts in the U.S. government and abroad than had Terpil himself.

Such a man was Edwin P. Wilson. To all who knew him, Wilson seemed very much a part of the Washington power structure. Wilson, a Virginian who made his career in the CIA, did so well while still in the

Agency that he was able to buy a fifteen-hundred-acre farm at Upperville, Virginia, that abuts an estate of Senator John Warner.

Wilson, who was born in 1929, worked in the CIA's Office of Security in 1951, even before he did his military service in the U.S. Marines. In 1955 he joined the CIA on a full-time contract basis. He infiltrated the Seafarers International Union and also handled their congressional liaison. Among the operations he was involved in, before his interest turned to North Africa, was the Bay of Pigs invasion of Cuba by CIA-trained Cuban mercenaries in 1960; Wilson handled procurement of equipment and pay for the invasion force. In that operation he worked with Theodore G. Shackley, one of the key officials in the CIA's clandestine service. According to evidence unearthed by Seymour Hersh, Shackley was of great help to Wilson and Terpil later with their Libyan operations for Qaddafi.

After the Bay of Pigs, Wilson helped establish a new Washington firm called Consultants International, Inc. (CI), a front for CIA and U.S. Naval Intelligence activities. It was during this period, according to federal investigators, that Wilson and his associates were able to earn benefits well in excess of their salaries from commissions and kickbacks for exporting U.S. security and intelligence technology. One of Wilson's fellow board members on Consultants International was the leading Republican public relations man Robert Keith Gray, who was cochairman of Ronald Reagan's inaugural committee. Gray denied ever knowing that Wilson was on the CI board, but said he found Wilson "charming and very much a red-blooded American."⁹

In 1971, according to CIA officials, Wilson left the Agency. He set himself up as part of Task Force 157, a secret component of the Office of Naval Intelligence charged with monitoring Soviet shipping. One of its specialties was keeping track of shipments of Soviet arms around the world, and also watching for traces of Soviet nuclear weapons, something the CIA had to do later on in Libya.¹⁰

When President Nixon visited Peking in 1972, the China mainland operations were halted by Washington. CIA officials, Hersh discovered, were surprised to find much of the sensitive equipment intended for use in China turning up for sale on the international arms market.

During the 1972–74 period of close CIA liaison with Egypt and Israel, which included the October 1973 Arab-Israeli war, Agency business in Libya was probably supervised by John Henry Stein. He was appointed in July 1981 as deputy director of operations of the CIA, in charge of all of their clandestine operations overseas. Stein was transferred from Phnom Penh, Cambodia, to Libya in 1972, and served as political officer at the American Embassy in Tripoli until 1974. A former CIA official said Stein was CIA station chief in Tripoli at the time.[11]

It is unclear when Terpil and Wilson, as private individuals, first began their operations for Qaddafi, but all accounts agree that their main commitment, as charged in the U.S. federal indictments against them, began in 1976. According to U.S. Justice Department files, Terpil began recruiting former Green Berets and former CIA staffers for work in Libya; the recruits were told they would be clearing mines and other unexploded ordnance in Libya's deserts and harbors. Instead, they were asked to manufacture ashtrays, phony rocks, and lamps and other ornaments containing explosive devices. By August 1976 Terpil and a small group of Americans were installed in luxury on the outskirts of Tripoli, in the former palace of King Idris, which had been christened by Qaddafi the "People's Palace." The palace, for some unknown reason was code-named "Swanee." Wilson appears to have been traveling in and out of Libya by this time, and was himself, according to the federal prosecutors, engaged in the arms business with Qaddafi. Qaddafi's intelligence chiefs liked to take trusted visitors to the People's Palace to show off both the terror devices and the American mercenaries who were teaching Libyans to fabricate them. One informant who helped build the U.S. case against Terpil and Wilson heard a Libyan lieutenant explain that the devices were intended to "eliminate certain people" because Qaddafi "would feel more comfortable if they were not around."[12]

By the time Terpil and Wilson had made a formal deal with Qaddafi to sell their experience, know-how, and contacts, U.S. federal authorities had a full report. In the fall of 1976, Kevin P. Mulcahy, a partner of Terpil and Wilson's at the time, briefed government agents on the clandestine operations that he thought were sponsored by the CIA during his first three months with Terpil and Wilson. Mulcahy admitted that he had worked with his associates in selling items such as somewhat outdated computer systems and cryptographic equipment, as well as more lethal items such as embargoed ammunition sold to South Africa. Like his associates, Mulcahy had served in the military (in his case the navy) before joining the CIA in 1963; once again, cryptography seems to have been his specialty. He had resigned from the CIA in 1968 to enter the private electronics industry. Alcohol, a rough divorce, and change led him to a new job as a drug and alcohol counselor in

Virginia. Barbara Wilson, Edwin Wilson's wife, acting as a real estate agent, rented Mulcahy a house in 1975, and one night Mulcahy accepted an invitation from the Wilsons for dinner on their fifteen-hundred-acre Virginia farm.

As an inducement to work with Wilson and Terpil, Mulcahy accepted Wilson's gift of another nine-bedroom farmhouse he could use as a refuge for the young people he was counseling, and agreed to a guaranteed $500,000 annual income plus expenses. Wilson then introduced Mulcahy to Terpil. The three men became equal partners in Inter-Technology, Inc., one of many Wilson-Terpil companies in the United States and Europe. In May of 1976, before a trip to Libya by Wilson and Terpil, Wilson arranged a meeting at Shackley's house (Shackley, one of the CIA's leading experts on secret warfare, was then serving as deputy director for covert operations). Harry Rasstatter, another of Terpil's business associates, turned over to the CIA information he had obtained from SAVAK, the Shah of Iran's security service; and intelligence operations in Turkey, Iran, and Libya were discussed. When Wilson told Shackley that he and Terpil planned a trip to Libya to meet Qaddafi (Wilson was later to deny that he had ever met Qaddafi), Mulcahy concluded that the whole Inter-Technology operation with Libya was indeed a CIA front. Shackley later insisted that neither he nor the Agency had ever given Wilson any indication of this.

Inter-Technology's biggest contract with Qaddafi was for the purchase of hundreds of thousands of timers capable of detonating explosives at programmed times. To sell them to Libya, they had found the American Electronics Laboratories of Colmar, Pennsylvania, and Falls Church, Virginia, which had been supplying the CIA with classified electronics gear. An active CIA employee, Patry E. Loomis, then operating under cover for a West Coast aircraft company, had also been recruited by Wilson and Terpil for the Libyan operation. According to Seymour Hersh, William Weissenburger, another associate of Wilson's, and two American Electronics employees (one of them also a CIA official) worked privately over a weekend to produce ten prototype timers to demonstrate to Qaddafi's security officers in Tripoli. The timers were sold at the grossly inflated price of $1,500 apiece (their real cost was about one-tenth that).[13]

In June 1976 Mulcahy set up an exhibition of security products in Brighton, England. It was a no-expense-spared affair that included ample food, drink, and party girls for possible customers of the firm. Sayyed Gaddaf Qaddam, Muammar al-Qaddafi's cousin, was present on this occasion, as he was during many future episodes in the U.S.-Qaddafi relationship. A Syrian company, Abdallah Engineering, purchased with ease some sensitive high-speed communications gear; Terpil apparently arranged the export licensing. Cryptographic and radio-monitoring materials, which the Syrian and other Arab armies desperately needed to compete with Israel's electronic-warfare wizardry, were part of the package sold to Syria. Irish Republican Army officials also appeared to bid for surplus U.S. Army M-16 rifles, available to arms dealers like Wilson and his associates from Vietnam war stocks.

What was most important about the Brighton interlude was that it marked the start for Terpil and Wilson of the Omar al-Meheishi affair. This became the core issue of their association with Qaddafi and his operations, and one of the keys to understanding why Qaddafi's relationship with Palestine Liberation Organization Chairman Yasir Arafat and his mainstream guerrilla organization, al-Fatah, deteriorated after 1976. The Meheishi affair was also the most important episode in Libyan internal politics since Qaddafi and his fellow RCC conspirators had come to power.

Omar al-Meheishi was one of the most important members of the original twelve-man RCC. An early and constant companion of Qaddafi from their school days on, he formed the revolution's "first cell" in Misurata. Meheishi, as minister of planning and assistant to Bashir Hawadi (another RCC member who chaired Qaddafi's brief and halfhearted attempt to form a Nasserist political party, the Arab Socialist Union), wanted Libya to invest all its earnings in agriculture and industry. He was especially interested in heavy industry; Misurata's iron and steel complex, which many foreign firms in 1981 were competing to complete, was Meheishi's favorite project.

An intense, nervous man, Meheishi was at first fiercely loyal to Qaddafi. During the first trials of the *ancien régime*'s senior members in late 1969 and early 1970, Hawadi served as president of the court and Meheishi as public prosecutor. But after the revolution, there was friction inside the RCC, and in May 1975 it emerged openly. The government was discussing possible austerity measures. Meheishi demanded that Qaddafi reduce the arms budget and the large sums being spent on supporting foreign terrorism and other ventures that did the Libyan people no good. Such spending represented the "dissipation of public funds in order to foment unrest" in other Arab countries, as Meheishi put it. Abdel Salem Jalloud stoutly defended the government's defense expenditures and its projects for supporting guerrilla warfare and subversion in Arab states such as Egypt, the Sudan, and Tunisia, which had dodged Qaddafi's projects for unification with Libya.

In the summer of 1975, Meheishi, together with Hawadi and another RCC member, Awad Hamza, plotted a coup against Qaddafi. With them were about twenty other officers, many of whom, like Meheishi, came from Misurata. Whether or not the CIA or other foreign intelligence agencies helped Qaddafi once again, the conspiracy was discovered and Hawadi and Hamza were arrested. Meheishi escaped to Tunisia. Qaddafi exerted enormous pressure on President Bourguiba, who nevertheless refused to return Meheishi to a country that had sent saboteurs into Tunisia and would-be assassins after Bourguiba. Meheishi went on to Cairo, where he apparently felt President Sadat could offer him a safer haven.

Qaddafi never explicitly admitted the existence of the Meheishi plot. But on September 1, 1975, his revolution's sixth anniversary, he publicly denounced "some felonious and fascist officers who want to introduce changes by force in Libya" and announced a purge of the army.

The public aspects of the Meheishi affair, which friends of Qaddafi say affected him deeply, gradually became known in Cairo. On March 8, 1976, the Egyptian authorities announced that a seven-man Libyan terrorist squad, assigned the mission of kidnapping Meheishi and returning him to Libya, had been arrested in Cairo. The former Tunisian foreign minister, Muhammad Masmoudi—the same Muhammad Masmoudi who had signed Tunisia's brief unity agreement with Qaddafi in January 1974, and whose career in Tunisia was ruined by that short-lived accord—was also questioned by the Egyptians in connection with the Meheishi affair.

From Masmoudi and from other sources,[14] the Egyptians and the CIA learned that the Meheishi affair had led to a new crisis in Tripoli and a new defection from Qaddafi's RCC inner circle. This time the defector was Abdel Moneim al-Hony—the former Libyan counterintelligence chief who had tried to recruit "James Kent" to kidnap Omar Shalhi during the Hilton assignment. Hony, who toured eye clinics throughout Western Europe and the United States in desperate attempts to restore his failing vision, also during his travels contacted the CIA sometime between 1972 and 1975. He may have been feeding information to Tripoli station chief John Stein, or to Stein's superiors in Washington.

Hony left Libya in late 1975 without proclaiming his defection. He went first to Cairo, then to Rome. On March 6, 1976, Italian police arrested three Libyans at Rome's Fiumicino airport for plotting to hijack a Cairo-Rome flight to Tripoli. Hony, supposed to be on board, had escaped his would-be kidnappers by taking another plane at the last minute. The hijack attempt, said Egyptian security sources on March 8, 1976, had followed failure of a mission by Masmoudi—under orders from Qaddafi—to "persuade" both Hony and Meheishi to return to Tripoli peacefully.

The Tripoli government denied the Egyptian accusations. On March 12, Meheishi, interviewed by *Al-Ahram*, denied having tried to instigate a coup against Qaddafi. He and other officers had been merely seeking a way of "correcting Qaddafi's errors," he said. Meheishi added that he had personally asked Qaddafi to resign, and described him as a "dangerous psychopath"—one of the earliest public references to Qaddafi's supposed insanity—and a "despot."

On Christmas Day, 1976, a Libyan military court sentenced twenty-three officers of the Meheishi group to death, and on April 2, 1977, Egyptian newspapers reported that twenty-two of them had been executed. These were probably the first executions Qaddafi had carried out since he came to power. They were not the last. Since then, Meheishi has suffered a mental breakdown. Friends reported in 1981 that he was in a Kuwait hospital.[15]

The Meheishi affair and its side effects weakened Qaddafi's ruling circle. By the end of 1975, the original twelve-man RCC had only five members left. Besides Qaddafi and Jalloud, only Abu Bakr Yunis Jabir, Mustafa al-Kharoubi, and Khoweildi Hamidi remained. The ouster of Muhammad Najm, another RCC insider, had preceded the defection and flight to the United States of Mokhtar al-Karawi in August 1975, another officer not a member of the RCC. Muhammad al-Mugarieff (not to be confused with Muhammad Mugarieff, Qaddafi's most formidable opponent, who in 1981 was alive, well, and traveling abroad) died in an automobile accident on August 21, 1972. More and more, Muammar al-Qaddafi felt himself alone and surrounded by enemies.

This was all the more reason why his brother Sayyed Qaddam was probably the creator of the proposition put to Mulcahy by Terpil in England in June 1976. Would Mulcahy like to earn five thousand dollars simply for taking a detour to Cairo before flying to Tripoli and delivering a "cold gun" (one with no identifying serial number)? No thanks, Mulcahy told Terpil; let someone else take care of that. Later, Mulcahy deduced that the gun was one of the weapons to be used in a new and complicated plot to assassinate Meheishi, despite the protection afforded him by Sadat's security men.

Mulcahy reported this, along with many other alarming aspects of the

Inter-Technology operation with Libya, to U.S. federal authorities, and was advised to go underground in the United States for his own protection. Meanwhile, as the federal indictments against Wilson and Terpil show, the Meheishi affair developed as follows. Early in October 1976, John Henry Harper, a former bomb technician for the CIA recruited by Wilson for Qaddafi, returned home from Libya. Hearing of Mulcahy's break with Wilson and Terpil, Harper decided to go to the CIA and describe the program he had participated in. Harper, whose information was incorporated into the evidence against Wilson and Terpil, said an initial task had been to set up a Tripoli bomb laboratory to make murderous objects out of innocent ones, like ashtrays, lamps, and fake rock formations.

Next, Wilson and Terpil hired three Cuban émigrés who had formerly worked for the CIA. Their mission was to kill Meheishi, for which they would be paid one million dollars by Qaddafi. Wilson paid the Cubans thirty thousand dollars in advance by a personal check drawn on his Middleburg, Virginia, bank account. At first, said the Cubans, they believed their target would be none other than the international terrorist Carlos Ilyich Ramirez, alias "The Jackal," reputed to have planned, among other outrages, the 1972 Munich Olympic attack on the Israeli athletic team. When they learned that Meheishi was the target, they fled to Europe and then flew back to the United States.[16]

Angered and frustrated by this failure, Qaddafi is said by Palestinian sources to have asked Yasir Arafat, the PLO chairman, to have al-Fatah men "take care" of Meheishi. Nothing doing, Arafat in effect told him. The PLO was not in the business of liquidating the opponents of one Arab regime or another; what it wanted to do instead was *unite* the Arabs. Raging at Arafat, Qaddafi closed all the al-Fatah offices in Libya.[17]

The misfired Meheishi conspiracy was only the beginning of a series of clandestine operations in which Wilson, Terpil, and other Americans worked closely with Qaddafi's operatives. One of these others, previously mentioned, was Pat Loomis, then still an active CIA staffer. Loomis and others met with Green Berets at Fort Bragg, North Carolina, where the John F. Kennedy Center trains U.S. Army special forces and commando and covert-action personnel from "friendly" countries. Here they persuaded U.S. personnel to quit the Army and join the group in Libya. Since President Gerald Ford had placed tight new restrictions on the CIA's covert activities overseas, Mulcahy believed for a time that Wilson and Terpil must have been "operating" with the CIA's tacit approval in order to circumvent the new rules.

By late 1976 or early 1977, the FBI, at the request of the Justice Department's Foreign Agents Registration section, was investigating the Libyan ties of Terpil and Wilson. The big problem for the FBI then, and in subsequent investigations, was that there are no U.S. federal laws that prohibit aiding terrorists overseas, or even committing terrorist acts abroad.

One morning in April 1977, Admiral Stansfield Turner, President Carter's old Navy friend and his choice as CIA director, picked up his copy of *The Washington Post*, read through an article about the Justice Department investigation of Wilson and Terpil, and grew very angry. Turner then read Mulcahy's reports on the Libyan operations. He called in Pat Loomis and Bill Weissenburger, and fired them. Later he shook up the CIA's clandestine services, replacing both Shackley and William Wells, Shackley's superior. Then he sent a warning to CIA posts abroad not to continue any association with Ed Wilson.

None of this stopped the Wilson-Terpil weapons-import business. By late 1977, Qaddafi had sent Wilson to provide support and expertise to Qaddafi's friend, Idi Amin Dada, the Ugandan dictator, and to Robert Astles, Amin's British security chief.

Investigating the arms-traffic charges against Wilson and Terpil that finally led to their arrest and first arraignment in New York in December 1979, New York State undercover agents taped conversations with Terpil in which he boasted that he had personally trained Carlos, one of the world's most notorious terrorists, years after the Venezuelan's earlier training in the USSR. Was this true or merely one of Terpil's many exercises in self-glorification?

Certainly Terpil's claim is plausible. In late August of 1973, Carlos, seeking a secure base in London, rented flats in Bayswater and Apple Court as places of refuge. Carlos, who had never been to Libya, desperately wanted to meet Muammar al-Qaddafi and offer him his services. On September 10, 1973, Carlos contacted Hamid Habib, a young attaché at the Libyan embassy in London who was one of Qaddafi's close friends. Habib told Carlos that George Habbash, the Christian Palestinian physician who headed the Popular Front for the Liberation of Palestine, one of the most radical of the Palestinian organizations, had recommended Carlos to the Libyans. After twelve days of reflection, Habib asked Carlos to fly to Tripoli.

Qaddafi, according to two authors with close connections to Israel's secret service, talked with Carlos and agreed to help him. He insisted as the only condition that Hamid Habib should act as paymaster. In typically canny fashion, Qaddafi was ensuring that the funds he dispensed in liberation causes would not be passed out aimlessly.[18]

Early in 1976, David Martin, a British newsman working for the *Observer* of London in Africa, initiated a conversation on an airliner in southern Africa with a Libyan civil servant. Several times the Libyan insisted that Qaddafi had masterminded the OPEC raid in Vienna. The Saudi oil minister, Ahmed Zaki Yamani, is certain beyond the shadow of a doubt that it was Carlos who was in charge of the terrorist group that kidnapped Yamani and ten other Arab oil ministers from the OPEC meeting in Vienna in December 1975 and took them on a wild flight to North Africa before they were safely released in Algiers—and is certain that Qaddafi had sponsored the affair.[19] Yamani even asserted that he was convinced that Carlos had "intended to kill all of us" had he not been prevented from doing so by the Algerians, at the end of the operation in Algiers.

There was other evidence that Carlos was working with Qaddafi. The Carlos gang was repeatedly sighted in Libya. Hans-Joachim Klein, one of its German members, was shipped there and hospitalized, according to diplomats in Tripoli, after his wounding during the OPEC raid. The *Sunday Telegraph* reported that Qaddafi had set up Carlos in a seaside villa (later reported to have been one of the buildings that had served as officers' residential quarters at Wheelus Field, rechristened Okbah ibn Nafi Air Base), and paid him about a million pounds sterling for the raid. Klein was said to have been paid one-tenth that amount in compensation, and a doctor was flown from Germany to treat his wounds.

Yamani's assertion of Qaddafi's complicity may have stemmed in part from conversations heard by Yamani and Captain Manfred Pollack, the pilot of the plane given the kidnappers. Carlos complained about the tougher aspects of working for the Libyans. He also muttered darkly about the unfortunate killing of the Libyan OPEC delegate in the initial shooting fray at the Vienna meeting.

British journalist Colin Smith asserts however that Qaddafi did not plan the raid or even know about it until after the fact. The raid and the manner in which it was carried out, especially the murder of the Libyan delegate, angered Qaddafi. Smith feels that this was the reason for the Libyans' reluctance to cooperate with the terrorists when the

Austrian Airways DC-9 landed at Tripoli before heading on to Algiers, where the oil ministers were set free.

On September 23, 1976, Frank Terpil met Carlos (the two had met earlier in the summer at a boat party in England) and Dr. Wadi Haddad, the chief of a clandestine terrorist branch of the Popular Front for the Liberation of Palestine. Haddad had broken with PFLP chief George Habbash when Habbash renounced airplane hijackings and other "external" terrorist acts outside Israel. Haddad had continued such work; he masterminded the July 1976 hijacking of the Air France jetliner to Entebbe. The meeting took place in Robert Astles's house in Kampala, the capital of Uganda. The meeting at Astles's house was Terpil's introduction to Amin's entourage, and was the beginning of a series of deals for weapons and communications gear for Astles's goon squads. Torture equipment, including electronic shock guns used on Amin's victims, accounted for much of the equipment forwarded by Terpil and Wilson to Astles.[20]

While their business flourished in Uganda during Amin's last months of power, Wilson was meanwhile expanding his explosives business with Qaddafi. He had found a Pomona, California, explosives manufacturer, Jerome S. Brower, to supply the Libyans. Brower also began recruiting bomb experts for Libya. At least two of them—Robert E. Swallow and Dennis J. Wilson (unrelated to Edwin Wilson)—were civilian employees of the U.S. Navy's secret China Lake Naval Weapons Center in the Mojave Desert in California, where the CIA and the Navy both test sensitive weapons and electronic devices. Swallow and Dennis Wilson spent their annual leave in 1977 at Edwin Wilson's guerrilla training site in Libya, working for Qaddafi. Both returned to their China Lake jobs without bothering to report on where they had been or what they had been doing. In 1981 a federal grand jury in Fresno, California, indicted six men on charges of stealing night-vision scopes, a low-light television camera ideal for night surveillance work, and a remote-control, James-Bond-type helicopter from China Lake. Federal investigators found strong indications that the equipment had gone to Libya.[21]

Actually, Wilson and Terpil had been selling such equipment to Qaddafi, usually at great profit, for some time, without obtaining the legal clearance documents needed from the State Department's Office of Munitions Control and the export control division of the U.S. Department of Commerce. One prototype U.S. Army vehicle with night-surveillance equipment, which Qaddafi needed for night work on Libya's borders, was first sent to Canada and transshipped to Libya. It cost Wilson and Terpil $60,000 in the United States; they sold it to Qaddafi for $990,000. Infrared night-vision scopes for snipers' rifles also went by the hundreds to Qaddafi and other buyers, some probably front men for terrorist groups.[22]

The word had spread earlier among international arms dealers that night-vision devices were items for which Qaddafi, with his love of gimmicks, would pay fabulous prices. Qaddafi's security services were especially eager to get the Startron device manufactured in the United States by Smith and Wesson, and used with devastating effect in Vietnam and also by the Israelis in the 1973 war. It magnifies stray light rays 65,000 times, and illuminates objects up to 600 yards away. Competing devices are produced in France, Sweden, Switzerland, and the Soviet Union. Palestinian, IRA, and other guerrillas hoped to obtain them from Libya, and almost certainly did. The American Startron is strictly regulated; one of the main items on the State Department's Munitions List, its shipment requires an export license.

In 1975 two Frenchmen, Georges Starkmann and Claude Demont, resolved to get a piece of the Libyan arms action for themselves before Terpil, Wilson & Co. got it all. They started out by rounding up 110 authentic Startrons in France and selling them to Libya for $7,000 each. They easily obtained export licenses, since France did not then recognize or apply the U.S. ban on their export. To handle the transactions, Starkmann and Demont created a phony company they called Régie Monceau.

Qaddafi's military, though delighted with their 110 Startrons, had originally ordered 300. When Demont and Starkmann tried to supply the remaining 190, French authorities clamped down and prohibited their export to Libya—there was at the time considerable tension in French-Libyan relations, partly because of Qaddafi's intrigues against the French-supported regime in Chad. Qaddafi increased the original order for 300 Startrons to 3,000 for a total price of $15,282,000. Seeing fortune within their grasp, the two Frenchmen mounted an elaborate scam: they got an optical-instruments manufacturer in France to prepare 3,000 fake Startrons—black metal tubes with very ordinary glass, but looking exactly like the real thing—for $96,000. French customs inspectors checked out the shipment while it was still in the warehouse and apparently passed it for export.

The black tubes were shipped to Madrid. There, a Libyan purchasing agent verified the count, and cabled approval for release of the $15,282,000 payment to the account of Demont and Starkmann in the Zurich branch of the Bank of America. After the money had been paid over to the two entrepreneurs, the Libyans discovered that the tubes were, as they put it, "not in conformity with the specifications" and shipped them back to Paris. Régie Monceau next informed the Libyans that the French authorities had discovered and banned the shipment and confiscated the genuine goods. By the time Qaddafi's men discovered how they had been swindled, Demont and Starkmann had already started another deal for nonexistent U.S.-designed 155 and 175 mm. cannons for $151 million. French newspapers reported that a partial payment of $60 million had already been deposited in Zurich.[23]

The Startron swindle was certainly one of the factors in Qaddafi's decision to rely more and more on Wilson and Terpil for gimmickry, and on the Soviets for heavy arms. Even their wares, however, were far from perfect: in July 1976 John Henry Harper, the former CIA ordnance expert, demonstrated ten timing devices sent to Libya by the American group. Two of the timers failed, apparently because Harper had miswired them. Later, some exploded at the wrong time. Nevertheless, the Libyans ordered 100,000 and then increased their order to 300,000. A Texas firm, Scientific Communications, which had already handled many similar contracts for the CIA, agreed to provide the timers. Joe Halpain, the firm's director, personally delivered the timers, hidden in plastic pharmaceutical containers, to a motel near the Langley headquarters of the CIA. Mulcahy and Wilson picked them up there.

Arranging export of the explosives was more difficult: TNT and plastic explosives could not legally be shipped on passenger or cargo planes. Wilson and Terpil contacted Jerome S. Brower in California. Wilson and Terpil assuaged Brower's fears, and paid him $38,000 as a down payment to prepare and pack the chemicals for shipping to Libya. RDX, the most sensitive of the explosives, was sent to Washington's Dulles Airport, marked "industrial solvent." It was packed into one freight container with the tools and workbenches needed for the Libyan explosives laboratory, and shipped without knowledge of Lufthansa to Frankfurt, and on from there to Libya.[24]

One item that guerrilla and terrorist groups from the Palestinians in Lebanon to the Polisario guerrillas fighting the Moroccan army in the Sahara urgently wanted was a good shoulder-launched antiaircraft missile. An al-Fatah operative in Beirut as far back as 1968 said that the Palestinians would pay very large sums for the Short "Blowpipe" missile, or its copy, manufactured in Communist China (eventually they obtained the SAM-7 "Strela" Soviet missile in large quantities instead).[25] Somehow, however, Qaddafi's ordnance experts decided that the U.S. General Dynamics "Redeye" was the missile for them, and probably also for the Palestinian, Irish, Filipino, South African, and myriad other guerrilla groups that were by now Libya's clients.

In late August of 1976, Kevin Mulcahy was on a business trip to Copenhagen when he received an urgent cable from Terpil and Wilson in Libya to return to Washington and open negotiations with General Dynamics, Redeye's manufacturer, for purchase of one of the heat-seeking missiles, whose export to Libya and most other countries was and still is banned. Mulcahy told Hersh that a foreign military attaché in Denmark warned him that Qaddafi could want a Redeye only for a terrorist attack, and "we speculated that Qaddafi probably wanted to be first to shoot down a 747."[26]

Mulcahy never went through with the Redeye commission from Terpil and Wilson. It was at this point that he flew back to Washington and began to fill in the federal authorities on what was going on in Libya. After a year of inquiries, the Foreign Agents Registration Office of the Justice Department decided in December 1977 that Wilson and Terpil, despite "nefarious" business activities, had broken no American laws. This prompted an assistant United States attorney named Eugene M. Propper, who wanted to pursue the matter further, to get Mulcahy to give his evidence on Wilson and Terpil to a grand jury. Still, however, the investigation dragged on interminably until 1978. The Federal Bureau of Alcohol, Tobacco and Firearms assigned two of its investigators, Richard Wadsworth and Richard Pedersen, to investigate whether Wilson and Terpil could have broken laws inside the District of Columbia in their dealings with Libya. In early June of 1979, after Wilson and Terpil had spent some of their earnings to buy over $4 million worth of real estate in England and the United States including a hotel in Crewe, England, and a townhouse in Lancaster Mews in London, the U.S. Attorney's Office told Wadsworth and Pedersen that there was not enough evidence to charge Wilson and Terpil with illegally exporting prohibited explosives to Libya. But a newly assigned U.S. attorney, Lawrence Barcella, authorized the two persistent investigators to go over Brower's records again. This time, they found evidence of the summer 1976 explosives shipments. Brower agreed to cooperate with the government, and eventually got only a four-month prison sentence, which he finished serving in 1981.

Terpil and Wilson continued their travels to and from Libya. On

September 1, 1979, among the guests invited by Qaddafi for his revolution's tenth anniversary were Billy Carter and President Carter's sister, Ruth. Brother Billy, who was yet to get his well-publicized $220,000 loan from Libya, later told congressional investigators that on that occasion, Terpil was on hand to describe and interpret for him at the parade of military equipment Qaddafi proudly held for his guests. By this time, as *The New York Times* disclosed in October 1981, Wilson was actively recruiting U.S. pilots for Qaddafi's civil airlines, though the Carter family may have ignored this.

Less than four months later, at the end of December 1979, Terpil and George Gregory Korkalla, another associate in the Libyan business, were arrested in New York. This was the end of an undercover operation, not by the U.S. federal authorities but by New York City police. Two New York detectives had posed as agents for a Latin American revolutionary group eager to purchase any kind of weapons. Manhattan District Attorney Robert M. Morgenthau, who ran the investigation, acquired two hours of taped conversations in which Terpil boasted to the undercover agents of his three years of work for Libya and of his team of former Green Berets willing to travel anywhere to train terrorists.

Puzzled by the slowness or reluctance of Washington officials to pursue the case, and hampered by the unwillingness of almost everyone except Mulcahy to discuss the Qaddafi-CIA connection, the New York authorities arraigned Terpil and Korkalla on the arms-traffic charges, then released them on bail after they pleaded not guilty.

Finally, after persistent work by Barcella with Mulcahy's support, Wadsworth and Pedersen arrested Terpil as he was attending a security equipment show at the Secret Service training academy in Maryland. Terpil, Wilson, and Brower were all indicted for conspiracy to export equipment in contravention of federal law. A federal magistrate reduced Terpil's initial bond from $500,000 to $75,000, of which only $15,000 had to be cash—not a difficult amount for anyone on Qaddafi's payroll to raise. On September 3, 1980, the day before he was supposed to stand trial on the New York firearms charges, Terpil, unchallenged and with a valid passport, flew to Europe, then on to Beirut, where he was spotted in a small hotel owned by a Viennese couple.[27]

In July 1981 a *Newsweek* reporter, Elaine Sciolino, visited Tripoli for a Qaddafi interview and a cover story on Libya, and found Wilson using "a two-story luxury villa as a home and office; most of his assistants are American Vietnam veterans." He was, said *Newsweek*, "a charming and gregarious man in a polyester safari suit." Wilson asserted that he had never met Qaddafi. He said he was just "a little man here, a man who runs a business . . . trying to promote American products where we can—things like clothing and nonlethal, nonoffensive military equipment. . . . I've never seen a terrorist in my life and I wouldn't know what one looked like."[28]

The question asked by intelligence insiders in Washington, London, Bonn, Paris, and many other places was whether the CIA would know either.

There is one crucial main area in which Qaddafi's early CIA connections have exercised no influence, or next to none, over his support of guerrilla and liberation causes—his advocacy of the cause of the liberation of Palestine and his support for the Palestinian armed guerrilla movement. Qaddafi's relationship with the mainstream leadership of the Palestine Liberation Organization, and indeed with most of the individual guerrilla organizations inside and outside the PLO, has been a difficult and uneasy one at best. There were many reasons for this, but the most fundamental one has been Qaddafi's belief that Yasir Arafat, leader of the largest and most conservative Palestinian group, al-Fatah (Arafat became chairman of the PLO after the 1967 Arab-Israeli war, even before Qaddafi took power in Libya), is interested in negotiating a compromise peace with Israel. Qaddafi believes, in fact, that Arafat is the Anwar al-Sadat of the Palestinians.

Since the relationships between Libya and the PLO have become so important for the future of Mideast and perhaps world peace, it is worth moving backward in time for a look at the Libyan-Palestinian relationship. Like Libya's oil boom, this was not something born with Qaddafi, but rather a phenomenon he inherited from the Libyan monarchy. Although the Algerian nationalist leadership had established early working contacts with Arafat and the other leaders of al-Fatah, the Palestinians found uneasy and sporadic support in Libya.

Even after the Arab League created the PLO in 1964, al-Fatah was a clandestine organization. In late 1964 it sent emissaries to a number of the Arab countries to seek support and advice on Fatah's plan to launch the first guerrilla operations against Israel—a plan that was to begin with an attack on the main Israeli water pipeline on January 1, 1965. When two of Arafat's principal aides, Salah Khalef (alias Abu Ayad) and Farouk Kaddoumi (Abu Lotf),[29] visited Libya on that important survey trip, King Idris refused to receive them at Beyda and instead delegated

Prime Minister Abdel Hamid Bakkouche. Their reception from him was extremely hostile. Their movement, he told them, would lead to nothing, and would certainly not free Palestine from Israeli rule. The only reason he was receiving them, Bakkouche added, was that the popularity of the Palestinian cause and their resulting wide support in Libya obliged him to. "Unfortunately," he told them, "the Libyans are a people of imbeciles."

Abu Ayad's recollection of the meeting to Eric Rouleau is that he replied to Bakkouche that, in that case, they would make the Libyan prime minister's opinion of his own people public at once, and there was no need to continue the conversation. Abu Lotf then reminded Bakkouche that he understood nothing of the Palestinian cause and held his own people in contempt, even though he, Bakkouche, had been a Communist during his student years. Libyans, Abu Lotf added, were well aware that Abdel Hamid Bakkouche had taken part in shady arms deals. The prime minister immediately changed his tone, offered his visitors coffee, and told them to come back and see him in his Tripoli office to determine how Libya could help them. The Libyan popular committees formed earlier then proceeded to collect about $30,000. Bakkouche received them cordially in Tripoli, and they left for points east with a total of almost $100,000 in Libyan dinars, which they badly needed at the time—and which was probably more than they could then get from even enthusiastic supporters such as Algeria.[30]

By the time Qaddafi came to power, the Palestinian resistance movement had already emerged in the wake of the 1967 war, and had fought and lost some of its most dramatic battles against Israel. None of the Arab governments hosting or supporting the PLO and its guerrilla groups had been willing to play the role of a North Vietnam or Cambodia in supporting a truly widespread "popular resistance war" à la Vietnam against Israel. Probably realizing that the PLO faced a showdown with King Hussein of Jordan, whose own country was the target of constant Israeli retaliation for the attacks of the *fedayeen* across the Jordan River, and that the regimes of Jordan, Lebanon, and other "reactionary" Arab states were threatened as a result, Qaddafi in early 1970 established in Libya a *jihad*, or holy war, fund to help sustain the Palestinians. It was supported by an 8 percent payroll tax on the ten thousand or more Palestinians employed in Libya. Within another year or two, after visits by leaders of al-Fatah and the politically far more radical Popular Front for the Liberation of Palestine (PFLP) of George Habbash, training camps were set up under his personal supervision. It is possible, though by no means certain, that Edwin Wilson, Frank Terpil, and other Americans were involved later in the training done in these camps, chiefly at Tokra, Tajjuna (also to be the site of the Soviet-supplied experimental nuclear reactor, outside Tripoli near the former Wheelus Field), Misurata, and Qaddafi's home region of Sirte. It was probably at Tajjuna that Carlos did his brief period of work for Qaddafi, though not under the auspices of the main PLO guerrilla organizations.

During the earliest months of his regime, Qaddafi struck the al-Fatah leadership as a man, in Abu Ayad's words, with a "poor knowledge of Arab affairs, but great enthusiasm for the Palestinian cause." When King Hussein launched his showdown offensive against the guerrillas in Jordan, in Black September of 1970, Qaddafi raged and railed against Hussein's "treachery" and, as we saw earlier, appeared, wearing a revolver, at the peace conference called in Cairo by the already dying Nasser. Earlier he had assured Abu Ayad, "Let Nasser betray the [Palestinian] cause or not, I'll always be with him."[31] During the first months of the Sadat era in Egypt, Qaddafi stood by the Palestinians, despite his impatience at their relative inactivity.

But by early 1973, when it looked as though Arab fortunes were at their lowest ebb, and relations were growing strained between Qaddafi and most other Arab regimes, he began to criticize the PLO leadership harshly. In an interview with a Beirut newspaper in February 1973, Qaddafi said the Arab forces, including the Palestinians, had lacked courage in the 1967 fighting and deserved death, whereas Israeli forces had shown courage and a bold military initiative and had therefore deserved victory. At the same time, Qaddafi's "cultural revolution," following the principles of *The Green Book*, was starting in Libya, creating administrative turmoil and confusion and causing the temporary closing of some of the training camps.[32]

Another reason for the cooling of relations with some of the Palestinian groups during this early period was their leftist ideology and propaganda, in particular that of the PFLP of George Habbash. Sometime in 1972, Qaddafi appears to have formed his own Palestinian guerrilla group, composed mainly of discontented militants of some of these groups, as well as of al-Fatah's clandestine arm, Black September, who were anxious to move from ideology and propaganda to more effective terrorist acts. The result was an organization called National Arab Youth for the Liberation of Palestine (NAYLP). Its leader was neither Palestinian nor Libyan, but rather a Lebanese named Ahmed al-Ghaffour, formerly a close associate of Arafat's, and sent by him as a PLO representative to Libya. Disapproving of Arafat's growing accent on diplomacy and international political maneuvering (as opposed to terrorism), Ghaffour deserted and helped Qaddafi set up NAYLP. It was probably the group behind a machine-gun attack on passengers preparing to board a TWA flight at Athens airport on August 5, 1973, in which three passengers were killed and fifty-five wounded. Another of NAYLP's squads threw two thermite bombs into a Pan American World Airways plane at Rome airport on December 17, 1973, killing thirty-two people and wounding eighteen. The attackers hijacked another plane to Kuwait, and surrendered there and told the Kuwait police that Qaddafi himself had ordered the attack as a substitute for another plan to assassinate Secretary of State Henry Kissinger.

Eventually NAYLP appears to have split up and its members moved into other groups. Al-Fatah held a trial of Ghaffour in absentia and condemned him to death. However, Ghaffour was so sure that Qaddafi would protect him that he ignored the death sentence and returned to Beirut. There he was captured by al-Fatah security men and was probably executed; in any case, he was not heard from again.

Hostility between al-Fatah and Qaddafi continued through the period of the October 1973 war. One of the reasons, as Palestinian leaders in Beirut told me at the time, was the improvement in relations between the PLO and the Soviet Union (Qaddafi's ties with the USSR had not yet warmed up to the point they had reached in May 1974, when Jalloud made his first arms-buying visit). Following the October 1973 war, when Libya and Iraq both supported the new "rejection front" of Arab states opposed to a separate Egypt-Israel peace settlement, Qaddafi and Iraqi leader Seddam Hussein both suspended their aid to al-Fatah again.

The great tide in the affairs of the PLO came with the 1973 war. Whereas the aftermath of the 1967 war had seen the Palestinians emerge in Arab folklore, popular arts, and even literature as a force in the Arab world, the 1973 war gave them international political standing. By the fall of 1979, 106 governments had given the PLO some form of recognition of its claim, confirmed by the Arab summit conference in Rabat in 1974, to be the "sole legitimate representative of the Palestinian people."

Qaddafi's relations with the PLO, however, continued to be troubled. Largely ignoring the mainstream leadership, he gave money and arms to the PFLP, to the Democratic Front for the Liberation of Palestine

(DFLP) of Nayef Hawatmeh, to the PFLP-General Command of Ahmed Jibril, and to other smaller groups. After ideological hostility toward Hawatmeh's group, caused by Hawatmeh's endorsement of the mainstream PLO program for a "two state" system in Palestine— implying peaceful coexistence of Israel and a future Palestinian Arab state in the Jordan West Bank and Gaza—Hawatmeh visited Qaddafi in Tripoli and restored their relations. For the first time, the DFLP opened an office in Libya. In May 1976 the PFLP newspaper in Beirut, *Al-Ahdaf*, praised Libya as the only Arab country truly willing to support the "rejectionist" forces against the idea of a political settlement. George Habbash began to visit Tripoli again, and Libyan funds apparently flowed once more to the PFLP.[34]

During the Egypt–Israel–United States and the Syria–United States–Israel disengagement talks that had followed the 1973 war until the conclusion of the second Sinai accord in September 1975, neither Libya nor the PLO had been able to exercise much influence on the course of events. Then Sadat's Jerusalem visit threw the entire Arab world into an uproar. Arafat and his chief aides attended the "rejectionist" Arab summit conference in Tripoli December 2–5, 1977. With the Libyans, the PLO agreed to establish a "united front" of Libya, Syria, Iraq, Algeria, and the People's Democratic Republic of Yemen (South Yemen) to stand against "capitulation to imperialists, Zionists and those Arabs serving them" (chiefly Sadat). Iraq was condemned (though not by name) for attending the conference and then opposing creation of the front. UN Security Council resolutions 242 and 338, under which all Mideast nations would have the right to peaceful existence within recognized boundaries once Israel had withdrawn to its 1967 borders, were rejected, as were all international committees or conferences based on those resolutions. The Tripoli summit also agreed on "action to implement the right of the Palestinian people to return [to Palestine] and to self-determination in the framework of a national independent state in each part of Palestinian land that will be liberated —without granting peace or recognition or involvement in negotiation." Finally, a boycott was imposed on Sadat's regime in Egypt, resulting in the breaking of diplomatic relations by most Arab governments with Egypt.[35]

Though Libya and the PLO leadership could agree on all these points, what they could not agree on was the PLO's expressed determination to pursue a two-track policy: continuing to fight and to oppose all those favoring association with the Egypt–Israel–United States process while pursuing simultaneously a political line that encouraged contacts with any Western elements willing to listen to the Palestine case, with the ultimate purpose of a dialogue with the United States. It was this latter course that Qaddafi could not stomach.

What actually transpired at that Tripoli conference has been related by Rouleau and Abu Ayad, and illustrates the problems between Qaddafi and Arafat. In the presence of President Houari Boumedienne of Algeria, Qaddafi told Arafat at Tripoli airport that he refused to greet him, and that "Sadat had been able to fly to Israel [in November], thanks to an airplane with one wing bearing the insignia of Hafez Assad (President of Syria) and the other with that of Yasir Arafat." [In other words, according to Qaddafi, both Syria and the PLO had acquiesced in, or helped make possible, Sadat's peace mission—a patently absurd charge.][36]

Arafat was so furious at this that he shouted at Qaddafi and tried to drive to the Tunisian border, where he was intercepted and returned to the conference by the Libyan police. When Major Jalloud, on the conference floor, backed the uncompromisingly Palestinian revolutionary line of George Habbash, Abu Ayad challenged the Arab presidents present to go out and talk with their own domestic opponents, since they were obliging the PLO to spread out its own internal problems on the table for all to see.

Next, Qaddafi tried to persuade President Assad of Syria to renounce UN resolutions 242 and 338. This would have been tantamount to denouncing Assad's own cease-fire with Israel. With strong support from President Boumedienne, Assad said there was no point in this. Resolution 242, he recalled, was not the cause of President Sadat's journey to Jerusalem. Nasser himself, whom Qaddafi so admired, had supported 242 in the UN Security Council without prostrating himself before the Israelis. Assad and Boumedienne won their point; Qaddafi lost his.[37]

In a way, the dispute between the PLO and Libya that developed after this became the most serious of any of the many PLO quarrels with an Arab government. This was because Qaddafi challenged the PLO's status as the sole representative of the Palestinians—recognized since the 1974 Rabat Arab summit by virtually all Arab regimes, including that of King Hussein of Jordan, who was the ruler most directly concerned.

In a long interview with *Der Spiegel*, Abu Ayad explained on behalf of Arafat:

*We have had a long history of dispute with Qaddafi since 1975. . . . He always wants us to do his bidding fully. We have to be the friends of his friends and the enemies of his enemies . . . what he wants is a paid revolution and he treats us like paid mercenaries. He never abided by the decisions made at the different Arab summit meetings to give us financial support. He is moody. If you do not satisfy him, you get a kick. He owes us contributions amounting to between $80 and $90 million. However, we are not prepared to submit to any Arab capital. . . .* [38]

One of the immediate causes of the embittering of this dispute was Qaddafi's accusation that the PLO had neglected the principles of its revolution, and that it was therefore unfit to represent the Palestinian people. He ordered closure of PLO and al-Fatah offices in Tripoli and Benghazi. He called on Palestinians, in Libya and elsewhere, to establish "People's Councils" and "Revolutionary Committees" along Libyan lines to represent Palestinians. At the November 1979 Arab summit, Qaddafi charged, the PLO had "surrendered" to demands of Arab moderates that it suspend operations against Israel from across the Lebanese border. A revolution, he said, could not be restricted by laws; it should instead fight to the end regardless of them. Qaddafi pointed out that the best tactics to be adopted by the Arabs would be to threaten navigation in the Suez Canal and at the entrance of the Red Sea. Ships carrying goods to Israel, he added, should be hit and Arab oil "should be destroyed, if it is not used for the liberation of Palestine."[39]

Shortly after this, Major Jalloud flew to Beirut for meetings with Jibril, Habbash, Dr. Samir Kushah of the Palestine Popular Struggle Front and Majid Hassan, a leader of Syria's Palestinian organization, *al-Saiqa*—all organizations that shared Libya's interest in weakening Arafat and ending al-Fatah control of the PLO.

In a throwback perhaps to their earlier reported quarrel over Arafat's refusal to become involved in efforts to neutralize Omar al-Meheishi, the PLO now complained that Libyan security personnel had surrounded and were "besieging" PLO and al-Fatah offices in Libya. The Libyans denied this, claiming the "besiegers" were Palestinians who had formed revolutionary committees as Qaddafi had urged them to do.

Al-Fatah responded with an editorial in its newspaper, *Filastin al-Thawrah*, on December 11, 1979. It was "sad," the editorial said, that Colonel Qaddafi had expelled the PLO representative and not the

U.S. ambassador, and had apologized for the burning of the U.S. embassy in Tripoli December 2 while claiming this had been done by Palestinians who had "infiltrated" the demonstrators. The accusation, said al-Fatah, was unfounded: "Those who burned the U.S. Embassy are . . . heroic Libyans who reject these showy demonstrations organized by Qaddafi and his intelligence services who dare not touch the huge U.S. interests in Libya."[40]

Major Jalloud set out to mediate the dispute, and Syria tried to help in the person of its foreign minister, Abdel Halim Khaddam, who announced that the problem had been solved. It hadn't been, because on January 8, 1980, Libya announced the breaking of all ties with al-Fatah. An uneasy compromise was finally reached at the fourth "rejectionist" summit in Tripoli, April 13–15, 1980. Through persistent lobbying, the Syrians secured Qaddafi's reluctant consent to al-Fatah's attendance, and sent Arafat to Tripoli in Assad's personal plane. At first Qaddafi refused to let Arafat into the conference hall and made no mention of the PLO in his keynote speech. Then, after more conciliation, Arafat pledged to Qaddafi that he would follow the "revolutionary line," whatever that meant, in the future. The conference resolutions recognized the PLO as sole representative of the Palestinian people, as before, but not unconditionally. This time it was recognized as "the leader of the armed struggle of the Palestinian people"—with stress on this—as well as its legitimate representative.[41]

Though apparently Qaddafi and Arafat still cannot stand one another, al-Fatah was able to operate to a limited degree in Libya in 1981; still, there was no indication that Qaddafi was meeting his arrears in payments. In June and July 1981, Israel's air attacks on the Iraqi nuclear reactor near Baghdad and on the Palestinians and Lebanese in Beirut and South Lebanon stirred some brief demonstrations of unity. Arafat, who spends better than half his working time seeking to mediate conflicts between Arab and Islamic rulers (even in the conflict between Iraq and Iran), acted as point man for a reconciliation between Qaddafi and King Hassan of Morocco. Hassan's support for the Arab cause in Palestine—such as sending about seven thousand Moroccan troops to fight Israel in the Golan Heights in October 1973 and chairing the Jerusalem Committee established by a summit conference of the Islamic states in 1978—was tempered by his encouragement to Sadat and Israel to talk over their peace moves secretly in Morocco in 1977. In the summer of 1981, Arafat's mediation seemed to work: Qaddafi suspended arms aid to the Polisario guerrillas fighting Morocco in the

Western Sahara. Hassan and Qaddafi halted propaganda attacks on each other and reestablished diplomatic relations, to the discomfiture of both Algeria and the Polisario. At two important conferences, Hassan relaxed his previous pressure on Qaddafi to clear out of Chad.

Yasir Arafat, never at home in Libya, had thus eased the way for Muammar al-Qaddafi to overcome the objections of many African states, and become chairman of the African Unity Organization (OAU) in 1982. What Qaddafi could or would do for the PLO, during the next round of conflict that seemed to be brewing in the Mideast following President Sadat's murder, remained to be seen.

**M**uch has been written and reported about Qaddafi and terrorism. What can finally be separated from the mass of hearsay, second- and thirdhand accounts, propaganda and disinformation, are a few generalities. Qaddafi, like other world leaders of his time, has not hesitated to use Libyans or hired foreigners to eliminate, upon occasion, his enemies at home and abroad, often by violent means. In Europe, for example, about ten Libyans who opposed him, mostly people of modest station who played no important role in the Libyan political opposition, were murdered between March and June 1980, when Qaddafi seems to have called a halt to the killings and indirectly disavowed the zealotry of the "hit teams," which he claimed were activated not by him but the Libyan "revolutionary councils." Over the years, terrorists or guerrillas trained and/or funded in Libya are known to have operated in Europe, the Arab world, and possibly in North America, though at this writing the shooting of a Libyan student in Fort Collins, Colorado, in November 1980 by former U.S. Green Beret Eugene Tafoya had not finished its slow passage through the courts of law, and neither the CIA's relationship nor Libya's connection with Tafoya had been clarified. Tafoya had been convicted for attempted manslaughter, but his jail sentence was appealed.

In Africa, Qaddafi's support of "terrorism" has most often been connected, as we shall see in some detail later on, with aiding well-established African liberation movements, as well as with help to dissidents trained in Qaddafi's "Islamic Legion" to subvert and overthrow their home governments, when and if opportunities arise.

Qaddafi has often denied that he supports international terrorism. He has tried to turn the tables by accusing the United States of being the "chief terrorist" through what he sees as its bullying of Libya, Cuba, and other countries. In 1978, after considerable pressure from the Carter administration, and obviously hoping to gain release of embargoed American aircraft, Qaddafi signed an international antihijacking convention. Since then, and until this writing, he has apparently abided by this: no hijacked planes have been allowed to land in Libya, and there are no publicly recorded cases since then of hijackers taking refuge in Libya. The activities of Carlos and other international terrorists who operated briefly out of Libya in the mid-1970s seem to have been centered elsewhere.

By contrast, Qaddafi has continued to aid with funds and training (though probably to a lesser extent than other Arab states including Algeria and Saudi Arabia) the PLO and its various guerrilla groups, despite his poor opinion of the PLO leadership and its goals. In the case of Palestine, probably no existing Palestinian guerrilla group, whether dependent upon the PLO or upon an Arab government or governments, could be "pure" and fanatical enough to satisfy Qaddafi. His most recent concentration on only two matters he apparently considers of the utmost importance, Palestine and the inclusion of Chad in a Libyan-dominated power system, seems to indicate that he has let drop, one by one, the causes less important to him: the IRA in Northern Ireland, the Moros in the southern Philippines, and Basque, Corsican, and other "ethnic" causes in Western Europe.

If Qaddafi's image as a Daddy Warbucks of world terrorism (to use Claire Sterling's phrase) is an unfair one to pin on the Libyan leader (and it is obviously one he wants to get away from if he can), then perhaps this image can be ascribed to a combination of two factors. First, in his early, most idealistic days, Qaddafi probably made little distinction, if any, between "bad" terrorists and "good" freedom fighters, but has since become more sensitive to Western views on the subject. Second, the information media of both the Western and Third Worlds are constantly in search of villains, and are inclined to overplay one when they find one. The unproved charges in December 1981 that Qaddafi had infiltrated "hit teams" into the U.S. to murder President Reagan and other American leaders did little to change the minds of either Qaddafi's friends or his foes. On Muammar al-Qaddafi and his final place in the history of world terrorism and guerrilla warfare, the final verdict is not yet in.

# NINE

## THE EXPORT OF THE REVOLUTION

If you take the drive into Tripoli from its international airport, you will pass a large ocher stone and plaster building capped with attractive green tile domes in the old Libyan-Arab-Ottoman style. This palace, partially obscured from the access road by gardens, was a favorite of King Idris before he lost his throne to Qaddafi in 1969. Now it is called the People's Palace. Most noticeable about it now are the odd antennae that sprout all over it and the web of attached wires and cables.

Since the late 1970s, the palace has been the main seat of the Arab Liaison Bureau. With its own elaborate telecommunications system, the Bureau has become a kind of foreign ministry (the old one was abolished with the coming of "people's government" in 1977), dealing mainly with the foreign "bureaus," which replaced the older Libyan embassies. In non-Arab countries like the United States and France, these embassies were called People's Bureaus, in Arab countries they were Brotherhood Bureaus. In late 1981, the function of relations with foreign countries in general had been taken over by Abdel 'Ati al-Abaidi, one of Qaddafi's stalwart supporters from early RCC days; he headed the *Maktub al-Iktissal*, the Foreign Liaison Bureau. One of its functions was to deal with non-Arab foreign guests; another was to send emissaries on cryptodiplomatic and goodwill missions abroad, such as those performed by Ahmed al-Shahati, who dealt with Billy Carter.

Intelligence professionals insist that both the Arab Liaison Bureau and the Foreign Liaison Bureau have other, more sinister functions as well—to recruit agents of influence and professionals in propaganda, subversion, and sabotage, and to send arms, munitions, and sabotage devices imported to Libya or developed in Libya through Libyan diplomatic pouches to overseas destinations.

Covering both the Arab and the Foreign Liaison Bureaus, and working in close concert with Qaddafi's military intelligence and security services, is the *Maktub Tasdir al-Thawra*. This means, literally, "Bureau for the Export of the Revolution." Its directing brain trust is composed of top associates of Qaddafi, ideologues utterly devoted to him and to the principles of *The Green Book*. They carefully scan the words and actions of statesmen, parliamentarians, congressmen, newsmen, editors, commentators, businessmen, and academics the world over for signs of sympathy toward Qaddafi personally and toward the Libyan revolution in general; and then they try to cultivate the most pro-Qaddafi among them. Ahmed al-Shahati and, probably, Ali al-Houdery, the last chargé d'affaires of the Libyan People's Bureau in Washington before the Bureau was expelled in June 1981, have been members.

In more recent years, as Qaddafi's arms deals with the Soviets and his series of technology and oil deals with the East bloc have increased, the Bureau for the Export of the Revolution has undoubtedly had more to do with the Soviet, East German, Cuban, Czech, and other East bloc experts sent to Libya.

After looking at Qaddafi's various misconceived and failed union efforts with Egypt, the Sudan, Tunisia, and most recently Syria, it is easier to understand how and why the efforts of the Bureau for the Export of the Revolution have turned increasingly to Qaddafi's non-Arab Black African neighbors, especially the predominantly Muslim ones or those with large Muslim minorities.

The Bureau for the Export of the Revolution has one principal adversary in the sub-Saharan states of Black Africa, its widest field of operation. That adversary is not the American CIA, nor was it President Sadat of Egypt, nor is it President Nimeiry of the Sudan. It is, rather, France. In Chad, the only African country overtly invaded by Libyan forces, and in a cluster of other French-speaking black states, France has tried to defend local independence as well as its own remaining (and major) strategic and economic interests. To understand what has happened in Chad and the other African countries that are the objects of Qaddafi's attention, it is first necessary to understand the background of the Franco-Libyan confrontation.

France's long and lucrative but generally uneasy diplomatic and commercial relationships with Libya have been played out against a somber background of covert action by her intelligence services and mercenaries in Africa. Just as Qaddafi has used former American Green Beret and CIA operatives, he has also used French hired help, especially during his lengthy involvement in Chad. At the same time France—a secret de facto ally of Egypt—has sought Qaddafi's destabilization and downfall.

North Africa, especially Algeria and its two flanking former French protectorates, Tunisia and Morocco, has always been a principal focus of French intelligence and covert activities in the Arab world. Reinforcing the history of defending direct French strategic interests in the area is the tradition of clandestine Free French-U.S.-British collaboration in North Africa during World War II, after the Allied landings of the November 1942 "Operation Torch" in Morocco, Algeria, and Tunisia.

During his exile years in London, Charles de Gaulle set up his own separate Gaullist security and intelligence network, the Bureau Central des Renseignements et de l'Action. The Free French forces working with the Allies in North Africa, meanwhile, established their own military counterintelligence service based in Algiers. Yet a third Free French resistance network, the Direction Générale des Services Spéciaux (DGSS) existed too. After France's liberation, the three organizations were merged into a single service that later became known as the Service de Documentation Extérieure et du Contre-Espionage (SDECE). Frenchmen and intelligence professionals of other countries often refer to it today as the "Sedick" (stress on the second syllable). The SDECE is the closest thing France has to the American CIA or the British SIS (Secret Intelligence Service). Since the election of French Socialist President François Mitterand in May 1981, the chief of SDECE has been former Air France director Pierre Marion, a staunch Socialist and close friend of Mitterand.

The SDECE's mandate since its founding has been "to seek, outside national boundaries, all information and documents that might inform the French government." Inside France, counterespionage and internal security operations are supposed to be carried out by the Défense et Sécurité du Territoire (DST). Like the American FBI, the DST has the power to arrest; the SDECE, like the CIA, is not supposed to operate internally and does not have the power to arrest. In practice, the DST and the SDECE have often been rivals, trying to operate in each other's territory, especially in what was formerly French North Africa.[1]

At the outbreak of the Algerian revolution in 1954, the main concern of both SDECE and the DST became the cutting off of arms supplies that flowed from Egypt, Libya, Tunisia, Morocco, and Europe to the Algerian National Liberation Front (FLN). During the earlier years of the Algerian war, before de Gaulle returned to power in France in 1958, the French agencies worked closely with Israel's Mossad. There was a strong community of sympathy and interests between the French Socialist governments of those days and Israel; after all, as the DST's Roger Wybot recalls in his memoirs, in 1947 French agents helped Jewish intelligence in Europe against Britain's SIS, which was then trying to track and neutralize the terrorist Stern Gang, Irgun Zvai Leumi, and other Zionist groups operating in British-ruled Palestine.[2]

The British, Israeli, and French services were all cooperating closely to unseat Nasser (then being aided by the Soviets) when Nasser nationalized the Suez Canal in 1956. The nationalization provoked an Anglo-Israeli-French attack on Egypt. When that operation failed, Socialist SDECE chief Pierre Boursicot, who had also failed to prevent Libya's Prime Minister ben Halim from supplying the Algerian FLN with arms, was replaced by a military man, General Paul Grossin. As the Algerian war progressed, French intelligence and Mossad collaborated to great effect, as when French warships intercepted the *Athos*, a ship loaded with arms for the FLN heading through the Mediterranean from Alexandria. The SDECE suspected the CIA of pro-Algerian sympathies, especially after Senator John F. Kennedy in 1957 publicly declared in favor of Algerian independence, and after the rightist French press in spring 1961 accused the CIA—wrongly, as it happened—of supporting the attempted Algerian putsch by French generals to overthrow de Gaulle.

As de Gaulle skillfully and shrewdly managed Algeria's disengagement from its French motherland between 1958 and the mass exodus of the French from Algeria in 1962, France and her security services moved slowly away from Israel and toward collaboration with the Arab world. By the time Qaddafi's group controlled Libya in late 1969, Gaullist France was growing hostile toward both the United States (de Gaulle had already quit NATO's military wing) and the Soviet Union, and was trying to steer France along a more independent course. As SDECE's links with Libya, Egypt, and other Arab countries slowly improved, they correspondingly worsened with Israel's Mossad. At the same time, the CIA's counterintelligence section, under James Angleton, was drawing great advantages, chiefly from Israel's then almost unique sources in the Soviet Union, from the CIA's ever-closer association with Mossad.

SDECE and another rival organization set up by Jacques Foccart, de Gaulle's senior adviser on African affairs and specialist in covert actions on the African continent, operated in Black African states like Guinea and Chad, former French colonies. Foccart's men, called *les barbouzes* ("the bearded ones," implying the false beard, which like the cloak and dagger is supposed to be a trademark of European secret agents), soon began to run up against Qaddafi's Libyan network spreading the word of Allah as interpreted by the "Brother Colonel."

In the Mideast, de Gaulle's relations with Israel steadily worsened after the 1967 Arab-Israeli war, when de Gaulle and his intelligence director, Etienne Burin du Rozier, embargoed French arms sales to punish Israel for being the first to attack. But strong pro-Israel factions remained in both SDECE and the DST. They resented the French government's new pro-Arab line, and especially its pro-Qaddafi policy (which resulted in the SDECE's helping to crush the Hilton assignment). The pro-Israel elements in the French services chalked up a spectacular victory: helping the Israelis take the five French-built Saar-class missile boats out of Cherbourg harbor and guide them swiftly through the Mediterranean to Haifa in December 1969.

When Qaddafi's spokesmen (if not his paymasters) supported the Black September terrorist murder of eleven Israeli athletes at the Munich Olympics in September 1972, France, like West Germany, set up a special antiterrorist unit. In France it was, and still is, called the Groupe d'Intervention de la Gendarmerie Nationale (GIGN). The SDECE, the DST, and the military and police security services improved their coordination, and began to share intelligence about privileged sanctuaries of terrorism, including Algeria and Libya, as well as France's one-time colonies in the Middle East, Syria and Lebanon. Under its then director, Alexandre de Marenches, the SDECE became the only Western intelligence service to predict the October 1973 Yom Kippur war.

Some of these terrorism operations were controlled by Carlos, who in June 1975 killed two DST inspectors and his former colleague in terror, Lebanese Michel Moukarbel.[3] Then came the retirement of James Angleton in the United States, and what the Israelis regarded as the growing "softness" of the Ford administration in Washington toward the Arabs, Libya and the PLO in particular. As a consequence, Mossad in its war against Carlos and his extremist Palestinian, European, and Latin American allies, improved its own links with other intelligence agencies, such as West Germany's Bundesnachrichtendienst (BND).

Sometime early in 1977, SDECE chief Alexandre de Marenches summoned his second in command, Colonel Alain Gagneron de Marolles, to de Marenches's office in what Frenchmen call "La Piscine" (the swimming pool), the SDECE headquarters in the French army signal barracks on the Boulevard Mortier in northern Paris.

Marenches, who from La Piscine directed the work of about two thousand analysts and undercover agents in North Africa, the Middle East, and the rest of the world, had new orders from President Valéry Giscard d'Estaing, successor to de Gaulle's chosen heir the late Georges Pompidou. Qaddafi and his regime in Libya, the Elysée pointed out, had become more than just an annoyance to France and her friends in Africa and the Arab world; they were a threat. Fresh information from other European services and the newly organized Saudi Arabian secret service indicated that President Sadat was now disposed to help Omar al-Meheishi and his fellow Libyan exiles strike at Qaddafi.

Colonel de Marolles appears to have been definitely involved in assisting Sadat and Meheishi's would-be Libyan government-in-exile during the lead-up to the four-day Libyan-Egyptian war of July 1977.[4] Strange as it might at first appear, Israel and the Mossad were strongly opposed to this French involvement (the CIA, on the other hand, had apparently encouraged it). According to the Paris newspaper *Tribune Juive*, and hints from Israeli sources, Tel Aviv took a dim view at the time of the possibility that Sadat, then maneuvering toward his forthcoming trip to Jerusalem and the ensuing peace negotiations, might be strengthened by the setting up of a pro-Egyptian government in Libya.[5] Failure of the Marolles-Meheishi plan therefore led to some sighs of relief in Jerusalem, if not in Washington.

It was at this point that the situation in Chad, long a festering sore between France and Libya, suddenly became a major preoccupation of La Piscine, as well as of the French foreign ministry on the Quai d'Orsay. It was becoming Qaddafi's main concern too, as was indicated by his engagement of hired French soldiers of fortune in one of the most bizarre episodes in the secret Franco-Libyan war.

It became clear to Qaddafi that Frank Terpil, Edwin Wilson, and Green Beret and former CIA operatives recruited in the United States were highly useful, despite the failures with Omar al-Meheishi and Herman Eilts. Qaddafi and his intelligence advisers decided to augment the American mercenary force with some Frenchmen, who, because of their knowledge of French military and intelligence involvement in

Africa, might prove invaluable in combating those who were fighting Qaddafi's designs in Chad.

The air cover for the French security force in Chad was provided mainly by several Jaguar fighter-bombers based at N'Djamena air base. The Jaguars were tough, versatile combat planes already proving highly useful in air-to-ground attack operations against the Qaddafi-armed Polisario guerrillas then threatening French interests in the iron mines of Mauritania in Western Sahara. Qaddafi's high command apparently decided that direct Libyan air action against the N'Djamena base to destroy the Jaguars would be too risky. It might involve Libya in open warfare with France at a time when Qaddafi wished to cultivate, not deteriorate, his relations with all Western countries.

By this time, Wilson, Terpil, and their American colleagues had trained a forty-man elite commando force of Libyans. What they wanted was to find expert guides and advance men for a concentrated assault on the French air base (N'Djamena) in order to make their knockout of the Jaguars look like the action of the Chad forces controlled by one of Chad's leading politicians, Goukouni Oueddei.

A Paris businessman, known to the principals as Bonouvrier (literally, "Mr. Good Worker"), found Qaddafi three veteran French mercenaries who seemed just right for the job: Michel Winter, Roland Raucoules, and Philippe Toutut.

From the Libyan point of view, Raucoules was certainly one of the best men possible for the task. He was a *pied noir* born in Algeria who had flown small planes as a sergeant for the French air force. His brother had been killed in combat by the Algerian FLN. When part of the French military in Algeria turned against de Gaulle, accusing him of selling out Algeria to the Arabs, Raucoules joined the Secret Army Organization (OAS) and took the code name "Sebastopol."

On February 18, 1962, as the last months of the Algerian war began, Raucoules and Lieutenant Marcel Hoerner had flown a highly unauthorized strafing mission against the FLN base near Oujda, Morocco, on the Moroccan side of the border, evading pursuit and then escaping French military justice by fleeing to Spain. Later, Raucoules appeared as a mercenary in Nicaragua and then as personal pilot for President Omar Bongo of Gabon, who liked to entrust his personal safety to Frenchmen whose loyalty could be bought, if not guaranteed by the French government in Paris.

After the duty with Bongo, Raucoules flew combat missions for the Ibo rebels of Biafra in the Nigerian civil war. There he met Michel

Winter, another ex-OAS man with a past of African adventures who had returned to France as a "marketing agent." Politically, like so many of Qaddafi's other friends or hirelings in Europe, Winter belonged to the extreme right; he was a close adviser of Pierre Sidos, chief of a neo-Fascist movement known as l'Oeuvre Française.

Early in June 1978 in Toulouse in southern France, Raucoules, who had been piloting a Fokker Friendship for a charter company called Uni Air Rouergue since 1976, asked a friend who flew air taxis, Pierre Tesseydre, to find him a DC-4 he could use on a job for Monsieur Bon-ouvrier in Paris. It was, Raucoules assured his friend, a good deal for the right people, with a lot of money involved.

Pierre Tesseydre found his friend not a DC-4 but an old DC-3, the property of Robert Boname of General Air Service, a Nice charter company. On July 21, 1978, they bought the DC-3 for 474,000 francs cash, later telling Boname they planned to use it to ship some cargo to Thailand. At this point, Raucoules recruited a third man, Philippe Toutut, a twenty-eight-year-old pilot with Uni Air. Tesseydre, not liking the looks of the whole thing, dropped out.

Libyan intelligence had procured the plane for the purpose of flying it to Goukouni's stronghold, Zouar, in northern Chad. There it was to pick up all or part of the forty-man Wilson-Terpil commando unit. The DC-3 was then supposed to head for N'Djamena to attack and destroy the French Jaguar squadron on the ground.

Raucoules, with Toutut as copilot and Winter as a passenger, took off from Toulouse on July 27, 1978, filing a flight plan for Palermo, Sicily. (Air Total, the French service company at Toulouse airport, had refused, for safety reasons, to fill a requested ten extra two-hundred liter cans of gasoline.) At 5 P.M., the DC-3 landed on schedule at Palermo, where it picked up two additional passengers. These two have never been identified; perhaps they were Libyan intelligence men or members of a Mafia-type Sicilian group who were also serving as intermediaries between the Libyans and Americans they sought to recruit as agents of influence. On the next day, July 28, the DC-3 made a short hop to Catania in Sicily, and managed there to load four hundred liters of extra gasoline. Raucoules filed a flight plan for Brindisi, Italy, and took off.

Seven minutes later, the Catania control tower lost contact with the DC-3, which at this point disappeared forever from the radar screens of Western Europe. Neither Raucoules, Winter, nor Toutut were ever seen again in Europe. But no wreckage or any other trace of the "Phantom DC-3," as the French flying trade came to call it, was ever found.

What happened, according to persons close to Qaddafi's French and American mercenaries and a Chadian close to the Frolinat leadership, was as follows. The DC-3 arrived at Zouar, more or less on schedule, late on July 28. With Winter in charge of the operation against the French at N'Djamena, the DC-3 took off with its full load of mercenaries around midnight July 30, bound for the Chad capital. Weather and fate were both against them. A heavy cloud cover and a total cutoff of radio and navigational aids—possibly ordered by French air force intelligence at the N'Djamena base—caused them to miss the darkened air base, turn tail, and return to Zouar. There they were to await arrival from Libya of new fuel and supplies for another try.

What happened next was one of the relatively rapid changes of alliance that characterize Qaddafi's mercurial relationships with his allies. Though the Libyans had been pushing Frolinat to take the offensive against the Chad government, or perhaps because they were pushing too hard, relations between Frolinat and Goukouni Oueddei went bad. Goukouni Oueddei's men clashed with their former ally Hissène Habré, who was very much on their former ally's "hit list" because he had earlier kidnapped and held for ransom for over two years a French lady scientist, Madame Claustre, in the rugged Tibesti mountains, the Toubou tribal stronghold.

The bad Habré-Goukouni relations quickly became bad Frolinat-Libyan relations. In August 1978, Libyan forces evacuated their three bases in northern Chad: Saya, Bardai, and Zouar. Instead of receiving the 500,000 French francs apiece they had been promised for successful completion of the Chad operation, Raucoules, Winter, and Toutut found themselves transported north to Sebha as prisoners of the Libyans. Nothing has been seen or heard of them since.[6] Perhaps they are out of prison and still with Qaddafi.

Qaddafi's interest in Chad—apart from his animus against past French and more recent Israeli connections there—centers on the vast country as a meeting place of two religious worlds: Muslim North Africa in the northern and eastern regions, populated with more than half the total national population of about 4.5 million; and the Christian and animist south, which under French colonial rule was the economic and political center of power. Qaddafi's Trojan horse for bringing all of Chad under his influence has been the restless Toubou tribes of the north. Nomads, warriors, and herders of livestock like the tribes in other parts of the Sahara, the Toubous number only about seventy thousand, or about

2 percent of the total population. Many of them have always moved freely between the Libyan and Chad sides of the frontier. Since falling under the influence of the Sanussi religious order in the last century, they have been naturally and traditionally the allies of whatever regime governed Libya.[7]

The first French settlers in Chad, around the turn of the century, were more interested in the northern steppes and deserts than in the tropical or subtropical southern regions. This was because the vast herds of Toubou livestock, when they could be rounded up, bred, and sold, provided quick profits. Around 1920, with the completion of new railroad links from the interior of Black Africa to the Atlantic Coast, the French began to realize that the south was ideally suited to growing cotton, a cash crop. Cotton fields in southern Chad had the added advantage of not being a threat to the livelihood of the locals, unlike the ranching activities of the early settlers in the north. From then on, French investment and interest was withdrawn from the north and focused on southern Chad, which the French, as in so many other colonies, called the "useful" part (*le Chad util*).

When independence came in 1960, the government in the southern capital, N'Djamena, then called Fort Lamy, dominated the north politically but neglected its economic development. In 1966 a Chad exile named Ibrahim Abatcha founded in Khartoum, Sudan, the Front de Liberation Nationale du Tchad, or "Frolinat" for short. Its purpose was to organize the northern Toubou tribes under the banner of Islam and "liberate" their ancestral homeland from the infidels in the south. The government forces of Félix Malloum, Chad's French-educated first president, killed Abatcha in a battle with the Toubou rebels in 1968 and paraded his head through the northern villages on the point of a spear.

Abatcha's successor as Frolinat's chief was Dr. Abba Seddik, who had both European and traditional Muslim education, and who was fiercely opposed to non-Muslim, "neo-colonial" black power in the south of Chad. Seddik was therefore a natural ally for Qaddafi, who enthusiastically opened training camps for Frolinat's new holy warriors. Qaddafi's support developed the Toubou rebellion into a major threat to the N'Djamena government.

After repeated accusations that Qaddafi was trying to topple the N'Djamena government, the new president, François Tombalbaye, broke diplomatic relations with Tripoli. In order to restore peace between them, Qaddafi demanded the following conditions of Tombalbaye: expulsion of the Israeli diplomatic mission in N'Djamena (following the coup attempt in Libya by the "Black Prince");[8] evacuation of the French garrisons in Chad; creation of an Arab university in Chad and eventual adoption of Arabic as the official language; and the establishment of a joint Libyan-Chad organization to control mineral resources in the Libyan-Chad frontier regions.[9]

This last condition was probably made because a Soviet geological survey mission that visited the sixty-mile-wide northern band of Chad, the Aouzou Strip, had filed a secret report with the Libyan government that the area contained both oil and uranium ore.[10] This has remained unsubstantiated by other sources, but in 1973 Libyan troops occupied the Aouzou strip and have remained there since. Qaddafi's 1976 atlas showed the Aouzou band, as well as a substantial chunk of Niger and pockets of Algeria rich in oil and gas,[11] as parts of Libya. As far as Qaddafi is concerned, this affair is closed, and Aouzou is as Libyan as Sirte, Benghazi, or Tripoli.

Qaddafi's swallowing of the Aouzou Strip, however, was a major factor in the gradual discrediting of Dr. Seddik among his Toubou followers. It was time for Libya to find a new Toubou ally. At first it looked as though Qaddafi would support a new two-man tandem leadership of the Chad rebels, the Conseil des Forces Armées du Nord (which came to be known by the short title FAN), led by Hissène Habré and Goukouni Oueddei, both Muslims. But Qaddafi liked Goukouni better because Goukouni enjoyed the prestige of being the son of a man called the Derdei, a kind of religious and temporal superchief of the Toubou tribes. Replacing Habré as chief on the FAN in 1976, Goukouni was soon master of about half of the territory of Chad. His capital, in the northern town of Faya-Largeau, was well positioned for logistical support and military aid from Qaddafi. Despite this, Goukouni contended that he was opposed to the Libyan occupation of Aouzou; he even proposed to President Félix Malloum "a national truce to confront the Libyan occupation."

Qaddafi now played the peacemaker. In March 1978 he persuaded Frolinat and the Malloum government to sign an armistice allowing Frolinat troops and a Libyan-Niger joint commission freedom to move around all of Chad's vast territory to "check on the presence of foreign troops in Chad."[12] By "foreign troops" Qaddafi of course meant the French.[13]

In the winter and spring of 1979, the civil war's raging full force in Chad finally led to an agreement among the various African states supporting Chad factions, signed at Kano, Nigeria, in August. A "provisional executive council" was formed. Qaddafi's man on the council was Acyl Ahmed, Chad foreign minister and former deputy in parliament. French intelligence knew him as an adversary of French interests who, after acting as a close adviser to President Tombalbaye, had defected to Frolinat in 1975 and gone to Libya in 1978 during the dispute that erupted between Qaddafi and Goukouni following the failed attack on the French fighter base at N'Djamena.

The Kano agreements led to the fall and exile of Chad's Christian president, Félix Malloum, the friend of France. Goukouni Oueddei, a Muslim and Qaddafi's old friend, returned as provisional president with the approval of the African Unity Organization (OAU) committee set up to watch over the Chad situation. By March 1980, the Kano agreement had broken down completely. Battles raged among the rival Chad factions in N'Djamena itself, where normal life gradually broke down. Unable to defeat his rival Habré alone, Goukouni in June 1980 signed a treaty of mutual defense with Qaddafi, who at once began to beef up his military base in the Aouzou Strip for the winter 1980–81 campaign to reconquer Chad for Goukouni Oueddi.

Though French interests were definitely suffering from Qaddafi's advance in Chad and neither President Carter nor anyone else in the West seemed to care, the men back at La Piscine still had a few tricks up their sleeves. Even if Chad was going down the drain, there were other ways to make life unpleasant for the obstreperous Libyan colonel, other fronts on which to operate against him. In January 1979, while President Giscard d'Estaing and his chief "spook," SDECE's Alexandre de Marenches, were harboring the Ayatollah Khomeini and allowing Khomeini, with Libyan support, to send his revolution messages to the Tehran revolutionaries then finishing off the Shah's tottering regime, de Marenches removed the former SDECE head of research, Colonel Candelier. In his place he named Colonel de Marolles, who had tried to work with the Egyptians in the failed 1977 operation against Qaddafi. De Marolles, friendly with Giscard, was thus able to bypass his superior, de Marenches.

By this time, Giscard had a special reason to want Qaddafi's downfall. Libyan sources in France had helped, or at least encouraged, publication, first by the satirical newspaper *Le Canard Enchaîné* and later by the sober *Le Monde*, of the damaging stories about Giscard's acceptance of a gift of diamonds from Jean Bédel Bokassa, the self-crowned "emperor" of the Central African Empire whose reign was finally ended by French troops in fall of 1979—ironically enough while Bokassa was visiting Qaddafi in Libya.[14] The diamond story was certainly a factor in Giscard's loss of the 1981 presidential elections to François Mitterand.

De Marolles's new "action" policy against Qaddafi got under way by early 1980, a whole year before Reagan's administration in the United States saw fit to do likewise. First, de Marolles sent new SDECE agents into Libya. One obvious cover was the French embassy in Tripoli (burned by a Libyan mob in January 1980, eleven months before the attack on the U.S. embassy that marked the beginning of the end of the Carter administration's efforts to get along with Qaddafi). Other cover for the French agents, outside the French diplomatic establishment, was the semi-state-owned French oil company, ELF.

On January 26, 1980, SDECE was called in to help crush and then counteract the Libyan-based guerrilla assault on Gafsa, Tunisia. A man known to fellow intelligence professionals only as "Colonel Bruno," it was reported, had set up an anti-Qaddafi liberation front along the Egyptian-Libyan border, and Colonel de Marolles once again was able to operate from Egypt. French media carried interviews with Qaddafi's opponents, and there was heavy promotion in France for a political novel, *The Fifth Horseman*, by Larry Collins and Dominique Lapierre, in which Qaddafi blackmails President Carter by concealing an "Islamic" nuclear bomb in New York. Some French newsmen got either scoops or controlled leaks about France-based terrorist operations financed by Qaddafi, with Interior Minister Christian Bonnet hinting that Libya was responsible for a bombing campaign by the Front de Libération Nationale de la Corse (FLNC), the Corsican autonomists.

Whether or not there was French participation in the August 1980 attempted mutiny in Tobruk led by Libyan Major Idris Shehaibi, the French media eagerly picked up the story, and the semiofficial Agence France-Presse (AFP) put on its wires an unsourced report hinting that "Colonel Qaddafi might have died in a shooting accident." After the Tobruk affair, de Marenches removed de Marolles. When Qaddafi invaded Chad in force in November 1980, de Marenches failed to convince Giscard d'Estaing to intervene with French military force.[15]

Qaddafi's intervention in Chad in the winter of 1980–81 gave him his first real military success, as well as a substantial political victory in Africa, though both were largely forgotten when he withdrew his army from Chad in November 1981. His successful occupation of the ruined city of N'Djamena, sacked and pillaged by all factions in the Chad civil war, proved to military observers that the Libyans were learning well the tactics and logistics taught them by their American, Soviet, and East

German instructors. As the Chad offensive progressed, the Carter administration in its final weeks awakened to the danger. The White House agreed to suggestions from the Pentagon that African heads of state, including Tunisian Prime Minister Muhammad M'Zali, be shown U.S. satellite photos of the Libyan movements in Chad and Libyan troop concentrations near their own borders. This was done in the final days of October and the first few days of November.

For Tunisian Foreign Minister Hassan Belkhodja, there was no doubt that Qaddafi's African venture coming after the attack on Gafsa at the beginning of that year represented the most serious threat Tunisia had yet known. This, he implied, was the reason why Tunisia had asked and accepted new French and U.S. military support. "You in the West won World War II in North Africa. If you don't act promptly enough to end the threat from Qaddafi, you may lose World War III here!"[16]

Senegal's outgoing president, Léopold Sédar Senghor, acting on the U.S. photos and on reports given him by France's SDECE, broke diplomatic relations with Libya. So did Ghana and Gambia. During a visit to France, followed by a trip to Cairo to discuss the Libyan threat with President Sadat, Senghor accused Qaddafi of wanting to destabilize not only Chad, but also Senegal, Niger, and Mali. Qaddafi's propagandists, and the colonel himself at a news conference in Tripoli in early December, claimed that the Touareg tribes, Saharan nomads who normally wander between Algeria, Mali, Niger, and Libya, are in reality good Libyans all and should accept the protection of their Libyan motherland.

Qaddafi's purpose, Senghor asserted, was to set up a giant new Saharan republic controlled from Tripoli. This would link up with the Algerian and Libyan-backed Polisario guerrillas, who were then still battling with King Hassan's Royal Moroccan Armed Forces for control of Western Sahara, from which Spain had withdrawn in 1975. Hassan had reason to worry; not only had Qaddafi's regular supplies of heavy arms to the Polisario continued through the old desert channels to the main Polisario base at Tindouf, Algeria, but they were also arriving sporadically by combined airlift and truck convoys that took the long southern Saharan route through Niger and Mali. Even more steadily, they were reaching the coasts of the Sahara and Mauritania directly by boat from Spain's Canary Islands.[17]

Even before a fanatical tribe of Muslim extremists devastated the northern Nigeria city of Kano in December 1980, Qaddafi had antagonized Nigeria's federal government and the conservative Muslim leadership in northern Nigeria by sending recruiting agents for his Islamic Legion to exhort, wheedle, and buy support and recruits from among the Nigerian Muslims. In Senegal, Islamic fundamentalist leader Ahmed Niasse acted as Qaddafi's recruiting agent for the Islamic Legion. Though Libyan participation in the Kano troubles was never proved, there were somewhat stronger indications of a Libyan role in the little tropical country of Gambia. After Senegalese troops had crushed a coup against its portly, British-educated president, Sir Dawda Jawara, in July and August 1981, Gambia elected to sign a union agreement with Senegal.

In late 1980, however, Gambia was still sandwiched between thick surrounding slices of Senegalese territory. Gambia broke off diplomatic relations with Libya on October 30.[18] To help keep order, Sir Dawda Jawara borrowed some of the Senegalese troops who in July 1981 were to save his regime. In both the first Senegalese intervention in Gambia in late 1980 and the final, conclusive one the following July, the new Senegalese president, Abdou Diouf, a Muslim but not given to Qaddafi's brand of Islamic zealotry, obtained the approval of his French advisers in Dakar for the first Senegalese military action.

Qaddafi's blows in Chad created shock waves in all of Chad's black, French-speaking neighbor republics, which enjoyed varying degrees of protection from France. In Gabon, President Albert-Bernard Bongo (changed to Omar Bongo when he converted to Islam at the urging of and financial inducements offered by Qaddafi) had what most of his neighbors lacked: oil, as well as manganese and uranium, and a resulting per capita national income of $3,580, one of Africa's highest. Since he had taken power in 1967, President Bongo's main protection had consisted of a French air base with four hundred French commando troops and the usual complement of French military and political advisers. Morocco's King Hassan loaned some of his own security personnel to the presidential guard. During the halcyon days of Jacques Foccart's ascendancy as master of clandestine French intelligence operations in sub-Saharan Africa, French mercenary Bob Denard operated out of Libreville, the Gabonese capital. For these reasons, Qaddafi realized that Gabon was no pushover. While he was busy promoting Libyan relations elsewhere to bolster the operation in Chad, converting many of the regular Libyan embassies to People's Bureaus manned by students and other young stalwarts whose loyalty he felt was unquestioned, he broke relations with Gabon in early 1980. Libyan statements indicated Tripoli felt that Libreville was hopelessly inside the

French sphere of influence and unlikely terrain for a "liberation" movement.

Not so for another neighbor, the much poorer Republic of Niger. This was another remnant of the once-vast French colonial empire, proclaimed independent in 1960 under the presidency of Hamani Diori. He was a moderate prepared to continue cooperating with France and was eager in particular to develop Niger's rich uranium resources. Niger did not enjoy the relatively tranquil infancy of the Ivory Coast or Senegal; nor did its internal strife tear it apart quite on the scale seen in Chad. But a radical politician, Djibo Bakary, heading the Sawaba political party, which was close to the French Communists, tried unsuccessfully to take Niger out of the French community in a 1958 referendum and then made life difficult for Diori. The drought that devastated most of the sub-Saharan Sahel region in 1973 impoverished the country, and, with some of the farmers and nomads literally starving, on April 15, 1974, the familiar and expected happened: an army coup. The successful officer was Lieutenant General Seyni Kountche, a French-trained professional soldier; he arrested Diori and his supporters, dissolved the national assembly, and governed with a Supreme Military Council. He maintained Niger's firm ties with Europe and the European Community, but put much more emphasis on Niger's largely Muslim culture and improved relations with all of the Arab world, including Libya.

Qaddafi had good reason to cultivate Kountche. Since 1971 a French company called the Société des Mines de l'Air (SOMAIR) that was owned by a cousin of Giscard d'Estaing, had been mining the Arlit uranium deposits in north-central Niger. Success led them to begin mining also at Akouta, Azelik, and Imouraren. By 1975, a year in which Qaddafi offered cash to Pakistan for her nuclear program and was beginning himself to make uranium purchases, Niger was one of the world's major producers. Since 1975, Libya and Pakistan have each been buying "yellowcake" (semirefined uranium ore) from Niger. Accurate figures are rarely if ever published, but French and U.S. intelligence believe that Libya purchased *tons* of yellowcake in 1980 alone.

Qaddafi thoughtfully made Kountche's balancing act between Libyan cash for uranium and the Libyan propensity to back militant Muslim rebels somewhat easier for the Niger leader. He provided Libyan cash and credits for the building of an Islamic university in Niamey, the Niger capital. Before the Chad invasion, he encouraged Kountche to play a diplomatic role in Chad affairs and seemed less bothered by the small but extremely watchful French security presence (upward of one thousand troops, special security guards for the uranium mines and the usual military and political advisers) than he had been earlier by such presence in Chad, Gabon, Senegal, and the Central African Republic.

In a rare interview with *Jeune Afrique* in 1981, Kountche explained, however, that he considered Qaddafi a threat—Kountche was sponsoring nationwide "patriotic" rallies to protest Libyan interference by then.[19]   Although Kountche accused the world's largest uranium producers (the United States, Canada, Australia, and South Africa) of coordinating their efforts to drive world uranium prices down partly in order to intimidate Niger because of the yellowcake sales to Libya and Pakistan, Kountche accused Qaddafi, whom he had recently asked to close his People's Bureau in Niamey, of attempting to "subvert" the trans-Saharan tribes by telling them that Libya is their homeland. "In Niger," Kountche contended, "they are perfectly conscious that they belong to the national community. . . . I can even say that if one day the Touareg had to choose a promised land, it wouldn't be Libya. . . . The Arabs in general, and the Libyans in particular, have no more regard for the Touareg than for blacks generally. For them, they're all slaves." Kountche promised that if Libya mounted a direct attack on Niger (something he said he didn't expect), "we'll fight with everything we have, even bows and arrows if need be." Kountche said he knew that Qaddafi was recruiting Niger people for subversion in Niger and had also appointed a Mauritanian merchant, Liman Chaffi, who earlier lived in Niamey to organize and lead the opposition. Chaffi was one of the main authors of a coup attempt in March 1976. Arms sent by Libya to the rebels had been found in Chaffi's home. Of the possibility that Qaddafi might occupy northern Niger as he did the Aouzou Strip in Chad in 1973 (there are known to be unexploited uranium beds in the northern zone of Niger), Kountche thought there was no danger "for the moment." Niger (and, he might have added, the French) "will defend itself, if anything like that happens." In the meantime, Niger would continue to work for "return of peace and free elections" in Chad.

Amid the furor caused by Israel's July 1981 bombing of the Iraqi nuclear reactor near Baghdad, Niger published for the first time a complete list of those to whom it had sold uranium during the first half of 1981. Iraq, for the first time, was among the purchasers, with 100 tons. Libya's purchases during the same period—1,212 tons—had increased sixfold over those in the same period of 1980. France had increased her purchases from 1,344 in 1980 to 2,293 in 1981. No sales at all were shown for Pakistan.[20]

The safeguarding of President Seyni Kountche and his uranium in Niger was vital to France. But it was only one aspect of the holding operation that Paris found itself obliged to fight against Qaddafi's Bureau for the Export of the Revolution in Africa. Chad was in many ways the main French bulwark in Africa, safeguarding as it did the air and land corridors of communication to the countries in the heart of Black Africa with their mineral and human riches. As the countries south of the Sahara became increasingly polarized by the developing war against white domination in southern Africa and as the issue of Soviet and Cuban aid in Angola, Mozambique, and the other "front-line" countries gathered force, there arose the equally important question of whether Qaddafi's Libya would be a proxy for Soviet penetration of Africa from the north.

No one was more conscious of the importance of Chad in this political puzzle than France's leaders. Though French troops had remained in Chad ever since independence in 1960, the first time they had helped the Chad government resist Libya and its Chadian allies was during the Toubou rebellion in 1968. In 1975 President Tombalbaye had been killed in a coup in N'Djamena. The French government had complied with a demand by the new Chad rulers to clear its combat forces out of their bases. The French did, however, retain over one thousand French "peace corps" type civilian workers, as well as teachers and some military advisers and instructors.

Then in 1978, the year in which Qaddafi tried to employ French mercenaries against other Frenchmen in Chad, the French sent paratroops and Foreign Legionnaires back into the country under a military aid agreement signed with President Félix Malloum in 1976. This time, their mission was to support Malloum and his regime against new and more powerful offensives by the Toubou rebels and their Libyan allies, which included Qaddafi's American mercenaries.

In April 1979, the French wanted to pull out but Goukouni Oueddei, who had just become provisional president, urged them to stay on. A year later Goukouni invited the Libyans into Chad.

Fighting flared up and died down periodically until March 1980. But the French avoided involvement in the new fighting. They concentrated on humanitarian aid to a Chad that was witnessing the massacre of its people and the decimation of its cotton crop and other agricultural riches. The French army continued to supply medical aid, electricity, water, and emergency oil supplies. Allies of President Goukouni, however, accused the French command of helping Hissène Habré. The Libyans, whose principal goal was to get the French out altogether, enthusiastically endorsed these charges. Amid growing criticism at home of Giscard d'Estaing's African ventures, the French government announced on April 27, 1980, that it would pull out its troops. Withdrawal of all but medical teams was completed by May 17. The French embassy in N'Djamena and the remaining foreigners mostly moved to Cameroon territory across the river from N'Djamena.[21]

At the American embassy, Ambassador Don Norland and his small staff had to lock up their offices and get out in a hurry, and then cross the river to Cameroon. What few people realized at the time was that they had left their communications and secret coding equipment behind in the embassy. When Norland was able to return to his office for a cleanup following the Libyan occupation in December, he found everything untouched: the Libyan invaders had either by accident or by design avoided violating any of the diplomatic missions. What might have been a disastrous compromise of U.S. codes and equipment had been avoided.[22]

After the French had left in April 1980 the Goukouni-Habré clashes continued. By June 6 Habré's men had captured the important northern Chad base of Faya-Largeau, about five hundred miles northeast of N'Djamena. Goukouni then flew to Tripoli on June 15 and signed with Qaddafi an eight-point "friendship treaty" that was not made public until the following September. The treaty called for Qaddafi to send in his troops if requested to do so by the Chad provisional government.

By October 1980 the main Libyan military thrust developed, with at first 3,000, then up to 7,000 Libyan troops and Islamic Legionnaires participating. On November 11, French Defense Minister Robert Galley said that the Libyan forces in Chad totaled 4,000 men stationed at Douguia, Faya-Largeau, and areas north of N'Djamena. By this time the U.S. satellite pictures had been shown to both the French and the African heads of state, confirming, as Pentagon sources told Washington newsmen November 19, that a large Libyan force was "preparing to attack" N'Djamena.

Qaddafi's air force began intervening in mid-October, strafing and bombing Habré-held areas around Faya-Largeau on October 18 and attacking again throughout most of November. In N'Djamena, Lieutenant Colonel Abdel Kader Kamougue, an important southern tribal leader who rejected the Libyan intervention and turned against Goukouni, tried to organize the capital's defense. The OAU's ad hoc committee on Chad, including Benin (whose forces were fighting with Qaddafi's Islamic Legion), Togo, Congo, and Guinea all met in Freetown, Sierra Leone, and then again in Lome, the capital of Togo, to try to find and apply a formula for a cease-fire.

On November 28, an agreement was drawn up for an armistice. It set up a monitoring committee composed of Benin, Congo, Guinea, Togo, and Sierra Leone to go to N'Djamena to supervise the cease-fire. Once again, Benin, Congo, Guinea, and Togo were supposed to send troops for an OAU peacekeeping force in Chad. The principal heads of state concerned, including Goukouni Oueddei, all signed. Habré, however, said on November 28 that he would not come to Lome and sign as long as the OAU (specifically, President Kerekou of Benin, the Togolese secretary-general of OAU) refused to denounce Libya's intervention and expel "Libyan agents" from the peace talks. The committee issued a separate call for evacuation of "all foreign forces" from Chad, and asked Nigeria to convene a meeting of all signers of the last Chad agreement signed in Lagos in 1979. Later, as it turned out, there were no African funds available in the OAU treasury for the peacekeeping force.

In December, while Qaddafi's well-oiled military machine, including his newly initiated Soviet T-54 and T-55 tanks, attacked and then mopped up N'Djamena, Habré was finally induced to travel to Cameroon. At the urging of Cameroon's President Ahmadou Ahidjo a cease-fire was signed on December 16, though Habré reserved for himself the right to continue the struggle to oust the Libyans later. Habré appears to have begun making serious contacts in Cairo and Khartoum; these later resulted in Egyptian military aid approved by the United States and France. Mostly secondhand Soviet equipment, rather than new first-line American supplies, was channeled to Habré through the Sudan to the region of Abeche (eastern Chad) near the Sudanese border. This became in 1981 a new focus of fighting and a possible flash point for Sudanese-Libyan hostilities. On December 24, 1980, the OAU tried in vain to organize a reconciliation of the Chad factions in another conference, again at Lagos.

The French reaction continued to be timid and hesitant. Just before the fall of N'Djamena, on December 13, Giscard d'Estaing's office issued a warning that France was "gravely concerned." It would "support any collective effort by African states to restore peace in Chad, preserve its unity, and maintain its independence.[23] Libya was not mentioned. French Foreign Minister Jean François-Poncet spelled out the French warnings in more detail to Qaddafi's much-traveled personal envoy, Ahmed al-Shahati, in Paris on December 22. But there was never a threat to back the warnings with force, save for the gesture of sending four Jaguar aircraft and some ground support planes to the main air base in Gabon.

Qaddafi totally ignored these signs of French displeasure. He basked in the success of what for him, after his defeat in Uganda three years earlier, seemed like a military tour de force. He and his Soviet advisers had, after all, managed to transport seven thousand troops, sixty tanks, and heavy artillery across over seven hundred miles of desert by airlift and tank transporters.

The setback to French prestige was not lost on France's client states. On December 29, as the guns fell silent in N'Djamena, President Bongo of Gabon, who wanted to stay friends with both the French and Qaddafi, claimed that France had not fulfilled its responsibilities toward Chad. It had abandoned the Chadians to "subversion" exerted by "certain big powers," letting the Chadians "kill one another."[24]

For weeks African leaders, stunned by the shock of the Libyan success, exchanged visits and missions. A tripartite meeting scheduled between Nigeria, Chad, and Libya did not take place because Nigerian President Shagari, mindful of the stiffening Western attitude toward Qaddafi and especially of the toughness of the new Reagan administration in Washington, refused to receive Qaddafi. He did, however, allow Major Jalloud to visit him, and they had a long talk in Lagos on February 14. Jalloud assumed the same soothing tone of Libyan propaganda broadcasts in Africa. He announced a major program of Libyan economic aid to Chad. Libyan petrodollars would henceforth meet the payrolls of Chad's hungry bureaucracy and President Goukouni Oueddei's army and would assist in reopening the Chad Central Bank. Later in N'Djamena, Jalloud dangled the prospect of Libyan "aid" to the French company CDRT, which still controlled Chad's cotton plantations. He offered contracts to buy "Chadian cotton production as well as loans to farmers worth between $50 million and $100 million."[25] By the end of 1981, however, no one seemed to know whether this promise of aid to revive Chad's most important cash crop had really been kept.

Following the Jalloud-Shagari meeting, a terse Nigerian statement was released stating that Libya "appeared" to have accepted the concept of an Africa peace force in Chad "in order to facilitate the establishment of a properly organized national army as well as popularly elected government" there. Goukouni Oueddei counterattacked with accusations that France was "mobilizing against Chad and using its African aid program as a weapon." In an interview with French television, Qaddafi repeated that Libya intervened or aided other African states only when asked to, and Goukouni had asked.

Nigerian officials in Lagos circulated a story that Nigeria was considering a plan with Libya under which Libyan troops would leave Chad if France in turn pulled out of the Central African Republic. But France was continuing to participate in Africa. Its Central African Republic contingent had, since the Chad invasion, been beefed up from 900 to 1,600 troops and had newly transferred Jaguar jets. More French instructors arrived in Niger. A French arms-sales mission was welcomed in Khartoum by Sudanese President Jafaar al-Nimeiry.

Throughout the winter and early spring of 1981, Libyan troops had begun making sporadic "hot pursuit" raids from Chad into Sudan, trying to eliminate the force of two thousand or so of Hissène Habré's partisans who were still resisting in the Abeche region and along the badly demarcated seven-hundred-mile Chad-Sudan border. The Libyans apparently never engaged any Sudanese troops, and the reports of incursions dropped off after President Sadat on several occasions promised that "if a single Libyan soldier enters Sudan, Egypt will act with its own forces."[26] Meanwhile Sudan, already host to hundreds of thousands of refugees from Africa's other wars in Eritrea and between Ethiopia and Somalia, found itself obliged to care for about ten thousand refugees from Chad.

The Sudanese, in the light of the 1976 coup attempt and other past experiences with Qaddafi,[27] feared Tripoli's Bureau for the Export of the Revolution far more than they feared a direct invasion by Qaddafi's tanks. The Sudan's western provinces of northern and southern Darfur, bordering Libya and Chad, are areas peopled mainly by nomadic tribes akin to those in Chad. The region was included within the borders of Sudan in one of the post–World War I agreements in 1919. Darfur is remote from Khartoum or any other major city, and is probably the least-developed region of Sudan's Muslim north. Poverty and the troubles it breeds are endemic. During one local revolt in January 1981 to protest appointment of a non-Darfuri governor, government troops were brought in to the regional capital, El Fasher, with fighting and casualties resulting. President Nimeiry had to back down and appoint a local man as governor.

Qaddafi and Libya were not initially blamed for the January 1981

Darfur troubles. But the local conditions—a tribal love of guns and an acute need for food and money—seemed to invite the attention of the Bureau for the Export of the Revolution in Tripoli. Nimeiry's continuous exchange of insults with Qaddafi in 1981 (each said the other should be put to death by his own people) added to the explosiveness of the situation. The nearly universal condemnation of Qaddafi's action in Chad and the Egyptian and Sudanese warnings caused Qaddafi to declare, in an interview with West German radio in February 1981 and in a speech in Tripoli in March, "We have no wish to send our troops beyond Chad. We are bringing all military confrontations to an end, including the one with Sadat's army."[28]

The Sudan was one of the African states pressing hardest for action to get Qaddafi's forces out of Chad. At the OAU ministerial conference in Addis Ababa on February 23–March 2, 1981, the Sudanese and some of the French-speaking states vehemently protested statements by Goukouni and the Libyan media in January that the two countries had decided on a merger of Libya and Chad. Both the Libyan and Chad delegations insisted to their OAU colleagues that these announcements meant only that there was a *proposal* for a merger. This would have to be decided by a referendum in both countries. Peter Onu, the OAU's deputy secretary general, had just completed a trip to New York with the Sierra Leone foreign minister to try to raise money for an OAU peacekeeping force in Chad and he had nothing positive to report. The OAU was broke.[29] Only Libya could afford to foot the mounting bills for the preservation of the economy and the body politic of Chad, even in its present war-blasted, decrepit condition.

The diplomatic jockeying over Chad within the OAU finally succeeded in bringing Qaddafi and Goukouni to a mini-summit meeting with the presidents of Sierra Leone and Nigeria at N'Djamena on May 23, 1981. It was a miserable failure. Qaddafi rejected Nigerian President Shagari's appeal for a Libyan withdrawal, reminding Shagari that only Goukouni, who had invited the Libyans in, could invite them out again. Qaddafi refused to recognize the jurisdiction or good offices of either the OAU or of Nigeria. Goukouni, according to Nigerian diplomats, remained silent when it was suggested that he now request the withdrawal. And, the Nigerians added, President Stevens of Sierra Leone, the 1981 OAU chairman (Qaddafi was next in line) was too timid to demand to Qaddafi's face that he pull his men out of Chad. After the meeting, however, a Sierra Leone statement issued in Freetown said Qaddafi had repeated earlier offers to withdraw once an

African peace force was sent in. Sudanese Foreign Minister Muhammad Mirghani Mubarak angrily commented that the N'Djamena meeting had been a Libyan effort to "close the file on Chad." And "Libyan dinars," he continued, "that had succeeded in buying some people would not succeed in closing the file on Chad until Libyan forces were fully withdrawn." He charged flatly that President Stevens was a "pawn" of Libya.[30]

The French socialist government of President François Mitterand, a politician who had been instrumental in France's long and laborious exit from Algeria between 1954 and 1962, has done more than just reorganize the French intelligence services in North Africa. It has taken a new, hard look at Qaddafi's Libya, and pondered how to reconcile the considerable French commercial interests there with Mitterand's old sympathies for Israel and his desire for more balance in the Arab-Israeli conflict than Giscard d'Estaing had had. A decision announced on July 15, 1981, lifted the arms sales ban that Giscard had imposed on Libya following the Chad invasion. All existing contracts, in arms and other areas, were to be honored, but France would open no new arms negotiations with Qaddafi while Libyan troops remained in Chad, nor could political relations be normalized before Libya finished rebuilding the French embassy in Tripoli, wrecked by mobs in February 1980. Among the arms no longer denied Qaddafi were ten fast gunboats not dissimilar to those France sold to Israel, thirty-four Mirage F-1 fighter-bombers, some Alouette III helicopters, and, perhaps most important to Qaddafi, four Daphne-class submarines of French design being built in Spain but presently held up there by Franco-Spanish agreement. What France would get in return was a relaxation on a hold order against the French oil company, ELF-Aquitaine (with a 67 percent French government interest), to go ahead with an oil exploration contract announced in the heat of the Chad crisis in October 1980.[31] In addition, Mitterand's Minister of Cooperation and Development, Jean-Pierre Cot, called in Qaddafi's senior diplomat in Paris, Said Afiana. He told Afiana that France expected Libya to abide by decisions made at the OAU summit held in Nairobi June 24–28; that the long-discussed OAU peace force composed of units from Benin, Congo, and Guinea should be sent to Chad; that neighboring states were to pledge solemnly not to meddle in Chad affairs; and that the OAU would help Chad rebuild its shattered national army.

What all this meant was aptly summed up by an American analyst in Paris. France would have normal or near-normal commercial dealings with Libya but reduced political contact—not unlike what the Reagan administration is doing. Libya and its neighbors were put on notice that the French would keep troops in the African states because they perceived a threat from the Bureau for the Export of the Revolution, and France would be ready to help in Africa if necessary. France would stop its covert assistance to dissident Chad factions, including the now Sudan-based leader Hissène Habré, and would be ready to respond favorably to Goukouni Oueddei's aid requests so that he might feel confident enough to dispense with Libyan support. French diplomats would begin new efforts to press Qaddafi to withdraw his troop force, now down to five thousand, entirely from Chad. Heavy French criticism of South Africa for its apartheid politicies, the Mitterand administration hoped, might make French policies toward Libya more credible and acceptable to the African rulers who had been shaken by Giscard's failure to oppose the Libyan military intervention in Chad.[32] Meanwhile, Qaddafi's time of extreme unease with France, and the past attempts of the French intelligence services to unseat him, seemed to be coming to an end. On September 1, 1981, after the air battle in which U.S. Navy fighters shot down two of his jets over the Gulf of Sirte and the signing of a tripartite defense pact with Ethiopia and South Yemen, Qaddafi, in his speech marking his revolution's twelfth anniversary, had not a word of reproach for France.

Jean-Pierre Cot, the French minister most concerned about Qaddafi's influence in Africa, clearly spelled out the Mitterand policies toward Libya in Chad, and Libya in general, in Washington in the early fall of 1981. Referring to Namibia, Latin America, and other areas as well as North Africa where the Reagan administration indicated the United States was determined to counter Soviet influence, Cot said: "We hope the Reagan administration will not drag the East-West conflict into the South. This will only help to spread Soviet influence—in Libya or Chad as everywhere else. If the United States obliges countries to take sides, it will make things easier for the Soviet Union. The way you [Americans] handled the Angola crisis was a mess, as compared with the skillful way the British handled the independence of Zimbabwe."[33]

As for Chad, he said, France would henceforth work to "create the conditions to help the country to regain its integrity." France would do this both by taking certain actions and by abstaining from others. First of all, it would "cease help to any of the factions in Chad." Qaddafi would have a good pretext, said Cot, to stay as long as "others" —an implied reproach to Presidents Sadat and Nimeiry as well as to the United States, their chief backer—kept on helping Habré. The attitude of the Giscard d'Estaing administration, Cot added, was "messy, to say the least."

France would help Chad in positive ways too—first of all, by helping in the reconstruction of N'Djamena and encouraging the return of French technicians, businessmen, and others there. "We must return a French presence to the capital," he said. "We have friends there and we must show them that we stand by them." At the same time, France would try to enlist international cooperation in investment and aid, though this would admittedly be difficult so long as Chad were occupied by the Libyans. Most definitely, France would put as much "political pressure" on Qaddafi as possible to get Libya out of Chad. No "wholesale" French or other Western aid would be possible until the Libyans were gone. France, the young minister continued, would help the OAU to put together the long-delayed African peace force, because "the security problem has to be managed by someone." France was willing to help with financial and logistical support, but no French troops would get involved again. Goukouni Oueddei wanted French help, said Monsieur Cot, to rebuild the Chad national army, but he would not get it, because "France cannot and will not do this." If other African states want to help do it, this would be fine: "In other words, we want to strengthen the independence and sovereignty of Chad in every way we can. This is difficult and the chances are not good that we will succeed, but if we fail, we will have proved the real nature of the Libyan presence." Of Qaddafi's wider designs in Africa Cot responded, "We think there is a Libyan problem. We are prepared to stand by our friends and to help them resist any pressure. Libyan ambitions in Africa are to be taken seriously, but perhaps not in an extremely drastic sense." In wondering whether France could meet the threat alone, or whether there was an American role that could be helpful, Cot shrugged. "Resources for meeting the threat are limited. The Libyan problem should neither be exaggerated nor minimized, but rather looked at with *un regard froid* [cold objectivity]." France had made many past errors. "The attitude of the former French administration was one of schizophrenia. On the one hand we treated Libya as an enemy and on the other we pushed greater trade relations with her. This absurd situation reached a peak when we sold arms to both sides [Libya and its opponents in Chad] during the Chad war." As for the United States, he added quickly, "We can't take lessons from people who have been buying ten times as much oil from Libya as we have been doing."

President Mitterand's decision to execute old arms contracts with Libya but sign no new ones would stand: "We will not sell new arms as long as Libya has this present attitude in Africa. We won't sell so much as a pistol or a bullet as long as it has this attitude."

By Christmas 1981, Libyan troops had quit Chad and an African peacekeeping force headed by Nigeria moved in to take their places. But the effort collapsed in mid-1982 and Habré returned and drove out Goukouni's faction.

The dilemma for French presidents since de Gaulle has been whether, where, and how to combat Qaddafi's encroachment on formerly sacrosanct French spheres in Africa. The dilemma in the case of Italian leaders has been quite different. With major Libyan investments in the Italian economy, and eighteen thousand or so Italians working in Libya in 1982, Qaddafi's leverage over Italy is far greater than Italy's leverage over Qaddafi. Many Italians who belong to the more or less conservative establishments of business, government, and the professions regard Qaddafi with great alarm. Not only is he seen as the upstart boss or godfather, in Mafia terms, of the North African country that Italy "civilized" earlier in this century; he is regarded as the paymaster, if not the fomenter, of at least some of the terrorism that has racked Italy's society and demoralized parts of its establishment over the past decade. And yet some Italian businessmen, such as Fiat's director-general, Gianni Agnelli, find Libyan markets and petrodollars indispensable.

Italian economic dependence upon its former colony is, of course, largely a function of Italy's energy situation. Sicily is rapidly growing into one of the largest European energy bases, with its Ragusa, Gela, and Fontanarossa districts producing over 30 percent of Italy's domestic crude-oil production in 1979 and 1980.[34] Yet Italy is at the same time one of the most vulnerable Western nations in any new oil crisis. Total Italian domestic production of around 1.5 million tons a year is only a tiny fraction of its 100-million-ton annual requirement. Though the Italians seek to increase imports from non-Arab sources such as Nigeria, Venezuela, and Mexico, 68 percent of Italy's energy needs are still furnished by the Arab world,[35] including 15 percent or more from Libya. Dependence on North African oil even grew in 1980 when ENI, the Italian state oil company, was faced with suspension of Saudi oil deliveries because a political scandal erupted over a commission kickback scheme. Libya's purchase in 1974 of a 10 percent interest (about $415 million) in the Fiat industrial complex added to Libyan leverage. Despite periodic ups and downs, which have included the imprisonment of Italian businessmen in Libya and occasional detention or arrest of Libyans in Italy in connection with terrorist activity, Rome governments have sought to have the best relations possible with Libya and to continue to secure lucrative contracts in Libya for Italian construction firms and other specialized companies and services, including the arms industry. When Libyan personnel were expelled from Malta in August 1980 because of a bitter Libyan-Maltese offshore oil dispute, the Italian foreign ministry justified the aid Italy offered Malta in soothing, diplomatic terms, and tried to make it palatable to Qaddafi.[36]

As the Hilton assignment partially disclosed, Italy's intelligence and security services were divided sharply about how to react to Qaddafi —indeed were even divided on the issue of Libya's real or imagined involvement in terrorism and drug smuggling inside Italy. In the immediate post–World War II period, before the Italian peace treaty ended the Italian colonial empire and ensured that Libya would become an independent state, the main Italian secret service was the Servizio Informazione Forze Armate (SIFAR). Its leaders included men who had held similar posts under the Fascist regime of Mussolini. Its goals in Libya were simple: collect as much information on trends in the territory as possible with a view toward safeguarding remaining Italian interests, especially the rights of Italian settlers.

Unfortunately for SIFAR, its director in the early 1960s, Carabiniere General Giovanni de Lorenzo, became enmeshed in political conspiracy. After a trial of the principal conspirators, SIFAR was disbanded. De Lorenzo became a member of parliament representing the neo-Fascist Italian Social Movement (MSI) party. SIFAR's successor was the Servizio Informazione Difesa (SID), supposed to be concerned with counterintelligence. The bombing of Milan's Agricultural Bank in December 1969, killing seventeen people, was first blamed largely on extreme leftists out to destabilize the country. A series of trials and investigative reports by Italy's colorful, if not always objective newspapers and magazines, indicated that the extreme right, aided by the SID, had a hand in this and other attacks. Later an SID agent, Guido Giannettinni, was given a sentence of life imprisonment for the explosion of a bomb at the central railway station in Bologna on August 2, 1980, the worst single act of terrorism in Western Europe since World War II. Although the MSI denied involvement and demanded death penalties for anyone convicted of the bombing, extreme rightists were blamed. An Italian staff officer, who in 1981 became one of the most senior military men in the Italian armed forces, said that the authorities had evidence that Libya had paid the terrorists but that it was unlikely any Italian government would ever dare to make this evidence public, or even admit to its existence, because of Libyan economic leverage.[37] Subsequently, SID chief General Vito Miceli was asked to resign because of his service's supposed involvement in terrorism. After a short jail sentence, he became an MSI deputy just as his predecessor, de Lorenzo, had done. Italian commentators linked Miceli with a pro-Arab, mainly pro-Libyan, faction of SID that stood in opposition to a pro-Israeli and pro-U.S. faction headed by General Gianadelio Maletti, who served in SID under Miceli. Premier Giulio Andreotti dissolved SID in 1977, partly in an effort to improve Italian relations with the Arab world and also to prevent involvement of Italian intelligence services in further rightist conspiracies.

Andreotti set up two new security services, a civilian and a military one. The idea was that each would watch the other and neutralize any wrongful acts. In practice, however, the military service, the Servizio Informazione Sicurezza Militare (SISMI), took precedence in most matters over the civilian Servizio Informazione Sicurezza Democratica (SISDE). SISMI's commander was General Giuseppe Santovito; SISDE's was General Giulio Grassini. Italian rightists moved into SISMI and soon the parliamentary committees charged with the oversight of both services could do little to interfere. In their ensuing rivalry, SISDE became generally more leftist (in Italian terms) and more pro-Arab and pro-Libyan in foreign relations. SISMI worked much more closely with the CIA and with Israel's Mossad, though not without hesitation in the case of the CIA because of leaks and disclosures about the CIA's covert operations in Washington.

The struggle against terrorism by the leftist Red Brigades, the kidnappers and murderers of former Premier Aldo Moro and perpetrators of many other misdeeds,[38] was showing some success by 1977. A secret document attributed to the CIA, but which may have been a plant by KGB or another "disinformation" agent, purported to urge the continuation of terrorism so that the terrorist groups could be infiltrated, much as the FBI in the United States had come largely to control the American Communist party. Attempts by the next premier, Francesco

Cossiga, of the leftist wing of the Christian Democratic party, to reduce the Pro-CIA SISMI's powers mostly to the benefit of the pro-Arab SISDE were discredited in media campaigns. As the result of one of these, Silvano Russomanno, deputy chief of SISDE, went to jail and SISDE was discredited.

A series of political scandals then buffeted Italy among the crosswinds of Arab, Israeli, Western, and Communist influence. First, in the spring of 1980, ENI chairman and Italian oil boss Giorgio Mazzanti was removed from office after charges, never proven in court, that he had helped Italian politicians take commissions on a Saudi oil deal. Next, customs police chiefs were accused of passing off (with the help of private oil companies) kerosene as heating oil, which is less heavily taxed. A profit of $2 billion was made over five years from this super-tax-evasion scheme. The fraud allegedly took place with the knowledge of leftist elements inside the Christian Democratic Party, with Libya supplying the oil at special prices outside normal distribution channels.

This wasn't a new story. Mino Pecorelli, the editor of a magazine called *OP*, had been murdered by an unknown assassin in 1979, immediately after publishing the story of the customs fraud in his magazine. His information had come from none other than Gianadelio Maletti of SID, who had begun investigating in 1974 as soon as the rumor of Libyan involvement reached him. Maletti was regarded as pro-Israeli; he had taken a number of junkets to Israel; and he retired to South Africa when he left SID in 1976. Maletti, his SID superior, and Admiral Mario Casardi were tried in the summer of 1981 for the leak. Later, Maletti's two chief aides in SID, Colonel Antonio Viezzer and Antonia La Bruna, were arrested on charges of espionage and terrorism.

The pro-Libyan and Palestinian factions in Italian security locked horns in several minor engagements in the secret intelligence war. Farouk Kaddoumi (Abu Lotf) was the Palestine Liberation Organization's shadow "foreign minister" with the title of chief of the PLO Political Department. Kaddoumi promised the Italians that there would be no more anti-Israel terrorist operations in Italy like the December attack at Fiumicino airport that had killed thirty-two persons aboard a Pan American World Airways flight. Clandestine terrorists under PLO jurisdiction were quietly recalled from Italy.[39]

In December 1979, three Italian leftists and a Jordanian were arrested on the Italian Adriatic seacoast with two SAM-7 missiles in their possession. Statements by the pro-Libyan PFLP leader George Habbash to the Italian court trying them claimed the four men had been helping the PFLP to take the SAMs, which were old and damaged, to a ship at Ortona that was supposed to carry them to Lebanon. All four were given seven-year jail sentences. The PFLP claimed it had negotiated an understanding with the Italian authorities through SISDE that the missiles could be discreetly gotten out of the country. It said the missiles were only in transit through Italy. However, the pro-Israeli SISMI seems to have gotten wind of the operation, with or without the help of Mossad. Italian police squads, like those that had helped save Qaddafi from the mercenaries of the Hilton assignment, swooped down and caught the four transporters red-handed. A new media campaign blaming the Palestinians for terrorism in Italy followed, with scant mention of Libya.

The next episode followed the Bologna bombing.[40] The PLO in Lebanon, engaged sporadically since the 1975–76 Lebanese civil war in a battle with the rightist Falange Party, had arrested four West Germans. They admitted to being rightists who had trained in Falangist camps in Lebanon. They belonged to a rightist terror band called the Karl Heinz Hoffman group, later linked to the 1980 Oktoberfest bombing in Munich. When the four Germans told their interrogators that they had overheard discussion by Italians on a "big bang" that was to take place in Bologna, a city ruled by Communists, PLO chairman Yasir Arafat's deputy, Salah Khalef (Abu Ayad), relayed the information to the Italian authorities (probably SISDE), but the tip was ignored. Bologna magistrates investigating after the incident discovered that several of the Italian neo-Fascists, together with rightists from Belgium, France, and Spain, had been trained by the Falangists in Lebanon. Other neo-Fascists charged with other crimes escaped to the Falangist-ruled part of Lebanon. In September 1980, after flying to Beirut to investigate, Italian newsman Italo Toni and newswoman Graziella de Palo disappeared from their Beirut hotel. There was a strong outcry in the Italian press that they had been kidnapped by the Lebanese rightists (though some attributed the disappearance to Palestinians or Libyans).

The single most mysterious act of terrorism or international piracy (if, as circumstantial evidence indicates, it was either of these) rocked Italy on June 27, 1980. On that day, as several Italian investigative reporters discovered, a Florentine magistrate named Giovanni Tricomi had booked an airline flight from Bologna to Palermo. Tricomi was on his way to the tiny Italian island of Pantelleria, about sixty miles south of the Sicilian coast, a steppingstone between North Africa and Italy since ancient times. Umberto Giovine, editor of the center-left Italian magazine *Critica Sociale,* disclosed that Tricomi was deep into an investigation of traffic in drugs between Libya and Palermo, the main distribution point for the drugs in Sicily. "Pantelleria," wrote an Italian newsman sympathetic to Giovine and his research, "has become a kind of trading post, where drugs, military information, arms and money are exchanged." Terrorists of the terrorist Prima Linea ("first line") group had also been reported to have used the island at one time or another, Giovine discovered.

About an hour after takeoff from Bologna, near the island of Ustica in the Tyrrhenian Sea sixty miles north of Palermo, the DC-9 suddenly vanished from Italian air controllers' screens after a violent explosion. All of its eighty-seven passengers, including the inquisitive magistrate, were lost in the disaster. What could be ascertained from the few bits of debris fished up from the sea suggested either a bomb inside the plane, or a missile outside it. Italian SISMI and carabiniere personnel leaked the rumor that there was evidence that the plane had been shot down by an air-to-air missile fired by a MIG-23 fighter. Among the Mediterranean countries, only Algeria and Libya possess such planes. U.S. and NATO intelligence sources were silent when asked whether Libyan planes had been in Tyrrhenian airspace at the time.

Lacking any proof, suspicion fell upon Libya. Algeria could have no possible motive either for such an act of piracy in general or for liquidating the troublesome Italian judge in particular. Qaddafi, on the other hand, had a motive, if it was true that the judge's investigation might have brought more exposures and undesirable publicity. The idea, farfetched as it sounded, haunted the offices of Italy's secret services and newspapers, and troubled the sleep of all in the country concerned with the battle against terrorism or relations with Libya.[41] It was perhaps inevitable that later Communist "disinformation" reports hinted that an American plane had shot down the airliner. The bomb theory, I was told in Rome in January 1982, looked like the most plausible.

For Italy, NATO, and the United States, another important aspect of Libyan operations in the Mediterranean concerns the island of Malta. Malta is now an independent island country, about 150 square miles in all, with 320,000 inhabitants of its own and more than twice that number of foreign tourists visiting each year.

Malta's possible value to Qaddafi, and the reason he has devoted so much attention to it, was stated during World War II by Sir Winston Churchill. Churchill called Malta "the only unsinkable aircraft carrier in the Mediterranean." It dominates all the sea routes between the Atlantic Ocean and the Suez Canal connection to the Persian Gulf as well as many of the north-south sea and air lanes between Europe and North Africa. As a British colony in 1941, it was a point of refuge and formation for Allied convoys supplying Allied forces in the eastern Mediterranean and Middle East. The main island's harbor and rocky fortresses at Valetta, the capital, were pounded relentlessly, month after month, by German and Italian bombers. It was scant comfort for the Maltese, who had to live underground during the worst Axis attacks, to be awarded the George Cross by Britain for their heroic steadfastness.

To Qaddafi and to Major Jalloud and other aides who regularly visited Malta after it won independence in 1965, the Maltese situation looked promising. In language and culture, the Maltese themselves must have looked to Qaddafi like semi-Arabs. They speak a tongue that is a mixture of Arabic, Italian, and English. The spires of Malta's churches (the Maltese are about 98 percent Roman Catholic) mingle harmoniously enough with architecture that is clearly Arab and reminds visitors constantly of past centuries of Arab domination.

In February 1982, the Maltese reelected to leadership Dom Mintoff's Labor Party in a close and controversial election. For more than fifteen years Mintoff has been the leader of the island's ruling Labor Party, which has followed an openly pro–Arab and pro–Third World policy. Opposing him was the pro–European Nationalist Party of Dr. Eddie Fenech Adami, a lawyer. Mintoff's long honeymoon with Qaddafi, which many Maltese wrongly predicted would cost him the 1982 election, soured and developed in August 1980 into an open break. Libyan technicians and military personnel were expelled from the island, and Libya seemed to be losing the foothold Qaddafi had painstakingly built up over the past decade. But no one knew who or what could replace the vast monies Qaddafi had invested in Malta. "You can be sure," one of Adami's Nationalist supporters told me, "that this is only one round in a long battle to come. Neither Qaddafi nor NATO is ever going to leave us in peace to be what we want to be—a little piece of Europe, floating in the Mediterranean, with no obligations to Africa."

Libyan operations in Malta shifted into high gear after final withdrawal of British and NATO naval and air forces from the island in 1979, though Qaddafi's patient and skillful wooing of Mintoff—

reciprocated by the same sort of behavior on Mintoff's part—had begun soon after Mintoff and his party came to power in 1971. Libya financed a technical and vocational training school in Valetta, and also helped with money for two newspapers, one of them, the *Jamahariya Mail*, a newspaper that reflected Libyan news and views but was published in English, the island's dominant language.

Qaddafi's propaganda and information specialists even set up their own radio station, beaming the revolutionary news from Tripoli throughout the Mediterranean area over Malta's powerful transmitters, and competing with Malta's own programs and those of the BBC medium-wave relay station in Malta. Libyan investment poured into several Maltese factories. Young Libyan soldiers, officials, and students, eager to escape the Islamic austerity at home and anxious to sample the pubs and cafés of Malta, its cheap whiskey and the friendship of Malta's attractive girls, swarmed over the island, especially on weekends.

What most troubled NATO and Israeli intelligence officials, however, was Qaddafi's discreet but insistent military penetration of the island.Only a month after Qaddafi's coup in Libya, on October 1, in 1970, the British army ceased responsibility for training and equipping the Maltese armed forces. The Maltese territorial units, hitherto maintained by the British army, were transferred to the control of Mintoff's government, and coordinated into the Malta Land Force. Qaddafi saw his opportunity to help Malta develop its own helicopter force in 1972, when West Germany donated four Bell 47G-2 choppers to Malta, and Maltese pilots and technicians returned home from helicopter training in Fassburg, West Germany.

In 1973 Libya took its cue and presented Mintoff with a five-seat Bell 206A Jet Ranger, complete with a flight instructor who set up a conversion course in Malta for four Maltese pilots and technicians. Malta's little five-helicopter force began flying regular search-and-rescue missions over the Mediterranean. Soon Libyan air-control technicians were at work in the Operations Center at Luqa, the airport in Valetta. In September 1978, Qaddafi sent three French-made Alouettes and a Super Frelon. During the October 1979 floods on the islands, the choppers saved many people trapped by torrents of water in the Marsa area. By this time, about forty-seven Libyan military personnel were based at Luqa, some of them following courses in the technical school the Libyans had established; others engaged in ground maintenance and communications for the Malta helicopter force. Clearly, Libyan intelligence now had an excellent post for watching and listening to central Mediterranean sea-lanes and airspace.

When Italian and other Western diplomats and the Tunisian government, still in shock following Qaddafi's attack on Tunisian soil at Gafsa in January 1980, warned the Maltese about Libya, the Mintoff government began to hedge its bets. Since Tunisians, as well as Libyans, could handle the French-made helicopters, several Tunisian instructors were assigned to Luqa in mid-1980. They were ready to take over flight training duties whenever Mintoff's showdown with Qaddafi occurred—and it did in the late summer of that year.[42]

What brought this showdown about was, quite simply, oil. In June 1980, Qaddafi cut off preferentially priced oil shipments to Malta. The oil was part of the many package deals that had established the Libyan presence on the island. Both Mintoff and his nationalist opponents hoped ultimately that Malta could emulate its former colonial master, Britain, and become self-sufficient from its own offshore oil. In Malta's case, this hope centered on the large Medina Bank, sixty-eight miles southeast of the main island. Malta claimed jurisdiction over waters to a distance of ninety-eight miles south of its southern coast, which was the halfway point between Malta and Libya.

Qaddafi, however, as part of maritime claims that included the entire Gulf of Sirte (which is where his planes clashed with F-14s of the U.S. Sixth Fleet in August 1981), insisted that Libya owned two-thirds of the entire sea area, up to a point just 65.5 miles from the same southern coast of Malta. Though Libya and Malta had agreed in 1976 to submit their quarrel by June 30, 1980, to the International Court of Justice in The Hague (as Tunisia and Libya had done over their similar oil problem in the Gulf of Gabes[43]), and though Malta had refrained from prospecting there until a settlement was reached, the Libyan National Oil Company had gone ahead with its own soundings in the area.

Exasperated with Libyan behavior in general, Mintoff in July 1980 asked the Texaco Oil Company of the United States to resume earlier Maltese operations on the Medina Bank under contract to the government of Malta. In August, Texaco chartered an Italian oil rig, the *Saipem-II*, from the Italian state oil company ENI and sent it out to the area. Almost immediately, one of Qaddafi's Soviet-made submarines appeared and began harassing the rig, training its deck gun on it and making it clear that discretion would be the better part of valor. Next a Libyan frigate appeared and told the rig's crew to leave or face the consequences. The Italian foreign ministry advised the captain, through the oil company, to begin winding up its operations. Italian patrol boats appeared and, together with the Libyans, watched as the *Saipem-II* wound up its cables and abandoned the site.

On August 26, Mintoff placed his helicopter force and several other light planes constituting the republic's air force "on alert." The next day, he expelled the forty-seven Libyan military personnel. On August 30, a Maltese government statement, read over Valetta radio within Qaddafi's range of hearing, accused Libya of endangering peace in the Mediterranean. It added that Malta hoped that Colonel Qaddafi had "not been aware" of what had happened on the Medina Bank. Mintoff then followed through by demanding—and getting on September 4—a UN Security Council session to consider Libya's "illegal action," pointing out that when Malta had notified Libya in November 1979 that it intended to resume drilling, Libya had made no objection. The Libyan delegate at the Security Council protested Qaddafi's good intentions toward Malta. The meeting adjourned without any action.

In the Farnesina, the Italian foreign ministry in Rome, the lights burned late. In Naples, there was concern in the headquarters of U.S. Admiral William Crowe, Jr., the supreme commander of NATO south. The concern centered on who or what (including possible Soviet aid that would almost guarantee access of Soviet ships or aircraft to Malta) might now replace the lost Libyan funds in Malta's economy.[44]

The Italian government had been mandated by the European Community in 1976 to reach a pact of neutrality with Malta and had long been brooding over its status. Italy now had a plan. Ever since Mintoff came to office in 1971 he had vainly sought formal guarantees of Malta's neutrality from Italy, Libya, Algeria, and France. He considered them the Mediterranean powers most concerned, and most in a position to offer such a guarantee. None had ever been forthcoming, but now, on September 15, 1980, the Farnesina came through. Malta and Italy exchanged notes agreeing on Italian recognition of Malta's future neutrality. Malta promised not to join any alliance, not to allow foreign troops or bases to use the island, and not to allow either U.S. or Soviet warships to use docking facilities. Libya was not mentioned, but everyone understood that the agreement would exclude any early return of the Libyans to Valetta.

To clinch the agreement, Italy undertook to guarantee Malta's neutral status. If Malta were threatened by outside forces and considered its neutrality so menaced, Italy would consult with Malta over providing military help as well as giving diplomatic support. An interesting clause in the agreement established that both countries would try to conclude similar Maltese pacts of neutrality with other European countries. The financial clauses guaranteed Italian economic aid to Malta; Mintoff said on September 20 that this would amount to $60 million over the period 1979–83, together with a loan of $15 million and an annual contribution of $4 million for five years to be used for "cooperative projects." Italy confirmed the figures, and Malta then issued a solemn declaration of its neutrality.

Since then Qaddafi has tried, without success, to move his propaganda apparatus formerly located in Malta to Cyprus by dangling the prospect of cheap oil before the Greek Cypriot government in Nicosia. But Israel and several neighboring Arab states have advised Cyprus against this. Cypriot Foreign Minister Nicos Rolandis stated in Nicosia in September 1980 that there was not the faintest chance that the Cyprus cabinet would ever agree to any such thing.[45] Periodically, Qaddafi has attacked the United States and Italy in his speeches since then for "trying to drive a wedge between the friendly peoples of Malta and Libya." As in most other cases, Qaddafi's most violent criticism is aimed at the United States.

**O**ne crucial factor in Qaddafi's growing patience and skill in his strategy for the export of his revolution has been his ability to cut his losses when he is not winning. Upon occasion, he can even be seen to play a constructive diplomatic role in trying to resolve peacefully a situation that he has helped to stir up. When British authorities in 1973 seized the *Claudia*, a ship loaded with arms for the provisional IRA, Qaddafi seems to have halted his direct arms aid to the IRA and confined himself to "moral and political" support for the Irish cause, which he has expressed on many occasions. He has regularly flirted with or aided one or another faction of the Palestinian movement, only to withdraw support when it became apparent that its tactics or objectives were not to his liking. The outstanding example, however, of attempts at constructive Libyan diplomatic action in a crisis where Qaddafi was shipping arms to one side is that of the Moros guerrilla movement in the Philippines. There was no clear positive outcome, but Qaddafi did prove that he can be persuaded, at times, that it lies in Libya's interest to try for constructive action.

Since 1971 a fairly well-organized Muslim guerrilla movement, the Moro National Liberation Front (MNLF) has been conducting terrorist, guerrilla, and, at times, full-scale military operations to end the control of Manila and attain self-rule of the thirteen southern provinces of the Philippines. Of the total Philippines population of about 50 million, about 6.5 million live in these provinces. The MNLF claims that about 5 million of them are Muslim; the Philippines government of President Ferdinand E. Marcos says the real number is about 3 million. For years, the MNLF obtained outside aid from various Islamic countries, including funds from Saudi Arabia and both funds and arms from Libya. The Islamic Conference organization showed special interest in the problem of Muslim rights in the Philippines, and so the outside concern was far from being Qaddafi's alone. In November 1976 Marcos seems to have concluded on the basis of all the evidence available to him that Qaddafi was the main source of arms, funds, and incitement, and that the key to a solution might lie in Tripoli. Accordingly, he sent his sophisticated wife, Mrs. Imelda Marcos, who has successfully conducted many diplomatic and business missions, on the seven-thousand-mile journey to Tripoli to charm Muammar al-Qaddafi into lending his own charisma and prestige to the MNLF to help find a settlement.

Qaddafi, duly charmed and impressed by Mrs. Marcos, readily agreed to do what he could. A month later, talks took place in Tripoli, half a world away from the scene of the Moro conflict, between Philippine government emissaries, Islamic Conference envoys, and MNLF representatives. Nur Misuari, the MNLF leader, came in person. Libya's fellow members of the Islamic Conference, Saudi Arabia, Somalia, and Senegal, attended too. On December 23 the conferees initialed a "preliminary" peace accord and ordered a cease-fire on Christmas Eve, December 24. The "preliminary" accord was signed on December 30 in Tripoli.

Back in Manila, President Marcos said on December 27 that the southern region would have its own regional institutions including an assembly and Muslim courts, but these would stay under control of the central government. So would a new regional security force for the Moro region. The conferees would return to Libya, Marcos said, in early February in order to conclude a final agreement for signature by early April. Meanwhile, a commission including equal numbers of Philippine and MNLF representatives and a four-man committee from Libya, Somalia, Senegal, and Saudi Arabia was supposed to supervise the cease-fire.

From this point on, however, Marcos appears to have gradually tugged the reins of decision out of Qaddafi's hands, and the role of Libya as a constructive catalyst gradually faded. President Marcos announced January 4 that a referendum would be held in the thirteen southern provinces to determine which wanted to be "part of an autonomous Muslim, the realm of the sovereignty and territorial integrity of the Republic of the Philippines." Other cultural areas, Marcos had said earlier, could have referenda too, and therefore autonomy in the south would have no specifically Muslim character. This of course was not to Qaddafi's liking, since his support had always been based on the Moros' Muslim character. More to the point, however, the MNLF disliked the whole idea of a referendum, and flatly rejected it.

Marcos skillfully held Qaddafi's interest in the matter by granting, on February 5, 1977, a conditional amnesty for Muslim rebels in the south, and then promulgating new laws for Muslims covering civil law matters and a Muslim court system. This was supposed to be a curtain-raiser for a new round of negotiations that began February 7 in Tripoli. They dragged on for nearly a month before breaking off on March 3 without visible progress. The Filipino envoy returned home to consult President Marcos, and the MNLF threatened to start the war up again if the government did not meet its further demands (its demands included a separate army, flag, and administration in the Muslim region, and incorporation of three predominantly Christian provinces— Palawan, South Cotabato, and Davao del Sur, where there was both offshore oil and good farmland—into the Muslim area). Military clashes between government forces and insurgents in Mindanao resumed March 7.

At this point, Imelda Marcos returned to Tripoli for another try. Qaddafi received her graciously, and presented her and the delegation accompanying her with a new Libyan peace plan. It involved creation of a new autonomous area, and a provisional administration to govern it and to supervise the referendum. In this respect he had taken his distance from MNLF, which insisted upon no referendum. In a cable to President Marcos, Qaddafi predicted the agreement would end the war and "open a new page in the relations between the Philippines and the Islamic states." In a marathon television and phone-in broadcast that lasted for four hours on March 29, President Marcos told his countrymen that the provisional administration would contain more Christians than Muslims, because their proportion in the population was greater. However, it would be subordinate to the martial-law regime and depend upon the outcome of the referendum. Colonel Qaddafi, Marcos added, had agreed to "persuade" the MNLF to accept the plan, including preparations for election of a regional assembly. Marcos claimed that Nur Misuari, the MNLF leader, would leave his asylum in Tripoli and return to take part in the new arrangements, which he had approved. (Misuari did not return, and said he disapproved.)

When the referendum was held April 17, official results showed 97.93 percent of votes in the thirteen provinces *against* the Qaddafi-MNLF proposals for autonomy under MNLF rule. About 75 percent of the 4,025,000 registered voters had voted. The MNLF boycotted the voting, claiming the first Tripoli agreement hadn't provided for such a referendum. Subsequent talks in April and May in Manila broke down, with Philippines Foreign Minister General Carlos Romulo blaming MNLF demands for total control in the south. The Islamic Conference members, including Libya, blamed Marcos's departure from the original Imelda Marcos–Qaddafi agreement in Tripoli. General Romulo attended an Islamic Conference meeting in May, where the MNLF was granted observer status with the Conference organization. In an interview with *Le Monde*, Misuari said the MNLF had abandoned its compromise efforts and would now battle for total independence of the south. The Philippines, he said, were helped mainly by the United States and Israel, while the MNLF had received help only from Muslim countries.

What happened next undoubtedly helped to make Qaddafi lose interest in the Moros. The MNLF split, first into two and finally into three factions, each with a separate host country. Nur Misuari, backed by Libya, stayed on in Tripoli. Misuari's aide, Hashim Salamat, head of the MNLF political committee, was picked up by Egypt and moved his base to Cairo, where Qaddafi's bitter adversary President Sadat became his host. Later another third faction had emerged and was living the life of pampered exiles in Saudi Arabia. To make matters worse from both the MNLF and the Libyan point of view, various ethnic and regional groupings in the Philippines themselves lined up behind the triad of émigré groups. After the Philippines problem was raised at an Islamic Conference meeting in May 1979 in Fez, Morocco, Moroccan Foreign Minister Muhammad Boucetta visited Manila and told President Marcos that King Hassan would be only too glad to help with the Moro problem in any way he could, adding another prospective cook to stir the Philippines broth. On September 20, the Libyan ambassador in Manila, Mustafa Dreiza, candidly admitted that although Libya would like to continue helping, this was growing very difficult since there were three factions to deal with. Another bit of bad news, from Qaddafi's point of view, was the contamination of the purely Muslim cause of the Moro rebels by their reported association, in 1980 and 1981, with the Maoist New People's Army, another anti-Marcos political group that was actually an armed wing of the pro-Chinese faction of the banned PKP, the Philippines Communist Party.[46] Qaddafi intensely dislikes any group associated to this degree with Communism. Little has been seen or heard of aid by Qaddafi to the rebellion since. Mrs. Marcos paid no further visits to Qaddafi to work her diplomatic wiles upon him. The old charges of his aiding the rebels have not been revived. Clearly, from Qaddafi's point of view, there are some revolutions it just doesn't pay to support.

The story of Qaddafi's "expansion" into the Caribbean, the backyard of the United States, is another aspect of the Libyan colonel's activity that like the Philippines episodes does not exactly fit the pattern of constant support for terrorism. However, it cut so close to home that it only increased the grievances the Reagan administration had with Qaddafi. As *Washington Star* columnist Georgie Anne Geyer wrote on May 5, 1981, just before the closing of Libya's Washington bureau, "A new triumvirate of support for radical politics in the Caribbean seems to be forming there, as it already has formed in Africa: a blend of Soviet weapons, Cuban military manpower and Libyan money."

Interest focused most strongly on Nicaragua. At the very moment when the Reagan administration was trying to decide whether to send $75 million in promised economic aid, Colonel Qaddafi's Foreign Liaison Bureau in Tripoli took care of the matter to the satisfaction of the revolutionary Sandinista regime by offering $100 million in aid, an enormous amount for a country the size of Nicaragua. At the same time, the Soviet Union contributed needed wheat, and the Cubans sent military advisers. All this happened, as Geyer reported, only a short time after Tomas Borge, a top Sandinista leader, had visited Tripoli and praised the principles of Qaddafi's *Green Book*. Marxist leaders from El Salvador and Guatemala, also visiting Tripoli, were also promised Libyan oil in generous terms, once they had managed to seize power from the pro–U.S. regimes in their respective countries.

By sending the Sandinistas aid when he did, Qaddafi effectively nullified any pressure the United States might have wanted to exert on the regime. It seems also to have signaled the end of a long-standing Cuban policy of advising Latin American radicals to keep up good relations with the United States, so that U.S. financial aid would not be cut off and Cuba and the Soviet Union forced to foot the bills. Elsewhere in the Caribbean, Libyan funding became available sometime in 1980 for a huge new international airport being built by Cubans for the probable use of Cuban and Soviet planes in Grenada, a radically ruled island mini-republic. Libyan aid first materialized when the United States pressed Europeans not to provide funds for the airport because of strategic implications involved. Cuba itself was already being used for transshipment of Soviet arms to friendly governments and rebel groups in Latin America and Africa, and the opening of the Grenada facility, expected by 1982, would add considerably to the transshipment capability,[47] especially by permitting refueling of Cuban or Soviet flights to and from Africa.

In Venezuela, just as he had done in Malta and parts of the Arab world, Qaddafi in 1980 began funding newspapers and sponsoring a leftist newspaper. "Far leftists from small radical parties connected closely with Nicaragua for many years are sporting Libyan money and constantly traveling back and forth between Caracas and Managua," Geyer reported.

During the Nicaraguan revolution, the PLO had supported the Sandinistas morally and with money and arms, while Israel backed the dictatorship of General Anastasio Somoza right up until his fall in July 1979.[48] Qaddafi began to work with elements of the PLO in sending arms and other help to the leftist guerrillas in El Salvador using the PLO office in Managua as a point of transit. The introduction of Soviet missiles and aircraft into Libya might someday turn it into "the Cuba of the Mediterranean," and that seems appropriate given that his own interests in the Caribbean are not incongruent with those of Cuba and the Soviet Union. To Reagan administration analysts in Washington, this has made things look as though Colonel Qaddafi's Bureau for the Export of the Revolution was operating as far away as the very southern shores of the United States.

# NUCLEAR AMBITIONS

"**W**e put the production of nuclear weapons," said Muammar al-Qaddafi in June 1981, "at the top of the list of terrorist activities. As long as the big powers continue to manufacture atomic weapons, it means that they are continuing to terrorize the world. . . . I have nothing but scorn for the notion of an Islamic bomb. There is no such thing as an Islamic bomb or a Christian bomb. Any such weapon is a means of terrorizing humanity, and we are against the manufacture and acquisition of nuclear weapons. This is in line with our definition of—and opposition to —terrorism. . . . this does not mean that we will spare any effort to use atomic energy for peaceful purposes."[1]

This was one of the clearest and most positive of a number of Qaddafi's disavowals of any intent to make nuclear weapons in Libya. Yet he has repeatedly berated his underlings and even publicly expressed regret over the slowness of his government to "implement the nuclear projects." His intention that these projects should provide both the means to generate energy for Libya for that distant day when the oil runs out (perhaps in thirty years), and to challenge Israel's undoubted nuclear-weapons monopoly in the Middle East, has always been clear. So far, his attempts to reach both his peaceful and his warlike goals have proved futile. At the southern desert stronghold of Sebha in the desert of Fezzan, not far from the missile and suborbital satellite range operated by a West German firm called Orbital Transport und Rakenten-Aktiengesellschaft (OTRAG), personnel connected with another West German firm, Kraftwerkunion AG (KWU), were reported to be cooperating with Libya in the preparation of a nuclear reactor facility. Unlike Qaddafi's small Soviet-supplied research reactor outside Tripoli, this one, if successfully assembled, would ultimately have the capacity to manufacture weapons-grade enriched uranium, or plutonium. The reactor, ironically, was one which KWU, with the knowledge and approval of the West German authorities, had reserved for Nigeria after talks with the Nigerian army chief of staff in 1976. Nigeria had delayed buying until the Germans involved apparently despaired of the sale.[2] KWU tried to sell it to Libya instead but initially had been denied an export license. Preparation of the Sebha operation, code-named "The Hotel Project," finally began at the start of 1981, and active construction started in the early summer. Of course, it might be many months—years, even—before such a reactor could be equipped. Libya lacked a real industrial base or the infrastructure needed to process uranium, manufacture reactor fuel from the uranium, produce substances like heavy water, or reprocess spent fuel into either weapons-grade enriched uranium (U-235) or plutonium (P-238). But Qaddafi, with the aid of highly paid foreign scientists and technicians —including, it was reported, not only one of the reports on work done for the secret South African nuclear facilities but also the German consultant who wrote it—was trying hard. He was trying so hard that his efforts could hardly be concealed or even disguised.

**A**ccording to a story originally told by Egyptian journalist Muhammad Haykal, efforts had begun in 1970 when Qaddafi sent Major Jalloud to Peking in an attempt to see whether or not China might be tempted by a huge offer of cash to sell Libya at least one prototype atomic bomb.

"Sorry," Chinese Premier Chou En-lai told Jalloud in effect, "but China obtained the bomb through its own efforts. We believe in self-help." Neither the bomb nor the technology were for sale to Libya.

The next major Libyan effort, not unexpectedly in view of Qaddafi's early honeymoon with Washington, was directed at one of the leading U.S. suppliers of nuclear reactors and nuclear-fueled electric power stations, Gulf and General Atomics Corporation of Los Angeles. Would the firm like to sell Libya a complete reactor system, and perhaps some fuel—as highly enriched as possible? (More than 90 percent enrichment is needed for weapons.) Gulf and General Atomics executives told Qaddafi's envoys that they were ready to talk business. Contracts were drawn up and a prospective deal was blocked out for a reactor-powered electric generating station. By avoiding, evading, or cheating the international inspections and safeguards that were then being set up by the Western uranium suppliers' consortium and later by the International Atomic Energy Agency, IAEA in Vienna, skilled Libyan or hired foreign scientists probably would have been able to produce some plutonium as a biproduct of the electric power generating process, as India was then doing.[3]

When the White House and the State Department got wind of the deal, both stepped in—reportedly with the personal attention of Henry Kissinger, then presidential security affairs adviser—to kill it. U.S. export licenses for the equipment were denied.

Next, Qaddafi's men approached a new firm of American consultants, Adera Inc. This firm had been established by several Arab-American academics and businessmen to study the possibility of development projects in the Arab world. Telegrams they received from Tripoli made Adera's experts believe that Libya was interested mainly in a routine physics laboratory, or a small, safeguarded research reactor, generating no more than perhaps two megawatts of electricity. Several meetings held in Tripoli, New York, and other places soon convinced Adera that Libyan intentions were in fact quite different. One of those attending a meeting chaired by Omar al-Meheishi in 1974 recalls that Meheishi, when told by one of the Americans that the U.S. government could not spare U.S. aid money to help Libya get nuclear-generated power, and would not authorize export of nuclear materials to Libya, pounded his fist on the table, shouting: "You can provide three billion or so in aid to Israel every year, but not even a few dollars to an Arab country for its own development!" The Adera group, like Gulf and General Atomics before it, broke off the talks.

More and more, Qaddafi focused his nuclear efforts on an organization called the Arab Development Institute, a group of scientists recruited from abroad. Qaddafi offered large salaries, housing and excellent working conditions to scientists who came from Baghdad, Beirut, Damascus, Cairo, or other Arab centers of science and learning to work for him. One cynical Egyptian physicist who worked there for a while later told a friend: "Everyone at ADI is glad to get the money, but a great deal of work is not getting done."

At the same time, Qaddafi's closest aides were capitalizing on an excellent personal rapport between Qaddafi and Pakistan's brilliant populist politician, President Zufilcar Ali Bhutto. The two had become acquainted during Qaddafi's first years of power. They got on well, each respecting the other as a champion of the Third World.

Pakistan had sought a nuclear capability of its own, to match India's. Ali Bhutto was often quoted as saying and writing that if the "Christian" and "Jewish" civilizations were entitled to nuclear weapons, then the "Islamic" one was too. Talks began sometime in 1974 or 1975 on nuclear collaboration between Pakistan and Libya. Whether or not large sums of Libyan cash were actually sent to Pakistan to fund the Pakistani program, as was reported, seems highly uncertain. At least one Libyan check (for $400,000) was passed to Pakistan at a meeting of Pakistanis and Libyans in the Pakistani embassy in Paris.[4] Sales of Niger's yellowcake uranium ore to Pakistan, some channeled through Libya and some sent directly, are a matter of public record.

In 1977 and 1978, General Zia al-Huq gradually chiseled away Ali Bhutto's power and that of his Pakistan People's Party, and then ousted him. Ali Bhutto was executed over the protests of many world leaders after a Pakistani court convicted him of complicity in the slaying of a political opponent. Qaddafi and Ali Bhutto had gotten along at least as well with each other as Henry Kissinger and Anwar al-Sadat had done. With General Zia and Qaddafi, it was quite the opposite. By late 1977 and early 1978, Qaddafi was demanding various political conditions from Zia for continuing to put any Libyan money into the Pakistani nuclear program. He asked Zia to take Pakistan out of the pro-Western Central Treaty Organization (CENTO) and join the non-aligned bloc instead. Qaddafi also wanted to upgrade the military collaboration between Libya and Pakistan, and to be allowed to construct an anti-Shah broadcasting station (he was an enthusiastic supporter of the anti-Shah revolutionary movement that was finally to triumph in Iran in the winter of 1978–79) in Pakistan or, if possible, in Afghanistan. General Zia, as Pakistan's new chief of state, would go along with none of these. Sometime in early 1978, Libyan-Pakistani nuclear cooperation seems to have broken off completely.

At the same time Qaddafi approached the Indian government offering sales of cheap oil if India would share some of its nuclear technology. According to Indian diplomats, Prime Minister Indira Gandhi and later Prime Minister Morarji Desai agreed only to supply the same low-grade technical help already given to perhaps fifteen other Third World states in India's modest "atoms for peace" program— instructors in engineering and in laboratory isotopes for medical purposes. There was no objection, however, to allowing India's state power company, the Bharat Heavy Electric Company, to enter into contracts to build conventional Diesel-powered electric generating stations in Tripoli and Benghazi. Bharat built these projects, and was later granted a contract to supply electricity and other preliminary work to prepare the site in Sirte for the large Soviet-supplied nuclear-fueled electric power station that the Soviet Union promised, in a 1976 agreement, to sell Libya.

While the arrangements were under way with Bharat, Libya was already operating a small two-megawatt experimental reactor supplied by the Soviets and fully safeguarded by frequent inspections carried out by the International Atomic Energy Commission (IAEC) in Vienna. The research reactor was installed at Tajjura, outside Tripoli and near Okbah ibn Nafi Air Base (formerly Wheelus Field). The two principal Libyan scientists in charge of the Tajjura reactor, and of a nuclear engineering faculty at Tripoli's al-Fateh University, were Dr. Fathi Nooh, trained at the University of California at Berkeley (outstanding among perhaps five hundred Libyans schooled in nuclear theory and technology at American institutions), and Dr. Fathi Skinji, trained in India and Britain. At least one American consultant on loan to Libya from a major U.S. university was among the scientists who helped set up the nuclear engineering facility at al-Fateh University.[5]

Early in 1981, residents of Sebha began to notice preparations beginning for construction of a very large new installation in the Sebha oasis region. Libyans living nearby were apprehensive when construction of several buildings actually began in the early summer of 1981. They noted the comings and goings of foreign consultants and technicians. It was believed that at least some of them were connected with the West German firm KWU. Although the West German government in Bonn had denied an export license to KWU to sell to Libya the medium-sized 450-megawatt nuclear fueled electric power reactor originally intended for Nigeria, Libyans close to the program said Qaddafi still hoped, through money or other means, to acquire all or parts of the KWU system and perhaps combine them with other Soviet equipment cannibalized from either the delivered Tajjuna reactor or the undelivered Sirte one. His hope was to build a comprehensive system at Sebha that might eventually manufacture weapons-grade enriched uranium or plutonium. U.S. intelligence officials at the highest level denied knowledge of the project, but reports about it persisted.

**W**ell before first reports about Soviet SS-12 Scaleboard missiles in Libya, an ambitious German engineer and entrepreneur named Lutz

Kayser had introduced advanced missile and satellite-launching technology. Since October 1980, on a vast area that Kayser claimed Qaddafi had furnished free of charge, Kayser's firm, OTRAG, had begun testing rockets that Kayser said would eventually furnish Third World countries with their own "poor man's satellite" for telecommunications, education, and weather observation. For anyone who followed rocket and missile technology, especially at its still imperfect stage of development on the African continent, it was very difficult to believe that Libya would not draw many military, as well as peaceful, advantages from OTRAG's ground experiments and rocket launchings.

One of the best ways to irritate a West German diplomat or government official is to ask him about OTRAG. When West German Chancellor Helmut Schmidt was asked about where OTRAG could go when it was expelled from Zaire by President Mobutu Sese Soko in April 1979, Schmidt said, "Let OTRAG go to hell!"

OTRAG signed its first deal in 1976, not with Zaire or Libya but with the West German government in Bonn. The accord gave OTRAG permission to establish a rocket test-and-launch site in Zaire; such permission was necessary since OTRAG had its legal seat in West Germany. OTRAG then acquired an area of about 100,000 square kilometers, or one-tenth the total area of Zaire. It launched its first rocket in 1977, and announced that by 1981 it planned to send up reconnaissance and earth-resources and communications satellites (the latter in synchronous orbits) from the Zaire site. The original rocket was based on a building-block system, with a relatively small fuel tank and engine. Each such double unit constituted a module, which could be combined to form a larger vehicle. Cost was kept down by using as many mass-produced, off-the-shelf components as possible. After an international outcry from East bloc and African states, and also after many questions by Western intelligence agencies, Mobutu revoked OTRAG's contract. Kayser approached a number of Third World states that he thought might be interested in cooperating in the development of his satellites. "You need satellites," he told them in effect, "for communications, evaluation of natural resources, or just to keep an eye on your neighbors. If you don't have your own system, you will have to rely either on existing American systems, like Intelsat, or Soviet ones, like Stationer. These are expensive, and you have to take the information they provide on faith, because the owner can feed you whatever he wants." The firm used similar arguments in talks with Brazil, Indonesia, Sudan, Nigeria, Sri Lanka, Sierra Leone, Liberia, Syria, and China.

Many expressed polite interest; none would have OTRAG operating on their home ground. Then Kayser began talks with the Libyans.

At the beginning of 1980, Qaddafi's involvement in Chad and his interest in his other neighbors was growing. Quite probably, he was not entirely satisfied with the intelligence the Soviets might have furnished him from satellites, and he had access to no other system. In May 1980, Libya agreed to let OTRAG use the Fezzan site. Though the Soviets and East Germany (especially the latter) had screamed with indignation over OTRAG's operations in Zaire, they said not a word against its move to Libya.

From its very beginnings, OTRAG had Arab connections that intrigued Israeli intelligence. Kayser was well acquainted with the work of Wolfgang Pilz and several other German specialists whom President Nasser had hired in 1962 for his *Projekt Wasserfall,* an effort to build long-range rockets similar to Germany's World War II V-2 types with warheads that could strike Israel. Mossad moved energetically against the Germans in Egypt, sending several package bombs to one specialist and kidnapping the family of another. Nasser ended the experiments after all the Germans had withdrawn in 1967.

Once OTRAG had been installed in Zaire, the Arab League headquarters in Cairo contacted Kayser, expressing interest in possible applications of his research to Arcomsat—a project, later renamed Arabsat, for a pan-Arab communications satellite. Several other German firms were already involved, and the League committee dealing with the project reportedly signed an agreement with OTRAG to buy the first satellite successfully orbited from OTRAG's launching pad at Kapanitono, Zaire.

The site selected for OTRAG in Libya was an immense natural basin, bounded on the south by the Fezzan plateau and on the north by the Djebel al-Sawda, a low range of mountains above Sebha. This site is at the heart of Libya. The Egyptian frontier is about six hundred miles away; those of Algeria, Niger, and Chad each about half that distance. Sebha has a large, modern airport and lies at about the same latitude as Cape Canaveral, Florida, which is far enough from the equator to place satellites in orbit.

Kurt Wukasch, the OTRAG president, in Stuttgart, told several interviewers in late 1980 that Libya was "especially well suited" to OTRAG's purposes.

Moroccan officials in Rabat told newsmen in March 1981 that OTRAG had agreed to supply medium-range ballistic missiles, capable

of carrying nuclear warheads, to Libya. In Stuttgart, Wukasch responded, "There is nothing to these ridiculous reports." The Moroccan fears
appeared to be a reaction to a successful suborbital launch in Libya on
March 1. OTRAG said that as a result of the test, it was offering the
"smallest type from our rocket family as a science research rocket at a
price level defying competition," capable of carrying payloads of 220 to
880 pounds (100 to 400 kilograms) to the "upper atmosphere and
radiation zone."[6] A further test conducted May 17 was reported to be a
failure.

During the summer of 1981, U.S. intelligence and space specialists
formed an interagency task force to study OTRAG and similar commercial rocket development elsewhere. Joseph S. Nye, Jr., a former senior
administration specialist, said that the U.S. government has only begun
to face this new security problem, which is a form of advanced nuclear
proliferation. In September 1981, U.S. intelligence officials said they
had new evidence that OTRAG might be using its tests in Libya to hide
efforts to sell military technology not only to Libya but to Pakistan, Iraq,
and other countries. The Sebha operations, they added, were under
the jurisdiction of Libyan army officers connected with Libya's nuclear
program. OTRAG had intensified its efforts to buy or build a rocket
guidance system. When the United States, Egypt, and Morocco
privately urged the Bonn government to do more to curb OTRAG, the
reply was that there was little that could be done since OTRAG was a
private firm not under government control, and it was operating from an
Italian subsidiary in Sardinia.[7]

But the international outcry did have an effect. In December 1981,
OTRAG's executives told the news media that OTRAG would cease its
Libyan operations in early 1982 and move on to an undisclosed new
country.

If Soviet or Libyan missiles are ever launched from Libyan territory
against NATO's exposed under-flank in Greece, Italy, or France, and if
Libyan technicians are involved in firing them, they will probably have
been trained not in the Soviet Union, nor even in the former supersecret
installation in southern Libya by West Germany's OTRAG. The
training of those manning the missile launchers and the guidance
systems they use have a common origin: neutral Sweden.

The Swedish story goes back to the oil crisis of 1974. Soon after the
shock waves of the world oil price rises in that year struck Scandinavia,

Swedish Social Democratic Premier Olof Palme's government made a deal with Qaddafi. A treaty of friendship and cooperation, the deal involved technology in exchange for oil, and an agreement to train Libyan technicians in electronics and other skills in Sweden. Its details have never been made public, despite a clamor by concerned Swedes and their media, especially Stockholm's *Espressen*, which is owned by Sweden's Bonnier chain and often speaks for Sweden's pro-Israel lobby. Despite public outcries against the Libyan connection, by 1977 the Swedish state-owned military electronics firm, TELUB, formed with Libya's Military Procurement Authority an agreement to give one hundred of Libya's most promising technical graduates intensive training in military electronics.

At the same time, TELUB began selling Libya sophisticated remote-control systems for high-speed motorboats capable of being linked to radar surveillance systems also manufactured by TELUB. Another Swedish firm, Storebro, builds the necessary fiberglass motorboats and has helped set up a boatyard in Libya for the Libyan navy.

So as not to be seen violating Swedish laws against manufacturing "lethal" arms for export to areas of dangerous international tension, the Swedish War Supplies Directorate designated the boats and the radar control system "civilian" equipment. As weapons of terror, however, the remote-controlled boats could be formidable: packed with explosives or equipped with missiles or rockets, the boats could be launched at a speed of thirty knots over a twenty-mile range against targets at sea. TELUB's parent company, Forenade Fabrik, Verken's (FFV), has supplied to Tunisia, Libya's fearful neighbor and possible adversary, and to Kenya, one of the world's most advanced one-man rocket launchers —one that delivers precision, long-range high explosives or antipersonnel rockets and antitank heat-seeking missiles. There is no evidence at this writing that Libya has also been able to obtain these particular weapons.

In 1977, when Qaddafi's Swedish connection first began to get under way, a Swedish consultancy firm, Teleplan, with close ties to the Swedish defense ministry, sent two instructors to Libya to teach military electronics to Qaddafi's army. Perhaps they worked with some of the American experts whom Edwin Wilson and Frank Terpil brought from the China Lake Naval Weapons Center in the United States.[8] Another Swedish firm in the town of Gavle began training Libyans in military cartography. In December 1977, TELUB's director, former Air Force General Benkt Dahlberg, informed the Swedish foreign ministry that the proposed Libyan trainees in Sweden would be military personnel. In January 1978, Swedish Ambassador to Libya Bengt Holmquist sent a classified report to Stockholm in which he warned that the TELUB contract was for training Qaddafi's cadres in the techniques of guided missiles. He also mentioned that Libya was trying to recruit retired Swedish officers as advisers. The United States, he noted, was concerned about the transactions.

By 1979 the first of ninety-six Libyan trainees arrived in Sweden to begin their training under conditions of tight secrecy. Meanwhile TELUB had designed shock-absorbing plastic portable shields that were capable of protecting up to five men. Ostensibly these were nonlethal shields for riot control, but it soon became evident that they could be fitted with weapons and radio equipment. The price proposed to Libya was about fifteen thousand dollars apiece, but the deal collapsed when it was disclosed in the Swedish newspapers. General Dahlberg resigned in April 1980 after the details were published in Sweden.

In March 1981 it was disclosed that Libya's five large amphibious tank landing craft—three of them the newer Soviet Polnocny class, which can carry 240 troops and eleven tanks, and are often seen in Soviet maneuvers in the Baltic Sea—were being fitted with Sweden's 40mm Bofors rapid-fire cannon, just about the best in the world. Exploding with indignation, *Espressen* commented: "Swedish companies are forbidden to export weapons to Libya, which supports international terrorism. But once more the law has been circumvented—the cannons are being produced under license in Italy and Sweden has no control of deliveries from other countries."

Critics of the Swedish government began a general offensive against it for not disclosing details of the TELUB guided-missile training deal. The officials concerned, including Trade Minister Staffan Burenstam Linder, his predecessor Hadar Cars, Defense Minister Eric Kronmark, and Social Affairs Minister Karen Soder all said they believed the training was only "civilian" in nature. Three successive governments have been involved: the three-party coalition in power when the final TELUB-Libyan contract was signed in 1979; the Folk Party regime, which collapsed after a year in office over the question of whether Sweden should build nuclear power plants; and the more recent Center-Liberal-Conservative coalition cabinet of Prime Minister Thorbjorn Falldin, which took office on October 12, 1979. Various parliamentary committees and extra-parliamentary bodies investigated the agreement, but it stood firm and so did the Falldin cabinet.

Here was clearly a situation where Qaddafi seemed to hold all the high cards, just as he did in so many of his other Western European connections. TELUB in 1981 was in financial difficulty; but if it defaults on the contract, it would have to pay hefty damages to Qaddafi. So crucial was the training to the Tripoli regime that Libyan diplomats apparently threatened to break off all ties with Sweden if the contract were canceled. However, when the Stockholm government canceled it in January 1982, no such break occurred.

Sweden imported about $500 million in Libyan products, mainly oil, in 1980; it imported only half that much the previous year. Heavy construction and other contracts, linked to the TELUB contract and military business, has brought the value of Swedish work in Libya up from $60 million in 1979 to around $1.5 billion in 1980 and 1981. L. M. Ericson, the telecommunications firm, was awarded a contract to develop all of Libya's telephone network. A construction company, ABV, is to build a new city in Sirte. Skanska Cement is building hotels, mosques, tourist bureaus, restaurants, and shopping centers. Muhammed Jeladi, one of the senior Libyans at the Stockholm People's Bureau, told one newsman that all the relevant Swedish governments had known of the linkage between the crucial TELUB contract and the other Swedish business in Libya. "Cancel one contract," said Jeladi, "and there will be a chain reaction."

The ninety-six young Libyans who in 1981 were still learning how to guide missiles—perhaps some of the very ones being tested on the range near Sebha by West Germany's OTRAG firm—lived in a special Stockholm hostel that cost over $4 million in Libyan petrodollars. The hostel is complete with heated swimming pool and mosque. Photos of weapons training (basic small-arms practice that in the U.S. would be considered police-academy or gun-club curricula) led to new outcries in the Swedish newspapers against other parts of their course, which includes radar, electronic communications, computer data processing, physics, and mathematics. The Libyans also learned to apply all these skills to the guidance of missiles.[9]

Finally, in January 1982, the Swedish government canceled the contract, sent the Libyans home, and let it be known there would be no further such courses.

# IN THE SUPERPOWER WEB

On a summer day in 1981, not long after Qaddafi's celebration of the eleventh anniversary of the U.S. evacuation of Wheelus Field, a Soviet Tupolev T-26 Backfire-B bomber took off from a base in the Black Sea area. Instead of flying the usual routine patrol around Russia's southern reaches, the Backfire, swiftest and deadliest aircraft type in the inventory of *Aviatsiya Dal'mevo Desitviya* (Soviet Long-Range Aviation), flew westward over Bulgaria and Yugoslavia across the Mediterranean. Crossing the Libyan coast, the Backfire landed at the new air base in Kufra, King Idris's favorite oasis and now a stronghold of Muammar al-Qaddafi's military machine in southern Cyrenaica.

The Backfire, the first ever to visit Libya, stayed at Kufra barely long enough to be refueled, and to be photographed by U.S. or Egyptian reconnaissance. One of those who saw the photographs was Egypt's defense minister, Lieutenant General Muhammad Abu-Ghazala. "We think," he said, the Backfire landed at Kufra "only to find out if these runways are good enough. . . . The runways in Kufra and some other bases are now more than five miles long. Why did the Libyans build a base with five miles of runway unless they are going to be used by some other people? They don't have any such airplanes for the Libyans to fly."[1]

U.S. and Allied defenses had often spotted and peacefully intercepted the 3,750-mile-range Backfires along the northern perimeter of air defenses near Alaska, Canada, and northern Europe. Some Danish fighters had a run-in with several Backfires during NATO maneuvers in the North Sea at about the time of the Backfire flight to Kufra. But this was the first Backfire visit to a country "friendly" to the Soviet bloc, and it was close to NATO's southern flank. Coming as it did shortly before the U.S.–Libyan air battle of August 19, 1981, over the Gulf of Sirte, the visit flashed two signals. One, to the West, demonstrated that the Soviets are more and more involved in building their "strategic friendship," as one Soviet diplomat called it, with Libya. The second signal was equally clear and should have been understood by Qaddafi: his growing military and strategic ventures were drawing Libya out of nonalignment and back into the superpower web from which he and his young RCC companions had sought to extricate their country in their carefully planned coup of September 1, 1969. Proof of nonalignment was supposed to be the speedy evacuation of the British and U.S. bases, and denial of landing rights or port facilities to the Soviets as well. But after the Sirte battle, Soviet port visits and antisubmarine air patrols from Libyan bases began.

Far more chilling for Europeans and for Qaddafi's Arab neighbors was a report by London's authoritative International Institute for Strategic Studies (IISS) in September 1981 that the Soviets had deployed in Libya a dozen SS-12 Scaleboard surface-to-surface missiles capable of reaching Athens, Cairo, Cyprus, and southern Turkey. The IISS report closely followed Qaddafi's threat, shortly after the August 19 air battle with the U.S. Sixth Fleet, to retaliate against "U.S. nuclear arsenals" in Italy, Greece, and Turkey if U.S. forces again returned to the Gulf of Sirte. The U.S. Defense Intelligence Agency said Qaddafi had not received the SS-12s, but rather a radar system generally used with them. Scaleboards can be deployed on mobile launchers, and those deployed in the Soviet Union have nuclear warheads in the megaton range, more destructive than the U.S. Pershings that NATO countries had agreed to accept in Europe by 1983 to counter the USSR's SS-20s. Under the Nato program, Italy planned to base 121 Cruise missiles at Comiso, Sicily. The Italian foreign ministry expressed surprise and concern over Qaddafi's threats, and reminded him that the U.S. missiles would be aimed toward the USSR, not Libya. The London *Daily Telegraph*, reproducing the IISS report, said the newest Soviet missiles had been installed in bunkers cut into the hills outside Tobruk. Many new Soviet personnel had arrived in Cyrenaica, augmenting the one thousand or so Soviets and four thousand East Germans, Cubans, Czechs, and other East bloc personnel already in Libya.[2]

Ottoman Turkey, Italy, Germany, and finally Britain, the United States, and France had recognized Libya's strategic importance in the war and postwar years of the 1940s and 1950s. But it had been left to Joseph Stalin, in his try for a political and military foothold in Tripolitania in 1945,[3] to signal Libya's tremendous strategic importance to the superpowers, and the probably unwilling role it would play in any new world war.

In 1949, four years after Stalin's bid for the Soviet trusteeship in Tripolitania that would have given him North African bases for the first time, a committee of the U.S. Joint Chiefs of Staff, under the authority of President Harry Truman, drew up a U.S. contingency plan (one of many others prepared over the years) for World War III. It was called Operation Dropshot. Its basic assumption, for planning purposes, was that world nuclear war, probably over Berlin, would break out on January 1, 1957, following Soviet aggression in Central Europe and at other diversionary points. Dropshot was declassified in 1977 and became available through the Freedom of Information Act. Author Anthony Cave Brown obtained the plan and published it, with comment and analysis, in an extraordinary book.[4]

After a visit by Israeli Prime Minister Menachem Begin to the United States in September 1981, it was disclosed that the United States was considering its own strategic stockpiling of weapons in Israel. For years there had been planning and agonized debate over the U.S. Rapid Deployment Force that was to defend Persian Gulf oil. These plans were clearly complementary to the huge Soviet-supplied arsenal that Qaddafi had been building in the Libyan Desert since 1974, as well as to other stocks of Soviet material and equipment in Ethiopia, Mozambique, and Afghanistan. This is why a fresh look at Dropshot seems to be in order today.

In the plan as presented by Brown, there were two major assumptions that are no longer true today. One was that mainland China would fight with Moscow beside Moscow's Eastern European allies and such Far Eastern friends as North Korea. Another was that there would be no permanent Soviet military presence in the Middle East or North Africa that could seriously interfere with Allied war operations. Greece, Turkey, most Arab states, Israel, Iran, Turkey, and Pakistan would try to stay neutral but would join the Allies if "attacked or seriously threatened."[5] This took into account, of course, none of the Mideast events of the last thirty years—not the Soviet invasion of Afghanistan nor the collapse of the Shah's regime in Iran and the consequent end of that strategic presence on the southern Soviet borders, nor the loss of Wheelus Field, nor the Soviet toehold in Libya that was being acquired in the early 1980s. The North African portions of Dropshot are therefore of double interest and importance today.

Dropshot's emphasis on North Africa was no accident. When it was prepared, the chairman of the Joint Chiefs of Staff was General Omar Bradley, who had commanded the 2nd U.S. Army Corps during the North African war in Tunisia and in Sicily in 1943. Brown notes that Dropshot required the Allies to hold and defend against the Soviets all of the southern Mediterranean, Arab, and African coastlines between Tel Aviv and Dakar, to say nothing of the strategic Turkish Straits. But even though Algeria, Tunisia, and Morocco were still firmly under French rule and Libya was not yet even an independent kingdom, Dropshot, as Brown points out, foresaw resistance to the Allies from "extremely hostile native armies, especially in Algeria, Libya, and Egypt."[6] This would have been totally unlike the situation in World War II when local populations were, at best, either openly friendly to the Allies (like the Sanussi in Libya) or, at worst, disarmed and indifferent (like the Arabs of French North Africa, who were concerned most of all about ending French colonial rule).

Dropshot required the United States to provide air and naval defense for bases the United States had then at Port Lyautey, Morocco, and others at Casablanca. After Dropshot was drawn up, the United States constructed three other giant bases for the USAF's Stategic Air Command (SAC) in Morocco. These and Port Lyautey had all been turned back to Moroccan control by 1978. All could be reactivated in case of a global crisis, if King Hassan or his successor remained in the Western camp. Further east, Dropshot's defensive arrangements included the defense on ground, sea, and in the air of Gibraltar (still a British Crown Colony in 1981, though there is constant pressure from Spain for its return), Malta (no longer a British colony, and although under pressure from Qaddafi its neutrality guaranteed by Italy),[7] the Gulf of Gabes in Tunisia, and the big air and naval base complex at Bizerte in Tunisia. In Algeria, the equally important air and naval-base complex at Mers al-Kebir, outside Oran, and the port of Algiers both called for Allied protection. Brown, perhaps recalling the three-day Franco-Tunisian battle for Bizerte believes the United States would have to fight in order to get access to Bizerte.

As for Libya, Dropshot foresaw the need to defend Tripoli and the Cyrenaican ports. In specific military terms, Dropshot called for deployment to Libya of about one U.S. Marine division, with one fighter group, antiaircraft defenses, and naval local-defense forces between D-Day (the outbreak of war) plus one month and D-Day plus three months. Further forces were to be allocated for defense of Egypt and the Suez Canal and to Greece and Turkey.[8]

Dropshot foresaw the subsequent rapid expansion of the Soviet navy into the northern, western and Black Seas (the Black Sea was the home waters of the Soviet Mediterranean *eskadra*) and the Far East. It also projected the development of the present formidable Soviet submarine fleet and fast coastal and attack craft. In the Middle East, Dropshot's authors predicted that there would be a fierce sea and air war for control of sea-lanes that the Soviets have to use to transport Middle Eastern oil back home.[9] Among the probable Soviet strategic objectives in the imaginary war of 1957 was a Mideast campaign, which would include Greece and Turkey, the two quarreling neighbors on NATO's southeastern flank. The campaign's main purpose was to deny Mideast oil resources and the Suez Canal to the Western powers, and to increase the depth of Soviet air defenses for the USSR's southern regions. Dropshot estimated that the Soviets would try to seize and use such Mediterranean area ports as Pola, Split, and the Gulf of Kotor in Yugoslavia; the port of Palermo, Sicily; and Valona Bay in Albania.[10] When Dropshot was drawn up, however, there was little or no account taken of the additional possibility of Soviet airborne landings along the North African coast. This was something the Soviets must have had in mind at least for Egypt when they alerted their airborne divisions during the global alert by both U.S. and Soviet forces following the 1973 Israeli recrossing of the Suez Canal and the surrounding of the Egyptian Third Army in Sinai.

To support the defense of Greece from invasion by the Soviets, Dropshot recommended avoiding concentrating all of Greek army strength in Thrace and Macedonia in northern Greece because Soviet overland thrust through Bulgaria or Yugoslavia might destroy what Greek forces were there. Instead, the Greeks should plan a slow withdrawal south, harassing the invaders as much as possible, and as final fallback try to hold Crete. Dropshot's authors thought this could be done with about two Greek divisions and a fighter group, provided they had support by Allied air forces from the Egypt-Cyrenaica area.[11] It would be essential for the Western forces to hold the key Mediterranean islands of Sicily, Malta, Cyprus, and Crete. Qaddafi has shown considerable interest in all of these. On September 1, 1981, he warned that Libya would attack bases used by U.S. forces within his reach in all these areas if U.S. naval and air forces again entered the Gulf of Sirte.[12]

During the early years of Qaddafi's rule, prerequisites for any future Soviet-Libyan alliance hardly looked propitious. The United States and its allies seemed to be at least benevolently neutral toward Qaddafi's revolutionary experiment in Libya, and even willing to guarantee his regime's survival by providing it with protection. Qaddafi's distrust of both superpowers, his Islamic zealotry, and his visceral dislike of Communism all militated against any leanings toward the Soviet Union. Though Nasser's final years were marked by growing dependence on Moscow for economic and military aid, Qaddafi's anti-Sovietism was little affected by his enormous respect for Nasser. After Nasser's death on September 28, 1970, and President Sadat's assumption of power, Qaddafi's anti-Soviet attitude at first even seemed to strengthen. He approved of Sadat's moves against the pro-Soviet political forces in Egypt in May 1971. He assisted Sadat and President Nimeiry of the Sudan in crushing the Communist coup in the Sudan in 1971. Libyan diplomats in the United Nations and elsewhere, with their all-out campaign against Israel, displayed resentment of the Soviet attitude of caution toward Israel and of Soviet support for a negotiated Arab-Israeli solution on the basis of UN Security Council Resolution 242. In many editorials and speeches, Qaddafi and the RCC leadership in Libya also justified their hostility toward Moscow by their repugnance for atheism. They proclaimed their dislike of Marxism on the basis that it was a theory evolved in nineteenth-century Europe (one compelling reason for Qaddafi's production of his Third Universal Theory and *The Green Book*). They rejected the dictatorship of the proletariat, or that of any class over any other. They refused to be tied to the "Russian imperialist bloc."

The Soviets, however, rarely allow their objectives in a country or region to be thwarted by the existence of a regime with principles unfriendly to their own. Though conventional wisdom about Libya and Qaddafi would have it that serious Soviet arms deliveries to Libya did not begin until 1974, one senior U.S. diplomat who served in Tripoli early during Qaddafi's rule recalls that at least one shipment of Soviet tanks must have arrived in Libya *as early as December 1970*. British and U.S. observers both saw T-54 tanks, never before seen in Libya, moving in Tripoli streets on one occasion. A British defense attaché, whose own military had trained the royal forces of prerevolutionary Libya, concluded that Soviet instructor-drivers must have arrived secretly with the tanks; the Libyans, in their current state of training, "simply would not have had a chance to learn to drive them so well."[13]

By 1970, Western intelligence agencies also knew of the beginnings of the East German security assistance that has since proven so valuable to Qaddafi, and that has helped to save him from at least one coup attempt. The East Germans had begun training the Libyan People's Militia, and frontier guards were giving advice on premilitary training for students and for technical courses at the Libyan Military Academy in Benghazi. Later, Libyan students began attending security courses in Dresden, East Germany.[14]

During this early period, Soviet diplomats worked patiently for an improvement of the situation and for a rapprochement with Qaddafi.[15] Their efforts seemed to be getting results when Major Jalloud, then deputy prime minister and minister of economy and industry, visited Moscow briefly in late February 1972. His trip to Moscow, the first by any Libyan leader, brought about an economic and technical agreement signed on March 4, 1972. However, the better atmosphere this should have created was quickly fogged on the very next day. *Pravda* bitterly criticized the Libyan newspaper *Al-Jundi* for having published a story claiming there was a Soviet-U.S. agreement for maintaining the "no war, no peace" stalemate in the Middle East. On April 13, 1972, just four days after the signing of the fifteen-year Soviet-Iraqi treaty of friendship and cooperation, Qaddafi's government declared the Soviet-Iraqi pact was "contrary to the charter of the Arab League" and recalled the Libyan ambassador to Baghdad. In remarks on June 3, Qaddafi severely criticized the Soviets for their responsibility in maintaining the status quo between the Arabs and Israel, and later welcomed the July 22 expulsion of the Soviets from Egypt by Sadat. Qaddafi even supported Sadat in Sadat's developing conflict with Moscow. On February 20, 1973, Libyan Foreign Minister Abu Zayed Durdeh accused Moscow of having fomented student riots against Sadat in Egypt, and of having ordered all of the pro-Moscow Arab Communist parties to infiltrate the Arab student movements, especially the Egyptian one.

Up to then, the Soviets had maintained relative silence, but in June 1973 they were goaded into publicly criticizing Libyan "extremism." On August 15, Moscow followed this up by siding publicly with Egypt in the Sadat-Qaddafi friction over the unification of the two countries. To Soviet media charges of the "adventurism" and "anti-Sovietism" of Qaddafi, the Brother Colonel asserted on November 18, 1973, that the USSR was "just another superpower like the others," prepared at any moment to bargain over the aid it offered the Arabs, and to betray the Arab cause.

Sadat's rapprochement with the United States and the beginning of his journey toward peace with Israel was the crucial turning point in Qaddafi's slow but seemingly inexorable course toward a future strategic link with Moscow. The signing of the first Israeli-Egyptian disengagement agreement on January 18, 1974, through the efforts of Henry Kissinger, brought about an immediate crisis in Cairo-Tripoli relations. From this point on, it becomes possible to discern several major Libyan objectives in relations with the Soviet Union. First, in order to prepare the way for achievement of the other objectives, the ideological conflict between them had to be muted. Second, they reasoned, Libyan crude oil could be exchanged, in effect, for arms and technical assistance Libya could not obtain from the West. Third, limited cooperation with the Soviet bloc would help to end the growing international isolation in which Libya found herself after Sadat's rapprochement with the United States and Israel. (The same motive existed in Syria's somewhat parallel warming of its ties with Moscow.) Fourth, since in Qaddafi's eyes Sadat was handing over Egypt to "American imperialism" and this process might even lead to the presence of U.S. or Israeli forces in Egypt that could directly threaten Libya, Qaddafi needed a tactical alliance with the Soviet bloc for his own protection.

All of these goals coincided fairly neatly with Soviet ones. Egypt's defection from the sphere of Soviet influence had been a terrible blow to the Kremlin. Soviet naval ships and aircraft could no longer operate from Egyptian bases. Moscow had lost an immensely valuable source of raw materials, goods such as Egyptian cotton, an intelligence listening post astride the Suez Canal, and many other benefits. To counteract this, the Soviets tried to improve and consolidate relations with members of the so-called Arab rejection front. They had achieved notable success in this only with South Yemen and to a lesser extent with Syria. Libya would make a valuable new ally, if Qaddafi could be won over. [16]

The Soviet-Libyan rapprochement, like so many other critical political and strategic changes in the Middle East, began with oil. Moscow encouraged East European governments to bid and buy at a Libyan oil auction in January 1974; this would help ease satellite requirements for Soviet oil. Major Jalloud, in the spring of 1974, preceded his important Moscow visit with a series of stopovers to discuss oil deals in Bucharest, Warsaw, and Budapest. He was given red-carpet treatment and entertained in the lavish style in which he had often been entertained before in Paris, London, and Rome. This led to a series of long-term contracts between Libya and Soviet satellites, including one three-million-ton-a-year deal with Rumania.

Libya had already made one major military aircraft deal with France to buy over one hundred Mirage jets. Some of these were loaned to Sadat during the 1973 war, when Qaddafi had also bought seventy replacement MIG-21s for Egypt. When Sadat-Qaddafi relations soured, Libyan logistical support was lost. Egyptians training or serving in Libya were expelled and Egypt withdrew others, including its pilot instructors and remaining naval personnel. The Egyptians removed SAM sites and air defense radar that Egyptians had helped install around Libyan air bases in Tobruk, Benghazi, and Tripoli. Since this was a period when Qaddafi and Pakistan President Zufilcar Ali Bhutto were close friends, Pakistan was able to send about six hundred Pakistanis, including about thirty pilot instructors, to replace the Egyptians.[17]

But both the Libyans and the Russians now began to realize that neither Pakistan nor any other Third World country could provide the arms and the military services that Libya was finding it increasingly hard to obtain from the West. The Soviet media began to drop their hostility to Libya, and this was reciprocated. Soviet President Podgorny met Jalloud in Paris on April 4, 1974, to prepare the way for Jalloud's crucial trip to Moscow on May 14–24. That trip saw the conclusion of the first of a major series of arms deals that have amounted to about $12 billion—the largest purchases ever made by one country from the Soviet Union.

Soviet Antonov AN-22 transports from the Black Sea area, and also from South Yemen, Ethiopia, and Iraq delivered load after load of heavy Soviet weapons. Most were unloaded at Gamal Abdel Nasser Air Base (formerly al-Adem), near Tobruk; Okbah ibn Nafi Air Base (formerly Wheelus Field) near Tripoli; and at Bernina, the airport for Benghazi. In December 1980 the Libyans closed Bernina to all foreign civil airlines flights, apparently to mask the incoming Soviet shipments (as well as the use of Bernina as a staging base for Qaddafi's operations in Chad). Soviet and East bloc ships discharged their military and naval cargoes in newly built Libyan naval facilities between Tripoli and Zuara in the west, and between Derna and Tokra in the east. From these latter coastal points in Cyrenaica it is only a short drive to extensive, well-defended supply bases around Tobruk where the main arsenals have been assembled.

By 1979, Soviet shipments had included many squadrons of MIG-21s and MIG-23s. Also part of the Libyan arsenal were SAM antiaircraft missiles of various ranges and purposes; the supersonic Tupolev TU-22 bombers, which the Egyptian and Sudanese general staff feared could be used against relatively defenseless cities; and up to three thousand tanks of all the older and more recent Soviet series—T-54s, T-55s, T-62s, and T-72s.[18]

Soviet "subcontractors" such as Omnipol of Czechoslovakia and East Germany's Office for Industrial Technical Trade in Pankow, East Berlin, have handled a large number of the actual sales, all for hard cash with no discounts asked or given, and the actual deliveries. The East Germans have sent infantry arms including the classic Kalashnikov AK-47 assault rifle, the favorite of Palestinian and other guerrillas the world over, and RPGs (rocket-propelled grenades). Many of these have been sent on to Libyan friends such as the more radical Palestinian and leftist factions in Lebanon, where many of them were used to deadly effect in the Lebanese civil war in 1975–76. Other supplies, some of which were to see action in Chad, included an assortment of tracked and trackless military vehicles, helicopters, tactical rockets, missile boats, minesweepers, landing ships, flamethrowers, gas grenades, and engineering equipment. Sophisticated optical, infrared, and fire-control systems as well as avionics and some computer equipment were also included.

Upon occasion the Soviets have persuaded Syria and the PLO to transfer some of the Soviet hardware they have acquired to the Libyan depots. This is one of the few areas where the new "union" arrangements between Libya and Syria, announced in September 1980 but never implemented in the political sphere, have helped military cooperation between Tripoli and Damascus. U.S. Army sources reported in 1979 that shipments from Syria to Libya had included 200 T-62 tanks, more than 130 aircraft (including 40 MIG-23s and 18 MIG-21s), SAM systems, SCUD missiles (with a range of about 150 miles), 260 armored personnel carriers, and artillery that includes antitank guns.

So as not to become totally dependent on Soviet, East German, or Czechoslovakian suppliers, Qaddafi shrewdly relies for spare parts, maintenance, and alternative systems upon India (which manufactures MIG fighters), Rumania, Yugoslavia, and North Korea. His arms purchasing agents have persistently sought Western outlets too, even after the United States began to pressure its West European allies in the mid-1970s not to supply Qaddafi. Thus, when Britain in 1973 refused to sell Libya Chieftain tanks (mainly because of a British-Libyan dispute over a canceled three-hundred-million-dollar deal for a British Aircraft

Corporation air defense system ordered by the monarchy of King Idris), France's SOFMA military exports operation was ready to oblige. Two hundred French AMX-30 medium tanks and some 155mm self-propelled howitzers on AMX chassis were sold. During the heyday of French arms sales to Libya under Presidents Pompidou and Giscard d'Estaing, Libya ordered Crotale air defense missiles and about thirty-eight Mirage F-1 fighters, most of which had been delivered by the time Giscard's embargo was lifted by President Mitterand in July 1981.

Israel and Egypt became upset when the Libya-Syria union arrangements made it likely that Damascus would furnish Tripoli with the NATO-standard HOT and MILAN antitank guided missile systems, ordered by Syria from the Euromissile agency in Paris for Syria. Both, say U.S. Army ordnance men, are better than the standard U.S. TOW and Dragon systems. HOT and MILAN have full electronic guidance systems and ranges of 4,000 and 2,000 meters respectively, making them a formidable weapon if Qaddafi's tank forces ever tangle again with Egypt's. In 1981 the Egyptians still direly needed to replace their old Soviet equipment with newer American equipment that was on order. Another future weapons danger might be nearly $95 million worth of U.S. M-60 Chrysler main battle tanks that the U.S. agreed in 1981 to sell Tunisia to defend its long desert frontier with Libya. Qaddafi's Cascavel armored cars, purchased from Brazil, proved better than Sadat's old Soviet ones in the 1977 border fighting. Brazil has continued to be a major arms supplier of Qaddafi. In 1980 Libyan forces in Chad used to good effect some of the 200 EE-11 Urutu APCs ordered from the Brasilia regime.

Italian arms transfers to Libya, in view of the problems Italy faces with Qaddafi,[19] are rarely reported publicly. However, the standard open sources in 1981 agreed that since 1974 the Italians had supplied considerable portions of large Libyan orders for Italian OTOMAT naval missiles to equip ten new French Combattante-II missile boats Mitterand released to Libya in 1981; Chinook CH-47C helicopters, manufactured under U.S. license in Italy; some 75 out of 200 ordered Leopard I West German–made NATO main battle tanks; and four Wadi-class naval corvettes.[20]

Qaddafi by 1981 had ordered several more fast patrol boats from West Germany, but the Soviet Union, with which he seemed intent on building up a long-term naval relationship, remained his chief naval supplier. In 1981 he was operating three Foxtrot-class Soviet-made diesel submarines, *Al Fateh*, *Al Badr*, and *Al Ahad*, with another three reported on order; a British-made frigate of 13,000 tons, the *Dat As-sawari*; two 500-ton missile corvettes (with two more under construction in Italy); and six Osa-2–class missile boats, similar to those used by Nasser's Egyptian navy in 1967 to sink the Israeli destroyer *Eilath* off Port Said, also operated out of Libyan naval bases (with six more scheduled for transfer from the Soviet Union).[21]

According to Admiral William Crowe, Jr., the scholarly U.S. commander of NATO forces for southern Europe in Naples, and Italian officers who have worked in training and supplying the Libyans, Qaddafi's navy is hampered by lack of truly trained or skilled personnel, though about one hundred Libyans have completed submarine training in the USSR. Libya also lacks good facilities for maintaining and servicing her ships. For truly sensitive conversion jobs, such as the outfitting of one of the Foxtrot-class submarines berthed near Sirte as a kind of floating command post for Qaddafi to use in emergencies, the Libyans farm out refitting contracts in Western Europe (in the case of Qaddafi's command submarine, the work was done in Italy). What worries the Allied naval analysts the most about Libya's navy, either on its own or as an auxiliary of the Soviet Mediterranean flotilla in a war, is its obvious ability to harass oil tankers and merchant ships in the Mediterranean. The Soviet-made submarines, and four other French-designed Daphne-class U-boats built in Spain and authorized for future delivery to Qaddafi by the Mitterand government in July 1981, could lay mines in the Sicilian Strait or the Malta channel. This was proven in June 1973, when Qaddafi first began to make his point that the Gulf of Sirte was to be jealously guarded as Libyan territorial waters. Using Soviet-made mines supplied by Yugoslavia and Egyptian tugboats and small auxiliary boats still in Qaddafi's service, Qaddafi mined Libyan parts of the gulf, perhaps as an exercise. A Greek and a Lebanese ship were sunk, and another Greek ship was damaged. Strange as it seems, no one protested.[22]

Qaddafi's main problem areas in military and strategic supplies have been long-range transport aircraft, missiles, and, of course, his fervently hoped-for but still unrealized nuclear capability. In all three of these areas Qaddafi, early on, pinned high hopes on his American and other Western connections. In some limited and sometimes unexpected ways, these hopes have been at least partially fulfilled. In other ways, Qaddafi has been bitterly disappointed. At least in the cases of transport aircraft and nuclear weapons, the Soviets have not been willing or able to satisfy Qaddafi either.

Probably no incident in Libyan-American relations attracted as much attention and notoriety in the United States or abroad as the Billy Carter affair. In the Third World in general, and Arab societies like Libya in particular, it is customary to assume that the immediate blood relatives of a chief or ruler will exercise great influence over that ruler, whether he heads a family, a tribe, or a nation. It was therefore quite natural for Qaddafi's aides—Qaddafi himself seems never to have gotten personally involved—to assume that winning the friendship of the brother of the President of the United States would be a major coup—one that would certainly influence U.S. policies and that just might help to reverse the whole unfavorable trend of Libyan-American relations.

There was a deep and abiding strategic interest behind all of the Libyan gestures of friendship toward Americans, despite the genuine nature of some of those gestures.[23] Qaddafi has always seemed to hold a lingering, somewhat wistful feeling that if only he could get through to ordinary people in the United States, they would see through the unfavorable image of Libya projected by the American media. At the same time by influencing the White House, Qaddafi's aides reasoned that not only would the entire climate of Libyan-American relations be improved, but specific strategic goals, such as the release of long-range transport aircraft, might also be attained. The result of this colossal miscalculation by the Libyans was the Billy Carter affair, which ended up having the opposite effect of everything sought by Qaddafi's men.

The story of Qaddafi's constant search for more long-range aircraft is a story closely related to the decline and fall of the U.S.-Libyan diplomatic relationship since 1969. The Libyan state airline, founded under the monarchy but rechristened Libyan Arab Airlines after the revolution, got its start, like the fledgling Libyan air force, with American planes. Beginning in the early 1970s, the U.S. Departments of State and Commerce, which must license aircraft exports, permitted the sale by Boeing Corporation of nine 727s and one 707 commercial-model airliners. Eight Lockheed C-130s had been ordered by the monarchy for the Libyan royal air force; the Qaddafi government completed payments for these and requested their delivery. However, in 1973, when U.S. hopes for an accommodation with Qaddafi's policies began to fade, the Ford administration blocked delivery of the C-130s. (These embargo measures did not prevent Edwin Wilson, in addition to his other services to Qaddafi, from recruiting American pilots, crewmen, and aircraft mechanics for Qaddafi's civil and military air transport services.)

In March 1978, during a time when Ahmed al-Shahati and his

Foreign Liaison Bureau had begun "people-to-people" visits with Americans, and Libya was purchasing Idaho farm products and trying to buy Idaho's Oshkosh Corporation's heavy tractors, the Department of State recommended to the Department of Commerce that licenses for two recent orders by Libyan Arab Airlines for two Boeing 727s not be issued.

"Decisions on matters of this kind are always difficult," recalled former Ambassador to Libya and Under Secretary of State for Political Affairs David Newsom. "Significant U.S. commercial interests are involved, not only in the particular sale but in the maintenance of a market against increasingly strong European competition in commercial aircraft." (By this time, French personnel were heavily involved in Libyan Arab Airlines management and operations, and LAA was interested in buying the Airbus and other French aircraft.) After a good deal of pressure from the concerned U.S. aircraft companies and lobbying by the Libyans in the United States, Secretary of State Cyrus Vance got recommendations that the earlier decision to hold up the sale of the two Boeings be reviewed. Commerce favored the sale too, pointing out that "market conditions and the growth and route structure of Libyan Arab Airlines made it clear that use of these aircrafts was justified economically."[24]

During the summer of 1978, while a decision was still hanging in the balance, the Foreign Liaison Bureau shifted its "people-to-people" program into high gear. At this time, President Jimmy Carter's brother Billy entered the picture. In March 1978, in Atlanta, real-estate broker Mario Leanza visited his nephew in Catania, Sicily. There Leanza also met a Sicilian corporation lawyer named Michele Papa, who was a founding member of the "Sicilian-Arab Association" that had been working with the Libyans since the early years of the Qaddafi regime. Papa suggested that if Leanza could persuade Billy Carter to come to Libya, he could make a lot of money. Leanza did not know Billy Carter, but Thomas L. Jordan, another Atlanta real-estate broker, did. In late June 1978, Leanza and Jordan met Gibril Shalouf, former Libyan ambassador to Italy, in Atlanta. On July 4, Billy Carter met Shalouf for the first time in Billy's service station, and Billy received his first invitation to visit Libya.

On July 22 Jordan sent Shalouf a mailgram with a list of prospective visitors to Libya (including Billy) and asked for a $50,000 advance to "defray expenses." Annoyed by the size of the request, Shalouf later gave Leanza $3,000 for his and Jordan's "expenses." In September 1978, Shalouf met Billy again and gave him a more formal invitation. Donald Carter, another realtor and close friend of the Carter family (but not related to them) tried to dissuade Billy from going, pointing out that the Libyan regime opposed U.S. foreign policy and could try to use the trip to embarrass President Carter.

Billy was also advised, through his associate Randy Coleman, by Dr. William Quandt, Arab affairs expert on the National Security Council, that the trip would be unwise. Billy told Quandt on the phone that he "knew more about Libya than all you State Department bureaucrats put together." President Carter has insisted he didn't know of the trip Billy planned before he departed. The State Department did know, however. It cabled William Eagleton, the U.S. chargé d'affaires in Tripoli (there was no full ambassador, since State had not appointed a successor to Ambassador Joseph Palmer, who left in 1973), to brief Billy after his arrival. Billy and Randy Coleman, with six Georgian companions and Shalouf, flew to Tripoli via Rome on September 25–27. Eagleton and Shahati met them at the airport, and later Billy assured Eagleton that he would keep politics out of his talks with the Libyans. At one dinner, during which their Libyan hosts had provided the kind of drinks for Billy that the revolution's anti-alcoholic austerity proscribed for Libyans, Billy, who received four gold bracelets, a sword, a serving platter, and a silver saddle, was heard to say he would "try to do something" about getting the blocked C-130 transport planes sitting on the ground at Marietta, Georgia, released to Libya. Eagleton may not have known this when he cabled to Washington that Billy had shown "restraint" from political comments. President Carter passed one Eagleton cable on to Billy after his return to Washington with the handwritten note: "To Billy, you did a good job under the 'dry' circumstances."[25]

All this time, the State Department was sorting out the matter of the two Boeing planes. At this point, the Libyans needed neither Billy Carter nor other intermediaries. During the summer, Libya notified the State Department it was willing to accede to The Hague international convention on hijacking. It did this formally in October. It also agreed to give written assurances that the planes would not be used for military purposes, assurances actually written into the export licenses. After consulting key congressmen, the State and Commerce Departments both decided on November 2, 1978, to sell the two 727s. In January 1979, the State Department followed up on this by authorizing the sale of three Boeing 747s, on condition that the Libyans give similar strict assurances that the planes wouldn't be used for military purposes— which must have provoked some amused grins in Tripoli.

Meanwhile, back in Atlanta a mixed group of Georgia businessmen and lawyers were reviewing the business perspectives opened by Billy's trip. On November 2, Billy sent Shahati a written invitation to visit Georgia. An advance party of Libyans including Shalouf and Muhammad al-Burki, head of the Department of Parties and Popular Organizations in the Secretariat of the Libyan General People's Congress, arrived to set up arrangements for the trip. One of the Libyans mentioned that releasing the C-130s would be a welcome result of the trip. The State Department authorized the Billy Carter group to host the Libyans, but warned that the Libyans would try to use the visit to influence U.S. policy. After the advance delegation's visit, Deputy Assistant Secretary of State for Near Eastern and South Asian Affairs Morris Draper informed Randy Coleman that the U.S. blockage of the export of the eight C-130s was unlikely to change.

A large number of Libyans, including a dance troupe, toured the United States, stopping first in Georgia, in January 1979. Billy met them at Atlanta airport on January 8 and the next evening hosted a giant reception, attended by President Carter's mother Lillian, his sister Ruth Stapleton Carter, and hundreds of others. Billy was first to sign a petition circulated at the reception that called for the formation of a Libyan-Arab-Georgian Friendship Society. Billy then escorted his visitors to a meeting with Georgia Governor George Busbee, led a tour of the Carter family's peanut warehouse, and hosted several Libyans overnight at his home. A series of business meetings followed. President Carter's friend and former budget director Bert Lance, now a banker, suggested Robert L. Schwind as someone knowledgeable in commodities and foreign trade to talk trading with Shahati. Billy was to get at least 50 percent of the profit of any deal, as disclosed by a guarded letter from Schwind to Coleman that used the code name *Sandbox* for Libya, *The Man* for Billy Carter, and *B.L.* for Bert Lance.[26] Lance, the Georgia banker and Carter family friend, seems, however, to have played no important role.

It was during this Libyan visit that Billy's alleged anti-Israel or anti-Semitic remarks were reportedly made. According to an Atlanta television report that got into the White House press summary January 11, Billy claimed that Atlanta Mayor Maynard Jackson refused to receive the Libyans because of pressure from "the Jews." The next day, Billy was quoted as saying the Libyan visit was intended not for his own personal gain but for better U.S.-Libyan relations. He also was quoted as saying "there are a hell of a lot more Arabians than Jews." At about this time, Zbigniew Brzezinski, President Carter's national security affairs adviser, learned that Clinton Murchison, a wealthy businessman who owned the Dallas Cowboys, had advised Billy to register as a Libyan agent and that Billy had said he intended to. In Washington with Shahati and Burki, Billy asked State Department Libya desk officer W. Alan Roy about the status of "those Boeing airplanes." Roy assumed he meant the 727s. When he said they had already been delivered to Libya, Billy responded, "Good."[27]

Unfortunately for everyone concerned with getting the Lockheed C-130 planes released to Libya, Libyan planes were seen in February by newsmen and intelligence agencies in Uganda, helping dictator Idi Amin Dada's fight against the invading Tanzanian army. Qaddafi rushed supplies and up to 1,500 troops to Entebbe airport on the C-130s Libya had acquired before the Qaddafi regime took power, and on Boeing 727s (not the two just delivered) assigned to the Libyan Arab Airlines civil fleet. The planes also evacuated some of the 400 to 500 Libyans wounded in the fighting. "When these reports were confirmed," said David Newsom in his congressional testimony on the Billy Carter affair, "it left the State Department with no alternative but to regard the 747s for Libya, then being manufactured, as having a 'potential significant military application.'" In May 1979 the State Department vetoed their export, and they never left the United States.[28]

Billy Carter and Shahati, meanwhile, were both becoming television celebrities, appearing together on ABC's "Good Morning America" and the "Stanley Siegel Show." But, as his brother President Jimmy Carter recalled, Billy's drinking problems had been aggravated and in late February 1979, he began a series of hospital cures for alcoholism and acute bronchitis, even as his financial problems in the Carter family businesses in Plains, Georgia, increased. President Carter talked with Billy on February 23 and, through other friends including Randy Coleman, tried to "discourage Billy," in President Carter's words, "from making any other trip to Libya; to try to keep him out of the newspapers for a few weeks" and "let him regain his equilibrium."[29]

Oil deals were among the matters Billy and his associates had already discussed with the Libyans, and this seemed to be one way out of Billy's financial troubles. While Billy was in the hospital, Arthur Cheokas, an Americus, Georgia, businessman, and Randy Coleman flew to Rome on March 6 for meetings with Shalouf and Shahati. Billy chatted briefly with Shahati on the phone, apparently about the possibility of buying some oil privately from Libya, which was the subject of the Rome discussions. Coleman and Cheokas visited Athens and then returned to

Georgia by way of London, where they discussed the oil transactions with a London banker recommended by Bert Lance. A number of possible oil transactions were later discussed and suggested by a friend of Billy's, Jack MacGregor, executive vice-president of Carey Energy Corporation, which had old problems with Libya that were being resolved through Carey Energy's acquisition by a larger conglomerate, Charter Oil of Jacksonville, Florida. MacGregor was now a consultant to Charter Oil. The oil possibilities never seemed to have panned out for Billy, but his other great financial need—for a cash loan—eventually did.

In late July, Burki visited Plains and told Billy's associates that a Libyan loan to Billy could be discussed if all concerned would come to New York. On August 5, 1979, with family members and associates including an Atlanta attorney named Helen Medlin, Billy flew to New York, and then moved to a Washington hotel where Burki introduced them to Abdallah al-Saudi, chairman of the Libyan Arab Foreign Bank. The bank is Qaddafi's main commercial banking outlet, managing, among many other things, Libyan funds abroad and placements among the multinationals. Coleman said Billy wanted to negotiate a $500,000 loan. Medlin said this could not come directly from the Libyan government because of Billy's status as the President's brother, and because it would be contrary to U.S. law. Burki told Medlin after the meeting that negotiations would continue when Billy next visited Libya to attend the revolution anniversary ceremonies September 1.

Before he left, Billy had come in for attention from the U.S. Justice Department for his failure to register as a foreign agent. When FBI agents quizzed Mario Leanza, Leanza recalled hearing Billy say in Libya that he would help the Libyans get aircraft deliveries from the United States. However, Joel S. Lisker, the Justice Department official pursuing the Billy Carter affair, "concluded from government records and interviews that there were no indications Billy Carter had influenced the executive branch's decision-making on planes for Libya."[30]

Billy then requested foreign agent registration forms from Justice, but did not register at the time. Billy, his wife Sibyl, his son Buddy, and other friends were joined by Coleman in Tripoli for the September 1 celebrations. Frank Terpil, who was arrested in New York and indicted on New York state firearms violations only three months later, acted as Billy's interpreter at the parade and other ceremonies, during which Billy was photographed with many of the official guests, such as Yasir Arafat and some of the other Palestinian guerrilla leaders. Billy waited in vain for two weeks for a meeting with Qaddafi (whom he never met), spoke with U.S. envoy Eagleton several times, and finally returned to the United States after three weeks in Libya. While in New York for an appearance on the "Today" show, Billy and Randy Coleman met with Mansour Kekhia, Libya's senior diplomat at the United Nations. Kekhia, who was soon to resign and go underground, disgusted with Qaddafi's policies, at this time was concerned about a William Safire column in *The New York Times*[31] that linked Kekhia with Democratic Party Chairman John White. Kekhia offered to apologize if the article embarrassed the administration, and said the meeting with White had been a chance one on a motel terrace in Washington.

It was the Iranian hostage crisis that was to provide, for the White House, the supreme test of how valuable the Billy Carter connection in Tripoli might prove to the United States. Before the crisis broke, Billy had been talking both oil business and a major loan with senior Libyans including Shahati, Houdery, and Kekhia. Neither the oil purchases nor, at this time, the loan, had come through. The publicity already given Billy's troubles and travels had not served the Carter White House well.

The Iranian militants seized the U.S. embassy in Tehran and their sixty-five diplomatic hostages on November 4, 1979. One of the courses taken by the Carter administration was a series of appeals to Islamic countries to press for the hostages' release. On November 8, Under Secretary Newsom met with Mansour Kekhia, still Libya's ambassador to the United Nations at that time, and asked for Libya's support. Kekhia and other Libyan officials expressed private sympathy, but the public position of the media in Tripoli was hostile to the U.S. and favorable to the hostage-takers. A further setback in the efforts to enlist Libyan help was a statement by Libyan Foreign Secretary Ali Tariki that urged other Muslim countries to boycott trade with the United States in protest of the freeze on Iranian assets ordered by the administration. In the United States David Newsom and in Tripoli William Eagleton criticized the Libyan position in their conversations with senior Libyan diplomats and officials.

On November 19, Mrs. Rosalynn Carter phoned Billy from Camp David. Would his Libyan friends help release the American captives in Tehran, she asked. Mrs. Carter informed her husband soon afterward that Billy had answered that he thought they might help. The President then phoned Brzezinski, who in turn called Billy to "ask . . . if he could somehow be helpful in getting Libya to take a more constructive

posture on the hostage issue," suggesting that he, Brzezinski, might talk
to Ali al-Houdery, whom the White House had unsucessfully tried to
reach. Secretary of State Vance agreed that Billy might be useful in the
Iranian crisis, though he was skeptical. Vance told Billy he did not
object to his trying, and Billy spoke with the President briefly on
November 20 about it. President Carter said later of the meeting: "I told
him [Billy] and Zbig to get together and discuss what message we might
pass on to the Libyans." But before either Billy Carter or Brzezinski had
been able to speak to Houdery or any other Libyan official about the
hostage situation, the Libyan foreign-affairs secretariat in Tripoli issued
a formal statement that "in our view the hostages should be
released. . . ." Eagleton was summoned to the secretariat November 24
and told the statement was official Libyan policy, and that Libya would
try to use its good offices to achieve liberation of the American
prisoners. Later, President Carter justified the decision to seek Libyan
help:

> My major preoccupation was the release of the hostages, and I
> was ready to try any channel that could help us reach this
> goal. The Muslim community places great importance on
> family ties, and I believed that a request arranged with Billy's
> participation would be regarded as coming more directly from
> the President and might supplement the efforts already being
> made through normal State Department channels. I recog-
> nized there was a risk of criticism in asking Billy to help but I
> decided to take the risk.[32]

Billy's face-to-face efforts on behalf of the hostages began with a
meeting with Houdery at the Libyan mission in Washington on
November 27. Billy asked the Libyan diplomat whether he would meet
Brzezinski on the hostage matter; Houdery said he would have to refer
this to his government. That afternoon, Billy and Randy Coleman met
with Brzezinski in Brzezinski's office for twenty minutes. After some
small talk, Brzezinski asked Houdery for Libyan help in the hostage
affair, and the two agreed to stay in touch in the future. Billy reported
on the talks to the President, who noted that the "meeting was a good
one . . . the first time the Libyans had ever been in the White House
since I've been here." Houdery, said President Carter, had promised
that Libya would do all it could "with the students and with Khomeini
to get the hostages released. We told them that we would like to have

better relationships with the Libyans and with the government itself."[33]

The State Department was apparently not told of the meeting. It learned about it when Eagleton cabled Qaddafi's response to Brzezinski's November 27 message asking for help, and when Libyan desk officer Roy visited Houdery at the Libyan mission. During the days that followed, Billy and Coleman made several calls to Jack MacGregor of Charter Oil and the Libyans, all in connection with the still elusive Charter Oil deal. Billy denied telling MacGregor of the Houdery-Brzezinski meeting.[34]

Coming as it did after the November 1979 attack on the Grand Mosque by Muslim zealots and the ensuing burning of the U.S. embassy in Islamabad, Pakistan, the burning of the U.S. embassy in Tripoli by a Libyan mob on December 2 drew much less global attention than the earlier events. In Washington, however, it triggered a process that led to the rapid deterioration of the slender network of working relationships the Carter administration had woven with Qaddafi. The White House issued a statement condemning Libyan official complicity in the mob action. Houdery was summoned to see Deputy Assistant Secretary of State Morris Draper and Under Secretary David Newsom. The State Department resorted to a favorite device in time of crisis; it set up a "working group" to follow events and set U.S. policy toward Libya.

On December 6, Brzezinski summoned Houdery to the White House and took him to see President Carter, who first asked him to thank Qaddafi and then called the attack on the U.S. embassy "inexcusable and very serious to us."[35] An apology, a commitment to replace or repair the embassy, and an assurance from Qaddafi that U.S. diplomats would be protected in Libya in the future would make it possible for the United States "to try in every way to improve consultations with Libya and long-range relations with them."[36]

Houdery returned to Libya to confer with Qaddafi. It was then, on December 10, *The New York Times* published Qaddafi's statement that he had assurances from President Carter that U.S. Mideast policy would move toward "a more neutral posture" during the President's second term, if he were reelected. The *Times* quoted Qaddafi as stating: "We have received these assurances in the last few days through unofficial but reliable channels from President Carter. . . . We interpret them as meaning a more neutral American posture in the conflict between the Arabs and Israel."

The White House appeared to offset this by adding a vague disclaimer

to the effect that "The United States remains committed to a comprehensive peace in the Middle East. . . . This involves continuity and
not a fundamental change in policy." State Department officials helped
draft these sentences.[37]

Houdery returned to Washington on December 12 and gave
Brzezinski a personal message from Qaddafi: the Libyan leader was
distressed over the hostage crisis; messages and a Libyan delegation had
gone to Khomeini; the embassy attack in Tripoli was Libya's responsibility; remedial steps would be taken; and high-level Libya-U.S. communications should be improved, with the United States, Libya hoped,
taking a "more evenhanded U.S. policy toward Libya."[38] Secretary
Vance later complained he had not been informed of the meeting.
Billy, not a party to this meeting either, meanwhile continued to hope
for the Charter Oil deals with the Libyans. Randy Coleman planned to
press it in a new trip to Libya.

The main point about Qaddafi's efforts, real or imagined, on behalf
of the hostages in Iran was missed by nearly everyone on the Washington scene. Qaddafi could do nothing about the hostages because he had
no leverage with the Ayatollah Khomeini's regime in Iran. For months,
Libya had been wooing Khomeini, pointing to the assistance Libya had
given the anti-Shah movements (more encouragement and propaganda
than cash, it appears, but there was also some guerrilla training provided
in PFLP camps in Lebanon, and perhaps also in Libya). Later, Qaddafi
had sent planeloads of arms to the Iranians for their war with Iraq,
which broke out in September 1980. According to one of his former
associates, Qaddafi had pleaded in vain with the Iranians to reopen the
former Iranian embassy in Tripoli, closed after the Shah's overthrow.

If all of this was to no avail, it was equally hopeless to expect that
Qaddafi's intercession for the hostages would be listened to in Tehran
The reason, quite simply, was that there was blood between the Libyan
and Iranian regimes. The Imam Musa Sadr, the charismatic green-eyed
Iranian-born leader of the poor Shi'a Muslims of south Lebanon, had
been invited to Libya in August 1978, apparently to discuss, among
other things, how Qaddafi's funding of the Shi'a was being used. Musa
Sadr, by several accounts, had a violent, even tempestuous argument
with Qaddafi. On September 1, when he was supposed to have boarded
a flight to Rome, the Italian airport police reported that he never arrived
from Tripoli. Musa Sadr's own people in Lebanon believe that he was
murdered or permanently incarcerated in Libya. One version has it that
it was murder, committed by one of Qaddafi's overzealous subordinates

without Qaddafi's order and that Qaddafi severely punished the man afterward. Musa Sadr, like the "hidden Imam" of Shi'a religious history who is supposed to reappear at the end of time, has yet to reappear. His shadow stands darkly between Qaddafi and Khomeini—because Musa Sadr was married to a niece of Khomeini's. President Jimmy Carter and his well-informed National Security Council should have known that ties of family and blood come almost before ties of religion in the Mideast, and that there was never any hope of Qaddafi's being able to convince Khomeini to do anything, especially help the U.S.[39]

Both Coleman and Billy Carter had asked Houdery for an advance on the earlier sought-after loan of $500,000 from Libya. En route from Georgia to Tripoli on December 27, Coleman picked up a $20,000 check payable to Billy Carter and mailed it to Billy in Americus, Georgia. Billy deposited the check on December 31, telling one friend he understood it was an advance on the loan because loan negotiations were not yet complete.[40] Coleman flew to Tripoli with Houdery on December 28 and met with Shahati there on the next day. Shahati told Coleman that the oil deal had been approved. Coleman phoned the good news to Billy, and agreed to try to get the Libyans to send a telex to Charter Oil that its crude-oil allocation from Libya would soon be increased.

The telex was never sent. Coleman learned on the next day that Qaddafi had fired the oil secretary, and no new one would be named for three or four weeks. The Charter Oil deal would have to be renegotiated from scratch. After Coleman returned to the United States, Billy saw Houdery at the Libyan mission in Washington. Houdery expressed optimism, according to Billy, that the deal would still go through.

Billy had by now brushed elbows again with the Justice Department. Its agents, including one FBI man, had questioned him about his relationship with the Libyans in October 1979. Billy did not tell them of the Charter Oil talks, nor about the twenty-thousand-dollar check. There was no action, apparently, to get Billy to register as a foreign agent either. While on the campaign trail for his brother in February Billy spoke with George Belluomini, an importer in Bakersfield, and Belluomini's son-in-law, Ronald Sprague, a financial consultant. In Tripoli, meanwhile, one of Shahati's assistants, Mokhtar al-Jamal, had begun discussing the oil deal with Coleman by telephone.

On March 26, 1980, CIA director Admiral Stansfield Turner was given an intelligence report about Billy Carter's dealings with Charter Oil and Libya. Instead of turning it over to the FBI, as might normally be done when an American citizen's activities inside the United States are concerned, he sent it to the White House because, as Turner said later, "it indicated that the President might well be in contact with somebody who was the target of a foreign government that was trying to influence him, and I therefore felt that it was advisable that the President be aware of this."[41] Turner took the report to Brzezinski, who then called Billy and warned him against embarrassing the President. Billy's reply, said Brzezinski, was "less than affirmative." Meanwhile Sprague and Coleman were continuing their oil negotiations with the Libyans in Tripoli, and also dealing with the matter of Billy's loan. They met with Muhammad Layas, assistant general manager of the Libyan Arab Foreign Bank (LAFB). Shahati called the bank to expedite things, and it was agreed that the loan would be secured by Billy's real estate.

Sprague returned to Atlanta to tell Billy on April 3 that he must complete a preliminary title report of his properties and an appraisal of them. Because the U.S. Internal Revenue Service was pressing him for a payment on back taxes owed by April 16, Billy said he urgently needed the cash. Sprague twice telexed Tripoli, asking the LAFB to speed the loan. Coleman, after more delays on the oil deal, was finally told that a People's Committee would have to approve it and this might take several weeks or months. Coleman returned to Washington, saw Houdery, and picked up a check for Billy for $200,000 labeled "loan."[42] Billy immediately began paying off his back bills and taxes, and used nearly the entire $200,000 during the next four months.

On May 7, the State Department decided to expel several members of the Washington People's Bureau who were suspected of tracking and harassing anti-Qaddafi Libyan students in the United States. In a final phone call to the Foreign Liaison Bureau in Tripoli on June 1, Coleman was told that this expulsion had made the situation "touchy" and that he should wait on the oil deal.

Meanwhile, the Justice Department had received reports about Billy's loan and his dealings on behalf of Charter Oil. Attorney General Benjamin Civiletti appears to have treated them gingerly, perhaps (though this did not emerge in the public report of the investigation) because they were obtained by wiretapping or other intercepts. Civiletti instructed Assistant Attorney General Philip B. Heymann to keep the file open for additional information. Use of a grand jury to investigate was considered, and one White House aide was asked by the FBI whether Billy had been intervening on behalf of releasing the embargoed airplanes to Libya; the answer was negative. On June 11, Billy voluntarily came to the Justice Department (he was meanwhile under FBI surveillance to see if he received new payments from the Libyans) and admitted the $20,000 "reimbursement" and the $200,000 loan and the oil dealings. Billy then went to the White House and asked Brzezinski and presidential counsel Lloyd Cutler whether there were any national security reasons for not disclosing his role in arranging Brzezinski's meeting with Houdery on the hostage issue. The answer was negative. Upon Cutler's recommendation, Billy hired as his lawyers Steven Pollak and Henry Ruth, who had been counsel for White House aide Hamilton Jordan during an investigation that was eventually to clear Jordan of drug charges, and then returned to Georgia.

Pollak and Ruth sought to persuade Billy to register with the Justice Department as a foreign agent for Libya. After hesitations on all sides, President Carter phoned Billy on July 1, urging him to register. The next day, Billy agreed and the negotiations for his registration began shortly afterward. Under an agreement he reached with the Justice Department, which filed a civil suit against him, Billy complied with an injunction requiring him to file a "true and complete registration statement, describing his travel, gifts, and loans, but without mentioning his role in the hostage negotiations."[43] Under heavy pressure from the media and congressmen, the White House published a report on July 22 about the whole affair that basically minimized contacts between the White House and Justice Department concerning the investigation. Ultimately, Billy and his problems escaped the harsh spotlight of publicity they had suffered through much of 1979 and 1980. In the spring of 1981, after the Carter family were all private citizens again, Billy sent the People's Bureau in Washington a check for one thousand dollars as a down payment on repaying the apparently interest-free loan, and the affair was finally permitted to die. It left the realization of the considerable trouble and expense Qaddafi's aides would incur in order to influence U.S. policy. The Billy Carter affair further added to the general impression, so common in the Arab world and among Western Europeans, that Qaddafi enjoyed some kind of special relationship with Washington.

The U.S.-Libyan air battle on August 19, 1981, over the Gulf of Sirte was one of those incidents that regularly erupt in history at a time when two potential combatants seem to be spoiling for a fight. I happened to be in Tripoli at the time, testing the atmosphere and waiting for the return of Qaddafi from his trip to sign his new "rejectionist" alliance with South Yemen and Ethiopia. I had been warned by Dr. Khalifa Azzabi, the director of foreign press in the Foreign Liaison Bureau, that prospects were dim for Qaddafi's early return, since he was going on to visit the Gulf and possibly some other places. I finally abandoned my plan to wait in Tripoli in order to conduct an interview with Qaddafi. By the eve of the battle, I had booked a seat on an Olympic Airlines flight to Athens for the next afternoon.

It was a dark, sultry evening at the Beach Hotel, where most visiting foreigners are lodged in a rambling, seaside structure looking out to sea. After taking coffee, I sat out on the terrace facing the bay, listening to the BBC news on my radio. Later I watched the evening's alarmist reports on Libyan television, which quoted *Newsweek* magazine as saying that the CIA planned Qaddafi's murder or downfall, and that the U.S. Sixth Fleet was approaching, and that all Libyan forces had been mobilized in "a high state of alert." I phoned Jim Hoagland, assistant managing editor for foreign news of *The Washington Post*, and told him about the deliberate building up of anti-U.S. tensions in Libya.

Although it was the Reagan administration that had first begun to depict Qaddafi in stark terms as International Public Enemy Number 1, and to talk openly of "destabilization" of Libya and to leak rumors about CIA plots to murder the Brother Colonel, there was nothing really new about U.S. military threats against Qaddafi or counterthreats from him. As far back as the Ford administration, in 1974, when the CIA was probably still more inclined to protect Qaddafi than to plan his demise, Henry Kissinger and other leading Washington figures had tried a policy of talking tough about oil prices to the Arab states who raised them or who might threaten U.S. supplies. Even in those days, *Newsweek* took the lead: in October 1974, it ran a long article, entitled "Thinking the Unthinkable." Official sources, it said, had talked of psychological warfare, covert operations, and open American military intervention such as paratroop attacks—supplemented by Israeli military moves—to seize Arab oil fields. Columnist Jack Anderson had written, on November 8, 1974, that a military takeover of the Libyan oil fields would require only a couple of U.S. Marine divisions.[44]

In January 1974, *New York Times* military analyst Drew Middleton noted that while some hawkish strategists such as Professor Robert Tucker had urged U.S. military intervention in the Persian Gulf, others preferred Libya. They argued, Middleton pointed out, that surprise was difficult in the Gulf because of the distance needed to fly in airborne troops from the Mediterranean or Indian Ocean. In Libya, however, surprise could be achieved through a combined air and sea strike. But that could be risky too. Two former U.S. Navy men usually rated as "superhawks," former Chairman of the Joint Chiefs of Staff Admiral

Thomas H. Moorer and former Chief of Naval Operations Admiral Elmo Zumwalt, Jr., warned that "it is dangerous for the United States now to deploy, in a bilateral confrontation with the Soviet Union in the Eastern Mediterranean, its fleet because the odds are that the fleet would be defeated in a conventional war."[45]

Be that as it may, the Gulf of Sirte apparently looked to Pentagon planners like an ideal place to confront Qaddafi. In 1973 he had warned that the entire Gulf was Libyan territory, despite the accepted international norms of three or twelve miles as the limits of territorial waters. In 1976 Libya reasserted the special character of the Gulf in a document submitted to the United Nations, drawing a straight line across the Mediterranean from a point near Benghazi across to the western headland bounding the Gulf. The United States had made it clear, however, that it considered everything outside twelve miles from the coast, including the zone inside the Gulf prohibited by Libya, as international waters. There had been many near confrontations between U.S. Navy planes and Libyan jets, including some piloted by Syrians and Palestinians, during the years since 1976. In September 1980, President Carter ordered the Sixth Fleet to stay out of the Gulf because he feared a serious clash there could harm the American hostages in Iran, whom Qaddafi was shortly going to be asked to help.

In February 1981, the Reagan administration, as *Newsweek* reported, began planning the Sixth Fleet maneuvers to be held in the summer. It was decided to hold them below 32 degrees 30 minutes north latitude, the line drawn by Qaddafi in 1973. Sixth Fleet task forces had held target practice against pilotless drone aircraft three times there in the past seven years. It was decided to do it there, as one official said, "because the principle of the open seas is important—and because we wanted to tweak Qaddafi's nose."[46]

On August 18, the day I was seeing and hearing the signs of Libyan nervousness in Tripoli, the Sixth Fleet task force, built around the nuclear-powered U.S. aircraft carrier *Nimitz*, began the exercise. Libyan interceptors rose to meet them, flying thirty-five missions into the exercise region, a 3,200-square-mile area of the Mediterranean that included the Gulf of Sirte. Most of the Libyan patrol flights were in pairs, including MIG-23s, MIG-25s, and several types of Mirage fighters. The Libyans converged on the area from bases to the south, east, and west. Six entered the maneuver area, which the U.S. Navy had formally announced in Notices to Airmen and Mariners and in an advisory to Flight Information Regions with jurisdiction over civil flights.

According to Vice Admiral William H. Rowden, U.S. Sixth Fleet commander, there was little commercial air and sea traffic or fishing activity in the region on that day. As the various Libyan planes approached, U.S. Navy planes signaled them to leave and escorted them away. Early on August 19, Libyan intruder flights were heavy. At 7:15 A.M., two Grumman F-14 fighters, flown by Commander Henry M. Kleeman and Lieutenant Lawrence M. Muczynski, patrolling at 20,000 feet south of the *Nimitz*, spotted two "bogies" on their radar. They were two Sukhoi Su-22 "Fitter" fighter-bombers. The *Nimitz*, cruising about 100 miles from the Libyan coast, ordered the two navy pilots to move south of their combat patrol orbit to intercept the two Libyans and get them out of the area. Kleeman and Muczynski spotted the two Sukhois. Kleeman reported that he then rolled his F-14 into a 90-degree bank to the left, trying to make a 150-degree turn to the left to fly formation with the Libyans. Kleeman's F-14 was about 500 feet above one of the Sukhois and about 1,000 feet from him when the Libyan launched a missile from his wing. Kleeman and Muczynski both saw the launch and broke hard to the left; the missile passed harmlessly below Kleeman's aircraft.

The second Sukhoi broke hard right and climbed. Kleeman reversed his turn and came down behind the Su-22. Waiting until the Libyan pilot was clear of the sun, and Kleeman was no longer staring into it, Kleeman launched an AIM-9L Sidewinder heat-seeking missile, hitting the Sukhoi in the rear fuselage. The Libyan pilot ejected and his parachute opened. Meanwhile, Muczynski was chasing the second Sukhoi and launched his Sidewinder from behind it. The missile hit the Sukhoi's tailpipe, and exploded with the rear fuselage tearing off the rest of the aircraft. The pilot ejected, but the American pilots did not see his parachute open. (Later, both Libyan pilots were produced, safe and sound, for Libyan television, after a well-organized Libyan search-and-rescue mission for them. They claimed they had shot down one U.S. F-14, a claim denied by the U.S. Navy.)

Later, aboard the *Nimitz*, American pilots involved in the operation said the quality of the Libyan pilots was uneven; those flying the French-built Mirage aircraft appeared to perform better than those flying the Soviet-built planes. They speculated that the French air force training had been superior to that offered by the Russians. The Libyan pilot who fired the missile had done so from an aircraft not well suited to air-to-air combat, and the missile had been fired from a "tactically poor position."

After the battle, Admiral Rowden said the two U.S. pilots had acted correctly: "The two U.S. aircraft under attack, and in an act of self-defense, shot down the two attacking aircraft. The aircrews correctly reacted in self-defense. They did not require or ask for any specific authorization from the task force commander, Rear Adm. James E. Service, or anyone else." Kleeman's often-quoted phrase was, "I didn't hesitate to fire, although it occurred to me at the time that it might cause a ruckus." The engagement took place about thirty miles from the Libyan coastline.[47]

I nearly missed my plane connection out of Tripoli to Athens that afternoon—or so I thought, as I arrived at the airport barely a half hour before my flight's scheduled takeoff time. After the brisk and thorough clearance through police controls and customs, I arrived in the passenger lounge only to discover that all outgoing foreign flights had been held up. Probably this was due to the aftermath of the air battle about six hours earlier. I and my fellow passengers were ignorant of the clash. The only hint we had was a raucous blast from the airport P.A. system, broadcasting a fragment of a Tripoli radio communiqué about a "cowardly attack" by the "American imperialists." At that point, we in the lounge wondered if we were going to get away that day at all—or any other day. But three hours later my flight departed, and flew through a flawless summer sky eastward over the sea, which showed no trace of the strife and turmoil then beginning to hit the airwaves.

In Athens I picked up Tripoli radio, which was relaying a communiqué from Qaddafi in Aden warning that the American attack had "endangered peace." In California, half a world away, President Ronald Reagan's aides had waited hours before waking him to tell him of the dogfight, which most of the American media represented as a famous victory. Most Arab governments and their media reacted nervously, some crankily, to the incident. Newspapers in countries with as little love for Qaddafi as Tunisia and Saudi Arabia accused the United States of behaving like a bully.

Qaddafi's nose had truly been tweaked. The day after the battle, the Texas firm of Brown & Root, which had done many construction jobs for Libya in the past, received a telex from Libya inviting it to bid on the construction of a giant new airfield to be built near Sebha. Two weeks later, on the September 1 revolutionary anniversary, Qaddafi threatened instant retaliation against American bases in the Mediterranean area if it happened again—and let the story be put around that he was considering signing a treaty of alliance with the Soviets.

Had the tweaking been worth it? And was the United States now embarked irrevocably on a collision course with Qaddafi? Or had it truly sent a message of power to Qaddafi's Soviet friends, who were remaining carefully aloof? Some of the Libyans I spoke with just before leaving Tripoli on that August day were apprehensive. As former defense secretary Harold Brown noted to one Washington columnist: "What the administration is really saying is that we are weaker than the Russians— but stronger than the Libyans." And that, the columnist added, was "hardly a measure of U.S. power that this particular administration, above all, should want to celebrate."[48]

The Reagan-Qaddafi confrontation seemed to reach an apotheosis in December 1981. The U.S. administration leaked reports that no fewer than fourteen Libyan assassins had entered the United States with the apparent intention of murdering President Reagan, Secretary Haig, or perhaps other American leaders. Antisniper patrols were seen crouched on the White House roof in Washington. The comings and goings of President Reagan and Vice-President George Bush were surrounded by ruses and artifices, such as decoy limousines and phony motorcycle-escorted convoys, to throw the supposed "hit team" off its supposed target. Though the reports were never substantiated, and sounded highly improbable to analysts abroad, Washington took them very seriously. The President retaliated by ordering between 1,500 and 2,000 Americans, many of them oil workers still in Libya, to leave. Reluctantly and under protest, the companies (except for Exxon, which in November had already announced it was suspending all Libyan operations) told their employees they would have company support and would get new jobs if they departed, since the U.S. State Department— though not the companies themselves—felt their security was in danger. When I visited Tripoli just before Christmas 1981, several hundred of the Americans had glumly complied. None said they felt threatened in any way, and Qaddafi's government, despite its constant polemics against American policy, was encouraging them to stay. By February 1982, however, the Libyan Oil Ministry was recruiting Iranian, Canadian, European, and Arab oil technicians to take the places of those Americans who had left.

The American attitude toward Qaddafi, as well as that of Western European countries, from this time forward could have an extremely important effect on the Libyan's colonel's future course. In the end, however, every statesman's fate is determined by how his own people react to him. Qaddafi's future is in the hands, above all, of the Libyans themselves.

# WHITHER QADDAFI?

After more than a decade of rule by Muammar al-Qaddafi, Libya has risen in the eyes of the world from a little-known, underpopulated desert country into a wealthy international gadfly. Internally, its people have become prosperous, and seem to lack nothing materially. Externally, Libya is flanked by fearful or jealous neighbors, and has few real friends. With Qaddafi bidding for leadership of radical Arabs everywhere, from the Palestinian refugee camps in the Middle East to disputed land or sea borders with Algeria and Tunisia, there were more questions than answers as 1982 began. Has Qaddafi fundamentally transformed Libya? If he were no longer there to lead would his influence disappear, like the trail of a comet that flashes briefly across the skies, then evaporates in the mists of space? Or would the changes he had wrought in Libya's economy, politics, and society linger? Will Libya remain in the vanguard for the propagation of *The Green Book*'s revolutionary ideas in the wider world outside?

The Libya that would emerge at the end of Qaddafi's rule and during the first years of the post-Qaddafi era would depend, in part, upon the economics of oil and the workings of these economics in Libya and abroad. It would depend on how the superpowers treated any new regime. It would depend upon the strength and organization of Qaddafi's loyal followers and partisans at home, and upon the same qualities of his serious Libyan opponents at home and abroad. In the manner of Qaddafi's departure from the scene might lie the seeds of the post-Qaddafi Libya.

What was left of Libya's oil revolution by the 1980s was, in the final analysis, impressive enough: an annual income of about twenty billion dollars for a population of fewer than three million people. That income has been enough for spectacular, if sometimes wasteful, development at home, with many billions left over to finance the causes of liberation, guerrilla warfare, terrorism, and the promotion of the Muslim faith throughout much of the world. But 1981 brought bad news for Qaddafi, and for Africa's other major oil producers (Algeria, Nigeria, and Gabon): the beginning of a world oil glut, possibly only a temporary one, but one that made their high-priced oil suddenly much less interesting to world markets.

One of the fundamental reasons for Qaddafi's animosity toward the Saudi Arabian monarchy was the Saudi action, taken from the 1980 Gulf war between Iran and Iraq, to raise Saudi production from 9.5 million barrels per day to 10.3 million barrels per day. Saudi Oil Minister Sheikh Amed Zaki Yamani said on several occasions that the oil glut on world markets, caused in part by decreased Western consumption and the "swing" Saudi production, was something the Saudis wanted in order to stabilize world prices and prevent the gouging demands of the radical Arab nations such as Iraq and Libya. By the summer of 1981, there was such an oversupply of oil that the Saudis decided to cut back their production in the third quarter of that year by 450,000 bpd from 10.3 million bpd to 9.8 million bpd. By the fall of 1981, the Saudis and most other non-African OPEC members were cutting prices from the $40-and-over price per barrel charged by Libya and the other radical Africans. In October 1981 OPEC established a uniform $34 price, but Libyan oil still cost more.

As Qaddafi has repeatedly refused to lower Libyan prices, the international oil companies, including the six American ones, have begun cutting back their production. In June 1981, these six companies and many other American ones operating in Libya refused to heed U.S. State Department recommendations to curtail their operations and withdraw their two thousand personnel. The Department of State wanted to enlist the companies' support in the Reagan administration's pressure campaign on Libya, and considered the personnel potential hostages to Qaddafi. Market forces worked for the administration: Conoco, Exxon, Mobil, and BP all expected to be pumping little or no oil by the end of 1981, and Exxon in January 1982 accepted $92 million in Libyan payments for all of its assets as it closed all operations in Libya. By September 1, 1981, when Qaddafi accused the Western companies of "boycotting" Libya, production had already dropped from 1.3 million bpd at the beginning of 1981 to around 600,000 bpd, and was still dropping fast—and oil experts in the United States believed that it might be 200,000 bpd or less within a few months. Income was projected to drop from $20 billion in 1980 to $7 billion or less in 1981 [1]

Qaddafi used oil as a weapon most recently in March 1981 after a Libyan MIG-23 pilot had flown his plane to the big NATO base at Souda Bay, Crete, on February 11, 1981, and asked for asylum in the United States. The pilot got his asylum, and U.S. and NATO intelligence officials got a good look at the plane, repeatedly stalling Libyan air controllers who radioed frantically that they were sending a cargo aircraft to pick it up. The plane was returned in pieces in a crate. The Libyans were furious, and on March 19, Greek officials confirmed that not only had several Greek ships been temporarily seized in Libyan waters, but Libyan oil deliveries to Greece, about 15 percent of Greece's needs, had been suspended. The suspension may have also been intended to punish Greece for the first visit of a high-level Greek official, Finance Minister Athannassios Cannellopoulos, to Israel. The suspension was ended about three weeks later, but Qaddafi had made his point with the Greeks. They were very careful after that not to join Italian, French, and other European foreign ministers in denunciations of Libya for Qaddafi's September 1981 threats to retaliate against U.S. "nuclear" installations in Greece, Italy, Cyprus, or Turkey in case of a U.S. "attack" in the Gulf of Sirte. [2]

How would the oil glut and the growing Reagan administration pressures against Qaddafi, following President Sadat's murder in October 1981, affect U.S. oil business still operating in Libya and, therefore, Qaddafi's economy? In the early stages of the Reagan administration's pressure moves against Qaddafi, the oil companies and other U.S. business serving Libya appeared little affected. "We're not concerned at all," the California-based Food Development Corporation said. The U.S. Commerce Department said American companies would continue to get licenses to sell their goods to Libya. This was later qualified when the State Department reaffirmed its ban on exporting U.S. commercial aircraft after it was discovered that the Libyans were seeking to buy aircraft for United African Airways, a new Libyan cargo line that Egypt and the Sudan suspected was being used for military or paramilitary purposes.

At the beginning of the eventful summer of 1981, about half of the two thousand U.S. nationals in Libya were associated with the oil companies. Exxon had a staff of 90, with 150 more dependents. Mobil had 35, with 47 dependents and 62 other staff working on a rotation basis. Occidental had 100 employees in Libya. Amerada Hess, Conoco, and Marathon Oil, who together owned 40 percent of the Oasis group, employed about 100 Americans. Total Libyan oil exports to the United States were running at around 640,000 bpd, about 40 percent of Libya's total exports and about 10 percent of total U.S. imports. Behind Saudi Arabia and Nigeria, Libya was America's third largest foreign oil supplier.[3] All of these oil figures were greatly reduced by the end of 1981.

Libya's cash shortage from its oil cutbacks began to affect foreign contractors seriously by the winter of 1981. Italian firms reported that tenders for new projects were withdrawn in September and that payment of some contracts had been held up. Cuts in the development plan and in specific projects were already becoming evident; obviously a 1981–85 development plan worth nearly $62.5 billion would be undermined if oil revenue fell to $5 billion or lower in 1982.

One of the projects where the cuts were first felt was a huge steel plant at Misurata. Eleven West German firms working there were offered payment in oil rather than in cash, and they held out against accepting this. Contractors from Western Europe, South Korea, and Japan were being offered such barter terms for turnkey contracts—the kind of contract where a firm delivers a completely finished industrial system and hands over the keys to its new Libyan proprietors. Many of these firms, such as Daewoo of South Korea, with thirty-three projects under way in Libya worth an average of $30 million apiece, were in a poor position to refuse.

The suggested barter terms being offered by the Libyans mostly provided for 30 percent payment in crude and the balance in cash. The real haggling came over the value assigned to the crude oil. Libya was insisting in late 1981 that it had to be $40 per barrel; most of the companies were offering $7 to $10 less. Brazil, already a major supplier of military hardware to Qaddafi, was the last country left in the world to manufacture Volkswagen Beetles, and it offered to trade some of them for Libyan oil. "Libya," commented *The Economist*, "whose streets are jammed with far flashier models, was not interested."[4]

Qaddafi's regime has so changed the basic fabric of life in Libya that there are a number of new kinds of social classes, some of which oppose him. The rise of "people's government" has replaced and alienated the old traditional tribal leaders, family notables, and career bureaucrats who survived the passing of the monarchy in 1969. The traditions of Islam, and the imams (those who read or lead prayer in the mosques) in Libya's mosques who preached it, have been censured, modified, or replaced by Qaddafi's own notions about reform and orthodoxy. The central government now controls almost completely the faculties and student bodies of the universities. In nationalizing private shops, even down to the *suq*, or market, level Qaddafi has alienated many thousands of Libyans who made their livelihood in retail trade and commerce. The military itself, the vital backbone of any radical state like Qaddafi's, has been the setting for plots and conspiracies, and Qaddafi has consequently promised on several occasions to eliminate the regular army officers' corps and replace it ultimately with militia officers who come from the "people."

Since the spring of 1980, Qaddafi has been conducting fairly frequent and systematic purges of government employees, university teachers and students, imams, and military men. The avowed purpose of the purges, which are often accompanied by lurid denunciations and confessions carried on Libyan television, is to root out graft and corruption. But political enemies at home and abroad were also targeted—sometimes literally. In fact, Qaddafi ordered his expatriate critics to come home "where they could be protected" from the "wrath" of the people's revolutionary councils. Some of those who refused were then murdered by "revolutionary volunteers" who Qaddafi later implied were not under his control.

Qaddafi has occasionally referred publicly to his opponents. In a speech on March 1, 1981, he talked of "demagoguery" among certain revolutionary committees, and of tribal differences, of popular resistance to the "people's" government system, of internal disunity, and of apathy. Scholarly critics of the Qaddafi regime have often noted Qaddafi's repetition of that last word. Qaddafi's greatest disappointment is that he has been unable to arouse great popular enthusiasm for his revolutionary program. In this, as in his foreign policy, he seems to be learning the quality of patience the hard way. His oil-funded welfare state has vastly raised the living standards of virtually all Libyans, but they are wont to ignore the revolutionary philosophy of *The Green Book*, or pay it only perfunctory lip service so long as the better material life his regime has provided continues.

There remain the special interest groups, or subdivisions of Libyan society, which Qaddafi has antagonized: the religious community; the traditional tribal leadership; the university community; the writers, journalists, and intellectuals; and last but potentially most dangerous, the armed forces. The émigré Libyan opposition leaders in other Arab countries, in Europe, and in the United States seek alliances among most or all of these domestic interest groups. Only a firm "national link" (the name of one of the external opposition factions) between those factions inside and outside the country could, they believe, succeed.

Opposition to Qaddafi on religious grounds is not to be confused with the opposition of *men of religion*, the sheikhs and imams of the traditional religious establishment. The Muslim asceticism of the RCC in its early years was written into law. By the end of 1972, Koranic punishments, such as amputating the hand of a thief, had been included in Libyan legal codes. Though these were not applied, they were intended to please the *ulama*, the Islamic scholars whose support Qaddafi wanted, at least in earlier years, in order to justify the "dismantling of the Sanussi establishment of the old regime."⁵

As time wore on, Qaddafi and his associates said less and less about religion in public, and their general principles were set down in the generalities of *The Green Book*. By 1978, Qaddafi had begun to criticize the *ulama*. In his most often quoted attack on them, he called them "a class of superfluous priests." Islam was supposed to be a faith whose members communicated directly with God, under which all people were equal before God. In a speech in a Tripoli mosque on the Prophet Muhammad's birthday, Qaddafi announced that the Muslim calendar should be revised, and should start not with the Prophet's flight from Mecca, or Hijra, as it had for fourteen centuries, but ten years later, with the Prophet's death. He also called into question the value of the *hadiths*, or oral traditions, about the Prophet that are handed on from generation to generation. To base religion on anything outside the Koran, he said, was blasphemous. In May 1978, European newspapers reported that the Libyan regime had replaced imams in Tripoli, Benghazi, Zuara, Homs, and Tajjura, because the imams were thought guilty of heretical or even atheistic preaching. More imams, according to Libyan émigrés, were purged in the spring of 1980.⁶

None of this, however, adds up to a serious "religious" opposition to Qaddafi at home. Sudanese charges in April 1981 that Libyan troops had massacred leading Chadian imams, or the disappearance in Libya of the Shi'a imam Musa Sadr from Lebanon in September 1978, were the cause of bad publicity for Qaddafi abroad, but they did little to affect his position at home. Though he has prohibited the Muslim Brotherhood and similar groups in Libya, and therefore created the possibility of such groups being backed by Saudi Arabia or others, religious factors alone could hardly coalesce to overthrow Qaddafi. They do, however, enter into the calculation of Qaddafi's adversaries, who seek to spread gossip or engage in sometimes childish "disinformation" about his own alleged departure from ascetic Islamic norms, such as his supposedly active sex life.[7]

The possibility of tribal opposition against Qaddafi has always attracted the attention of his adversaries abroad. The 1970 plot by King Idris's distant cousin the "Black Prince" and members of the Seif al-Nasr clan was an early example. Egyptian newspapers claimed in April 1976 that Qaddafi's own tribe from Sirte had been favored with the best officer appointments in the armed forces, and this aroused protest. In April 1980, as the wave of domestic purges began, the Cairo newspaper *Al-Ahram* reported strong resistance by tribal leaders to Qaddafi's plans to abolish the tribal system. Arrests of nearly two hundred tribal sheikhs led to splits in the army and "mutinous discord" among Libyan oil-field workers, the newspaper claimed; Qaddafi canceled his order to dissolve the tribal structure.[8] One of Qaddafi's opponents abroad, Mustafa al-Barki, founder of a major opposition group called the Libyan National League, claimed there was dissidence in the Barassa and Ubaydah tribes in Cyrenaica, and even among the al-Qaddaf, the Brother Colonel's own tribe. But with the population moving more and more to the affluent cities and villages and the rural tribal population declining, tribalism, like religion, seemed hardly a factor that could work alone to undermine Qaddafi. In *The Green Book* Qaddafi finds tribes to be a divisive force with no role to play in building the kind of revolutionary society he says he wants.

In the university community, Qaddafi encountered some of his most determined opposition along with some of his most fanatical support. At the beginning, most university students were behind Qaddafi. The trouble started when he began to subordinate student groups to the failed Arab Socialist Union, and put the government in charge of matters such as the election of student councils. In his 1973 cultural revolution, Qaddafi concentrated on the universities. Some of the first People's Committees were formed on the campuses in Tripoli and Benghazi. As in cultural revolutions elsewhere, professors were fired, curricula were changed, and school terms were cut short to enable students to join volunteer construction or agricultural projects and to do their compulsory military training for the People's Militia.

In January 1976 there was serious fighting at Benghazi University when government police tried to impose the election to student councils of Arab Socialist Union–backed candidates over nongovernment independents. Despite official denials, there was shooting and several killings. The student protest movement against the regime spread to Tripoli University, and Libyan students abroad demonstrated at their embassies in Washington, London, and Bonn. Some public executions followed.[9]

Qaddafi and Jalloud personally exhorted the Tripoli students in April 1976 to cooperate in driving out "reactionary" opposition. There were serious clashes between pro- and anti-regime elements. The government closed Tripoli University. When it was reopened, it was renamed al-Fateh University (not a direct reference to the Palestinian group, but rather to the term *al-fateh*, meaning the September 1 revolution). Further clashes were reported by the Egyptian press between students and security forces in 1977, and many former anti-regime demonstrators —the "usual suspects"—were rounded up again by the security police.

It is only fair to point out that students have also taken the lead in forming and steering the regime's revolutionary institutions, especially the revolutionary committees that supervise and direct the local People's Committees and the basic popular congresses. Students have responded to Qaddafi's calls to take over the domestic information media, including the radio and television services, and to convert Libyan embassies abroad into People's Bureaus, like the one the U.S. government closed down in Washington in May 1981. A small committee representing the approximately four thousand Libyan students in the United States was allowed to operate out of a rented building in McLean, Virginia, but no diplomatic status was granted. At least three hundred of the four thousand Libyan students in the United States were, according to U.S. State Department information, studying nuclear physics, and were often polarized between pro- and anti-Qaddafi elements. In Colorado, for instance, Qaddafi's supporters were mainly at the University of Denver and at the University of Colorado in Boulder. Their opponents' stronghold was at Colorado State University in Fort Collins. There, one of their number was shot and wounded by Eugene Tafoya, the former U.S. Green Beret who had ties to Edwin Wilson in Tripoli. Pro- and anti-Qaddafi Libyan students demonstrated in Washington, D.C., on May 23, 1980, among other occasions.

Qaddafi obviously takes the student threat more seriously than he does that of religious or tribal leaders. But supporters of Qaddafi among the students, as well as elements controlled by the revolutionary committees in Libya, appear to infiltrate the dissidents and keep them in check. Like the émigré students, those inside Libya are disorganized and divided into factions, and are under constant pressure from the security forces. However, an alliance between the student groups, if they were better organized, and some added element such as the military, might give Qaddafi some very serious trouble.

Intellectuals, writers, and journalists who have dissented from Qaddafi's views and actions have probably fared no worse than similar dissidents in most other countries in Africa, Asia, and Latin America. Several have been murdered, a few have been executed after legal proceedings, and many have been imprisoned. More attention has been paid to them by Amnesty International and similar groups than to other Libyan opponents of Qaddafi, and for this reason somewhat more is known about them in the outside world.

Like other revolutionary leaders, Qaddafi from the beginning tried to coopt Libyan intellectuals and win their support and collaboration. In the early 1970s a "Revolutionary Intellectual Seminar" organized by the RCC was intended to serve as a dialogue between the regime and those who wrote or studied about Libyan politics and society. Qaddafi personally controlled the seminar, despite some speeches by Major Jalloud, Omar al-Meheishi, and others. During the seminar meetings, intellectuals and writers were repeatedly condemned by the regime's spokesmen for their supposed responsibility for the inability of the Arab world to solve its own problems, and for "importing alien theories and ideas." These could be atoned for only by teaching the principles of "direct democracy" and the ideas and ideals of the revolution to the "masses." At one seminar session, Ali Mustafa al-Misurati, a respected journalist and the editor of *Al Shaab*, tried to defend the freedom of the press and the need for independent comment. Both Qaddafi and Meheishi attacked him and accused the print media in Libya of being a corrupt extension of the old regime. Free comment on Libya's future development was unnecessary, since the new people's government understood the country's goals and needs and would take care of meeting them without the help or criticism of outsiders.

When the revolutionary seminars had helped lead to creation of the Arab Socialist Union (ASU), the Ministry of Information was shaken up. In January 1972, twenty-nine editors and broadcasters, some of them well known and popular, were arrested and tried by the People's Court for financial corruption and allegedly corrupting public opinion

under the old regime. Eight were acquitted, some after publicly re-
canting their past political beliefs and promising to follow the revolution
in the future. Others were fined. One Minister of Information under
the monarchy was given eight years in prison. Journalists and others in
the media took it as a warning.

At the founding conference of the Arab Socialist Union in 1972,
Qaddafi again attacked prerevolutionary intellectuals for allowing them-
selves to be influenced by Marxist ideas and by the ideas of the Baath
Arab Socialist Party, which ruled in Iraq and Syria. A new press law
issued in June 1972 forbade newspapers to criticize the revolution or
Islam or to call for rule by any class or individual in Libyan society.
Though there was no formal prepublication censorship, there were
severe penalties for violating the rules.

Meanwhile, ten newspapers had been suspended by the government
after *Al-Rayed*, a Tripoli daily newspaper, had said in an editorial that
journalists should be able to criticize the authorities if they felt it was
necessary. Fadel Massaud, a columnist in another paper, *al-Maidane*,
criticized the way *Egyptian* newspapers had been implying that Libya
should provide funds for the proposed Egypt-Libya-Sudan union even at
the cost of its own development. This was still the period of relative
harmony between Sadat and Qaddafi, and Massaud became the first of
many Libyan journalists who had to flee abroad to escape official wrath.
Many Libyan writers refused to contribute to the Qaddafi government's
official gazette, *al-Thawra*. The private newspapers that had been
suspended were eventually replaced by government-controlled newspapers and periodicals. Though these publications often change their
names or managers, they still dominate the Libyan media scene today.

When Qaddafi launched the cultural revolution in April 1973, he
demanded the removal from Libyan culture of the imported and
poisonous doctrines that could "influence feeble minds." People's
Committees in Tripoli and Benghazi began censoring bookshops' stocks
and demanding changes in school textbooks. Course changes were
made in the schools and universities, and symbolic book-burnings were
held. Around this time about one thousand intellectuals were arrested,
and a group of forty university professors, lawyers, and writers were
accused of links with Marxist, Trotskyist, Baathist, and Muslim Brotherhood organizations. After a year's detention without trial they were
released by a court order, and then immediately rearrested. Some were
released after making televised confessions and promising to do better.
Again editors and writers fled the country.

In 1977 and after, there were further signs of protest from intellectuals. A Benghazi student, Mansur Abu Snaf, wrote a play called *When the Mice Rule*, a direct, satirical attack on the Qaddafi regime. He was last reported serving a life sentence in prison. A poet named Shultami spent a year in prison without trial for criticizing the regime. In 1978 and 1979, the nationalization measures destroyed the few private publishers who remained. Arbitrary arrests continued. In 1978, eighteen journalists working for two newspapers, *Al-Fajr al-Jadid* ("The New Dawn") and *Al-Usbu al-Thaqafi* ("Cultural Week") were arrested in Benghazi after they attended a commemorative meeting for a dead poet. Accused of belonging to Marxist groups, they were held without trial until March 1980, when they were tried before a revolutionary council court; their sentences were not disclosed. Others who have been critical have languished in prison for years without trial, such as two university lecturers held from 1970 until 1979. Seven others were reportedly held under sentence of death, without being executed, for between three and ten years.[10]

Only Amnesty International has shown serious, sustained interest in the plight of intellectuals and other political prisoners—AI prefers to call them "prisoners of consience"—under Qaddafi. In 1980 the organization had "adopted," as it does in other countries, seventy-seven such prisoners, and was investigating new cases of journalists and writers who were arrested in December 1978, accused of forming a Marxist organization. Most of those whose cases AI has tried to follow are held either in Tripoli's Central Prison (the old "Hilton" of the Hilton assignment) and Kuweifiya Prison in Benghazi. Prisoners awaiting the outcome of their trials were held in Jdeida Prison, about eight miles outside of Tripoli.

In March and April 1980, an Amnesty mission was permitted to observe parts of two trials of its adopted prisoners of conscience, and to confer with Libyan justice officials. The first trial included eighteen journalists and writers, most of whom had been arrested during a cultural festival in Benghazi in December 1978. Some were alleged to have been beaten in detention and held in solitary confinement for three months; they were not allowed to see a lawyer or their own families during that time. Believing in Marxism and forming an illegal Marxist organization were the main charges at their trials, along with trying to infiltrate and "dominate" two state-owned weekly newspapers. Their defense lawyers contended the trial was mainly concerned with the freedom of expression and opinion. All received prison sentences.

In February 1980, official Libyan newspapers published a declaration issued by the revolutionary committees meeting at Gar Yunis University in Benghazi. It authorized "physical liquidation" of enemies of the revolution abroad, as well as of others said to be obstructing the revolutionary changes in the country. By June 11, 1980, ten Libyans had been killed abroad. Amnesty International also received reports of deaths in detention, including that of Amer Deghayes, a former Baathist who died a few days after his arrest. There were many reports of mistreatment of those arrested. On April 25, 1980, Amnesty International condemned the killings of Libyans abroad, including that of the well-known Libyan journalist Muhammad Ramadan, a BBC employee in London, killed there on April 11, 1980. AI called upon the Libyan authorities to renounce "physical liquidation," and was then told, in talks with the government, that the program had *not* been applied. Despite this, only two days later, Qaddafi announced that opponents abroad should return; and the next day, April 28, 1980, the official newspaper *Al-Azhaf al-Akhdar* ("The Green Road") said the "liquidation" program had begun and warned of reprisals against families of Libyans abroad who, when summoned home, did not return. AI received reports of torture—use of electricity, and beating of the soles of the feet—against prisoners held by the intelligence service. Applications to visit four adopted prisoners in Tripoli and Benghazi were refused.[11]

The only group or institution that could seriously threaten Qaddafi's rule is the one from whence he and his fellow officers came: the army. On the whole, the 45,000-man regular army and its officer corps have remained loyal. But a few plots have been reported regularly since December 1969. Nearly one hundred officers were said to be implicated in an anti-Qaddafi conspiracy at the time of Omar-Meheishi's defection in August 1975. There were persistent reports in February 1978 of brewing military unrest. Captain Muhammad Idris Sharif, who then directed military intelligence; his brother-in-law, Air Force Captain Muhammad al-Saayid; and several other officers were reported to have been arrested in a plot against Qaddafi and Jalloud. Sharif, according to information received by Western intelligence, was said to have refused to obey an order from Qaddafi to cease the funding of some of the international terrorist groups then on Qaddafi's payroll (most probably, those dealing with hijacking; this was shortly before Qaddafi announced his intention to sign an antihijacking convention and then withdrew from the hijacking game altogether). JANA, the official Libyan news agency, called the reports published in Cairo and Europe "Egyptian lies." The rumors arose again in March 1978. Members of a visiting German delegation were killed in a helicopter crash, said to have been part of an assassination attempt against Qaddafi, and several high-ranking air force officers were reportedly arrested.

The Tobruk mutiny of August 1980, put down with the help of East German security men in Libya, fit into the pattern of Egyptian and French efforts to "destabilize" Qaddafi. At a public rally on March 28, 1981, commemorating the eleventh anniversary of the British evacuation, Qaddafi announced that regular troops had been removed from their military positions in the Tobruk region. Army camps, Qaddafi said, would be converted into education centers. The People's Militia, Libya's citizen army of fifty thousand or so, would take their place, with the regular army ready to return if needed.[12] On a live American TV news interview program in early May, Qaddafi said he did not trust the regular army.[13]

*Newsweek* reported on July 20, 1981, that in May of that year Qaddafi was warned of a plan by opponents to shoot down his plane upon his return from a visit to the Soviet Union. The Soviets reportedly had lost a decoy plane to hostile Libyan fire in the incident. By autumn of 1981, Qaddafi and Tripoli Radio were regularly reporting CIA plots to murder Qaddafi by poison, shooting, stabbing, or even bombing from the air.[14]

To protect himself, Qaddafi makes use of the East Germans and of his own al-Qaddaf tribe, organized in a "deterrent battalion" that he apparently considers totally loyal. All of its members are drawn from the Sirte region. Women soldiers are included in a larger Jamahariyah Guard, which comprises "revolutionary elements" and is intended to "safeguard the revolution and defend the Jamahariyah regime." Initially its members were supposed to consist of unpaid volunteers.[15]

Qaddafi's decision to withdraw his troops from Chad in November 1981 was certainly a response to African political pressures, and perhaps to his desire to reach a modus vivendi in Africa with the new French government of President François Mitterand in 1982, the year when Qaddafi was to become chairman of the African Unity Organization. Qualified Libyan observers also believed it was in part a move to placate dissatisfaction and incipient mutiny, which might have broken into the open if Libyan casualties in Chad had continued to increase or if the Chad operation had turned into another debacle on the scale of the

Ugandan intervention of 1979. By February 1982, Nigerian and other African peacekeeping troops were well established in Chad, but they had not even tried to prevent new advances by Hissène Habré, the old enemy of President Goukouni Oueddei and the Libyans. The Habré forces seemed to be engulfing much of Chad. The several hundred casualties from Uganda, some of whom were flown to hospitals in Malta and thus shielded from the eyes and ears of Libyans, apparently deeply affected the military. Some senior officers, especially Abu Bakr Yunis Jabir, the chief of staff, had opposed the Uganda operation and were thought by many Libyans to have doubts about the Chad one.

Further points of friction between Qaddafi and the military would be a decision to sign a defense treaty with the Soviet Union, or the implementation of Qaddafi's often-announced plan to phase out the professional military in favor of People's Militia. There have been persistent stories, none of them very satisfactorily confirmed, of tension between the Libyan military and their East bloc advisers, especially the Russians—tension of the sort that helped to spoil relations between the Egyptian military and the Russians when Sadat expelled the Soviets from Egypt in July 1972. One of the factors causing the downfall of President Ahmed ben Bella of Algeria, who was ousted by Colonel Houari Boumedienne and his fellow Algerian army officers in June 1965, was ben Bella's buildup of the militia as a counterweight to the regular army and the propensity shown by some of ben Bella's advisers for a closer Soviet connection.

It is more than possible that the Soviet Union, in its infinite wisdom, has been training or grooming some future military rival of Qaddafi for the day of Qaddafi's downfall, in order to replace him with a more reliable ally—a Libyan Babrak Karmal, the puppet who tries to rule Afghanistan for the Soviets. Qaddafi and the Soviets both believe they are using each other, and both are correct. But the Soviets might have to wait a long time, or indefinitely, for the set of favorable circumstances that would enable their candidate to take power in an Arab country like Libya. That is something they have been able to achieve so far in the Arab world only in South Yemen. Under Qaddafi, Libyans probably have even less love for their East bloc advisers than their fathers did for the West bloc ones under King Idris.

During the months that followed the air battle over the Gulf of Sirte, the signs of a growing will by the Reagan administration to increase the pressure on Qaddafi grew and multiplied. President Sadat's assassination on October 6, 1981, by Egyptian assassins doing Qaddafi's work for him, increased that pressure, if only verbally. During his last visit to Washington shortly before his death, Sadat was told by the United States that if war should develop between Egypt and Libya, arising from the Chad affair or Libyan action against the Sudan, the United States would undertake to deter any Soviet action in favor of Libya. This was a return to a similar commitment given Sadat by the Ford administration in 1976—one that President Carter had backed away from, preferring to restrain Sadat from any further adventures against Qaddafi after the desert skirmishes of July 1977. The commitment was repeated to Egypt's new president, Husni Mubarak, after Sadat's funeral. Though the assurances did not include encouragement to Mubarak to attack Libya (something he was unlikely to do anyhow), the Reagan administration left no doubt in Mubarak's mind that if the Soviets threatened Egypt or Sudan because of hostilities between them and Qaddafi, a U.S. protective umbrella would be available for Egypt.[16]

Meanwhile, what had the Reagan administration actually done about Qaddafi or about either strengthening or weakening the hands of Qaddafi's Libyan enemies? From the beginning of the Reagan era in January 1981, Secretary of State Alexander M. Haig, whose own position was being weakened at home by what Haig termed "guerrilla warfare" waged against him by White House advisers, had it in for Qaddafi. Publicly, he referred to him as a leading sponsor of "international terrorism." Privately, he talked of Qaddafi as a "cancer" that might have to be cut out. Vice President George Bush was equally vehement in tone.

Public figures in both the Western and Arab worlds repeatedly suggested an oil boycott or a military campaign against Qaddafi, or both. Former President Richard Nixon visited Saudi Arabia, Tunisia, and Morocco after Sadat's funeral, and came home suggesting that rulers in those countries favored the oil boycott.

This call was echoed from Khartoum, Sudan, fast becoming the main capital for the Arab opponents of the Libyan colonel. Muhammad Yusuf al-Mugarieff, generally considered to be the opposition leader most acceptable in Khartoum, said that the West should boycott Qaddafi's regime. His opposition group, the National Front for the Salvation of Libya, was planning "imminent" military action against Qaddafi. His followers, he said, included "diplomats, officers, lawyers, doctors, and Libyans inside and outside Libya from all walks of life." Their clandestine radio station was "heard in Libya and also by our soldiers in Chad." The West should stop buying oil and so make easier "the sacred task of getting rid of Qaddafi, which is a Libyan responsibility."[17]

Mugarieff's words and existence were both worthy of careful attention in the West. Mugarieff is a well-educated former lecturer at Benghazi University's faculty of economics and commerce, and he was still young at the time of the Qaddafi revolution. He did his teaching from May 1971 to July 1972, and was then recruited by Qaddafi and the RCC to head the state comptroller's commission, a job he held from 1972 until November 1977, when Qaddafi made him ambassador to India and sent him to Delhi. He left his post there and announced in Cairo in October 1980 that he was joining the Libyan opposition; he accused Qaddafi of having abandoned all legal and human values, of executing innocent people, and of fostering "dictatorship, tyranny, and corruption." Later, in London, he criticized the United States for the CIA's protection of Qaddafi during the regime's early years. Repeatedly he asked the United States at least not to interfere with, even if it had no plans to participate in, Qaddafi's overthrow.

The day after Mugarieff's statement in Khartoum, the U.S. Senate, voting 47 to 44, shelved a measure to ban all U.S. imports of Libyan crude oil. Instead it decided on a new six-month study by the U.S. administration of "concrete steps" to confront Qaddafi. This was a minor victory for the Reagan administration because President Reagan had expressed public doubt that a U.S. oil boycott of Libya would be joined by Libya's European customers, though the boycott was finally enacted in March 1982.

So, during a winter of 1981–82 that promised to be rich in new developments in the Middle East situation—the United States and Israel being increasingly isolated by Western European interest in a Saudi-sponsored peace initiative aimed at creating a Palestinian state—the United States studied its Libyan options. Oil was foremost. Paradoxically, even as United States–Libyan political relations had declined, trade was still rising. The value of U.S. exports to Libya in 1980 was about $509 million, and during the first five months of 1981 had already totaled $349 million—a 63.2 percent increase over the same period in 1980. This period of expansion in U.S. sales to Libya in 1981 coincided exactly with the expulsion of the People's Bureau from Washington, Secretary Haig's pleas to the American oil companies to get their personnel out of Libya, and the air battle over the Gulf of Sirte. In 1980, U.S. imports from Libya, almost entirely oil, were worth $7.1 billion. First-quarter U.S. imports were worth $1.97 billion, down from

$2.32 billion during the same period of 1980. The drop reflected the decline in oil bought by the United States due to the worldwide oil glut.

Qaddafi has always favored U.S. oil technology. By the end of 1981, about fifteen hundred American personnel, most of them in the oil business, were working in Libya. They were being repeatedly assured by Qaddafi that they were in no personal danger whatever the state of U.S.-Libyan political relations. However, after the "hit team" scare and U.S. instructions to leave in December 1981, they did begin to go home. The Libyan oil industry was about 70 percent dependent on American oil companies and American oil expertise. Libya was the only OPEC country still permitting foreign company participation of up to 49 percent in oil concessions, and the Libyan industry minister told me in Tripoli December 18, 1981, that this situation would not change. American companies enjoyed their widest profit margin on Libyan oil. By November 1981, the United States was still buying about 40 percent of Libyan oil production, but this represented only about 7.7 percent of total American oil imports. In early 1982, it had sunk below 3 percent.

If West Europe joined the United States in an oil boycott of Libya, the Libyan economy would face an almost total cutoff of revenue within months. Libya would then be forced to live on its financial reserves, which most economists believe are sufficient to finance about two years' imports, or a total of about $40 billion. New buyers willing and able to take over the 80 percent of Libyan production dropped by the United States and Western Europe would be hard to find, and all the harder if the 1981 world oil glut continued. France, Italy, and West Germany might well be unwilling to sacrifice their trade with Libya for an American policy with which they disagreed. But even if they did refuse to boycott, in a time of worldwide glut it was not too likely that they would move in to buy up the Libyan oil left over from an American boycott.

According to leading Arab oil analysts, only Abu Dhabi among the OPEC states of the Persian Gulf would support Libya if a boycott were imposed, but that support would be largely rhetorical, and based on domestic United Arab Emirates' political considerations. Saudi Arabia, on the other hand, has rejected all calls for solidarity of OPEC states in case the West boycotts Libyan oil. Saudi Arabia might even be willing to offer standby oil on attractive terms to countries that want to stop buying Qaddafi's oil. Nigeria, like fellow OPEC member Saudi Arabia, would, because of Qaddafi's past behavior in Africa and its own economic needs, be only too happy to sell oil to Libya's customers. In late 1981 it appeared that Algeria, because of its mistrust of Qaddafi and its frontier dispute with him, would be unlikely to go beyond condemnation of Western measures of Qaddafi, though that would depend upon the circumstances. However, by January 1981, Saudi Arabia had restored its broken diplomatic links with Libya, and Algerians and Libyans were again holding joint oil talks.

There remains Qaddafi's prospective new ally, the Soviet Union. The USSR, some leading analysts believe, could buy much more Libyan oil for itself or allow its satellites to buy more than it does now, and then try to resell it. This happened in 1980 in a small way, when Greece took a total of 850,000 tons of Libyan oil directly from the Soviet Union in addition to the 3 million tons or so it bought directly from Libya. Still, it is doubtful that the Soviets could find enough new buyers for more than an insignificant quantity. And the Soviet political and strategic partnership with Libya is a conditional one, with many ifs and buts. Likewise, neither Qaddafi himself, nor his possible successors, seems likely to accept any massive Soviet oil purchases because they would almost inevitably be linked with unacceptable political conditions.

Therefore, concluded many thoughtful observers in the winter of 1981–82, U.S. economic sanctions against Qaddafi seemed more likely than military ones. The United States finally did initiate a Libyan oil boycott to please domestic critics clamoring for action against Qaddafi, and to assure foreign friends like Israel that the Reagan administration was serious about its anti-Qaddafi pronouncements. The Exxon Corporation, the largest U.S. oil company, seemed to be taking the lead in this effort when it announced a withdrawal from all operations in Libya beginning November 4, 1981.

It could also be that military action, shielding an offensive by Muhammad al-Mugarieff and other Libyan opponents of Qaddafi from Egypt and the Sudan, would set the entire Mediterranean and North African area in flames. What would happen then—whether the United States and the Soviet Union would confront one another in the deserts of Libya as foreseen by General Omar Bradley and the authors of the Dropshot plan—would depend on decisions made not in Tripoli, but in Washington and Moscow.

Either way, the Libyan sandstorm that began before dawn on September 1, 1969, has swept across several countries and continents, into the very council chambers where great decisions about the future of the world are made. Muammar al-Qaddafi himself, his disciples and his detractors, had worked this singular series of historical events. It remained not for them, but for the fates and perhaps the God in which Qaddafi, like his Bedouin forebears, so fervently believes, to write the epilogue.[18]

**H**alf a generation after that dawn over the Gulf of Sirte when Abu Meniar al-Qaddafi and his wife first heard their son's words at sunrise over the transistor radio he had given them, Muammar al-Qaddafi and his people are living in a new country. Oil and the "Green Revolution" have transformed the simple Bedouin encampment where Qaddafi first saw the world into a teaming center of new construction, industry, and human activity. The shores of Sirte now sprout not the Mediterranean palm trees and remnants of ancient European colonization but the chimneys and the surrealistic array of refinery towers, natural gas plants, tanker loading terminals. At Ras Lanuf, amid the ancestral homeland of the al-Qaddaf tribe, a new city is being constructed by contractors lured from all four corners of the world by the profits from Libya's oil boom. Not far away, the bulldozers and road-building machinery of other builders have prepared the site for Qaddafi's first nuclear electric power generating station.

Somewhere along that coast, a lonely figure, his bodyguards watchful and nearby, stands gazing out at the eternally blue waters of the Gulf of Sirte. He has lifted his desert realm out of obscurity, and his people out of poverty and the shadow of underdevelopment. Yet his zeal has turned half the world outside into enemies. The sun rises swiftly in this desert land, warming its farthest corners and spreading life to every remote city alley and distant oasis. But the desert day in winter is short. The night will descend swiftly and with chilling effect. Unseen threats lurk at sea or in the air, beyond the Mediterranean horizon, behind the enveloping hills of the desert beyond Sirte.

Like so many others before him who have tried to lead entire nations or peoples to greatness, Muammar al-Qaddafi now knows how it feels to be totally responsible and, in the end, totally alone.

# NOTES

Note: Because of the problems inherent in transliterating Arabic, I have chosen certain styles of spelling; however, occasionally there are variations between the book's style and English translations by other people. Where this is the case, my choice for style will appear in brackets following the spelling that will appear on a given source.

## One: A SEPTEMBER DAWN

1  Full text of the proclamation appears in the Appendix of *Middle East Journal,* vol. 24, no. 2 (Spring 1970), documents section.
2  This account comes from several Libyan émigrés who knew Qaddafi, and from Hamza Kaidi, "Kaddafi et les Grands," *Jeune Afrique* (Paris), no. 1063 (May 20, 1981), pp. 57–58.
3  Ruth First, *Libya: The Elusive Revolution* (Harmondsworth, England: Penguin, 1974), pp. 108–10.
4  Ibid., p. 110. Another source was my personal conversation with someone who must be anonymous, as he was imprisoned by the new regime and his life could be endangered. The impact of the al-Aqsa mosque fire, which took place when I was visiting the Jordan-Israel cease-fire line with a Jordan army officer, has been described for me by a number of Libyans, both inside the Qaddafi regime and outside it.
5  Conversations with Daryl Penner in Washington, D.C., June 6, 1981, and with U.S. military personnel who served at Wheelus Field in 1969.

6   Mohamed Heikal [Muhammad Hasseinine Haykal], *The Road to Rama-dan* (London: Collins, 1975), p. 69.

7   It is likely that Colonel Abdel Azziz al-Shalhi, and possibly Omar, had word of the joint Soviet-Egyptian fleet maneuvers, and these helped them choose the date of September 4 for their own planned coup. In any case, whatever the Soviet intent, the Red Fleet had Qaddafi's thanks. It was therefore no accident that Qaddafi, after his swing to Soviet arms, training, and advisers, put such heavy stress on the Libyan navy and that the first group of Libyans sent to the Soviet Union in 1974 went for submarine training.

8   Nasser was apparently ready to use force to protect Qaddafi even at this early stage. According to a report that was later proved to be false, several Egyptians who remained in Benghazi cabled to Nasser that the West German government was "helping the Turks to mount an expedition by sea which would have the aim of reinstating King Idris." Nasser was so concerned he ordered General Fawzi to "calm things down on the Canal front with Israel and prepare for action in the West." An armored brigade was moved to Marsa Matruh, near the Libyan border, and two destroyers and several Egyptian submarines were dispatched westward from Alexandria.

9   Anwar al-Sadat, *In Search of Identity: An Autobiography* (New York: Harper & Row, 1977), p. 201.

10  Personal communication.

11  Among the first measures announced by the RCC—which included doubling the minimum wage for working people, halving the salaries of cabinet ministers, and banning the Latin alphabet on all signs and in government forms and substituting Arabic—Qaddafi, the puritan, banned alcohol and frivolous entertainment and ordered Tripoli's cabarets and nightclubs closed. Taking a squad of military police with him, he descended upon the Bowdlerina nightclub, one of the favored night spots of the Italian community and also of the Libyan jet set. Drawing his gun from its holster, Sheriff Qaddafi and his posse walked into the midst of the floor show. Customers and performers scattered. "This place," Qaddafi said in effect, "is officially closed."

12  Omar I. al-Fathali and Monte Palmer, *Political Development and Social Change in Libya* (Washington, D.C.: Lexington Books, 1981), p. 39.

13  Patrick Seale and Maureen McConville, *The Hilton Assignment* (New York and Washington: Praeger, 1973), pp. 50–52.

14  He is currently a leader of the émigrés who oppose and vow to overthrow Qaddafi.

15  Joe was killed by a stray bullet in Tehran during the Iranian revolution in February 1979. As always, Joe felt that his duty to his readers was to be where the action was, and, much more than that, to explain why it was

happening. Joe's friendship helped me and many other colleagues through many a tight situation during the years I was privileged to know him.

16 We both knew ben Bella and many other Algerian leaders. I had written a book about the role of Islam in the struggles of all four North African countries to be rid of their foreign rulers. John K. Cooley, *Baal, Christ and Mohammed: Religion and Revolution in North Africa* (New York: Holt, Rinehart and Winston, 1965).

## **Two:** THE SHORES OF TRIPOLI

1 Majid Khadduri, *Modern Libya: A Study in Political Development* (Baltimore: Johns Hopkins University Press, 1963), p. v.

2 Ruth First, *Libya: The Elusive Revolution* (Harmondsworth, England: Penguin, 1974), p. 33.

3 John K. Cooley, *Baal, Christ and Mohammed: Religion and Revolution in North Africa* (New York: Holt, Rinehart and Winston, 1965), pp. 73–79.

4 Adrian Pelt, *Libyan Independence and the United States: A Case of Planned Decolonization* (New Haven: Yale University Press, Carnegie Endowment for International Peace, 1970), pp. 3–8.

5 Khadduri, *Modern Libya*, p. 71.

6 Nathan Miller, *The U.S. Navy: An Illustrated History* (New York and Annapolis: American Heritage Publishing, U.S. Naval Institute Press, 1977), p. 45.

7 Gentil Lamotte, *Revue de Cercle Militaire*, 1902, p. 12, quoted in Cooley, *Baal, Christ and Mohammed*, p. 180.

8 Muammar al-Qaddafi's fascination with submarines and submarine warfare—he once ordered an Egyptian submarine to attack the British liner *Queen Elizabeth II* when she was bound for Israel, and has prepared a specially equipped submarine for his own personal command or escape in time of danger—may stem from the importance that German undersea craft played in that war. Germany and Turkey, from 1915, were supporting an "independent Tripolitanian republic" along the narrow coastal strip between Misurata and Qaddafi's ancestral homeland of Sirte. Ramadan al-Suheily and his followers had annihilated an entire Italian column near Sirte. German and sometimes Turkish submarines ran a tight British naval blockade in order to bring in money, arms, and instructors for the Libyan partisans and to support the Sanussi partisans in Cyrenaica.

9 Pelt, *Libyan Independence*, p. 26.

10 Ibid., p. 41.

11 Letter from Prime Minister Alcide de Gasperi to the U.S. secretary of

state, August 22, 1945, *Department of State Bulletin*, vol. 13 (1945), pp. 764–65.

12  Khadduri, *Modern Libya*, pp. 113–14.

13  Ibid., pp. 115–17.

14  Ibid., p. 125.

15  Henry Serrano Villard, *Libya: The New Arab Kingdom of North Africa* (Ithaca, N.Y.: Cornell University Press, 1956), p. 24, as quoted in First, *Libya*, p. 67.

16  I worked from 1955 to 1957 with the U.S. Army Corps of Engineers based at Nouasseur, Morocco, which supervised the work in Libya, and earlier, in 1953, with Atlas Constructors, the main air-base contractor in Morocco.

17  Khadduri, *Modern Libya*, pp. 136–37.

18  Ben Halim succeeded in getting the French to evacuate their own garrisons in the Fezzan in the Franco-Libyan Treaty of 1955, even though the French were locked by then in their bitter and finally losing struggle with the Algerian, Tunisian, and Moroccan nationalists, and ben Halim was secretly aiding Algeria's FLN to smuggle major quantities of arms across the Sahara into Algeria to fight the French.

19  Andrew Carveley, *Non-Aligned Third World Annual*, 1970 (Washington, D.C.: 1971). Privately published by Mr. Carveley and his fellow editors.

## Three:  THE GREAT OIL BOOM

1  Professor Desio wrote some basic works on North African geography and oil and minerals potential: *Il Tibesti Nord-Orientale* (Rome: Reale Società Geographica Italiana, 1942); *Le Condizioni geologico-petrolifere della Libya, 18th International Geological Congress* (Great Britain, Reprint Part 6, 1950), and *La Vie della Sete, Explorizione Sahariane* (Milan: Ulrico Heepli, 1950).

2  Personal conversations with Mr. Mustafa ben Halim and Dr. Majid Khadduri in Washington, D.C., in April 1981; Majid Khadduri, *Modern Libya: A Study in Political Development* (Baltimore: Johns Hopkins University Press, 1963), p. 260; and a 1961 report of the U.S. State Department's Geographical Section in the Algero-Libyan frontiers, passim, with maps.

3  Khadduri, *Modern Libya*, p. 327.

4  J. A. Allan, *Libya: The Experience of Oil* (Boulder, Colo.: Westview Press, 1981), p. 91.

5  Christopher Rand, *Making Democracy Safe for Oil: Oilmen and the Islamic East* (Boston: Atlantic–Little, Brown, 1975), pp. 235–37.

6 Andrew Carveley, *Non-Aligned Third World Annual,* 1970.

7 *Who Was Who in America,* 1976; *Current Biography,* 1976 (Obituaries), p. 474; Rand, *Making Democracy Safe,* pp. 237–39, 242.

8 Milton Moskowitz, Michael Katz, and Robert Levering, eds., *Everybody's Business: An Almanac* (New York: Harper & Row, 1980), p. 497.

9 Rand, *Making Democracy Safe,* p. 246.

10 Wilbur Eveland, *Ropes of Sand: America's Failure in the Middle East* (New York: W. W. Norton, 1980).

11 Rand, *Making Democracy Safe,* p. 251.

12 Personal communication.

13 Moskowitz et al., eds., *Everybody's Business,* pp. 518–19.

14 The fertilizer-plant scheme dangled before the Libyans was to be signed later on—but with the Soviets, not the Libyans. In April 1973 Hammer announced a multibillion-dollar, twenty-year chemical fertilizer deal, promising U.S. technology for a Soviet fertilizer complex to be built by Oxy and Bechtel at Kuibyshev, north of the USSR's Orenburg gas and oil fields. In exchange, Occidental would get Soviet urea, potash, and ammonia to market abroad.

   Though he never lost sight of the riches in Libya, Hammer worked doggedly and successfully to keep the Soviet deal alive. It was interrupted when President Carter cut back U.S. agricultural exports to the Soviet Union in retaliation for the Soviet invasion of Afghanistan in December 1979. When President Reagan lifted the export curbs on April 24, 1981, Hammer just happened to be in Moscow. He reopened talks with the Soviets and on June 25, 1981, announced he had completed arrangements to exchange $250 million in phosphates for an equal value in Soviet ammonia. Occidental had built a special plant in central Florida, where most U.S. phosphates come from, to produce superphosphoric acid for the Soviets and invested $180 million in three special tankers to carry them to the Soviet Union, according to a *New York Times* report from Moscow on June 26, 1981.

15 Rand, *Making Democracy Safe,* p. 254.

16 *Wall Street Journal,* February 8, 1972, report by Stanley Penn on p. 1.

17 One company in the portfolio was the Hooker Chemical Company, which fell into deep trouble with the U.S. federal government in 1980 over pollution. *Current Biography,* p. 474; *Who Was Who in America,* 1976; Rand, *Making Democracy Safe.*

18 Babcock admitted this in court. AP dispatch and *The New York Times,* December 11, 1974.

19 Bechtel Corporation company brochure, 1979.

20 Rand, *Making Democracy Safe,* p. 257.

21 Ibid., pp. 259–62.

22 Allan, *Libya,* pp. 202–05.

## FOUR: OIL: WEAPON OF REVOLUTION

1 Cf. John K. Cooley, "The International Politics of Energy," in *Energy and the Way We Live*, Article Booklet, Courses by Newspaper (University of California Extension, San Diego; Boyd & Fraser Publishing Co., San Francisco, 1980), pp. 23–24.

2 Ali D. Johany, *The Myth of the OPEC Cartel: The Role of Saudi Arabia* (Dhahran, Saudi Arabia: University of Petroleum and Minerals, and Chichester, England: John Wiley), p. 10.

3 Edith Penrose, "The Development of Crises," *Daedalus*, vol. 104, no. 4 (Fall 1975), pp. 39–59.

4 "A Broad Outline of Revolutionary Oil Policy," in *Al-Mussawar* (Cairo), October 17, 1969.

5 Christopher Rand, *Making Democracy Safe for Oil: Oilmen and the Islamic East* (Boston: Atlantic–Little, Brown, 1975), pp. 279–80; and Peter Foster, *The Blue-Eyed Sheikhs: The Canadian Oil Establishment* (Toronto: Totem, 1979), p. 27.

6 Rand, *Making Democracy Safe*, pp. 280–81.

7 Arab World File (a carded information system, Beirut), June 15, 1977, no. 474 (Libyan oil series).

8 *Platt's Oilgram*, New York City, December 8, 1970.

9 Rand, *Making Democracy Safe*, pp. 281–83.

10 Milton Moskowitz, Michael Katz, and Robert Levering, eds., *Everybody's Business: An Almanac* (New York: Harper & Row, 1980), pp. 508–09.

11 Arab World File, no. 662, June 1, 1977; no. 674, June 15, 1977; no. 1160, January 3, 1979.

12 Testimony before the Church subcommittee to investigate the world oil crisis, U.S. Senate, January 31, 1974, cited in Rand, *Making Democracy Safe*, p. 287. Schuler in 1982 was an oil consultant in Washington.

13 Mira Wilkins, "The Oil Companies in Perspective," in *The Oil Crisis*, Raymond Vernon, ed. (New York: W. W. Norton and Harvard University Center for International Affairs, 1976), p. 167.

14 Rand, *Making Democracy Safe*, p. 291.

15 Wilkins, "Oil Companies in Perspective," p. 168.

16 Rand, *Making Democracy Safe*, pp. 33–34.

17 Ibid., p. 295.

18 *Petroleum Intelligence Weekly*, May 6, 1974.

19 Wilkins, "Oil Companies in Perspective," p. 169; and Arab World File, no. 1166, January 10, 1979.

20 A BP-Sohio executive told me this when I visited Prudhoe Bay, Alaska, in May 1980.

21 Moskowitz et al., eds., *Everybody's Business*, pp. 536–37.

22 Arab World File, no. 662, June 1, 1977.

23  Ibid., no. 674, June 15, 1977.
24  *Petroleum Press Service,* vol. 41, no. 10 (October 1974).
25  Federal Energy Administration, Washington, D.C., Office of Internation-
    al Energy Affairs, *The Relationship of Oil Companies and Foreign
    Governments,* June 1975, p. 110.
26  Marathon, one of the companies created by the breaking up of Standard
    Oil, was among the major stockholdings of the eighty-four members of the
    Rockefeller family; Amerada Hess was a combine of the small Amerada
    firm with a New Jersey marketing firm called Hess.
27  Jim Hoagland of *The Washington Post* and *The Christian Science Monitor*
    of July 5, 1973. Informed of the audience, the then U.S. ambassador to
    Saudi Arabia told us: "The Saudis have been saying that kind of stuff for
    weeks now. It's just Arab rhetoric. We don't take it seriously and we don't
    even bother reporting it to Washington."

    A highly classified U.S. government report apparently leaked to
    Seymour M. Hersh, who wrote about it in *The New York Times,*
    December 21, 1977, indicated that the Central Intelligence Agency and
    the National Security Agency had managed to eavesdrop on meetings
    between Faisal and Sadat. They reported, according to Hersh, that in
    August 1973, Faisal and Sadat agreed on war against Israel, Saudi
    economic aid to Egypt of $600 million for the war, and the use of oil as a
    political weapon.
28  Arab World File, no. 1166, January 10, 1979.
29  Wilkins, "Oil Companies in Perspective," p. 172.
30  Moskowitz et al., eds., *Everybody's Business,* p. 527; Arab World File, no.
    1166, January 10, 1979.
31  Arab World File, Ibid.
32  Personal conversations with Tunisian Prime Minister Muhammad M'Zali
    and Foreign Minister Hassan Belkhodja, Tunis, November 4, 1980.
33  *Petroleum Economist* (Beirut), vol. 42, no. 8 (August 1975).

### Five: QADDAFI'S WESTERN PROTECTORS

1  Carter's reply and covering letter dated August 4, 1980, to Senator Birch
   Bayh, chairman, Subcommittee of the Committee on the Judiciary, in
   Inquiry into the Matter of Billy Carter and Libya. Hearings before the
   subcommittee to investigate the activities of individuals representing the
   interests of foreign governments, Ninety-sixth Congress, second session,
   vol. 3, appendix, p. 1479. Referred to subsequently as *Billy Carter
   Hearings.* The sources for the Eilts conspiracy episode are former
   intelligence-community insiders who for obvious reasons must remain
   anonymous.

2  Claire Sterling, *The Terror Network: The Secret War of International Terrorism* (New York: Holt, Rinehart and Winston, 1981).

3  Statement by Richard T. Kennedy, under secretary for management, before the Senate Foreign Relations Committee on June 10, 1981, Department of State, Current Policy Papers, no. 285, June 10, 1981.

4  This information originates with Libyan émigrés, to whom it is an article of faith. Senior U.S. officials have refused to supply any details, but have never denied its truth.

5  "Black propaganda" is well defined by ex-CIA officer Miles Copeland in his book *The Real Spy World* (London: Sphere Books, 1978), p. 199: "the dissemination of information, true or false, which purports to come from sources other than the real ones."

6  The fact about Nasser seems to have contributed to the belief held by many anti-Qaddafi Libyans that the CIA also had foreknowledge of Qaddafi's revolution.

7  Information supplied by former Yemeni Prime Minister Hassan al-Amri in 1974. Cf. also Ruth First, *Libya: The Elusive Revolution* (Harmondsworth, England: Penguin, 1974), pp. 230–31.

8  Patrick Seale and Maureen McConville, *The Hilton Assignment* (New York and Washington: Praeger, 1973).

9  See *The New York Times* of July 11, 12, 13, and 14, 1971, and my dispatches from Rabat in *The Christian Science Monitor*, week of July 13–17. The Libyan broadcasts were monitored by the Foreign Broadcast Information Service, Washington, D.C.

10  Cf. all major newspapers, August 27, 1972, for King Hassan's news conference in Rabat, in which he reported this as an illustration of Oufkir's treacherous disposition (not of his own esteem for Qaddafi, which of course is and was nonexistent).

11  The reporter who wrote the story is, at this writing in 1981, a high official of the Lebanese government. He subsequently admitted that he "hadn't checked the story carefully enough." Playback of the story in the Arab world did indeed arouse Moroccan and other Arab suspicions against the United States for a time, especially because of the then current belief of Arabs in the Mideast that the United States was Qaddafi's ally.

12  The story made page one of the respected Beirut paper, and so, of course, was immediately flashed around the Arab world, where some media, including those in Libya, inflated it. But it proved to be a two- or three-day wonder. King Hassan was silent, amid indignant U.S. denials. Among the alleged ringleaders of the plot, all executed or given long prison terms, was Moroccan air force Captain Ghassan Touil, married to an American woman, Nancy Touil, who had lived at Kenitra; her husband, the Moroccan military court found, had signed the order to issue the ammunition to the F-5s. In 1981 Mrs. Touil had returned to the

United States and lost all contact with her husband, held incommunicado in a prison in southern Morocco where his health was reported to be failing. Amnesty International felt unable to investigate because they normally deal only with prisoners of conscience not charged with violent offenses. I interviewed Mrs. Touil by telephone several times in early 1981.

13  Richard Deacon, *The Israeli Secret Service* (New York: Taplinger, 1980), pp. 209–12. The ethnic and commercial links between the northerners were noted in chapter Two.

14  Seale and McConville, *The Hilton Assignment*, p. 74. See also First, *Libya*, pp. 117–18; authors' conversations in Tel Aviv in October 1980 and Washington, D.C., in June 1981.

## Six: THE QUEST FOR ARAB UNITY

1  Mohamed Heykal [Muhammad Hasseinine Haykal], *The Road to Ramadan* (London: Collins, 1975), p. 186.
2  Ibid., p. 189.
3  Anwar al-Sadat, *In Search of Identity: An Autobiography* (New York: Harper & Row, 1977), pp. 201–02.
4  All three were relieved of their posts, arrested, and convicted of conspiracy when, in May 1971, Sadat cracked down on the pro-Soviet faction in Egypt's ruling Arab Socialist Union for plotting to oust him.
5  Arab World File (a carded information system, Beirut), no. 207, February 19, 1975.
6  Heykal [Haykal], *The Road to Ramadan*, p. 190.
7  Sadat, *In Search of Identity*, p. 233.
8  I can remember making a stopover at Benghazi airport in 1972, and listening to a group of Libyan airport technicians and workers mocking in falsetto pseudo-feminine voices the dialect and mannerisms of Egyptian women.
9  Interview with author.
10  Heykal [Haykal], *The Road to Ramadan*, p. 191.
11  Conversation with a Libyan émigré, now an opponent of Qaddafi, March 1981. The *Queen Elizabeth II* affair is briefly mentioned by Sadat in his memoirs and in more detail by Heykal [Haykal], *The Road to Ramadan*, pp. 192–94.
12  Heykal [Haykal], *The Road to Ramadan*, pp. 194–96, and Arab World File, no. 208, February 19, 1975.
13  Saad al-Shazly, *The Crossing of the Suez* (San Francisco: American Mideast Research, 1980). The book was edited and printed privately by a

consultancy firm run by Shazly's daughter. It deserves much wider attention than it has received.

14  Ibid., p. 94.
15  Ibid., pp. 102–03.
16  Ibid., p. 108.
17  Ibid., p. 133.
18  Ibid., p. 136.
19  Ibid., p. 177.
20  Heykal [Haykal], *The Road to Ramadan*, pp. 197–98.
21  Radio Cairo, February 20, 1981 (author's notes taken in Beirut).
22  Arab World File, no. 208, February 19, 1975.
23  Ibid. Libyan émigrés confirmed there were such executions, though the number was in doubt.
24  Arab World File, no. 725, August 17, 1977. Along with former President François Tombalbaye of Chad, Jean-Bédel Bokassa, "emperor of the Central African Empire," General Mobuto Sese Soko of Zaire, President Omar Bongo of Gabon, and several other heads of state, Eyadema was the object of serious efforts by Qaddafi to convert him to Islam. Eyadema first refused Qaddafi's request, reportedly backed by an offered bribe, in November 1973. In February 1976, during an official visit to Togo, Qaddafi insisted again, indicating he had already picked out a Muslim name for Eyadema. Qaddafi dropped the subject only when Eyadema countered with the suggestion that Qaddafi should become "a Protestant like me."
25  Arab World File, no. 760, September 28, 1977.
26  I saw several of them at Larnaca airport in Cyprus.
27  Arab World File, no. 766, October 5, 1977.
28  See interviews conducted by myself and others with Bourguiba in March and April 1965, after his return from the Holy Land. Notably in a speech to Palestinian refugees in Jericho, he had suggested a return to the 1947 UN partition of Palestine into an Arab and a Jewish state—with Israel thus renouncing further expansion and making room for a neighbor state, Palestinian Arab.
29  *Al-Amal* (Tunis), January 16, 1974.
30  Arab World File, no. 893, March 1, 1978.
31  See page 77.
32  Arab World File, no. 899, March 8, 1978.

**Seven:**  QADDAFI'S NEW SOCIETY: *THE GREEN BOOK*

1  John Mason, *Island of the Blest: Islam in a Libyan Oasis Community*, Papers in International Studies, Africa Series, no. 31. Ohio University

Center for International Studies, Africa Program, 1977, Athens, Ohio, pp. 142–44.

2 Conversations in 1981 with Dr. Majid Khadduri, the distinguished Arab historian now at Johns Hopkins University, and with former Libyan Prime Minister Mustafa ben Halim, now a Saudi citizen. Examination of ben Halim's file, under the "Where did you get it?" law, uncovered no conclusive evidence either for or against his conviction or exoneration. However, after a kidnap-murder attempt against him by Palestinians in Beirut, possibly on behalf of Libya, he was in no mood to return to Libya and test the RCC's intentions toward him.

3 Omar I. Fathali, and Monte Palmer, *Political Development and Social Change in Libya* (Lexington, Mass.: D. C. Heath, Lexington Books, 1980), p. 59.

4 Ibid., p. 55.

5 John K. Cooley, *East Wind Over Africa: Red China's African Offensive* (New York: Walker, 1965).

6 Anne-Marie Cazalis, *Kadhafi, le Templier d'Allah* (Paris: Gallimard, 1973), p. 110. My translation.

7 Ruth First, *Libya: The Elusive Revolution* (Harmondsworth, England: Penguin, 1974), pp. 130–31.

8 Personal communication.

9 *L'Orient* (Beirut), January 31, 1971.

10 Arab World File (a carded information system, Beirut), no. 1857, April 1, 1981. On the Egyptian-Libyan union attempts, see chapter Six.

11 First, *Libya*, p. 137.

12 Arab World File, no. 376, September 10, 1975.

13 Muammar al-Qaddafi, *The Green Book*, 3 vols. (Tripoli, Libya: Public Establishment for Publishing, Advertising and Distribution, 1975–1978). *Vol 1: The Solution of the Problem of Democracy*, 1975; *Vol 2: The Solution of the Economic Problem*, 1977; *Vol 3: The Social Basis of the Third Universal Theory*, 1978. My own copies are well-thumbed, paperbound brochures printed in England with shiny green covers, celebrating the favorite color of all Muslims. They were given to me by the Foreign Press Department in Tripoli, and they carry notations inked in Malagasy, the language spoken in the Malagasy Republic (formerly Madagascar). They must have passed through the hands of one of the innumerable visitors from the Third World who are given the book for basic educational purposes.

14 Oriana Fallaci, *Corriere della Sera*.

15 Muammar al-Qathafi [Qaddafi], *The Green Book, Vol. 1: The Solution of the Problem of Democracy.*

16 Ibid.

17 Ibid.

18  Saab was killed by a sniper's bullet during Lebanon's civil war in 1976 (perhaps by one of the militiamen in Qaddafi's pay, perhaps by a member of one of the other lawless gangs that terrorized the city and eventually destroyed Lebanon). He told me this in a private communication.

19  Arab World File, no. 376, September 10, 1975.

20  Mason, *Island of the Blest*, pp. 144–45.

21  Interviews in Tripoli, August 1981, and John Paxton, ed., *The Statesman's Yearbook 1981–1982* (London: Macmillan, 1981), p. 799.

22  Fathali and Palmer, *Political Development*, pp. 141–42.

23  Harold D. Nelson, ed., *Libya: A Country Study* (Washington, D.C.: The American University, 1979), pp. 207–08. (One of a series of country handbooks by same publisher, used by the U.S. government.)

24  Tripoli Radio, domestic newscasts, August 17 and 18, 1981.

25  Ibid.

26  Ibid.

27  Ibid.

28  Tripoli JANA in English 1408 GMT, August 31, 1981, broadcast September 1, 1981, LD311640, FBIS, North Africa, pp. Q-10–Q-13.

29  Muammar al-Qathafi [Qaddafi], *The Green Book, Vol. 2: The Solution of the Economic Problem*.

30  Ibid.

31  Muammar al-Qathafi [Qaddafi], *The Green Book, Vol. 3: The Social Basis of the Third Universal Theory*, pp. 1–46.

## Eight: TERROR, INC.

1  Miles Copeland, *The Real Spy World* (London: Sphere Books, 1974), p. 211.

2  Henry Kissinger, *White House Years* (Boston: Little, Brown, 1979), pp. 421, 423, and 526.

3  William Quandt, *Decade of Decisions: American Policy Toward the Arab-Israeli Conflict* (Berkeley and Los Angeles: University of California Press, 1977), p. 174 n.

4  Quoted in Stephen Kurkjian and Ben Bradlee, Jr., "The Americans Who Are Training and Supplying Libyan Terrorists," reprinted from the *Boston Globe*, in the "Outlook" section of *The Washington Post*, March 22, 1981.

5  In a remark Mr. Copeland made to me in Cairo in 1969, and has made to many other friends.

6  Qaddafi seems not to have realized that an American mole may have been responsible for tipping off President Carter about the Eilts plot. See the opening pages of chapter Five.

7  Robert Pear, *The New York Times*, January 11, 1980.

8 Seymour M. Hersh, "The Qaddafi Connection," Part I, *The New York Times Magazine*, June 14, 1981, p. 56.

9 Ibid., p. 58.

10 Ray S. Cline, *Secrets, Spies and Scholars: The Essential CIA* (Washington, D.C.: Acropolis Books, 1976), pp. 167–68. The same unit was charged with moving clandestine intelligence operatives from Taiwan secretly into mainland China for espionage there, especially the planting of electronic sensors and surveillance devices. According to Ray S. Cline, former deputy CIA director who was station chief in Taiwan toward the end of the 1950s, there were long "heroic" flights over the Himalayas and into northwest China, where, before the Sino-Soviet quarrel erupted in 1959 and 1960, the Soviets had helped the Chinese establish their nuclear-weapons research facilities. It fell to Wilson to help run some of the aspects of the CIA's first proprietary companies, such as Air America, Civil Air Transport (CAT), and Air Asia, mainly composed of overage planes operated for and in some cases by the CIA. One of their main functions was to drop supplies to the Chinese Nationalist armies that had remained behind Communist lines in southwest China before implanting themselves permanently in the China-Burma-Thailand borderland wilderness.

11 Quoted by Judith Miller, *The New York Times*, July 15, 1981. Libyan émigrés have insisted that Terpil first met Qaddafi *before* the September 1969 revolution, when Terpil was a CIA courier, and when Qaddafi was plotting the coup. No official U.S. source would confirm this.

12 Quoted by Jack Anderson, *The Washington Post*, October 21 and 22, 1980.

13 Hersh, "The Qaddafi Connection," Part I, pp. 57–58.

14 Perhaps from the same American mole President Carter was to use the following year to thwart the plot against Ambassador Eilts.

15 Omar I. Fathali and Monte Palmer, *Political Development and Social Change in Libya* (Lexington, Mass.: D. C. Heath, Lexington Books, 1980), pp. 43, 46, 47, 56, and 60; Arab World File (a carded information system, Beirut), no. 1853, March 25, 1981, and no. 1857, April 1, 1981; also private conversations with a close friend of Meheishi's.

16 Hersh, "The Qaddafi Connection," Part II, *The New York Times Magazine*, June 21, 1981, p. 58.

17 A PLO official who must remain anonymous; corroborated by several Arab diplomats.

18 Dennis Eisenberg and Eli Landau, *Carlos: Terror International* (London: Corgi Books, 1976), pp. 187–88.

19 Personal conversation with Yamani.

20 Jack Anderson, *The Washington Post*, February 18, 1981. After the Tanzanian invasion of Uganda in 1979, when Qaddafi's troops sent to help Amin were routed with over four hundred casualties, Astles was

captured by the invading forces and returned to Kampala in chains. He was tried and acquitted of one of the murder charges in October 1981, but remained subject to other Ugandan charges.

21 *Newsweek*, July 20, 1981.

22 Hersh, "The Qaddafi Connection," Part I, p. 62.

23 Russell Warren Howe, *Weapons: The International Game of Arms Money and Diplomacy* (New York: Doubleday, 1980), pp. 424–25.

24 Hersh, "The Qaddafi Connection," Part II. Walter Doerr, a Lufthansa sales manager, had already refused to ship them to West Germany for transshipment to Libya.

25 Personal communication with the operative.

26 Hersh, "The Qaddafi Connection," Part II.

27 He had left the hotel when I passed through Beirut in early November 1980. Knowledgeable persons said: "Terpil has almost certainly returned to Tripoli, and he's likely to stay there." Later, he reappeared in Beirut, only to vanish again in November 1981 after an interview by CBS News.

28 *Newsweek*, July 20, 1981, p. 45.

29 Most of the PLO leaders have become better known in the Arab world by their noms de guerre. *Abu* means simply the father of whoever or whatever is used for the second part of the name (i.e., Arafat's nom de guerre, Abu Amar, means simply "the father of Amar," though he has no such son). The anti-Arafat, hard-line "rejectionist" leader, Sabri al Banna, is known as Abu Nidal, literally "the father of the call."

30 Eric Rouleau, *Abou Iyad, Palestinien Sans Patrie* (Paris: Fayolle, 1978), pp. 90–93.

31 Ibid., p. 205.

32 Personal communication with a Palestinian official in Beirut, September 1973. It was confirmed in another similar interview in Beirut in January 1982.

33 Christopher Dobson and Ronald Payne, *The Terrorists, Their Weapons, Leaders and Tactics* (New York: Facts on File, 1979).

34 Arab World File, no. 1420, November 7, 1979.

35 Aryeh Y. Yodfat and Yuval Arnon-Ohanna, *PLO Strategy and Tactics* (New York: St. Martin's Press, 1981), p. 6.

36 Rouleau, *Abou Iyad*, pp. 316–17.

37 Ibid.

38 *Der Spiegel*, December 17, 1979.

39 *Al-Siyasah* (Tripoli), December 7, 1979. All this was going on while the Carter administration was hoping that Qaddafi would help release the American hostages from Iran, and while Billy Carter was pursuing his business goals in Libya. See chapter Eleven.

40 Quoted in Yodfat and Arnon-Ohanna, *PLO Strategy*, p. 123.

41 Ibid., p. 124.

## Nine: THE EXPORT OF THE REVOLUTION

1 I worked with Atlas Constructors and the U.S. Army's Corps of Engineers in Morocco. Before Moroccan independence in 1956, French military security agents in Morocco worked closely with the DST, then run by the redoubtable Roger Wybot (whom some have called a French Allen Dulles). French air force security even tried to recruit Europeans, Moroccans, and Americans in Morocco to perform anti-FLN work for the DST, even though such work would have fallen under the mandate of SDECE.

2 Cited in *Middle East Magazine* (London), August 1981.

3 See Christopher Dobson and Ronald Payne, *The Carlos Complex: A Pattern of Violence* (London: Hodder and Stoughton, 1977), for the most complete account in English of Carlos's early operations and his connections with Qaddafi at that time.

4 See chapter Five.

5 *Middle East Journal*, August 1981.

6 Drelon-Mounier Remy, "Mission sans Retour du DC-3 Fantôme," in *Historia* (Paris), no. 406a (1980).

7 Except for the Italian and French colonials, against whom the Toubous regularly waged guerrilla wars.

8 See chapter Six.

9 Philippe Rochot, *La Grande Fièvre du Monde Musulman* (Paris: Sycomore, 1981), p. 126.

10 Information supplied by a former high Libyan official responsible for economic planning.

11 See chapter Three.

12 Rochot, *La Grande Fièvre*, pp. 126–27.

13 Goukouni's rival and Qaddafi's adversary, Hissène Habré, became prime minister of the Malloum government in N'Djamena with the support of SDECE and the French security force of 2,000, part of the small but well-armed and highly mobile rapid deployment force France has maintained in most of its former African colonies since their independence.

14 Though they had helped to install Bokassa's successor, President David Dacko, the French apparently did nothing to prevent Dacko's overthrow by his own army in Bangui, the Central African Republic capital. At the time of the military coup on September 1, 1981, there were about 2,500 French troops in the country.

15 *Middle East Journal*, Summer 1981.

16 His words reminded me of the warning sounded by General Maurice Challe, who had helped plan and lead the Anglo-French-Israeli expedition against Nasser at Suez in 1956. Challe tried to overthrow President de Gaulle of France in April 1961, hoping to prevent Algerian independence: "Do you want Europe's southern flank to be exposed to Soviet missiles in

North Africa?" France, more than any other European power, has always been sensitive to the strategic danger from Qaddafi's Soviet-supplied arsenal of weapons, then being used in the Chad offensive.

17 Moroccan military officers in Rabat and in the Sahara itself confirmed that the maritime route from the Canaries was the principal one being used by the Libyans, and the most difficult to control. This confirmation was made during my visit to Morocco and al-Ayun, the Western Saharan capital, in August 1981.

18 Cables received by the British embassy in Tripoli while I visited Libya about that time indicated that the Libyan ambassador in Banjul (formerly Bathurst), the Gambian capital, had been recruiting young Gambians for the guerrilla camps and encouraging teenage troublemakers.

19 Siradiou Diallo, "La Parole et au . . . Niger," *Jeune Afrique* (Paris), no. 1058 (April 14, 1981), pp. 46–50. Quotations that follow are from this article.

20 *New African Yearbook 1980* (London: I.C. Magazines, 1981), p. 251.

21 Just before the French withdrawal, between March 30 and April 3, 550 Congolese troops sent to N'Djamena in January 1980 as part of a neutral force organized by the OAU and supposed to supervise a cease-fire were withdrawn as fighting with heavy artillery raked through the city. The Guinea and Benin troops who were supposed to join them had never been sent.

22 Conversations with Ambassador Don Norland, March 1981. Qaddafi had already been able to purchase sensitive U.S. communications equipment through the good offices of Frank Terpil and his associates.

23 *Le Monde,* December 14, 1980.

24 *Keesings Contemporary Archives* (London), February 6, 1981, p. 30696.

25 *African Research Bulletin,* vol. 18, no. 2 (March 15, 1981), p. 5965.

26 Ibid.

27 See chapter Six.

28 *African Research Bulletin,* pp. 5966–67.

29 The bareness of the OAU treasury was dramatically spelled out in the 1981–82 budget figures: $19.4 million dollars, 11 percent more than the year before. Member states' contributions still outstanding amounted to $25.5 million. *Keesings,* May 15, 1981, p. 308066.

30 *African Research Bulletin,* p. 6048.

31 *Financial Times* (London), July 16, 1981.

32 *Herald Tribune* (Paris), July 17, 1981.

33 Conversations with Jeane-Pierre Cot at Carnegie Endowment for International Peace, Washington, D.C., September 28, 1981. The quotations that follow are also from these talks.

34 John Paxton, ed., *The Statesman's Yearbook 1981–82* (London: Macmillan, 1981), p. 726.

35 "Italy," special report of *Middle East Economic Digest*, November 1980, p. 3.
36 Private interview with a senior Italian diplomat, February 1981.
37 Personal interview in August 1980.
38 See Claire Sterling, *The Terror Network: The Secret War of International Terrorism* (New York: Holt, Rinehart and Winston, 1981), for a detailed account of terrorism in Italy.
39 Personal interview with a PLO leader in Beirut, May 1979.
40 My Italian officer friend blamed the bombing on funds from Qaddafi.
41 *Europeo* (Rome), August 3, 1981. Giovine is the highly respected editorial director of ISPI (Istituto di Studi di Politica Internazionale) and a professor at Stanford University's extension in Florence. He has a long record of "progressive" activity, including helping socialist leader Pietro Nenni set up a network to resist the 1967–74 dictatorship of the colonels in Greece.
42 Personal interviews in Malta, August 1980, and *Air International* (London).
43 See p. 127.
44 Personal conversation with Admiral Angelo Monassi.
45 Personal interview.
46 *Keesings*, July 8, 1977, pp. 28440–41.
47 Cf. "Soviets Boost Arms Shipments to Cuba," *Aviation Week and Space Technology*, October 12, 1981, p. 92.
48 Somoza's armed forces received, among other things, two Israeli-built Arava transport planes and smaller communications planes and helicopters. The PLO sent the Sandinistas the usual Kalashnikov rifles, grenades, and some heavier weapons such as mortars. See *The Statesman's Yearbook 1981–82*, p. 923.

## Ten: NUCLEAR AMBITIONS

1 *Time*, June 8, 1981, p. 31.
2 Robert D. A. Henderson, "Nigeria: Future Nuclear Power?" *Orbis*, vol. 25, no. 2 (Summer 1981), p. 414.
3 India detonated its first "peaceful nuclear device," as an Indian government statement called it, at a test site in the Rajesthan Desert in May 1974.
4 Confidential source.
5 Ibid.
6 Associated Press, March 12, 1981.
7 Judith Miller, *The New York Times*, September 9, 1981.
8 SIPRI *Yearbook* (Stockholm International Peace Research Institute) no. 9

(1978), pp. 79–80, and also *Jeune Afrique* (Paris), no. 1040 (December 10, 1980).
9  Personal communication, Stockholm, 1981.

## Eleven:  IN THE SUPERPOWER WEB

1  Benjamin F. Schemmer, interview with Egypt's defense minister Lieutenant General Mohammed Abu-Ghazala: "The U.S. Has Lost a Lot of Years," *Armed Forces Journal International*, September 1981, pp. 50–51.
2  International Institute of Strategic Studies, "The Military Balance 1981–82," quoted in "Soviet Missile Sites Reported Inside Libya," by Air Commander G. S. Cooper, *The Daily Telegram* (London), September 24, 1981.
3  See chapter Two.
4  Anthony Cave Brown, ed., *Dropshot: The American Plan for World War III Against Russia in 1957* (New York: The Dial Press/James Wade, 1978).
5  Ibid., p. 45.
6  Ibid.
7  See chapter Eight.
8  Brown, *Dropshot*, p. 53.
9  Ibid., pp. 235–37.
10  Ibid., p. 122.
11  Ibid.
12  Tripoli Radio in Arabic, which I monitored, September 1, 1981.
13  Conversation with David Mack in Tunis, August 1981.
14  *Military Review* (Fort Leavenworth, Kans.), no. 11 (November 1979).
15  One of these was Alexander Zotov, who in 1979–81 was the resident Soviet Middle East expert on Ambassador Anatoly Dobrynin's staff at the Soviet embassy in Washington.
16  For background on this period, see Arab World File (a carded information system, Beirut), no. 731, August 24, 1977.
17  *Military Review.*
18  Ibid.
19  See chapter Nine.
20  *Military Review*, no. 11; Russell Warren Howe, *Weapons: The International Game of Arms, Money and Dipomacy* (New York: Doubleday, 1980), p. 648.
21  Captain John Moore, ed., *Janes Fighting Ships 1981–82* (London: Janes, 1981), pp. 310–14.
22  Conversations with Admiral Crowe and an Italian staff admiral at NATO headquarters, both in August 1980; and a Greek diplomatic informant, March 1981.
23  Though only a handful of Washingtonians know this, one example came

at Christmas 1980 when the People's Bureau led by Dr. Ali Houdery distributed several thousand dollars' worth of generously large food packages to the poor of the Washington area—totally anonymously. Dr. Houdery asked that the origin of the food packages be concealed from the recipients, and that there be no publicity. The secret was well kept.

24 "U.S.–Libyan Relations Since 1969," *Current Policy*, no. 216, U.S. Department of State, Bureau of Public Affairs, testimony by David Newsom, August 4, 1980, pp. 2–3.

25 *Inquiry into the Matter of Billy Carter and Libya*, report together with additional views of the Committee on the Judiciary, Subcommittee to Investigate Individuals Representing the Interests of Foreign Governments to the United States, Senate, October 2, 1980, U.S. Government Printing Office, pp. 2ff.

26 "U.S.–Libyan Relations," p. 3.

27 *Inquiry*, p. 7.

28 "U.S.–Libyan Relations," p. 3.

29 *Inquiry*, pp. 8–9.

30 Ibid., p. 10.

31 Ibid., p. 15.

32 Ibid., p. 16.

33 Ibid., p. 17.

34 Ibid., p. 18.

35 Ibid.

36 Ibid.

37 *The New York Times*, December 10, 1979. See also *Inquiry*, pp. 19–21.

38 *Inquiry*, pp. 19–21.

39 Results of my own inquiries, including interviews with Iranian and Italian officials, in September 1978 and August 1980.

40 *Inquiry*, pp. 21–23.

41 Ibid., pp. 24–25.

42 Ibid., pp. 25–29.

43 Ibid., p. 30 and passim.

44 Cited in Marwan Buheiry, *U.S. Threats of Intervention Against Arab Oil: 1973–1979* (Beirut: Institute for Palestine Studies, 1980); IPS Papers, no. 4 (E), p. 22.

45 Buheiry, *U.S. Threats*, p. 31.

46 *Newsweek*, August 31, 1981, p. 11.

47 The best and most authoritative reports of the incident can be found in the following: *Aviation Week and Space Technology*, August 24 and 31, 1981; *Newsweek*, August 31, *New York Herald Tribune* (Paris), August 20 and 21, 1981. See also my two dispatches to *The Washington Post*, August 20 and 22, 1981.

48 Philip Geyelin in *The Washington Post* and the *European Herald Tribune* (Paris), August 29–30, 1981.

## Twelve:  WHITHER QADDAFI?

1  *The Economist,* September 5, 1981, p. 33.
2  Personal communication in Athens with an unnamed government official, September 1981.
3  Report from Washington by William Lee, *Middle East Economic Digest,* May 15, 1981.
4  *The Economist,* September 12, 1981, p. 72.
5  Lisa S. Anderson, "Religion and Politics in Libya," *Journal of Arab Affairs,* vol. I, no. 1 (October 1981), p. 68.
6  *L'Espresso* (Rome), Foreign Broadcast Information Service (FBIS), July 13, 1980.
7  Sudanese News Agency, quoted by Agence France-Presse, Paris, April 29, 1981, FBIS, April 29, 1981. Some of the "disinformation" took the form of a widespread campaign of telephone calls to journalists and others, recounting Qaddafi's supposed encounters with Western women.
8  *Al-Ahram,* quoted in FBIS, July 16, 1980.
9  George Henderson, "Free to Agree with Colonel Qaddafi," *Index on Censorship,* vol. 9, no. 6 (November 1980), p. 19.
10  Ibid., pp. 20–22.
11  *Amnesty International Report 1980* (London: Amnesty International Publications, 1980), pp. 244–47.
12  Tripoli Domestic Service, March 28, 1981; FBIS, March 30, 1981.
13  "MacNeil-Lehrer Report," U.S. National Public Broadcasting Network, May 7, 1981.
14  For example, United Press International, quoting Tripoli Radio November 4, 1981, said the U.S. military maneuver "Bright Star" in Egypt in late November was expected to involve bombing Libya from the air "in all the areas where Qaddafi might be thought to be" in order to kill the leader.
15  Tripoli Domestic Service, January 1, 1981; FBIS, January 2, 1981.
16  *The Washington Post,* November 8, 1981. The story was confirmed to me by senior analysts in the Reagan administration.
17  Arab Press Service (Beirut), SP 225, October 28–November 4, 1981, p. 14.
18  Arab Press Service, Operations in Oil Diplomacy, SP 37, October 28, 1981, pp. 1–6. I am especially grateful to APS editor Pierre Shamas and to Dr. William Mussen of APS for sharing with me many of their thoughts, both on paper and otherwise, on the Libyan opposition and on Libyan oil; as well as to Mr. G. Henry M. Schuler, former U.S. diplomat and now an oil consultant, for his insights and unique expertise on the North African oil scene.

# INDEX